African American History

MAGILL'S CHOICE

African American History

Volume 1

Abolition — Fugitive Slave Law of 1793

Edited by
Carl L. Bankston III
Tulane University

SALEM PRESS INC.
Pasadena, California   Hackensack, New Jersey

Frontispiece: Picketer protesting discriminatory hiring practices in Chicago in 1941.
(Library of Congress)

Some essays originally appeared in *American Justice* (1996), *Encyclopedia of the U.S. Supreme Court* (2000), *Great Events from History II: Arts
and Culture* (1993), *Great Events from History II: Human Rights* (1992),
Great Events from History: North American Series, Revised Edition (1997),
Great Events of the 20th Century (2002), *Racial and Ethnic Relations in
America* (2000), *The Fifties in America* (2005), *The Sixties in America* (1999),
and *Women's Issues* (1997). New material has been added.

Library of Congress Cataloging-in-Publication Data
African American history / edited by Carl L. Bankston, III.
   p. cm. -- (Magill's choice)
   Includes bibliographical references and index.
   ISBN-13: 978-1-58765-239-4 (set : alk. paper)
   ISBN-10: 1-58765-239-0 (set : alk. paper)
   ISBN-13: 978-1-58765-240-0 (v. 1 : alk. paper)
   ISBN-10: 1-58765-240-4 (v. 1 : alk. paper)
   [etc.]
1. African Americans--History. I. Bankston, Carl L. (Carl Leon),
1952-   II. Series.
   E185.A25355 2005
   973'.0496073--dc22

                                                              2005015348

First Printing

PRINTED IN THE UNITED STATES OF AMERICA

Contents

Contents

Complete List of Contents

Volume 1

Volume 2

Volume 3

Publisher's Note

This three-volume contribution to Salem Press's Magill's Choice series offers comprehensive coverage of the history of African Americans in the United States, from the arrival of the first African immigrants in British North America in 1619 through the first years of the twenty-first century. *African American History*'s alphabetically arranged essays cover the full sweep of the African American experience in North America, with articles on the major economic, political, legal, social, and cultural events and developments of nearly four centuries of history.

Subject Matter

Individual essays in *African American History* range in length from 200 to more than 3,000 words and average nearly 1,000 words each. The diverse subject matter covered in these volumes ranges from the origins of the peoples who make up the modern African American population to the impact of African Americans on present-day American culture and society. While the range of subjects covered is broad, the set has an unavoidable emphasis on rights issues. For, just as the history of African Americans has been dominated by struggles for freedom and equal rights, articles in *African American History* emphasize such issues as slavery (25 essays), the abolitionist movement (11), and civil rights (56). The set also has 33 essays on topics relating to discrimination and 26 essays on voting rights. Other subject areas covered in these volumes include arts and entertainment (9 essays), Black nationalism (13), crime and punishment (14), demographics (12), economic issues (10), education (21), military history (10), politics and government (12), the Reconstruction era (18), religion (9), riots and civil disturbances (14), and women's issues (8).

The history of the African American struggle for equal rights is closely tied to the history of U.S. Supreme Court decisions. With the set's emphasis on rights issues, it should thus not be surprising that 71 essays are on specific Supreme Court decisions and another 24 are on federal laws. There are also 113 essays on specific events and eras, 42 on organizations and government agencies, and 50 on such broad subjects as demographics, economic history, the entertainment industry, integration, literature, the military, music, and politics and government.

Information on individual personages in African American history is consolidated in the Biographical Directory in the appendix section of volume 3. The directory offers substantial entries on more than 100 notable figures from all periods of African American history and emphasize their individual places in black history. To tie *African American History*'s subjects together, the set is introduced by an original essay on African American historiography written by Professor Carl L. Bankston III, the editor of the set. In addition to the Biographical Directory, the appendix section at the end of volume 3 includes an extensive and up-to-date general Bibliography and a Time Line of African American history.

Using This Set

Each of the alphabetically arranged articles in *African American History* opens with the type of ready-reference top matter for which Salem Press's reference works are well known. Except in a small number of articles on subjects that require no explanation—such as Agriculture, Economic trends, and Education—the first entry following every title is a brief passage that defines or identifies the article's subject. Articles on such subjects as events, court cases, organizations, and laws have additional entries that provide dates and places, as relevant. The next item in every article is a brief italicized statement summarizing its subject's significance. Readers can thus see the most essential information about every topic at a glance.

Boldface subheads help guide readers through longer articles, and most articles are followed by up-to-date Further Reading notes. Additional bibliographical help can be found in the general bibliography at the end of volume 3.

African American History offers several features to help readers find the information they need. The first and most obvious feature is the alphabetical arrangement of the essays, whose titles are worded to make finding topics as straightforward as possible. Readers may either go directly to the articles they seek or look for them in the complete list of contents that can found at the front of every volume. Readers who cannot find what they need in the article titles will find substantial additional help in the set's detailed indexes of personages and general subjects at the end of volume 3. Volume 3 also has a Category Index which should help readers who are uncertain under what headings they should look. Finally, every article is followed by a list of cross-references to other articles on closely related subjects. Readers are encouraged to follow the paths that these cross-references provide.

Acknowledgments

About one-half of the 293 essays in *African American History* are taken from Salem's *Racial and Ethnic Relations in America*, which was published in 1999. The rest come from ten other Salem reference sets that include, most notably, *Great Events from History: North American Series* (1997), *Great Events from History II: Human Rights* (1992), *Encyclopedia of the U.S. Supreme Court* (2000), and *The Sixties in America* (1999). Bibliographical notes from those sets have been updated as necessary, and ten entirely new articles have been added.

As always, the editors of Salem Press wish to thank the many scholars whose contributions make publications such as these possible. More than 155 scholars contributed the articles in *African American History*. The editors would also like to thank the project's editor, Carl L. Bankston III of Tulane University. In addition to overseeing the project and writing the Introduction, Professor Bankston also wrote most of the new material appearing in this set.

Introduction to African American History

The techniques, approaches, themes, and theories that historians employ in their work are collectively known as historiography. Historiography recognizes that the discipline of history itself is a historical product. An African American historiography looks at how historians have thought and written about African American history. It also looks at the subjects and issues that have distinguished African American history from American history in general and at how African American history is connected to American history.

Most readers of this three-volume set are probably interested in specific topics in the history of African Americans. As they use this comprehensive work, however, they may want to remember that the topics covered in it are not here simply for their writers to set forth. They have emerged from more than a century of reflection on the past of African Americans by historians and the public. For this reason, I want to introduce these volumes with a brief discussion of how African American history has been studied and presented and the issues that have concerned those writing in this area. I will begin by examining how the discipline of African American history has developed, and then discuss the major issues that recur through this branch of history.

Generations of African American Historians

One of the most influential descriptions of the development of African American history comes from the work of the distinguished scholar John Hope Franklin. Franklin has argued that African American historians can be divided into four generations, from the late nineteenth century through the end of the twentieth century.

The first generation of historians consisted mainly of nonprofessional historians concerned with explaining how African Americans fit into American society. George Washington Williams (1849-1891) is often considered the first true scholar of African

American history. Educated as a minister and with a background in politics, Williams trained himself in techniques of historical research. With an extensive investigation into primary sources, he published the two-volume *History of the Negro Race in America from 1619 to 1880* in 1882. An ardent advocate of integration, Williams was concerned with presenting African Americans as Americans.

Although there were arguably no other major scholars of African American history in Franklin's first generation, the study of African American history attracted a great deal of interest. In Philadelphia, a group founded the American Negro Historical Society in 1897. A little over a decade later, in 1911, African American New Yorkers founded the Negro Society for Historical Research. In these groups, readers and writers were driven by the desire to find a positive identity for members of the racial group, and to locate African Americans within American society.

Franklin dates the second generation of African American historians from around 1915, with the publication of *The Negro*, by W. E. B. Du Bois, in that year, and with the founding of the *Journal of Negro History* the following year. The most important figure of this second generation was Carter G. Woodson, the new journal's first editor. Woodson is regarded by some historiographers as the true founder of African American history, since he brought together historians interested in the field and published their articles in his journal. He also encouraged them to write books and manuscripts, which he helped to publish through Associated Publishers, of which he was executive director. Woodson's own first major book was *The Negro in Our History* (1922). His best-known book today is probably *The Mis-Education of the Negro*, first published in 1933, which criticized the inattention to black history and its misleading portrayal in American schools.

This second generation (which some scholars consider to have been the first generation) of historians was overwhelmingly concerned with the achievements of African Americans in politics, art, music, and other areas. To a large extent, its historians were reacting against the negative portrayals of African Americans in mainstream history and in educational institutions. Writing in a time when segregation and discrimination had been institutionalized and even legally prescribed in many parts of the nation, the second generation of historians attempted to bring to light parts of the past that most white scholars overlooked.

Franklin dates his third generation in African American history to around 1935. Its characteristic work was again published by Du Bois, whose long career spanned many changes and who was a sociologist and political activist as much as a historian. Du Bois's *Black Reconstruction*, first published in 1935, emphasized cooperation between black and white people during the Reconstruction era in the South. A primary area of interest to historians of this generation was how black and white Americans have interacted and dealt with one another. Accordingly, many white historians began working in African American history during this time and published their research in journals devoted to the field. Historians of this third generation were among those who laid the groundwork for the Civil Rights movement of the 1950's and 1960's, and participated in it.

Franklin's fourth generation began around 1970. Made up of well-trained and primarily academic historians, this late twentieth-century generation was distinguished by the range of topics it studied and by the fact that African American history was, by then, considered an integral part of mainstream history, even as it continued to criticize the mainstream. Popular demand for African American history, small at the beginning of the twentieth century, had become great by the century's end and this led to a deluge of books on the subject.

The fourth generation saw the rise of black, or African American, studies programs as an academic discipline, frequently with political implications, and African American history often became part of this new discipline. African American studies gave rise to calls for Afrocentric perspectives on the past and future. For many historians, this meant that the primary task was no longer to identify African American history within American history, but to work from the premise that African Americans were at the center of American history. Some scholars have suggested that a new generation is now emerging from Afrocentric historians, one that will deal with African Americans not simply as participants in the nation's history, but as creators of it.

Across these generations, a number of topics have frequently predominated. These topics are well covered within the three volumes of *African American History*. At least three major issues tend to cut across most discussions of African American history: slavery and its heritage, the rural and urban backgrounds of African Americans, and racism.

Slavery and Its Heritage

Slavery is one of the key topics across all generations of African American historians, and it intersects with most other topics. One of the issues in the writing on slavery has been its impact on African American culture. Many historians, from the beginning, have maintained that slavery basically destroyed African culture and left slaves psychologically isolated and demoralized. An early challenge to this point of view can be found in the work of the Jewish American anthropologist Melville Herskovits, who argued in *The Myth of the Negro Past* (1941), that African Americans had, in fact, preserved much of their African culture through slavery.

During the 1950's, historians Kenneth Stampp and Stanley Elkins published influential works arguing that slavery left such deep psychological scars on the slaves themselves that it damaged social institutions that the slaves passed on to their free black descendants. A long line of African American historians have concentrated on slave revolts and resistance to slavery to counter the view of slaves as damaged, helpless, and docile. Toward the end of the 1960's and into the 1970's, especially, historians reacted against claims that slavery had damaged African Americans culturally and psychologically. More recently, Ira Berlin, in works such as *Generations of Captivity: A History of African American Slaves* (2003), has offered evidence that slavery varied greatly from one region to another and that therefore the impact of slavery on African American culture varied by region.

The influence of slavery on families has been an especially controversial issue for historians. The African American social scientist E. Franklin Frazier, in *The Negro Family in the United States* (1939), presented family instability and a tendency toward single-parent families as a consequence of slavery. This was later countered by Herbert Gutman's *Black Family in Slavery and Free-*

dom: 1750-1925 (1976). Gutman offered evidence that slavery actually strengthened black families.

Relationships between slaves and masters have been another hotly debated subject in historical writing on slavery. In the early part of the twentieth century, mainstream white historians often presented slavemasters as largely paternalistic, almost benevolent. Reacting to this, African American historians tended to emphasize the horrors of slavery. Insights into the brutal nature of slavery came from interviews with former slaves conducted as part of the Federal Writers Project during the 1930's, and these interviews became essential primary sources for later historians.

In 1974, Robert Fogel and Stanley Engerman published *Time on the Cross*, a statistical analysis of slavery that suggested it was actually a profitable and productive institution. Although Fogel and Engerman meant to emphasize black achievements through adversity, their work impressed some as an apology for slavery. *Time on the Cross* began a new round of historical investigations into how brutal master-slave relationships really were.

Rural and Urban Backgrounds

As the essay on demographic trends shows in the following pages, the African American experience in the years that followed slavery was one of a transformation from a mostly rural, agricultural population to a mostly urban one. Generally, the early second-generation historical works concerned with African Americans in urban settings concentrated on the movement from the countryside to the city. *Negro Migration During the Great War* (1920), by Emmett J. Scott, considered why African Americans had left the rural South for the cities during World War I and what that meant for their urban destinations. Many of the historical works that followed were concerned with the problems faced by African Americans in large cities, and they tended to concentrate on places such as Harlem and Chicago, which held the greatest black populations.

Toward the end of Franklin's third generation of historians, the development of ghettos became a topic of increased interest among scholars. Gilbert Osofsky's *Harlem: The Making of a Ghetto* (1966) and Allan H. Spear's *Black Chicago: The Making of a Negro*

Ghetto, 1890-1920 (1967) addressed concerns generated by the urban riots of the 1960's. In the years following, the development and maintenance of racial segregation in American cities became a central issue among historians and social scientists.

Racism

Racism is intertwined with nearly all areas of study in African American history, from its origins during the slavery era to its continuing influence on American society in modern times. The enthusiasm of African American historians for promoting black achievements during Woodson's era stemmed from a conscious desire to counter the negative views of African Americans in mainstream history. For example, Du Bois's *Black Reconstruction* (1935) responded to portrayals of African Americans as passive and corrupt during the Reconstruction period. Du Bois ended *Black Reconstruction* with a chapter criticizing the distorted portrayal of African Americans in history books. Historian Robert W. Logan (1897-1982), an associate of both Woodson and Du Bois enjoyed a long career as a historian. The historical impact of white racism on African Americans was a central theme in all his writings.

One of the key questions among historians dealing with racism has been how racist attitudes have been connected to social structures. In *White Supremacy: A Comparative Study in American and South African History* (1981), George M. Fredrickson argued that the institution of slavery created racism. Historians dealing with urbanization have often studied how racial attitudes led to racially segregated cities, even in the North. Studies of family and class position among African Americans have emphasized that these cannot be understood without taking white supremacy and racial prejudice into consideration.

Carl L. Bankston III

Further Reading

The best approach to African American historiography would be to read widely and deeply in the field. However, a good overview of the historiography can be found in *The State of Afro-American History: Past, Present, and Future* (Baton Rouge: Louisiana State

University Press, 1986), edited by Darlene Clark Hine. That book's chapter "On the Evolution of Scholarship in Afro-American History" by John Hope Franklin is particularly recommended. *The African American Experience: An Historiographical and Bibliographical Guide* (Westport, Conn.: Greenwood Press, 2001), edited by Arvarh E. Strickland and Robert E. Weems, Jr., looks at historical writing in twelve of the major topics in African American history. *Black History and the Historical Profession, 1915-1980* (Chicago: University of Illinois Press, 1986), by August Meier and Elliott Rudwick, offers five essays on the development of African American history. The essay on the career of Carter G. Woodson is especially useful for an understanding of the field.

Carl L. Bankston III
Tulane University

Contributors

McCrea Adams
Independent Scholar

Mary Welek Atwell
Radford University

Barbara Bair
Library of Congress

Carl L. Bankston III
Tulane University

Bernice McNair Barnett
University of Illinois at Urbana

Paul Barton-Kriese
Indiana University

Alvin K. Benson
Utah Valley State College

S. Carol Berg
College of St. Benedict

Milton Berman
University of Rochester

Cynthia A. Bily
Adrian College

Steve D. Boilard
Independent Scholar

James J. Bolner
Louisiana State University, Baton Rouge

Aubrey W. Bonnett
State University of New York, Old Westbury

J. Quinn Brisben
Independent Scholar

Michael H. Burchett
Limestone College

Byron D. Cannon
University of Utah

Glenn Canyon
Independent Scholar

Sharon Carson
University of North Dakota

Erica Childs
Fordham University

John G. Clark
University of Kansas

Thomas Clarkin
University of Texas

Robert Cole
Utah State University

William H. Coogan
University of Southern Maine

Tom Cook
Wayne State College

William J. Cooper, Jr.
Louisiana State University, Baton Rouge

Stephen Cresswell
West Virginia Wesleyan College

Laura A. Croghan
College of William and Mary

Edward R. Crowther
Adams State College

Gilbert Morris Cuthbertson
Rice University

Richard V. Damms
Mississippi State University

Sudipta Das
Southern University at New Orleans

Jane Davis
Fordham University

Theresa R. Doggart
University of Tennessee, Chattanooga

Davison M. Douglas
William and Mary Law School

Paul E. Doutrich
York College of Pennsylvania

Jennifer Eastman
Clark University

Robert P. Ellis
Worcester State College

Daryl R. Fair
College of New Jersey

John W. Fiero
University of Southwestern Louisiana

Brian L. Fife
Ball State University

Alan M. Fisher
California State University, Dominguez Hills

John C. Gardner
Louisiana State University, Baton Rouge

Karen Garner
University of Texas at Austin

Phyllis B. Gerstenfeld
California State University, Stanislaus

Richard A. Glenn
Millersville University

Robert F. Gorman
Southwest Texas State University

Lewis L. Gould
University of Texas at Austin

William H. Green
University of Missouri, Columbia

Jimmie F. Gross
Armstrong State College

Michael Haas
University of Hawaii at Manoa

Pamela D. Haldeman
Mount St. Mary's College

Irwin Halfond
McKendree College

Roger D. Hardaway
Northwestern Oklahoma State University

Contributors

Claude Hargrove
Fayetteville State University

Keith Harper
Mississippi College

Katy Jean Harriger
Wake Forest University

William M. Harris, Sr.
Jackson State University

Stanley Harrold
South Carolina State University

James Hayes-Bohanan
University of Arizona

Ronald W. Howard
Mississippi College

John Jacob
Northwestern University

Robert Jacobs
Central Washington University

Ron Jacobs
University of Vermont

Duncan R. Jamieson
Ashland University

Robert L. Jenkins
Mississippi State University

K. Sue Jewell
Ohio State University

Mabel Khawaja
Hampton University

Kathleen Odell Korgen
William Paterson University

Beth Kraig
Pacific Lutheran University

Jeri Kurtzleben
University of Northern Iowa

M. Bahati Kuumba
Buffalo State College

Linda Rochell Lane
Tuskegee University

Eleanor A. LaPointe
Ocean County College

Sharon L. Larson
University of Nebraska at Lincoln

Abraham D. Lavender
Florida International University

Jama Lazerow
Wheelock College

Thomas Tandy Lewis
Anoka-Ramsey Community College

Matthew Lindstrom
Siena College

Janet Alice Long
Independent Scholar

Anne C. Loveland
Louisiana State University, Baton Rouge

William C. Lowe
Mount St. Clare College

Robert D. Lukens
University of Delaware

Siobhan McCabe
Siena College

Grace McEntee
Appalachian State University

Robert E. McFarland
North Georgia College

Susan Mackey-Kallis
Villanova University

Paul D. Mageli
Independent Scholar

Jonathan Markovitz
University of California, San Diego

Chogollah Maroufi
California State University, Los Angeles

Thomas D. Matijasic
Prestonsburg Community College

Joseph A. Melusky
Saint Francis College

Beth A. Messner
Ball State University

Gregg L. Michel
University of Virginia

William V. Moore
College of Charleston

Charles H. O'Brien
Western Illinois University

Eileen O'Brien
University of Florida

Max C. E. Orezzoli
Florida International University

William Osborne
Florida International University

Jason Pasch
Independent Scholar

Craig S. Pascoe
University of Tennessee, Knoxville

Darryl Paulson
University of South Florida

Thomas R. Peake
King College

William E. Pemberton
University of Wisconsin, La Crosse

Marilyn Elizabeth Perry
Independent Scholar

Doris F. Pierce
Purdue University

Mark A. Plummer
Illinois State University

Marjorie Podolsky
Penn State University, Erie

David L. Porter
William Penn College

John Powell
Penn State University, Erie

Steven J. Ramold
University of Nebraska at Lincoln

R. Kent Rasmussen
Independent Scholar

E. A. Reed
Baylor University

Douglas W. Richmond
University of Texas, Arlington

Barbara Roos
Grand Valley State University

Courtney B. Ross
Louisiana State University, Baton Rouge

Irene Struthers Rush
Independent Scholar

Dorothy C. Salem
Cleveland State University
Cuyahoga Community College

Lisa M. Sardinia
Pacific University

Elizabeth D. Schafer
Independent Scholar

Larry Schweikart
University of Dayton

Terry L. Seip
Louisiana State University, Baton Rouge

R. Baird Shuman
University of Illinois, Urbana-Champaign

Donald C. Simmons, Jr.
Mississippi Humanities Council

Donna Addkison Simmons
Independent Scholar

James Smallwood
Oklahoma State University

Christopher E. Smith
University of Akron

Ira Smolensky
Monmouth College

Mary Ellen Snodgrass
Independent Scholar

David L. Sterling
University of Cincinnati

Leslie Stricker
Park College

Robert Sullivan
Independent Scholar

James Tackach
Roger Williams University

Vanessa Tait
University of California, Santa Cruz

Harold D. Tallant
Georgetown College

G. Thomas Taylor
University of Maine

Emily Teipe
Fullerton College

Christel N. Temple
University of Maryland

Nancy Conn Terjesen
Kent State University

Vincent Michael Thur
Wenatchee Valley College

Leslie V. Tischauser
Prairie State College

Brian G. Tobin
Lassen College

Mfanya D. Tryman
Mississippi State University

Annita Marie Ward
Salem-Teikyo University

Elwood David Watson
East Tennessee State University

William L. Waugh, Jr.
Georgia State University

Donald V. Weatherman
Arkansas College

Richard Whitworth
Ball State University

Lou Falkner Williams
Kansas State University

Harry L. Wilson
Roanoke College

Richard L. Wilson
*University of Tennessee,
    Chattanooga*

Thomas Winter
University of Cincinnati

Michael Witkoski
Independent Scholar

Trudi D. Witonsky
University of Wisconsin, Madison

C. A. Wolski
Independent Scholar

Gene Redding Wynne, Jr.
Tri-County Technical College

Clifton K. Yearley
*State University of New York,
    Buffalo*

African American History

Abolition

Definition: Efforts to abolish slavery

The abolition movement attempted to apply the concepts of Christian brotherhood and democratic egalitarianism to race relations; it helped to end slavery in the United States.

By the mid-eighteenth century, American Quakers such as John Woolman and Benjamin Lay were denouncing slavery as un-Christian. The rationalism of the Enlightenment, with its stress upon natural law, added ammunition to the arsenal of critics of slavery.

The egalitarian rhetoric of the Revolutionary era illustrated the irony of slaveholders fighting for liberty. As a result, most northern states abolished slavery by 1784. New York and New Jersey did so afterward. Southern whites believed that they could not afford to abolish slavery, yet they too felt the need to justify the institution on ethical grounds. They concentrated on humanizing the institution and argued that it was a "necessary evil."

Antislavery feeling receded after 1793 because of fear of slave revolts, the increasing profitability of slavery following the invention of the cotton gin, and new scientific theories that reinforced racism. The leading antislavery organization in the early nineteenth century was the American Colonization Society (ACS). The ACS attempted to resettle free blacks in Africa and encouraged voluntary emancipation without challenging the right to own human property. The colonization plan allowed liberal slaveholders and moderate members of the clergy to rationalize their guilt over slavery.

In 1825, a great Protestant religious revival swept the northeastern region of the country. Ministers such as Charles Grandison Finney preached a new perfectionist theology that sought to counter the growing worldliness of Americans. This revival sparked a host of humanitarian crusades designed to protect the rights of the disadvantaged and to cleanse American institutions of contamination.

By the early 1830's, many evangelical reformers began to view slavery and racism as sinful because racism violated the Chris-

The Oberlin Rescuers, an abolitionist body based in Oberlin, Ohio, in 1859. Oberlin was a major center of the abolitionist movement. (Library of Congress)

tian ethic of equality. Known as immediate abolitionists, these re-formers demanded the immediate and unqualified liberation of slaves and an end to racial discrimination. With the formation of the American Anti-Slavery Society in 1833, abolitionist speakers toured the northern states attempting to rally support for their cause. Abolitionists were frequently attacked by angry mobs, and their literature was destroyed in southern post offices.

The abolition movement failed to end racism in the North. It did, however, spark antisouthern feelings, which led to increased controversy within the national government. This conflict led di-rectly to the Civil War (1861-1865). During the war, abolitionists pressured the federal government to transform the conflict from a war to preserve the Union into a war to end slavery. Abolition ad-vocates were disappointed by the Emancipation Proclamation because it was based upon military necessity rather than moral principle, but they accomplished their central purpose with the passage of the Thirteenth Amendment, which ended slavery in the United States.

Garrisonian Ethics

One major faction within the abolition movement was led by editor William Lloyd Garrison. In a real sense, the publication of the first issue of *The Liberator* on January 1, 1831, established Gar-rison as the foremost abolitionist in the country. Garrison's harsh attacks upon slaveholders and colonizationists caused a national sensation even though the circulation of his newspaper never ex-ceeded three thousand.

Like all abolitionists, Garrison demanded that everyone recognize a personal responsibility to improve society. The three major tenets of his ethical philosophy were human liberation, moral suasion, and no compromise with evil. Garrison actively campaigned on behalf of legal equality for African Americans, temperance, and equality for women. Garrison rejected force and violence in human affairs. He sought the moral reformation of slave owners, not their destruction. He never advocated slave revolts, and he wanted the northern states to allow the South to secede during the crisis of 1860-1861.

Garrison sincerely believed in all that he advocated, and he would not compromise his principles. He rejected any solution to the issue of slavery that involved a program that would delay emancipation. He also demanded that his followers reject participation in the American political system because the Constitution was a proslavery document. Other abolitionists, such as Gerrit Smith and James Birney, attempted to use the political system as a way to gain publicity for the cause of abolition.

African American Abolitionism

In a sense, there were two abolition movements. The white movement was based on a moral abstraction, but African Americans were forced to confront the everyday realities of racism in nineteenth century America.

Frederick Douglass emerged as the major spokesperson for African Americans during the antebellum period. Douglass self-consciously attempted to use his life as an example to repudiate racist stereotypes. Because of his eloquence, Douglass gained an international reputation as a public speaker, and in doing so, he proved the humanity of African Americans.

Like Garrison, Douglass strongly supported temperance and women's rights. He was, however, willing to use any means to achieve the liberation of slaves, including violence and political action. He approved of John Brown's idea of using the southern Appalachians as an armed sanctuary for runaways. He also supported the Free-Soil and Republican Parties even though neither advocated the emancipation of southern slaves. He justified his positions as part of a larger struggle to advance the cause of racial equality in America. For Douglass, as for other African Americans involved in the cause of abolition, equality was the only acceptable ethical standard for a free society.

Thomas D. Matijasic

Further Reading

Books that provide additional information on the abolition movement include, Kevin C. Julius's *The Abolitionist Decade, 1829-1838: A Year-by-Year History of Early Events in the Antislavery Movement* (Jefferson, N.C.: McFarland & Co., 2004), Stanley Harrold's *The Rise of Aggressive Abolitionism: Addresses to the Slaves* (Lexington: University Press of Kentucky, 2004), Harrold's *Subversives: Antislavery Community in Washington, D.C., 1828-1865* (Baton Rouge: Louisiana State University Press, 2003), Richard S. Newman's *The Transformation of American Abolitionism: Fighting Slavery in the Early Republic* (Chapel Hill: University of North Carolina Press, 2002), Gilbert Hobbs Barnes's *The Antislavery Impulse: 1830-1844* (New York: Harcourt, Brace & World, 1964), *The Antislavery Vanguard: New Essays on the Abolitionists* (Princeton, N.J.: Princeton University Press, 1965), edited by Martin Duberman, Gerald Sorin's *Abolitionism: A New Perspective* (New York: Praeger, 1972), James Brewer Stewart's *Holy Warriors: The Abolitionists and American Slavery* (Rev. ed. New York: Hill & Wang, 1996), and Alice Felt Tyler's *Freedom's Ferment: Phases of American Social History to 1860* (Minneapolis: University of Minnesota Press, 1944). Nathan Irvin Huggins's *Slave and Citizen: The Life of Frederick Douglass* (Boston: Little, Brown, 1980) looks at the African American abolitionist, and Henry Mayer's *All on Fire: William Lloyd Garrison and the Abolition of Slavery* (New York: St. Martin's Press, 1998) and Russel B. Nye's *William Lloyd Garrison and the Humanitarian Reformers* (Boston: Little, Brown, 1955) examine the prominent white abolitionist.

See also American Anti-Slavery Society; American Colonization Society; *Amistad* slave revolt; Antislavery laws of 1777 and 1807; *Clotilde* capture; Emancipation Proclamation; Harpers Ferry raid; *Liberator, The*; National Council of Colored People; Negro Conventions; *North Star, The*; Slavery; Thirteenth Amendment; Underground Railroad

Abolitionist movement and women

Conflict over women's role in the abolitionist movement, which sought the immediate emancipation of slaves and an end to the institution of slavery, led to the women's rights movement.

Abolition emerged as a social movement in the United States by the early 1830's. U.S. women witnessed the example of British women in their call for total emancipation in the 1820's and 1830's, during which time more than a million people (mostly women) signed petitions for Parliament and prayed for the end of slavery. British women used passive resistance, free-produce societies, and active abolitionist tactics. Anne Knight and Marie Tothill gathered 187,000 women's signatures and achieved their goal of freeing 800,000 West Indian slaves in 1833.

Much of the early antislavery movement reflected the influence of the Society of Friends (Quakers), whose leaders, John Woolman and Anthony Benezet, opposed slavery in the late eighteenth century. Benjamin Lundy, a Quaker, became one of the first traveling antislavery lecturers and founded the antislavery paper *Genius of Universal Emancipation* in 1821. As early as 1829, Quaker Elizabeth Margaret Chandler, the first female correspondent for an antislavery publication, used her column, "Female Department," to urge U.S. women to take a strong stand against slavery.

The U.S. movement had ties to the British antislavery crusade. The associate editor of Lundy's paper was William Lloyd Garrison. On January 1, 1831, Garrison founded his own antislavery newspaper in Boston, *The Liberator*, which called for immediate emancipation without compensation to slaveowners. That same year, Prudence Crandall came to Canterbury, Connecticut, to establish a select school for young ladies. By 1833, she had opened the school to "young colored Ladies and Misses." When the town arrested her, abolitionists provided bond. Her problems drew the support of Garrison; the Tappan brothers, Arthur, Benjamin, and Lewis; and Samuel May. Her case became one of the most celebrated incidents in the denial of abolitionist civil rights. Antislavery delegates from throughout the Northeast gathered in Philadelphia to form the American Anti-Slavery Society in 1833.

The national abolitionist movement emerged from strong reform foundations.

Foundations for Reform

By the 1820's and 1830's, women in the United States had become increasingly aware of how the concept of "separate spheres" for the sexes restricted the role of women in social reform movements. Nevertheless, many women were able to use their perceived moral superiority to work in religious, charitable, and educational organizations. To avoid conflict over the issue of integrated female participation in reform, women participated through ladies' societies. Female moral reform societies addressed such issues as prostitution, male licentiousness, and double standards. Temperance became a women's issue, because a husband's drinking could drain the family income, lead to domestic abuse and neglect, and threaten the stability of civilized life. The most political of all reforms was abolition, a movement to abolish slavery. Quaker women were early leaders in the abolitionist movement. The beliefs of the Society of Friends encouraged egalitarianism, in which all souls were considered equal in the eyes of God. Quaker women exercised leadership as ministers, testified in front of mixed male and female audiences, and supervised the spiritual life of other women through meetings that expanded women's roles beyond the spiritual community. In 1828, the Hicksite Quakers split from their more traditional fellows and advocated a boycott of slave-produced goods.

The general divisions in the antislavery movement included the Garrisonians, evangelicals, and political abolitionists. The Garrisonians called for immediate emancipation, racial civil equality, and moral suasion as the means to persuade others to their cause. Rejecting gradualism, colonization, and political action, the Garrisonians embraced absolute human equality, criticized the institutions of organized religion and slavery, and used inflammatory rhetoric and tactics. The evangelicals remained committed to a conventional, revivalistic Christianity. The political abolitionists were directly involved in political activity in the establishment of third parties such as the Liberty Party, the Free Soil Party, and the Republican Party. Women were most active in the

Garrisonian wing, because they were accepted there as equal participants. Women also worked through female free-produce societies and separate female auxiliaries.

Female Free-Produce Societies

Free-produce unions promoted the manufacture and marketing of goods made entirely by free labor by boycotting products associated with slave labor. The free-produce movement was both racially and sexually segregated in the 1830's, as were the majority of abolition societies. Female free-produce societies tried to encourage other women not to purchase slave produce, such as cotton, sugar, molasses, rice, and tobacco, in order to put pressure on the slave-based economy of the South and the markets for such goods in the North. Members of free-produce societies patronized shops selling products and goods produced by free labor. Drinking tea without sweeteners, wearing coarse cloth without cotton, and avoiding foods from the South raised the consciousness of women and their families to their dependence upon slave labor, producing more of a moral than an economic impact.

Female Antislavery Societies

At first, only men addressed the members of antislavery societies, but soon women began to publish their own tracts and to speak. African American women were the first to organize antislavery societies, from their earlier religious, moral, benevolent, or literary societies. The first U.S.-born woman to deliver public antislavery lectures to mixed audiences was Maria Stewart, a black woman, in 1831. In 1832, Stewart called her "daughters of Africa" to dedicate their lives to abolition. In February, 1832, African American women in Salem, Massachusetts, joined together to form the first women's abolitionist society. Female societies emerged in towns throughout the Northeast, with leaders including Charlotte Forten, Harriet Jacobs, Sarah Douglass, and Sarah Parker Remond. By October, 1832, the Boston Female Antislavery Society began its work. It was followed by more than one hundred women's antislavery societies during the 1830's. Influenced by Garrison's abolitionism, Lydia Maria Child called for women to enter the fight against slavery in 1833, with *An Appeal in Favor of That Class of Americans Called Africans.* Garrison helped form the Philadelphia Female Anti-Slavery Society in December, 1833. Humanitarian Lucretia Mott, a member of a Hicksite group of the Society of Friends, had attended a meeting of the newly formed American Anti-Slavery Society with three other women. Seeking greater participation, however, she soon joined with other Quakers and seven women of color to form the Philadelphia Female Anti-Slavery Society. Women throughout the Northeast held meetings, organized societies, raised money, supported antislavery publications, and circulated petitions for the antislavery cause. Soon petitions called for Congress to put an immediate end to slavery in the District of Columbia. By 1837, *The Liberator* noted that the women of New England had sent nearly twice as many petitions to Congress as had the men.

Centered in New England, the female antislavery societies spread to New York and the West, especially in northeastern Ohio, an area settled by New Englanders. Garrisonian abolitionism gained followers, leading to the formation of the Ohio Anti-Slavery Society in 1835. In Quaker regions such as Salem, Ohio, men and women acted together and formed integrated societies.

By January, 1836, Ohio women were entering the abolition movement. That summer, the American Anti-Slavery Society appointed two female agents to serve as speakers and propagandists. The speaking tour of Sarah and Angelina Grimké, Quaker converts and daughters of a South Carolina slaveowner, produced a controversy that eventually split the antislavery movement and raised issues concerning the human rights of women. The Grimké sisters spoke to audiences throughout the Northeast. Among the young, idealistic women who heard or read their words and became converts to the antislavery cause were Lucy Stone, a young teacher in West Brookfield, Massachusetts, and Elizabeth Robinson, a young Quaker from Mount Pleasant, Ohio.

The first national convention of female antislavery societies met in New York in May, 1837, to begin an extensive campaign. After hearing the Grimkés speak about their tour, the convention leaders asserted that women had the right to move into this sphere, which they believed Providence had assigned. The pioneers included both experienced and new leaders, including

Mott; the Grimkés; Maria Weston Chapman, a volatile supporter of Garrison; Abby Kelley Foster, a Quaker school teacher from Lynn, Massachusetts, who would eventually leave teaching to become a full-time lecturer for antislavery; Susan Paul, the daughter of a Boston Baptist minister; and Forten and her daughters, founding members of the Philadelphia Female Anti-Slavery Society.

The women met in national conventions two more times, both in Philadelphia, before women were accepted as equals in the American Anti-Slavery Society, eliminating the need for separate conventions thereafter. Women raised money by selling original texts, writing letters, conducting petition drives, hosting bake sales, holding antislavery fairs, and lecturing. Women's work became increasingly essential to the antislavery movement as the decade progressed. As their presence became critical, the character of their roles came under scrutiny.

The Woman Question

The variety of ways that women participated in the abolition movement raised "the woman question." Should women work through gender-integrated associations, or should they serve in a supportive role through female societies? This question had no universal answer. The role of women in the antislavery movement was a point of contention that led to a split in the movement: In May, 1840, the American Anti-Slavery Society split over the equal admission of women. Those who favored a separate role for women formed the American and Foreign Anti-Slavery Society, headed and financed by Lewis Tappan. The majority of evangelicals left the American Anti-Slavery Society for the American and Foreign Anti-Slavery Society so as to continue working within U.S. religious and political institutions.

In June, 1840, the World Antislavery Conference in London rejected the credentials of U.S. female delegates. To further aggravate the official decision, the women were placed behind a screen to limit their participation. William Lloyd Garrison joined the women behind the screen to voice his disapproval. His demonstrated egalitarianism won militant women to his form of abolitionism.

Women continued writing tracts, poetry, and columns for the antislavery cause. Harriet Beecher Stowe's antislavery novel *Uncle Tom's Cabin* (1852) dramatized the cruelty of slavery and sold more than 300,000 copies in its first year of publication. A free woman of color, Frances Ellen Watkins Harper, used much of her income from her book of poetry *Poems on Miscellaneous Subjects* (1854) to support William Still and the Underground Railroad.

Some women edited antislavery newspapers. In the 1840's, Child edited the *National Anti-Slavery Standard*. By 1845, the *Anti-Slavery Bugle*, edited by Jane Elizabeth Jones and her husband, Benjamin, carried the Garrisonian message and later served as the organ for the radical Western Anti-Slavery Society, formed in 1846.

Following the passage of the Fugitive Slave Act in 1850, conditions worsened for free blacks and fugitive slaves. Many abolitionists advocated migration to Canada, where there was no slavery. For Ellen Craft, escape to Nova Scotia and then to England prevented her return to slavery. The Refugee Home Society, established by black Canadians and Michigan abolitionists, provided cheap land, self-government, and schooling to African Americans.

Mary Ann Shadd Cary, the first black American female editor, established *The Provincial Freeman* in 1853 to encourage fifteen thousand free blacks and fugitive slaves to emigrate to Canada. The less restrictive life there did not include integrated education, however. Mary Bibb, the wife of fugitive slave Henry Bibb, taught black children in separate schools in Ontario, while she supported the antislavery wing led by Lewis Tappan.

Following the examples of Stewart, the Grimké sisters, and Foster, many women became well-known lecturers. Stone, for example, entered Oberlin College to train in public oratory so she could become an antislavery lecturer. Free black women traveled the lecturing circuit. Harper launched her career as a lecturer with "Education and the Elevation of the Colored Race" in New Bedford, Massachusetts, in August, 1854. She became the first female orator for the Maine Anti-Slavery Society and, in 1857, spoke for the Pennsylvania Anti-Slavery Society. Remond, a member of several antislavery groups, started lecturing for the American Anti-Slavery Society in 1856, traveling in the Northeast and in England, Scotland, and Ireland to support the cause of abolition.

Former or fugitive slaves made excellent lecturers because of their firsthand experience with slavery. Many African American women were used on the antislavery lecture circuit to recount their miseries under slavery. (Light-skinned women were often sent out to lecture, to shock audiences into empathy with their plight.) One of the best-known speakers was Sojourner Truth, who was born a slave in New York State. Freed in 1826, she became an itinerant evangelist preacher who turned to antislavery issues, often sharing the platform with Frederick Douglass. Although she was illiterate, Truth used effective speaking techniques. Ellen Craft, a fugitive slave, lectured for the British and Foreign Freedman's Aid Society to avoid recapture in the 1850's and 1860's. Harriet Tubman, also illiterate, was a speaker for the antislavery movement, in addition to her more noteworthy role as a conductor on the Underground Railroad, which led three hundred slaves to freedom in the 1850's.

Impact

Women's role in the abolitionist movement was critical to its spread and survival. Their support financed antislavery newspapers, lecture circuits, societies, and conventions. Their moral spirit guided both written and spoken arguments for immediate emancipation.

Although most female antislavery societies fell within conventional notions of the woman's sphere, many female leaders showed no fear in arousing public wrath to carry out antislavery functions. Their activities gave inspiration and apprenticeship to many advocates of women's rights. The discussions about slave oppression raised awareness of racial and sexual oppression in the North. The Garrisonian abolitionism provided women with a worldview and a theoretical framework through which they could criticize social institutions. The antislavery movement also produced a political network of support among readers of antislavery newspapers, members of societies, and audiences who came to hear the speakers. Hence, the antislavery platform led both to the eventual gender and racial integration of the abolition movement and to the ultimate end to slavery. Women also gained the political expertise to develop an organized women's rights movement.

Dorothy C. Salem

Further Reading

Blackett, R. J. *Building an Antislavery Wall: Black Americans in the Atlantic Abolitionist Movement, 1830-1860*. Ithaca, N.Y.: Cornell University Press, 1989. Spans the ocean in the study of antislavery activity in Great Britain and the United States.

Cooper, Afua. "The Search for Mary Bibb, Black Woman Teacher in Nineteenth-Century Canada West." In *"We Specialize in the Wholly Impossible": A Reader in Black Women's History*, edited by Darlene Clark Hine, Wilma King, and Linda Reed. Brooklyn, N.Y.: Carlson, 1995. Studies the life of a freeborn black Quaker woman in Canada, who was a teacher and small businesswoman.

Hansen, Debra Gold. *Strained Sisterhood: Gender and Class in the Boston Female Anti-Slavery Society*. Amherst: University of Massachusetts Press, 1993. Discusses the conflicts within one of the most famous women's antislavery societies.

Hersh, Blanche. *The Slavery of Sex: Feminist-Abolitionists in America*. Chicago: University of Illinois Press, 1978. Shows the roots of women's rights in the female leadership of abolitionism.

Jeffrey, Julie Roy. *The Great Silent Army of Abolitionism: Ordinary Women in the Antislavery Movement*. Chapel Hill: University of North Carolina Press, 1998. An examination of women's antislavery societies and many of the women at the forefront of the movement.

Kraditor, Aileen. *Means and Ends in American Abolitionism*. New York: Pantheon Books, 1969. An analytical study of the various abolitionist organizations and leadership, with particular emphasis on women's roles.

Silverman, Jason, and Donna Gillie. "'The Pursuit of Knowledge Under Difficulties': Education and the Fugitive Slave in Canada." *Ontario History* 74 (1982): 95-111. Details the segregated education of blacks who came to Canada seeking freedom.

Sterling, Dorothy. *We Are Your Sisters: Black Women in the Nineteenth Century*. New York: W. W. Norton, 1984. One of the best collections of information about individual women and groups during the nineteenth century.

Yee, Shirley. *Black Women Abolitionists: A Study in Activism, 1828-1860*. Knoxville: University of Tennessee Press, 1992. Discusses black female leadership in the abolitionist movement and the women's perspectives of racial and gender discrimination.

Yellin, Jean Fagan. *Women and Sisters: The Antislavery Feminists in American Culture*. New Haven, Conn.: Yale University Press, 1989. Exposes the contradicting definitions between "true womanhood" and the role of women in the abolitionist movement.

See also Abolition; Slavery; Slavery and women

Adarand Constructors v. Peña

The Case: U.S. Supreme Court ruling on affirmative action
Date: June 12, 1995
In this decision, the U.S. Supreme Court held that broad affirmative action programs involving employment and contracts were unconstitutional but preserved the applicability of affirmative action to specific and limited circumstances of discrimination.

Randy Pech, a white contractor in Colorado Springs, Colorado, submitted the lowest bid for a federal road-repair project. The contract, however, was awarded to a company owned by a Latino man because of a 1987 law requiring that the Department of Transportation award at least 10 percent of its funds to companies owned by women or members of minority groups. Pech took his complaint to the courts. The case was decided by the Supreme Court at a time when criticism of affirmative action had become widespread both among the public and in Congress. In addition, the makeup of the Court itself had changed since the last federal affirmative action case in 1990; notably, Thurgood Marshall, a staunch liberal, had retired and been replaced by another African American jurist, Clarence Thomas, a conservative.

Overturning previous decisions offering support of federal affirmative action, on June 12, 1995, the Court voted 5 to 4 that the type of affirmative action program involved in the case was unconstitutional. In an opinion written by Justice Sandra Day O'Connor, the Supreme Court stated that the Constitution protects individuals but was not intended to offer special protections to groups. Treating "any person unequally because of his or her race" causes the person to suffer an injury that is not acceptable under the Constitution's guarantee of equal protection under the law. The law can treat people differently because of race "only for the most compelling reasons," and racial classifications by government agencies are "inherently suspect and presumptively invalid." The Court did say, however, that affirmative action programs could be acceptable to remedy specific, provable cases of discrimination.

The decision severely undercut all federal affirmative action programs, most notably those involving jobs or contracts required to go to members of minority groups ("minority set-asides"). In addition, federal law at the time of *Adarand* required firms that did more than fifty thousand dollars of business a year with the federal government and had more than fifty employees to have a written affirmative action policy, which meant that the *Adarand* decision could affect the policies of nearly all major employers in the United States. Reaction to the decision was strong and immediate. A leader of the Anti-Defamation League called it a "sea change" in the law. Many civil rights leaders protested the decision and urged the government not to abolish all affirmative action efforts. Conservative Republican leaders in Congress, in contrast, vowed to pass legislation to eliminate all racial preferences in federal hiring and contracting.

McCrea Adams

See also Affirmative action; *Bakke* case; Emancipation Proclamation; *Fullilove v. Klutznick*; *Griggs v. Duke Power Company*; Thirteenth Amendment; *United Steelworkers of America v. Weber*

Affirmative action

Definition: Programs of governmental agencies or private institutions designed to provide members of racial and ethnic minorities and women with access to opportunities in education and employment

Because of discrimination against women and minority members, governmental agencies, businesses, and educational institutions gave them special opportunities, which some people criticized as discriminating against nonminority members. A divided Supreme Court struggled with the question of when such programs are acceptable.

Affirmative action is a highly controversial means of pursuing equal access to resources in education and employment. Although the term affirmative action first appeared in an official document in an executive order issued by President Lyndon B. Johnson in 1965, affirmative action did not emerge as a government policy until the 1970's. In *Griggs v. Duke Power Company* (1971), the Supreme Court ruled that discrimination could be judged to exist when business practices resulted in limiting opportunities for members of minorities, even if there had been no evidence of intent to discriminate on the part of the employer. This altered the definition of discrimination, making it a matter of built-in racial bias.

Duke Power Company required either a high-school diploma or a passing grade on a general intelligence test for a job in its power plant. Fewer black applicants than white applicants passed this test. The plaintiffs argued that in this case, educational credentials and test results had no direct relevance to job performance, so no justification existed for a job requirement that disproportionately affected members of the minority race. The Court, under Chief Justice Warren E. Burger, found that employment practices that exclude African American job seekers and are not related to job performance are indeed discriminatory.

The concept of built-in discrimination established by *Griggs* helped lay the groundwork for political efforts to dismantle unintended barriers to full participation in American society. Affirmative action, according to the official government definition,

Milestones in Affirmative Action

Year	Event	Impact
1965	Executive Order 11246	Requires firms doing business in excess of $50,000 per year with the U.S. government to submit time tables and goals for diversifying their workforces.
1978	*Regents of the University of California v. Bakke*	Strikes down a policy that established a quota for minority admissions on grounds that it is unfair to a qualified white applicant ("reverse discrimination").
1979	*United Steelworkers of America v. Weber*	Upholds an agreement between an employer and a union, establishing goals for minority inclusion in a training program on grounds that any harm done to white employees is temporary and does not create an absolute barrier to advancement.
1986	*Wygant v. Jackson Board of Education*	Holds that right of seniority may take precedence over affirmative action plans when workforce is reduced.
1991	Civil Rights Act	Modifies effects of Supreme Court rulings that increased burden of proof on plaintiffs.
1995	*Adarand Constructors v. Peña*	Holds that broad affirmative action programs involving employment and contracts are unconstitutional, but preserves the applicability of affirmative action to specific and limited circumstances of discrimination.
1996	Proposition 209	California voters approve Proposition 209, a measure that ends state-supported affirmative action. Opponents of affirmative action in other states are encouraged by the passage of this measure.

involved action to overcome past or present barriers to equal opportunity. Two of the most obvious ways of overcoming such barriers were establishing quotas of minority members or women to be hired or admitted to educational programs and creating set-asides, positions reserved for minority members or women. These remedies, however, met with challenges by those in groups not benefiting from affirmative action, who charged that they were suffering from officially sanctioned discrimination.

In 1971 a Jewish man named DeFunis applied for admission to the University of Washington Law School but was rejected. The law school followed a practice of dividing its applicants into two categories, minority group members and majority group members, using lower standards for admitting minority group members. If DeFunis had been black, American Indian, or Latino, his test scores and grades would have gained him entry. He sued, claiming that his rights to equal legal protection, guaranteed by the Fourteenth Amendment, had been violated.

DeFunis v. Odegaard came before the Court in 1974. However, DeFunis had been admitted to the law school after a lower court found in his favor, and the school had said that he would be allowed to graduate, regardless of the Court's ruling. The Court ruled the case moot because a ruling would not affect the outcome for the plaintiff, and it dismissed the appeal. Justice William O. Douglas wrote a dissent expressing his view that DeFunis had indeed been denied equal protection under the law.

Increasing Challenges

Although the Court did not have to rule on preferential treatment of protected categories of people in the DeFunis case, challenges to affirmative action increased through the 1970's. One of the objections was the claim that affirmative action violated Title VII of the Civil Rights Act of 1964, which forbids discrimination on the basis of race. Many critics maintained that preferential treatment of minority group members could be viewed as discrimination against those who were not minority group members. In *United Steelworkers of America v. Weber* (1979), the court ruled that Title VII's prohibition against racial discrimination does not condemn all private, voluntary race-conscious affirmative action plans. Kaiser Aluminum and Chemical Corporation and the United Steelworkers Union maintained a training program. As long as the percentage of African Americans among Kaiser's plant employees was less than the percentage of African Americans in the local workforce, half of the openings in this program were reserved for African Americans. Brian Weber, a white man who had not been allowed to enter the training program, sued, claiming that he had been a victim of racial discrimination.

Justice William J. Brennan, Jr., writing for the majority of justices, maintained that Congress had not intended Title VII to prohibit private, voluntary efforts to overcome long-established patterns of racial discrimination in employment. In addition, the Fourteenth Amendment did not apply in this case because it did not involve any governmental actions. Whites, in Brennan's view, were not handicapped by the policy regarding the training program because no whites were fired and whites still had opportunities for advancement.

The *Bakke* Case

The best-known challenge to affirmative action to come before the Court was *Regents of the University of California v. Bakke* (1978). Allan Bakke was a white man who had been denied admission to the University of California medical school at Davis. In 1972 the thirty-two-year-old Bakke was a Marine Corps veteran who had served in Vietnam and an engineer at a research center of the National Aeronautics and Space Administration (NASA) near Palo Alto, California. While working at NASA, he decided to become a medical doctor. He took classes to prepare himself for medical school and served as a volunteer in a local hospital emergency room.

Despite receiving high scores on the Medical College Admissions Test and having strong letters of recommendation, Bakke was rejected by the University of California and ten other schools to which he applied. He wrote to the chairman of admissions at the University of California, Davis, requesting reconsideration, charging that racial minority members who were less qualified than he had been admitted through a special admissions program. Bakke reapplied for early admissions in 1973 and prepared to sue if he was again rejected. In the summer of 1974 Bakke's suit was officially filed in Yolo County Superior Court.

Bakke became one of the most celebrated court cases of the decade. It provoked national debate over affirmative action and brought wide attention to the practice of setting aside places in businesses or educational institutions for minority members. The California supreme court found that Bakke had suffered racial discrimination. In November, 1976, the Board of Regents of the University of California voted to appeal the decision to the Supreme Court.

Four justices, led by Justice Brennan, voted not to hear the case. Five chose to hear it, however, and it went on the Court docket. Ultimately, the Court reached a split decision. Four justices concluded that the University of California had clearly violated both the equal protection clause of the Fourteenth Amendment and the Civil Rights Act of 1964. Four other justices disagreed and wanted to uphold the constitutionality of taking race into consideration for education or employment. The swing vote, Justice Lewis F. Powell, Jr., essentially divided his decision.

The phasing out of affirmative action programs in several major universities' admission policies during the mid-1990's threatened to return American colleges and universities to the racially imbalanced student bodies of earlier eras. (National Archives)

He sided with the four who maintained that the minority set-aside program at Davis was unconstitutional; however, he also stated that although racial quotas were unacceptable, race could be taken into consideration. The majority opinion, written by Brennan, incorporated Powell's ambivalence. It stated that it was constitutional to take race into account to remedy disadvantages resulting from past prejudice and discrimination, but that race alone could not be the basis for making decisions about opportunities in employment or education.

After *Bakke*

Many legal scholars believe that *Bakke* established an unclear precedent. Although it did uphold the basic principle of affirmative action, it also left the door open for challenges to specific affirmative action policies. As a part of the 1977 Public Works Employment Act, Congress set aside 10 percent of all federal appropriations for public works contracts for minority contractors and subcontractors. This legislation came before the Court in *Fullilove v. Klutznick* (1980). Once again, a controversial issue split the members of the Court.

One of the differences between *Fullilove* and earlier affirmative action cases was that it involved the actions of Congress, which may act with greater power and authority than a private employer or a local school board and is also charged with seeking the present and future welfare of the nation. Chief Justice Burger's opinion, joined by Justices Powell and Byron R. White, recognized this, stating that Congress has the power to act to remedy social evils and that there was a compelling governmental interest in seeking to counteract the deep-rooted disadvantages of minority contractors. Thurgood Marshall, joined by Justices Brennan and Harry A. Blackmun, wrote a concurring opinion arguing that the actions of Congress were constitutional because the set-aside provision was related to the congressionally approved goal of overcoming racial inequality. Justices Potter Stewart, William H. Rehnquist, and John Paul Stevens disagreed. Stewart and Rehnquist maintained that an unconstitutional practice could not be constitutional simply because it came from Congress rather than from a lesser source and that the set-aside involved distributing governmental privileges based on birth. Stevens objected to the governmental favoring of some groups over others and pointed out that those who were likely to benefit most were the least disadvantaged members of minority groups, such as successful black or Hispanic businesspeople. Thus, although *Fullilove* established once more the principle of affirmative action, it also made it clear that there were fundamental disagreements on the principle, even among the justices.

Two major issues emerged from the *Fullilove* decision. One was the concept that affirmative action policies undertaken by the government merit a special deference because of the constitutional authority of Congress to make laws. The second was that because affirmative action is a means of pursuing governmental policies, agencies and organizations must be able to demonstrate that their affirmative action programs serve a compelling governmental interest. This second point placed the burden of justifying affirmative action programs on those seeking to establish the policies. Those seeking to pursue affirmative action policies must be able to demonstrate that these policies are narrowly designed to compensate for past discrimination or to bring about a clearly defined goal. For this reason, the Court decided in *Mississippi University for Women v. Hogan* (1982) that a college could not deny men entry into a nursing program on the grounds that this was intended to compensate women for past discrimination.

On the other hand, when past discrimination could be clearly demonstrated, affirmative action policies were deemed acceptable. A requirement in Alabama that one black state trooper be promoted for every promotion of a white state trooper was upheld by the Court in *United States v. Paradise* (1987) because it could be demonstrated that underrepresentation of African Americans at high ranks was caused by past discrimination by the Alabama Department of Public Safety. In *Richmond v. J. A. Croson Company* (1989), however, the Court ruled that the Richmond city government's minority business utilization plan failed to provide appropriate statistical data showing systematic underrepresentation of minority-owned businesses. Therefore, the Court found that the plan was not narrowly tailored to remedy the effects of prior discrimination and failed to demonstrate a compelling government interest for awarding a certain percentage of contracts to minority-owned businesses. Both the concept of the special status of Congress and of the legitimacy of affirmative action for compelling governmental interests were upheld in *Metro Broadcasting v. Federal Communications Commission* (1990), in which a majority of justices ruled that minority preference policies of the Federal Communications Commission were acceptable because they met both criteria.

Limits on Affirmative Action

During the 1990's there were a number of public challenges to affirmative action, notably in the Texas and California systems of higher education, where controversial laws passed in 1997 made it illegal to give preferential treatment to members of protected groups. Affirmative action proponent Marshall left the Court in 1991, and new justices appointed by Presidents Ronald Reagan and George Bush—including Sandra Day O'Connor, Anthony M. Kennedy, Antonin Scalia, and Clarence Thomas—appeared to be largely unsympathetic to affirmative-action-style policies.

In his book on affirmative action and the Court, Lincoln Caplan observed that in the middle to late 1990's Chief Justice Rehnquist and Justices O'Connor, Kennedy, Scalia, and Thomas never voted to uphold an affirmative action program based on race. Thomas, the only African American among these justices, was the strongest and most open opponent of the preferential treatment of members of minorities, which he derided as "racial paternalism." The limiting of affirmative action appeared in *Adarand Constructors v. Peña* (1995), in which the Court expanded the idea that programs had to serve a compelling interest. Affirmative action programs, the court ruled, must be observed with the strictest scrutiny and must be necessary to meet a compelling state interest.

By the end of the twentieth century, many observers were predicting that the Court would make a ruling that would end affirmative action. This perception made some defenders of affirmative action policies reluctant to bring cases before the Court. This happened, for example, in the case of Sharon Taxman. Taxman, a white teacher, had been laid off from her job by the school district of Piscataway, New Jersey, in 1991. The school district needed to reduce its teaching force and had to choose between Taxman and an equally qualified black teacher. Because black teachers were underrepresented in the district, the school system used its voluntary affirmative action program to decide between the two teachers. Taxman sued, claiming racial discrimination. The case was poised to go to the Court in late 1997. Fear that a Court ruling in favor of Taxman would further weaken affirmative action led civil rights groups to support the Piscataway School Board's decision to pay Taxman a $433,000 settlement in November, 1997, rather than risk an unfavorable Court decision.

The Court also showed a reluctance to hear affirmative action cases at the end of the twentieth century. In March, 1999, the Court refused to hear a case regarding a program in Dallas, Texas, that had been intended to benefit minority firefighters. A lower court, the Fifth Circuit Court of Appeals, earlier found that there was insufficient evidence of a historical pattern of discrimination against members of minorities in Dallas to justify preferential promotions for minority candidates. The two justices who had been appointed by President Bill Clinton, Stephen G. Breyer and Ruth Bader Ginsburg, issued a written dissent urging the majority of justices to take the case. Nevertheless, the Court let the decision of the lower court stand. Many observers maintained that this case and others like it sent the message that the majority on the Court saw racial preferences as a dying and disfavored strategy.

Carl L. Bankston III

Further Reading

An insightful work on affirmative action is Terry H. Anderson's *The Pursuit of Fairness: A History of Affirmative Action* (New York: Oxford University Press, 2004). Brian Pusser's *Burning Down the House: Politics, Governance, and Affirmative Action at the University of California* (Albany: State University of New York Press, 2004) and Greg Stohr's *A Black and White Case: How Affirmative Action Survived Its Greatest Legal Challenge* (Princeton: Bloomberg Press, 2004) are timely and valuable additions to the literature on affirmative action. *Up Against the Law: Affirmative Action and the Supreme Court* (New York: Twentieth Century Fund Press, 1997) is a short introduction to the role of the Supreme Court in the American debate over affirmative action that also offers explanations of the practices and consequences of affirmative action programs. A great deal has been written on the *Bakke* case. Timothy J. O'Neill's *"Bakke" and the Politics of Equality: Friends and Foes in the Classroom of Litigation* (Middletown, Conn.: Wesleyan University Press, 1981) is a detailed study of the case and of the political forces on both sides.

Readers who want to know about the *Bakke* case should consult Howard Ball's *The Bakke Case: Race, Education, and Affirmative Action* (Lawrence: University Press of Kansas, 2000) and *Behind "Bakke": Affirmative Action and the Supreme Court* (New York: New York University Press, 1988) by Bernard Schwartz. *The Color-Blind Constitution* (Cambridge, Mass.: Harvard University Press, 1992) attempts to discover the history of the argument that the Constitution prohibits racial classifications by agencies of the government. The last chapter, "Benign Racial Sorting," is particularly useful to those interested in the arguments surrounding affirmative action issues. For the ideas behind questions of racial preferences, readers may want to consult *Equality and Preferential Treatment* (Princeton, N.J.: Princeton University Press, 1972). This is a collection of essays by professors of law and philosophy that attempt to present arguments for and against racial, ethnic, or gender preferences in schooling or employment. Although the book is a little old, its arguments continue to be relevant. Dinesh D'Souza's *Illiberal Education: The Politics of Race and Sex on Campus* (New York: Free Press, 1991), a work strongly opposed to affirmative action, presents a view of affirmative action policies in universities before these began to be scaled back. *The Shape of the River: Long-Term Consequences of Considering Race in College and University Admissions* (Princeton, N.J.: Princeton University Press, 1998) by William G. Bowen and Derek C. Bok provides a positive view of affirmative action in higher education.

See also *Adarand Constructors v. Peña*; *Bakke* case; Civil Rights movement; Civil Rights Restoration Act; Education; Employment; Equal Employment Opportunity Act of 1972; Equal Employment Opportunity Commission; *Fullilove v. Klutznick*; *Griggs v. Duke Power Company*; Integration; *United Steelworkers of America v. Weber*

African Liberation Day

The Event: Internationally recognized anniversary commemorating the freeing of Africa from European colonization
Date: May 25, 1963
Place: Worldwide

African Liberation Day is a date honored throughout the African world, as a day on which to unite and denounce racism, capitalism, and Zionism.

In 1963, thirty-one African heads of state convened in Ethiopia for the Summit Conference of the Independent African States, with the overall goal of freeing African people from the yoke of European domination and white supremacy. On May 25, 1963, the Charter of the Organization of African Unity was signed, and it was decided to celebrate African Liberation Day every year on May 25. Sponsored by the All African People's Revolutionary Party, African Liberation Day has led to the concerted action of the member states of the Organization of African Unity to pool financial aid to revive, strengthen, and intensify liberation movements throughout Africa. As much as possible, the goal is to end exploitation and oppression of Africans at home and abroad by finding peaceful solutions through deliberations and frank exchange of views among the nations that are involved.

African Liberation Day has become an institution throughout the African world, being a day when all African people rally for unity and denounce racism, capitalism, and Zionism. On African Liberation Day, African people focus on what they share—their common past, set of problems, and future—as they pause to think about the plight of their African brothers who are under foreign rule and who are seeking to win their freedom and fundamental human rights.

Alvin K. Benson

See also Black Is Beautiful movement; Black nationalism; Black Power movement; Pan-Africanism

African Methodist Episcopal Church

Identification: Predominantly African American Protestant denomination

Date: Founded on April 9, 1816

The African Methodist Episcopal Church was a radically distinct denomination that became an advocate for the cause of abolition and a bulwark of the African American community.

On April 9, 1816, sixteen African Methodist delegates met in Philadelphia to unite as the African Methodist Episcopal Church. Delegates from Philadelphia and Attleborough, Pennsylvania, joined representatives from Baltimore, Wilmington, and Salem to elect a bishop. They elected Richard Allen, who was consecrated as the first bishop of the African Methodist Episcopal Church (AME Church) on April 11, 1816. From the original sixteen delegates in 1816, membership grew to 7,257 by 1822.

Allen, known as the father of African American religion, was born a slave in 1760 in Philadelphia. Sold to the Stokeley plantation near Dover, Delaware, Allen attended evangelical tent meetings and experienced a religious conversion when he was seventeen years of age. He joined the Methodist Society, which held classes in the forest under the leadership of a white man, Benjamin Wells. Allen became a convincing proselytizer, converting first his family and then his owner, who agreed to Allen's proposal to purchase his own freedom in 1777. Allen worked at many jobs and preached at his regular stops, developing broad contacts through his travels. As an aide to other itinerant preachers, he met Bishop Francis Asbury, who established the first General Conference of the Methodist Church in America in 1784. Allen declined to accompany Asbury on a trip through the South and returned to Philadelphia in February, 1786.

Allen joined such Philadelphia leaders as former slave clerk and handyman Absalom Jones and other members of the St. Thomas vestry: James Forten, William White, Jacob Tapisco, and James Champion. Allen and Jones became lay preachers throughout the city, including early-morning and evening services at St. George's Methodist Episcopal Church. As African American attendance increased, racial conflict became apparent. In November, 1787, African Americans worshiping at St. George's were ordered to the gallery. After mistaking the section of the gallery assigned for their worship, Allen, Jones, and White were physically removed while praying at the Sunday morning worship service.

The Free African Society

The humiliation of this incident led to a mass exodus of African Americans from this church and a movement to create a separate church. In the spring, these African American leaders established the Free African Society, the first mutual aid society established to serve their community. By 1791, they held regular Sunday services, assumed lay leadership positions, and made plans for construction of a church building.

The leaders differed over the issue of church affiliation, with the majority voting to unite with the Episcopal church. On July 17, 1794, the St. Thomas African Church was dedicated as the first African church in Philadelphia, a Protestant Episcopal church with Jones as pastor. Jones became the first African American priest in 1804.

Richard Allen, the founder of the African Methodist Episcopal Church. (Association for the Study of African American Life and History)

Allen withdrew from the Free African Society to form a separate church, the Bethel African Methodist Episcopal Church, on July 29, 1794. Allen declared the church independent in management but did not sever all relations with the Methodist Episcopal Church. The articles of incorporation ensured independence by allowing membership only to African Americans. Allen became the first African American to receive ordination from the Methodist Episcopal Church in the United States.

A Force for Change

Such church independence helped African Americans resist the insults and subordination resulting from slavery and racial prejudice and reflected a growing role of the church in the community. Sermons underscored the need for the African American community to become self-reliant through the church, schools, and economic organizations in order to gain group solidarity and recognition. Christian character, in turn, depended upon Christian education.

In 1804, Allen established the Society of Free People of Color for Promoting the Instruction and School Education of Children of African Descent. In 1809, he helped Forten and Jones organize the Society for the Suppression of Vice and Immorality in Philadelphia, to provide community supervision of the morality of African Americans and to establish means for their moral uplift. These leaders recruited three thousand members for the Black Legion during the War of 1812. The successful functions associated with African American churches led to greater membership. By 1813, St. Thomas had a membership of 560, while Bethel Church had 1,272 communicants.

The movement spread to other cities and along the seaboard states. Church leaders continued their pioneering efforts for group solidarity. In January, 1817, the First Negro Convention met at the Bethel Church to protest the plans of the American Colonization Society for emigration of free blacks to Africa. Also in 1817, Allen and Tapisco published the First Church Discipline as well as a book of hymns compiled by Allen, Daniel Coker, and Champion.

The church continued to improve the conditions for African Americans. It supported the use of boycotts to protest the eco-

nomic basis of slavery through the Free Produce Society of Philadelphia, which was organized at an assembly at Bethel Church on
December 20, 1830, to advocate purchase of produce grown only
by free labor. The First Annual Convention of the People of Color,
convened in Philadelphia in 1831, elected Allen as its leader
shortly before his death on March 26, 1831. The African Methodist Episcopal Church has survived as an integral part of the African American community and continued its strong leadership
role.

Dorothy C. Salem

Further Reading

Jualynne E. Dodson's *Engendering Church: Women, Power, and
the AME Church* (Lanham, Md.: Rowman & Littlefield, 2002) is
a helpful analysis on women and the AME Church. *Social Protest Thought in the African Methodist Episcopal Church, 1862-1939*
(Knoxville: University of Tennessee Press, 2000) edited by Stephen W. Angell and Anthony B. Pinn and *Disciples of Liberty: The
African Methodist Episcopal Church in the Age of Imperialism, 1884-
1916* (Knoxville: University of Tennessee Press, 2000) by Lawrence S. Little are serviceable additions to the literature on the
AME Church. James T. Campbell's *Songs of Zion: The African
Methodist Episcopal Church in the United States and South Africa*
(New York: Oxford University Press, 1995) examines the rise and
development of the AME Church in America and South Africa.
Katharine L. Dvorak's *An African American Exodus* (Brooklyn,
N.Y.: Carlson, 1991) provides the history and theology of the
nineteenth century African Methodist Episcopal Church. A num-
ber of books and articles describe Richard Allen and his life and
work, including Allen's own *The Life, Experience, and Gospel Labors
of the Right Reverent Richard Allen*, originally published in 1833
(Nashville, Tenn.: Abingdon Press, 1983), Carol V. R. George's
*Segregated Sabbaths: Richard Allen and the Rise of Independent Black
Churches, 1760-1840* (New York: Oxford University Press, 1973),
Richard Allen: The First Exemplar of African American Education
(New York: ECA Associates, 1985) by Mwalimu I. Mwadilitu
(E. Curtis Alexander), Charles Wesley's *Richard Allen: Apostle of
Freedom* (Washington, D.C.: Associated Publishers, 1935), and

Gary Nash's "New Light on Richard Allen: The Early Years of Freedom" in *William and Mary Quarterly* 46 (April, 1989).

See also African Methodist Episcopal Zion Churches; Baptist Church; Black church; Free African Society

African Methodist Episcopal Zion Churches

Identification: Predominantly African American Protestant denomination
Date: Founded in 1821

The church has historically emphasized advancement of black citizenship rights, expanded roles for women in church government, and ecumenicism among black and white Methodist churches.

The African Methodist Episcopal (AME) Zion Church is one of several black Methodist churches that originated in the northern United States in the late eighteenth and early nineteenth centuries. Organized in 1821, the AME Zion Church was conceived in the 1790's, when a handful of black congregations broke away from the predominantly white Methodist Episcopal denomination in search of greater autonomy and freedom of worship. These independent black Methodist churches eventually organized into three separate denominations: the Union Church of Africans; the African Methodist Episcopal (AME) Church; and the New York City-based AME Zion Church. Although largely similar in doctrine, these and other black Methodist churches operated separately, occasionally clashing over competition for membership and the question of which denomination was established first.

The AME Zion Church grew steadily before the Civil War, establishing congregations as far south as Louisville, Kentucky, and rousing white suspicion for its emphasis on abolitionism and religious self-determination. Emancipation and Reconstruction opened the postbellum South to black Methodist churches, sparking a dramatic expansion of AME Zion missionary activity in North America, the Caribbean, and Africa that increased AME Zion Church membership from 4,600 in 1860 to around 350,000 in 1896. In addition to missionary activity, the AME Zion Church has historically emphasized advancement of black citizenship rights, expanded roles for women in church government, and ecumenicism among black and white Methodist churches.

Michael H. Burchett

See also African Methodist Episcopal Church; Baptist Church; Black church

Afrocentrism

Definition: Philosophy of historical analysis and education articulated by Molefi Kete Asante

Afrocentrism offers an alternative to "Eurocentric" interpretations of history.

A professor of African American studies at Temple University, Molefi Kete Asante is the author of *The Afrocentricity Idea* (1987), *Afrocentricity* (1988), and *Kemet, Afrocentricity, and Knowledge* (1990), and other works that define Afrocentrism as the perspective of history that allows students to observe the world from the point of view of the African and African American. Asante created Afrocentrism as a reaction to "Eurocentric" interpretations of history, which, in Asante's view, marginalize members of ethnic and racial minorities by portraying them as victims and passive participants in European-dominated history.

Asante's philosophy advocates a "multi-centered multiculturalism" in which all racial groups are encouraged to write history from their perspective to replace the "monocentric," or European-dominated, historical perspective. Asante's philosophy does not advocate the elimination of the European perspective but rather invites the European perspective to be presented alongside the interpretations of other racial groups. Opponents of the Afrocentric model, however, accuse Asante and his supporters of historical inaccuracy and of using history to promote a racist political agenda. The philosophy of Afrocentrism borrows heavily from the writings of Carter G. Woodson, Asa Hilliard, and Cheikh Anta Diop.

Jason Pasch

See also Black Is Beautiful movement; Black nationalism; Education

Agriculture

Through most of American history, agriculture was the primary occupation of African Americans. It was only after World War II that African Americans joined the general shift of laborers away from agriculture.

African Americans have deep historical ties to agriculture. During the centuries of slavery, tending crops was the primary economic activity of enslaved African Americans. Along the South Atlantic Coast in colonial North America and in the young United States, tobacco depended heavily on slave labor. Later, rice, grown in parts of South Carolina and other states, and sugar cane, grown chiefly in Louisiana, became important cash crops grown by slaves. With the development of the cotton gin at the end of the eighteenth century, cotton became the most profitable agricultural export of the United States.

After the Civil War and emancipation, African Americans remained heavily involved in agriculture, particularly in the South. In the second half of the twentieth century, however, African American involvement in farmwork dropped dramatically, so that only a tiny proportion of African Americans were involved in agricultural labor as the twenty-first century began. While nearly two-thirds of African American workers were engaged in agricultural labor in 1870, only about 1 percent worked in agriculture in 2000.

Black Farmers After Slavery

After slavery ended in 1865, most African Americans still lived in the rural South, where farming remained the most important occupation. In order to farm, however, workers needed land, tools, farm animals, and seeds and other supplies. As a result, most African Americans farmed on white-owned land through tenant, sharecropper, and crop-lien systems.

Tenant farmers rented their plots of land for fixed sums—in money or the equivalent in crops. Under the sharecropping system, the farmers borrowed fertilizer, tools, seeds, and other necessities from landowners. They then paid off their debts, with interest, by giving the landowners shares of their crops. Since the landowners often charged high rates of interest and were also the primary keepers of business records, sharecroppers frequently fell steadily deeper into debt with each harvest.

The crop-lien system gave merchants and landlords who provided supplies to farmers mortgages on the crops that the farmers promised to produce. Again, high interest rates gave the advantage to the lenders and contributed to keeping most black farmers in perpetual debt and poverty. At the same time, concentration on the planting of cotton, encouraged by white landowners, further hampered black farmers in the South. Overproduction of cotton led to a drastic drop in cotton prices during the second half of the nineteenth century.

Some scholars have estimated that by 1890, nine out of ten African American farmers were sharecroppers. Despite the many handicaps that African Americans face and widespread white southern opposition to their owning land, a substantial minority of African Americans did manage to acquire their own land in the late nineteenth and early twentieth centuries.

In 1886, African American farmers joined together to form a mutual-support organization, the Colored Farmers' Alliance, modeled on the white Farmers' Alliance founded two years earlier. This cooperative endeavor supported its members and aided in the progress of independent African American farms. Meanwhile, the founding of black-owned banks and other financial institutions helped in their efforts. About fifty black-owned lending institutions were founded between 1880 and 1911. By

Contemporary drawings of slaves working a rice plantation in North Carolina.
(Library of Congress)

1910, around 200,000 African American families had managed to obtain their own farmland. Their holdings totaled something over fifteen million acres—an average of about 75 acres per family.

The Great Migration North

During World War I and the years immediately following it, African Americans continued to be concentrated regionally in the South and occupationally in agriculture. Two trends began to undermine these concentrations. First, U.S. entry into the war in 1916 created thousands of new jobs in northern cities, and northern black leaders urged the oppressed populations of the rural South to move north. Second, cotton prices fell again, depressing the southern economy. Although black farmers were still more heavily involved in cotton growing than white farmers, government farm aid went primarily to the white farmers. The new black-owned lending institutions that had helped promote African American land ownership were hit hard, were unable to collect on their loans, and many went bankrupt. The troubles of black farmers were compounded by the spread of the boll weevil, an insect that destroyed cotton crops.

These new problems forced many black landowners to consider returning to sharecropping or working for white farmers as laborers at deplorable wages. Between 1910 and 1920, about 300,000 African Americans left the predominantly rural South, mostly for northern cities, in a movement that became known as the Great Migration. During the 1920's, the exodus grew greater, as an estimated 1,500,000 African Americans left the South between 1920 and 1930.

The Depression

The 1930's were hard years for many Americans but were even harder on African Americans—especially African Americans who worked in agriculture or had commercial ties to it. Black-owned banks, dependent on loans to African American farmers, had already started failing before the Depression. Of the fifty black-owned lending institutions in existence in 1911, only about twenty-five survived to 1930. Three years later, when President Franklin D. Roosevelt tried to stop investors from withdrawing all the money from banks by closing banks for three days, only eleven black-owned banks remained in the entire United States.

As northern jobs dried up during the Depression, the movement of African Americans to northern cities slowed. Surplus agricultural labor became plentiful in the South, and agricultural wages dropped. Black tenant farmers found it increasingly difficult to come up with rent for land and the sharecropping system took on renewed life.

According to the U.S. Farm Security Administration, by the end of the 1930's, 47 percent of all African Americans in farming were sharecroppers, 32 percent were tenant farmers, and only 21 percent were landowners. In 1931, African American farmers, supported and encouraged by the Communist Party, joined together to found the Sharecroppers Union in Alabama. The union spread to other states and may have had as many as twelve thousand members by 1935. However, the union's connection with the Communist Party hindered its growth, as many black farmers were reluctant to become involved with an organization that had communist sponsorship.

Some government programs made the problems of African American farmers worse. For example, the federal Agricultural Adjustment Act (AAA), passed in 1933, paid farmers to cut back on their production of crops in order to stabilize crop prices. With an incentive to produce less, landowners frequently fired their farmworkers and evicted tenant farmers—workers who were predominantly black. Some funds paid by the Department of Agriculture were intended to go to workers or tenants, but the money went directly to landowners, who typically passed on little or none of it. In response, black and white tenant farmers in Arkansas formed the Southern Tenant Farmers Union in 1934. This organization spread to six other states and acquired an estimated 30,000 members. With little support from the federal government, however, the union gradually faded.

The Decline of African American Agriculture

With the entry of the United States into World War II at the end of 1941, the African American movement to northern cities that had slowed during the Depression began once again. In the years that followed the war, African American movement out of rural areas and out of agriculture grew rapidly. In 1940, slightly fewer than one in three African American workers were in jobs in agriculture; this proportion dropped to less than one in four by 1950. By 1960, fewer than one in ten African Americans were in agriculture.

The decrease continued steadily, so that by the year 2000, only slightly more than one in one hundred African Americans were in agriculture. Meanwhile, the small farms owned by African Americans had become outdated, as large-scale agribusiness took over farming throughout the United States. Demand for farmworkers declined steadily over the second half of the twentieth century. By the 1960's, the sharecropper system had virtually disappeared in most of the South, where mechanization had reduced the need for human labor.

In 1967, the federal government included agricultural workers under its minimum wage law. As a result, farmworkers immedi-

Percentages of African American and White Workers Employed in Agriculture, 1870-2000

Year	African American	White
1870	64.3	43.1
1880	59.8	38.6
1900	53.7	33.9
1910	47.6	27.9
1920	41.3	22.2
1940	31.2	15.5
1950	23.4	13.3
1960	9.1	6.5
1970	3.5	3.4
1980	1.6	2.9
1990	1.3	3.0
2000	1.2	2.8

ately became much more expensive for southern planters, who became even more reliant on machines and began controlling weeds with chemicals, instead of workers with hoes. After centuries of heavy African American concentration in agriculture, black agricultural workers had almost disappeared.

A decline in the numbers of black farmworkers was not the only change. The remaining farmworkers were growing much older. Few young African Americans were going into agricultural work by the end of the twentieth century. During the 1990's, the median age for black farmers was sixty years, one in every four was over seventy years old. These aging farmers held only a small percentage of America's farm land. Of the 960 million acres of agricultural land in the United States at the end of the twentieth century, only about 2.6 million acres—0.25 percent—were owned by African Americans.

Suing the Federal Government

Many African American farmers have argued that a long history of government discrimination against them has continued. In 1997, organizations representing them filed a class action lawsuit against the federal Department of Agriculture. The farmers maintained that the department had discriminated against them by denying them loans and other forms of aid. This discrimination, according to the farmers, contributed to the decline of African American agriculture.

In April, 1999, federal district court Judge Paul L. Friedman approved a settlement agreement on the case. African American farmers could file for compensation along two tracks. On the first track, they could file claims of past discrimination and receive automatic payments of fifty thousand dollars upon approval of their claims. The second track made possible greater compensation for farmers, but only after they went through hearings. The deadline for submitting claims was in September, 2000.

These settlements did not end legal action and did not end complaints about discrimination by the Department of Agriculture. Some farmers objected that the department had not sufficiently publicized the availability of compensation before the deadline passed. Others said that the department was slow in awarding compensation money and resisted paying out the money at every opportunity.

By July, 2002, the Department of Agriculture had awarded about $645 million in payments and forgiven loans. However, this was only a small portion of the amount that should have been paid, according to some observers. A report issued in the summer of 2004 by the Washington-based Environmental Working Group maintained that the Department of Agriculture had assigned Justice Department lawyers to fight claims. Among the 94,000 farmers who filed for compensation, according to the report, 81,000, or nearly 90 percent, were denied their claims.

Carl L. Bankston III

Further Reading

Banks, Vera J. *Rural Research Development Report No. 59: Black Farmers and Their Farms.* Washington, D.C.: U.S. Department of

Agriculture, 1986. U.S. government report on black farming in the United States.

Daniel, Pete. *The Shadow of Slavery: Peonage in the South, 1901-1969.* New York: Oxford University Press, 1972. Classic and widely cited work on rural race relations during the years when sharecropping was the major concentration of African Americans in agriculture.

Gilbert, Charlene, and Quinn Eli. *Homecoming: The Story of African American Farmers.* Boston: Beacon Press, 2000. A companion volume to Charlene Gilbert's film *Homecoming*, this book provides a compelling introduction to the history of African American farmers and contains an excellent selection of historic photographs.

Nieman, Donald G. *From Slavery to Sharecropping: White Land and Black Labor in the Rural South, 1865-1900.* New York: Garland, 1994. Thorough coverage of the history of black farmworkers during the transition from slavery to sharecropping.

Tolnay, Stewart E. *The Bottom Rung: African American Family Life on Southern Farms.* Urbana: University of Illinois Press, 1999. Provides an intimate look at how African American farmers lived.

See also Demographic trends; Economic trends; Employment; Great Migration; Sharecropping; Slavery

Albemarle Paper Company v. Moody

The Case: U.S. Supreme Court ruling on employment discrimination

Date: June 25, 1975

Referring back to Title VII of the Civil Rights Law of 1964, the Supreme Court found that an employer's screening tests were discriminatory and that the employer must provide back pay for employees who suffered monetary loss as a result of racial discrimination.

African American employees in a North Carolina paper mill, the Albemarle Paper Company, charged that the company's preemployment tests and seniority system perpetuated the discrimination that had existed before the passage of Title VII, and they sought back pay relief. By a 7-1 vote, the Supreme Court ruled in favor of the employees. Because the tests were judged to be not sufficiently job related to be valid, they had to be discontinued. The awarding of back pay, moreover, provided an appropriate incentive for compliance with the law. The *Albemarle Paper Company* decision provided a useful framework for resolving numerous claims under Title VII.

Thomas Tandy Lewis

See also Civil Rights Act of 1964; *Griggs v. Duke Power Company*

Alexander v. Holmes County Board of Education

The Case: U.S. Supreme Court ruling on school desegregation
Date: October 29, 1969

In this case, the U.S. Supreme Court ruled that southern school boards must desegregate their schools immediately and refused to grant several school districts a one-semester delay in proceeding with school desegregation.

In the late 1960's, many southern school districts still operated segregated schools, notwithstanding pressure from both the U.S. Office of Education and the federal courts to integrate. In the late 1960's, African American parents throughout Mississippi, with the assistance of the National Association for the Advancement of Colored People (NAACP) Legal Defense and Educational Fund, filed lawsuits challenging segregation in thirty Mississippi school districts. In 1969, the U.S. Court of Appeals for the Fifth Circuit ordered the districts to file desegregation plans by August 11, 1969, to take effect by the beginning of the 1969-1970 school year.

With the support of President Richard M. Nixon's Department of Justice, however, the school districts requested the court to allow them to postpone the submission of school desegregation plans until December 1, 1969. The proceedings, which marked the first time that the Department of Justice had asked for a delay in a school desegregation case, reflected the Nixon administration's lukewarm support for school desegregation. The Fifth Circuit granted the request, and the parents who had filed the original suits appealed to the U.S. Supreme Court.

The Supreme Court considered the case in an expedited fashion. On October 29, 1969—only twenty days after deciding to hear the case, and only six days after oral argument—the Court held that the court of appeals had erred in permitting the delay; the Court's decision stated that "the obligation of every school district is to terminate dual school systems at once." The Court ordered every affected school district to "begin immediately to operate as unitary school systems."

The *Alexander* decision signaled an unprecedented sense of urgency in school desegregation cases. After allowing local school boards to desegregate at a slow pace for much of the prior fifteen years, the Court had now indicated that further delays would not be tolerated—even delays until the end of a school semester or school year. In a sense, the *Alexander* decision constituted the Court's atonement for the "all deliberate speed" language of its 1954 decision in *Brown v. Board of Education*; although the *Brown* decision had been a landmark in the battle against segregation, the muted language of the Court's opinion had allowed another generation of African American children to remain in segregated schools. Beginning with its *Green v. County School Board of New Kent County* decision (1968), the Court had finally begun to insist upon meaningful desegregation. Faced for the first time with Justice Department recalcitrance in a desegregation case and a presidential administration with a questionable commitment to school integration, the Court acted in dramatic fashion to signal that the time for delay and "deliberate speed" had come to an end.

In the wake of the *Alexander* decision, courts throughout the South began to insist on immediate desegregation, in some instances in the middle of the school year. The *Alexander* decision dramatically altered the time frame within which school boards were required to meet their desegregation obligations.

See also *Brown v. Board of Education*; *Green v. County School Board of New Kent County*; Segregation

American Anti-Slavery Society

Identification: Northern abolitionist organization
Date: Founded in December, 1833
Place: Philadelphia, Pennsylvania
This organization unified two centers of radical abolitionism and called for immediate eradication of slavery.

In December, 1833, sixty delegates gathered in Philadelphia to form the American Anti-Slavery Society, electing Arthur Tappan, a wealthy New York businessman, as president. They also approved a Declaration of Sentiments, drawn up by William Lloyd Garrison, Samuel May, and John Greenleaf Whittier, that called for immediate, uncompensated, total abolition of slavery through moral and political action. In signing the declaration, the delegates pledged to "do all that in us lies, consisting with this declaration of our principles, to overthrow the most execrable system of slavery that has ever been witnessed upon earth . . . and to secure to the colored population of the United States, all the rights and privileges which belong to them as men and Americans." The American Anti-Slavery Society organized a system of state and local auxiliaries, sent out agents to convert people to its views, and published pamphlets and journals supporting its position. The society grew rapidly; by 1838, it reported approximately 250,000 members and 1,350 auxiliaries.

Immediatism

Before the 1830's, most opponents of slavery advocated moderate methods such as gradual and "compensated" emancipation, which would reimburse former slave owners who released slaves, or removal of free African Americans to Liberia by the

American Colonization Society, founded in 1817. The formation of a national organization based on the principle of immediatism, or immediate and total emancipation, symbolized the new phase that antislavery agitation had entered in the early 1830's—radical, uncompromising, and intensely moralistic. The shift to immediatism was a result of several factors, including the failure of moderate methods; the example of the British, who abolished slavery in the empire in 1833; and, probably most important, evangelical religion. Abolitionists of the 1830's inherited from earlier antislavery reformers the notion that slavery was a sin. This notion, coupled with the contemporaneous evangelical doctrine of immediate repentance, shaped the abolitionist doctrine of immediate emancipation. Abolitionists emphasized moral suasion over political methods. They hoped to persuade people to emancipate the slaves voluntarily and to form a conviction of guilt as participants in the national sin of slavery.

The American Anti-Slavery Society represented the union of two centers of radical abolitionism, one in Boston, the other around Cincinnati. Garrison, the key figure among New England

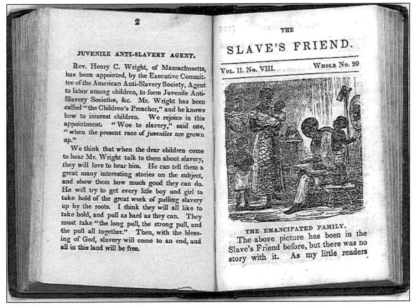

The Slave's Friend, *a publication of the American Anti-Slavery Society from 1836.* (Library of Congress)

abolitionists, began publishing *The Liberator* in 1831 and soon organized the New England Anti-Slavery Society, based on the principle of immediate abolition. In the Midwest, Western Reserve College and Lane Seminary were seedbeds for the doctrine of immediate emancipation. Theodore Dwight Weld, a young man who had been converted to evangelical Christianity by Charles Finney, organized a group of antislavery agents known as The Seventy, who preached the gospel of immediatism throughout the Midwest.

Although the leadership of the antislavery movement remained predominantly white, free African Americans played a significant role in its ranks. Before 1800, the Free African Society of Philadelphia and black spokespersons such as astronomer Benjamin Banneker and church leader Richard Allen had denounced slavery in the harshest terms. By 1830, there were fifty antislavery societies organized by African Americans, and African Americans contributed to the formation of the American Anti-Slavery Society in 1833. African American orators, especially escaped slaves such as Frederick Douglass and Sojourner Truth, moved large audiences with their impassioned and electrifying oratory. African Americans also helped run the Underground Railroad; Harriet Tubman led more than three hundred African Americans to freedom. Generally, African American abolitionists shared the nonviolent philosophy of the Garrisonians, but black anger often flared because of the racism they found within the antislavery ranks. Influenced by tactical and race considerations, white abolitionist leaders such as Garrison and Weld limited their African American counterparts to peripheral roles or excluded them from local organizations.

Internal Divisions

The late 1830's marked the high point of the movement for immediate abolition through moral suasion. Abolitionism was hard hit by the Panic of 1837, a nationwide banking crisis which reduced funds and distracted attention away from reform. At the same time, abolitionists faced an internal challenge as the American Anti-Slavery Society divided into radicals and moderates. One issue causing the split was women's rights. Moderate abolitionists tolerated and even welcomed women in the society, as long as their activities were confined to forming auxiliary societies, raising money, and circulating petitions. They refused, however, the request that women be allowed to speak in public on behalf of abolitionism or to help shape the organization's policies.

The other issue that divided abolitionist ranks was that of political action. Some abolitionists, convinced that political action, not merely moral suasion, was necessary to effect emancipation, formed the Liberty Party in 1840. In the 1840's and 1850's, the majority of abolitionists moved gradually into the political arena, where they became involved in the Free-Soil movement and other aspects of the sectional conflict leading to the Civil War.

Anne C. Loveland
Updated by Sudipta Das

Further Reading

Kevin C. Julius's *The Abolitionist Decade, 1829-1838: A Year-by-Year History of Early Events in the Antislavery Movement* (Jefferson, N.C.: McFarland & Co., 2004) is a valuable addition to the literature on antislavery societies. Stanley Harrold's *Subversives: Antislavery Community in Washington, D.C., 1828-1865* (Baton Rouge: Louisiana State University Press, 2003) is an insightful examination of an antislavery community. Louis Filler's *The Crusade Against Slavery, 1830-1860* (New York: Harper & Row, 1960) is a comprehensive treatment of the people and groups who made up the antislavery movement and the relation of the movement to other reform activities of the period. Lawrence J. Friedman's *Gregarious Saints: Self and Community in American Abolitionism, 1830-1870* (New York: Cambridge University Press, 1982) presents a fresh, challenging analysis of the antislavery movement, written from a psychological perspective and focusing on the first-generation immediatists. *Antislavery Reconsidered: New Perspectives on the Abolitionists* (Baton Rouge: Louisiana State University Press, 1979) edited by Lewis Perry and Michael Fellman contains fourteen original, thought-provoking essays based on a variety of interpretive and methodological approaches. Richard H. Abbott's *Cotton and Capital: Boston Businessmen and Antislavery Reform, 1854-1868* (Amherst: University of Massachusetts Press, 1991) examines the activities and ideology of a group of Bostonian businessmen who fostered abolition. In *The Liberator: William Lloyd Garrison* (Boston: Little, Brown, 1963), John L. Thomas surveys not only the antislavery movement but also the many other reforms in which the well-known editor was engaged.

See also Abolition; American Colonization Society; Free African Society; *Liberator, The*; National Council of Colored People; Underground Railroad

American Colonization Society

Identification: Organization dedicated to repatriating African Americans to Africa
Date: Founded in 1816
Place: Philadelphia, Pennsylvania
The society's work had little impact on North American slavery, but the slaves it helped send to West Africa founded the modern nation of Liberia.

Organized in 1816, the American Society for Colonizing the Free People of Color of the United States, commonly known as the American Colonization Society, attempted to resolve conflicts over slavery and racism by removing African Americans from the United States. Popular in many northern cities and in the upper South, it counted among its members national figures such as Henry Clay, Daniel Webster, and Francis Scott Key. The society planned to establish a colony in Africa to which free African Americans could voluntarily migrate. Although the society did not address the issue of emancipating enslaved African Americans, it hoped that the colonization scheme would prompt slaveowners to free their slaves, secure in the knowledge that the free blacks would not remain in the South. In 1822, the society helped to found Liberia, on the western coast of Africa, and supported a small settlement there. However, lack of financial support and the commitment to slavery in the lower South doomed the unrealistic plan to failure. Most important, almost all African Ameri-

American Colonization Society membership certificate from around 1840. (Library of Congress)

cans rejected the notion of colonization, declaring the United States to be their rightful home. Only fifteen thousand made the journey to Liberia in the years before the Civil War (1861-1865).

Thomas Clarkin

See also Abolition; American Anti-Slavery Society; Pan-Africanism

Amistad slave revolt

The Event: Capture of a Spanish slave ship by its human cargo
Date: 1839
Place: North Atlantic Ocean
The incident allowed abolitionists to win a victory in the judicial battle that followed an illegal importation of Africans as slaves.

Although the British-Spanish Treaty of 1817 banned African slave trading as of 1820, a highly lucrative covert slave trade existed, especially between Africa and Cuba. In April, 1839, a Portuguese slave ship left West Africa bound for Havana filled with more than five hundred illegally purchased Africans, mostly Mendis. After a two-month passage in which one-third of the Africans died, the ship reached Havana. Government officials receiving kickbacks provided paperwork declaring these Africans to be *ladinos*, slaves residing in Cuba prior to 1820, which would make their sale legal. Within a few days, José Ruiz purchased forty-nine adult African men, and Pedro Montes bought four children, three girls and a boy.

The Uprising

The slaves were loaded onto the schooner *Amistad*, which set sail for Puerto Príncipe, a few days' journey away. The Africans, unable to communicate with the Spanish-speaking owners or crew, became convinced that they were to be eaten. On the third night out, Joseph Cinqué picked the lock on his iron collar and broke into the cargo hold, where he and others found cane knives. The Africans took over the ship, killing the captain and the cook. The two crew members disappeared, perhaps having jumped overboard. Ruiz, Montes, and Antonio, the captain's slave cabin boy, were spared.

The Africans demanded to be taken to Sierra Leone. For almost two months, Ruiz and Montes pretended to comply. During the day they sailed southeast, occasionally landing to scavenge for food and water, but at night they headed north and northeast, in the hope of finding help. The schooner's decrepit condition

Contemporary illustration of the revolt aboard the Amistad *in 1839.* (Library of Congress)

and the many blacks on board aroused suspicion. The *Amistad* came to the attention of the USS *Washington*, whose captain, Thomas Gedney, ordered the schooner boarded. The thirty-nine surviving slaves, by now almost starved and unable to resist, were taken into custody.

The Legal Battle

Ruiz and Montes filed suits to have their slave property returned to them; Gedney claimed salvage rights to the *Amistad* and its cargo, including the slaves; the Spanish government demanded the fugitives be handed over to it; U.S. abolitionists clamored for the Africans to be set free. Although African slave trade was banned, slavery in Cuba was legal, and Ruiz and Montes had paperwork documenting their ownership. Moreover, there were U.S.-Spanish relations to be considered in determining whether or not the United States should recognize Spanish property rights to the Africans. Precedents from an earlier slaver incident, the *Antelope* case, had to be analyzed also. Perhaps most important, the *Amistad* affair carried grave implications for the slavery issue in the United States—and President Martin Van Buren hoped to avoid that issue in his upcoming reelection campaign, knowing that his success depended on maintaining his coalition of northern and southern supporters.

Newspapers across the land kept an interested public informed of the status of the case. For the most part, northerners were sympathetic toward the Africans, while southerners felt they should be returned to the Spanish government to be tried for piracy and murder. The affair probably would have been handled quietly and quickly if the abolitionists had not recognized its potential to raise the public's awareness of the moral and legal issues at stake in the slavery question.

Abolitionists and other opponents of slavery quickly formed the *Amistad* Committee, made up of Simeon Jocelyn, Joshua Leavitt, and Lewis Tappan, to raise money for legal counsel and to appeal to President Van Buren to allow the case to be decided by the United States court system rather than turning the prisoners over to the Spanish government. The committee employed James Covey, a native African who could speak the Mendi language, to communicate with the *Amistad* blacks, for so far depositions had been given only by the Spaniards and the cabin boy.

The legal proceedings began in mid-September, 1839, in the United States circuit court convened in Hartford, Connecticut. The case worked its way over the next eighteen months from circuit court to district court, back to the circuit court and finally to the Supreme Court. The abolitionists made sure that the case stayed before the public. The public, although ambivalent in its responses to the legal and moral questions, stayed interested.

The case also excited international interest, and the cause of the abolitionists was substantially aided when Richard Robert Madden, a British official living in Havana, gave a moving and informed deposition concerning the state of the slave trade in Cuba. He spelled out the means and extent of illegal activities and clarified the status of *ladinos*. He also stated that the children on board the *Amistad* were without doubt too young to be pre-1820 Cuban residents, and that he strongly believed that all the *Amistad* captives were *bozales*, newly imported Africans, not *ladinos*.

The Conclusion

In January, 1840, Judge Andrew T. Judson of the U.S. District Court of Connecticut ruled that the Africans could not be counted as property in the calculation of salvage value, nor could they legally be held as slaves, because their initial purchase had been illegal. The government appealed the case, and a few months later, Judge Smith Thompson of the U.S. circuit court concurred in Judson's decision. The government again appealed, and the case came before the U.S. Supreme Court in early 1841. John Quincy Adams argued passionately on behalf of the defendants. On March 9, 1841, the Supreme Court also ruled that Africans brought to Cuba illegally were not property, that as illegally held free men they had a right to mutiny, and that they should therefore be released. In November, 1841, the Africans sailed to Sierra Leone, accompanied by a small group of New England missionaries.

The *Amistad* decision was a great victory for abolitionists and raised the public's awareness of the slavery issue. The case fed secessionist sentiments in the southern states but helped opponents of slavery focus on legal attacks against the institution.

Grace McEntee

Further Reading

Iyunolu Folayan Osagie's *The Amistad Revolt: Memory, Slavery, and the Politics of Identity in the United States and Sierra Leone* (Athens: University of Georgia Press, 2000), Christopher Martin's *The "Amistad" Affair* (New York: Abelard-Schuman, 1970), and Howard Jones's *Mutiny on the "Amistad": The Saga of a Slave Revolt and Its Impact on American Abolition, Law, and Diplomacy* (New York: Oxford University Press, 1987) describe the case and its effects. William A. Owens's *Black Mutiny: The Revolt on the Schooner "Amistad"* (Philadelphia: Pilgrim Press, 1968) is a dramatized but well-researched rendering of the incident that includes information on the fate of the Africans after the trial. *The "Amistad" Case: The Most Celebrated Slave Mutiny of the Nineteenth Century* (New York: Johnson Reprint, 1968) contains correspondence between the U.S. and Spanish governments concerning the *Amistad* case.

See also Abolition; *Clotilde* capture; Slavery; Stono Rebellion; Turner's slave insurrection

Anderson's Lincoln Memorial concert

The Event: Recital by contralto Marian Anderson on the steps of the Lincoln Memorial
Date: April 9, 1939
Place: Washington, D.C.

The Daughters of the American Revolution (DAR) rejected contralto Marian Anderson for a singing engagement at Constitution Hall, but Anderson rescheduled her appearance outside the Lincoln Memorial.

Even with her rich, warm, evocative contralto, Marian Anderson, the first African American to perform with New York's Metropolitan Opera Company, did not arrive easily at fame and acceptance, particularly among prejudiced whites. The daughter of a poor Philadelphia widow, she got what training she could afford, then evolved an expanded vocal repertoire including material ranging from spirituals to folk songs and grand opera. She developed a significant following among classical music fans. In 1939, after requesting the use of Washington's Constitution Hall from the Daughters of the American Revolution, she was humiliated by a flat rejection.

A Promising Career

Marian, the first of three daughters of John and Annie Anderson, was born at her grandmother's house in South Philadelphia on February 17, 1902. Her father, a coal and ice seller, died of brain cancer ten years later, leaving his wife, a schoolteacher, to support the family by taking in laundry and working in Wanamaker's Department Store. Anderson, who progressed from the Union Baptist Church junior choir to public performances of duets and solos, also learned to play the piano and violin. She concentrated on a business curriculum at William Penn High School, then transferred to South Philadelphia High for music training and studied privately under voice coach Mary Patterson.

Public response to Anderson's extensive range and expressive talents brought invitations to a variety of public musical forums and Negro colleges as well as membership in the Philadelphia Choral Society. White philanthropists often donated funds to assist her obviously promising future in music. Despite the beneficence of a few, laws of segregation and local custom required her to travel on separate train cars, ride service elevators, and eat in substandard dining areas maintained for nonwhite patrons. Overnight accommodations in hotels proved so difficult to obtain that she usually stayed in private residences.

In 1921, Anderson received a church-sponsored scholarship for voice lessons with Giuseppe Boghetti, who strengthened her technique and stage presence and taught her operatic roles. With the help of accompanist and manager William "Billy" King, a black pianist, she increased her fee to a hundred dollars per performance. A period of low self-esteem arising from unfavorable reviews deflated her enthusiasm temporarily. The expertise she gained from learning foreign languages to augment her vocal talent, in addition to the backing of her mother, sisters, coach, and manager, restored her to earlier levels of confidence.

In 1925, after defeating three hundred contenders in a local competition, Anderson won the privilege of appearing with the New York Philharmonic at Lewisohn Stadium under the direction of Eugene Ormandy. Good reviews bolstered her competitiveness. As a result, in 1930, on a National Association of Negro Musicians scholarship, she traveled to Europe to study. While sailing on the *Ile de France*, she sang for distinguished passengers. The experience proved beneficial to her career, encouraging her to return to Berlin to immerse herself in the German language. Back in the United States, she demonstrated her cosmopolitan training with a cross-country tour.

Organized Bigotry

It was in the midst of this increasing professional success that Anderson was refused permission by the Daughters of the American Revolution (DAR) to sing at Constitution Hall in Washington, D.C., in 1939. The refusal came solely on account of Anderson's race. At the time of the turndown, Anderson was on tour in California. She met with interviewers to voice her sadness and shame. In characteristic low-key, nonjudgmental style, she refused to affix blame and noted, by way of explanation, that crusading for racial equality was foreign to her nature. She did, however, alter her personal criteria for performance sites and refused to sing where non-whites were refused admittance.

The refusal to let Anderson sing proved embarrassing to the two hundred thousand members of the DAR, an elite women's historical society founded in 1890 to honor descent from patriots, encourage patriotism and activities related to teaching history, foster genealogical research, honor the American flag and Constitution, found citizenship clubs, award scholarships and medals, assist veterans with disabilities, and generally further Americanism. To save face in response to press stories about their actions, the group's leaders cited a Washington, D.C., law restricting integrated performances. They insisted that the DAR had in fact challenged bigotry by publicizing the local restrictions that forbade

Contralto Marian Anderson performs for a crowd of more than 75,000 at the Lincoln Memorial in Washington, D. C., on April 9, 1939. (Library of Congress)

Anderson's performance. This story proved to be false.

Other entertainers and leaders came to Anderson's defense and protested the obvious attempt to hide racial discrimination. As a conciliatory gesture, Eleanor Roosevelt resigned from and broke all ties with the DAR and persuaded Anderson to sing a free Easter concert at the steps of the Lincoln Memorial. The Sunday performance, attended by more than seventy-five thousand people, including government dignitaries, representatives from Howard University, and the secretary of the National Association for the Advancement of Colored People (NAACP), showed Anderson's sincere response to the racist action of an elitist clique. Choked with tears at the sight of so many supporters, Anderson faltered on the words to the national anthem. She drew on her professional training and years of onstage experience to help complete her usual repertoire of hymn tunes, classical arias, and national favorites. She closed with a simple rendition of "America."

Anderson's performance at the Lincoln Memorial became the focal point of her career. To commemorate her public triumph, the Department of the Interior commissioned a mural. Fellow entertainers of all races boycotted future performances scheduled for Constitution Hall. For her self-control and positive attitude,

Anderson accepted honors from Eleanor Roosevelt and the king and queen of England. She later entertained at the White House for the inaugural galas of Dwight D. Eisenhower and John F. Kennedy. The policy at Constitution Hall changed in regard to use by nonwhites, and Anderson eventually gave her long-delayed performance.

The nationwide notoriety resulting from the Washington rejection and its triumphant aftermath brought Anderson a deluge of opportunities to travel, perform, study, and record. Reluctant to release many of her RCA recordings, she reworked studio performances until they reached her high standards. Her most popular disc, a soulful, intense rendering of "Ave Maria," marked by her characteristic vibrato and amplitude, sold a quarter of a million copies.

International Success

Twice Anderson toured Denmark, Sweden, Norway, and Finland, impressing Finns by singing in their language. Royalty, local fans, and notable musicians, especially composer Jean Sibelius, escalated her Scandinavian appearances from mere acclaim to "Marian fever." European and Asian audiences, particularly Russians and those in other nations under communist regimes, demanded encores of her spirituals, claiming "Deep River" and "Heaven, Heaven" as their favorites. Konstantin Stanislavsky carried a bouquet of lilacs to entice her to sing *Carmen*.

Returning to America in triumph, Anderson came under the management of Russian impresario Solomon Hurok. Under his direction toward new challenges, she accepted tours in Japan, Africa, and South America and gave standing-room-only concerts at New York City's Town Hall and Carnegie Hall and at the Philadelphia Forum. Far from her original rewards of fifty cents per performance, she earned hefty fees commensurate with her talents. Fans poured out their response to her compassion, which brought them comfort in times of personal crisis. Critics acknowledged her maturing grace, range, control, and musical technique. She performed more than seventy-five concerts per year and had many opportunities she could not accept without overextending her voice and sapping her energies.

Even with increased audience rapport, racism continued to crop up in correspondence, reviews, and public treatment, especially after Anderson was invited to sing before Nazis in the 1940's. Following her reply to their questions about race, Hitler's staff dropped their request for a concert. In the United States, she was presented with the key to Atlantic City, but white hotels refused her requests for a reservation. These unsettling public slurs were somewhat offset by awards and honoraria from fifty universities including Howard, Temple, Smith, Carlisle, Moravian, and Dickinson.

At the age of thirty-seven, Anderson received the Spingarn Medal, awarded annually by the NAACP to an African American achiever. A year later, in 1940, she earned the Bok Award, an annual $10,000 prize accorded a native Philadelphian. She used the money to endow the Marian Anderson Scholarship for students of the arts. To assure unprejudiced administration of the annual award, she placed her sister Alyce in charge.

In 1943, Anderson left the Philadelphia home she shared with her mother and married architect Orpheus Fisher of Wilmington, Delaware, whom she had met during her school years. The couple built Mariana Farm in a rural setting outside Danbury, Connecticut. Often absent from home on tour, she reserved the summer months for domestic pleasures, particularly sewing, cooking, and gardening. Her particular delight was the success of her strawberry patch. By choice, she had no children so that she could avoid the problem of separation from family while she devoted her life to music. To fill the gap left by voluntary childlessness, she immersed herself in the activities of her sisters' children, who were frequent visitors to her home.

Later Years

In middle age, Marian Anderson continued to achieve renown. At the bidding of German fans, she returned to post-Nazi Berlin to perform. In 1955, New York impresario Rudolf Bing organized her debut as Ulrica, the aged sorceress in Giuseppe Verdi's *Un ballo in maschera* (1857-1858; *The Masked Ball*). This performance at the Metropolitan Opera House was the first ever by an African American performer. It made extra demands on her limited stage experience, which she met by practicing her acting role and deliberately subduing stage fright. She reprised her part in the opera on tour in Philadelphia, where black fans mobbed the performance. Continuing to refine the role of Ulrica in later appearances, she commented that she felt that perfection of the small character part was an essential part of her training for the operatic stage.

At the age of fifty-four, Anderson wrote her autobiography, *My Lord, What a Morning* (1956), in which she revealed personal reflections on poverty and longing in her childhood, when performing before distinguished audiences lay far outside the grasp of a black singer. Late in her career, having toured Europe and the United States once more, she was named in 1958 as an alternate delegate to the United Nations for her support of human rights. In 1959, two years before formal retirement, she accepted from President Dwight D. Eisenhower the Presidential Medal of Freedom. At the age of seventy-six, she appeared at the Kennedy Center and, as the sole woman among fellow honorees George Balanchine, Arthur Rubinstein, Richard Rodgers, and Fred Astaire, received a national award.

The famed singer returned to the spotlight long after the end of her stage career. At the age of eighty-seven, to raise scholarship funds, Anderson, still regal and gracious, presided over a concert at Danbury's Charles Ives Center. Feted by admirers including Jessye Norman, Isaac Stern, William Warfield, Cicely Tyson, Phylicia Rashad, Connecticut's governor William A. O'Neil, and President George Bush, she graciously accepted the national acclaim that well-wishers extended. She later became more reclusive but remained a symbol of African American achievement and grace under pressure.

Mary Ellen Snodgrass

Further Reading

Anderson, Marian. *My Lord, What a Morning*. New York: Viking Press, 1956. Somewhat dated in style and tone, this autobiography nevertheless contains the most factual information on Anderson's childhood and developing career. Some of the information is sentimentalized, but the author avoids bitterness in recounting prejudicial treatment.

Keiler, Allan. *Marian Anderson: A Singer's Journey*. New York: Scribner, 2000. A definitive biography of Anderson's life and work.

"The Survivors." *Ebony* 46 (November, 1990): 28-33. A brief overview of black achievement during a forty-five-year period. The article helps set Marian Anderson among her black peers. Photographs capture worthy scenes of American entertainment history.

Sweeley, Michael. "The First Lady." *National Review* 41 (September 29, 1989): 65-66. A brief but articulate summary of Anderson's life and career, with particular emphasis on the open-air concert at the Charles Ives Center.

Tedards, Anne. *Marian Anderson*. American Women of Achievement Series. New York: Chelsea House, 1988. A superb illustrated resource for students, from the point of view of African American achievement. This volume is a must for educators who seek to instruct young people in American history.

"A Tribute to Marian Anderson: Famed Contralto Is Honored at Gala Concert in Connecticut." *Ebony* 45 (November, 1989): 182-185. A photographic tribute to Anderson's concert at the Charles Ives Center. The article fills in information about the singer's retirement and widowhood. Like most accounts of Anderson's career, the article mentions the DAR snub.

Vehanen, Kosti. *Marian Anderson, a Portrait*. Westport, Conn.: Greenwood Press, 1970. An undistinguished biography. The lackluster account of Anderson's life and career bogs down in detail but might prove useful to a researcher or student of music history.

See also Harlem Renaissance; Music

Antislavery laws of 1777 and 1807

The Laws: Earliest state and federal laws to abolish slavery
Dates: July 2, 1777, Vermont; and March 2, 1807, federal
In 1777, Vermont became the first of eight northeastern states to end slavery; the federal government outlawed the slave trade in 1807 but failed to condemn slavery outright, reflecting the young nation's moral ambiguity.

On July 2, 1777, Vermont became the first state to abolish slavery fully. Its 1777 Constitution outlawed "holding anyone by law to serve any person" as a servant, slave, or apprentice after he or she reached twenty-one years of age. In 1780, Pennsylvania passed a law gradually abolishing slavery. An attempt five years earlier had failed, partly because opponents argued that abolishing slavery would antagonize the South, where slavery was a deeply embedded institution, and break up the Union during the war for independence from England. Under the Pennsylvania law, any African American not registered as a slave by the end of the year would be considered free; however, children born slaves in 1780 would remain in service to their owners until they were twenty-eight years of age to compensate the owners for the cost of raising them. The law also enabled African Americans to testify against whites in courts and legalized interracial marriage.

Abolitionism in the States

In Massachusetts, opponents defeated a gradual emancipation bill in 1777, and three years later, voters rejected a constitution that declared all men free and equal and provided voting rights for free blacks. In 1781, however, a slave named Quork Walker sued for his freedom in a state court because his owner had severely abused him. The trial judge, Caleb Cushing, instructed the jury that the idea of slavery conflicted with state law, so Walker was ordered freed. Although the legislature refused to act, by 1790, slavery no longer existed in Massachusetts because of similar court actions in dozens of other cases.

During the American Revolution, the New Hampshire legislature gave freedom to any of the state's six hundred slaves who volunteered for the militia. Other slaves gained their liberty by running away and joining the British military. Thus, when the state's 1783 constitution declared all men equal and independent from birth, only fifty slaves remained in the state. Although slavery was never abolished legally, slave property was removed from tax roles in 1789 and eleven years later, only eight slaves remained in the state.

In 1783, Rhode Island passed a gradual emancipation bill after six Quakers petitioned the state assembly for immediate liberation for all human beings kept as property. The bill stipulated that all slave children born after March 1 would be apprentices; girls became free at age eighteen, boys at age twenty-one. After slaves were freed, their masters were required to post bonds with the state guaranteeing that the former slaves would never require public assistance.

Connecticut, the New England state with the largest population of African Americans, granted freedom to slaves who fought against England, but three times—in 1777, 1779, and 1780—rejected gradual emancipation. In 1784, however, the legislature declared that all adult slaves would be free by the end of the year and that black and mulatto (mixed-race) children would become free at twenty-five years of age. The state also passed discriminatory laws forbidding free blacks to vote, serve on juries, or marry whites.

Both New York and New Jersey freed African Americans who served in the army, but these states were slow to enact antislavery laws. New York's legislature rejected gradual emancipation in 1777. Eight years later, a freedom bill supported by the New York Manumission Society, whose membership included Alexander Hamilton, John Jay, and Aaron Burr, was defeated. In 1785, New York prohibited the sale and importation of slaves and allowed masters to manumit (free) their slaves, but only if they guaranteed that they would not require public assistance. The next year, New Jersey passed similar laws.

In 1788, New York declared that slaves would no longer be judged or punished under standards different from those used to judge whites. Although slave auctions ended in both states by 1790, New York did not pass an emancipation bill until 1799. The bill allowed owners to free their slaves regardless of age or condition but permitted them to keep boys until twenty-eight years of age and girls until the age of twenty-five. In 1804, New Jersey became the last of the original northern states to end slavery legally. Neither state allowed free African Americans the right to vote.

The 1807 Federal Bill

Although these northeastern states had ended slavery, the invention in 1793 of the cotton gin by Eli Whitney had made cotton a more profitable crop by greatly increasing the speed at which seeds could be separated from the picked cotton, thus increasing plantation owners' desire for more cotton pickers. It has been estimated that no fewer than twenty thousand new slaves were imported into Georgia and South Carolina in 1803 alone.

In December, 1805, Senator Stephen R. Bradley of Vermont introduced legislation that would prohibit the slave trade beginning in 1808, but the bill was stalled for some months. A similar bill was offered in the House of Representatives by Barnabas Bidwell of Massachusetts, again to no effect. Later that year, President Thomas Jefferson urged passage of the bill in his message to Congress. On March 2, 1807, Congress enacted a law specifying a twenty-thousand-dollar fine and forfeiture of ship and cargo for importing slaves, as well as other penalties for acts ranging from equipping a slave ship to knowingly buying an imported slave. The disposition of illegally imported slaves was left to the states, however. Enforcement of the law was delegated first to the secretary of the treasury and later to the secretary of the navy.

Antislavery forces rejoiced in this new and symbolically important law, but enforcement proved weak. An exhaustive census of the slave trade published in 1969 estimated that 1.9 million slaves were imported illegally between 1811 and 1870; more recent research has called that estimate low. Although more than one hundred slave vessels were seized and their officers arrested in the years between 1837 and 1862, and nearly as many cases were prosecuted, convictions were difficult to obtain, and judges often gave light sentences. Another weakness of the 1807 law was that it permitted the continuation of slave traffic between states. An owner could take his slaves into another slave state or, according to the Missouri Compromise of 1820, into a western territory south of 36° north latitude.

Robert P. Ellis
Leslie V. Tischauser

Further Reading

Books that discuss the end of slavery in the northeastern states include Gary B. Nash and Jean R. Soderlund's *Freedom by Degrees:*

Emancipation in Pennsylvania and Its Aftermath (New York: Oxford University Press, 1991), Arthur Zilversmit's *The First Emancipation: The Abolition of Slavery in the North* (Chicago: University of Chicago Press, 1967), and Robin Blackburn's *The Overthrow of Colonial Slavery, 1776-1848* (New York: Verso, 1988). John Hope Franklin's *From Slavery to Freedom: A History of Negro Americans* (5th ed., New York: Alfred A. Knopf, 1980), first published in 1947, is a pioneering study by an African American historian that contains a succinct summary of the enactment of the 1807 law and its aftermath. Warren S. Howard's *American Slavers and the Federal Law: 1837-1862* (Berkeley: University of California Press, 1963) is a copiously documented study of violations of the 1807 law during the quarter century before the outbreak of the Civil War. James A. Rawley's *The Transatlantic Slave Trade: A History* (New York: W. W. Norton, 1981) surveys the slave trade from its fifteenth century beginnings and places U.S. involvement in its international context.

See also Abolition; Emancipation Proclamation; Missouri Compromise; Proslavery argument; Slave codes; Slavery; Underground Railroad

Ashmun Institute

Identification: Institution of higher learning created for African Americans that later became Lincoln University
Date: Founded on January 1, 1857
Place: Chester County, Oxford, Pennsylvania
Lincoln University has remained a predominantly African American school and is proudly recognized as the oldest school with the purpose of educating African American youth.

Lincoln University originally opened its doors as Ashmun Institute, on January 1, 1857, in Chester County, Oxford, Pennsylvania. The institute's purpose was to give African American youth an opportunity to receive a sound, well-balanced education. Although many people through many decades helped to create the idea of a school devoted to the higher education of African Americans, John Miller Dickey was the man who put the idea to work.

Dickey, the son of a minister and of Scotch-Irish descent, attended Dickinson College in Milton, Pennsylvania. He was graduated in 1824 with a bachelor of arts degree; that fall, he entered the Princeton Theological Seminary to become a Presbyterian minister, following in the footsteps of his many relatives who also were ministers. In 1827, at twenty-one years of age, he was graduated from the seminary and received his first assignment, at the Presbytery of New Castle in Newark, Delaware. In 1829, he received a new assignment in Georgia from the Board of Missions. He found that the slaves in the area listened ardently to his sermons, and he was particularly impressed by their desire to learn.

On June 12, 1834, Dickey married Sarah Emlen Cresson, the daughter of a wealthy Quaker family. The marriage was frowned upon by the Quakers because Dickey was a Presbyterian, a religion that the Quakers thought did not hold the same beliefs as they did. For this marriage, Sarah was rejected from the Quaker meeting; nevertheless, the Quaker religion had helped her to develop and continue her support and concern for African Americans, which she took with her into her marriage to John Dickey.

Many circumstances led to the founding of Ashmun Institute. The past life of Dickey and his wife played an important role in the school's founding. John Miller, Dickey's grandfather, had given money for the education of African American youth in earlier years, and Miller's acquaintance, Benjamin Franklin, also saw the need for an African American school. Both Dickey and his wife had many relatives who were ardently opposed to slavery. Another reason for Dickey's interest, according to him, was the kidnapping of two young African American girls, Rachel and Elizabeth Parker. Although both girls were returned to their home, the incident helped Dickey to realize the inherent inequalities in the lives of the African American youth and the difficulties they experienced because they were not given the same opportunities that other young people enjoyed. The death of Dickey's own child was another factor in his decision to create the institute.

Breaking Ground

Sometime in 1853, Sarah picked the land on which they would establish an institute for the education of youth of African descent in science, art, and theology. In the same year, John Miller Dickey announced his plans for an African American university, which would be called Ashmun Institute. In order to bring the institute into being, a committee was set up to gather funds and secure the Ashmun Institute's charter through the legislature. By April 29, 1854, the Ashmun Institute Bill was signed by Governor Bigler, allowing for the construction of the new school. Because there were not enough funds to construct the buildings, Dickey used his own money (for which he would later be reimbursed) to finance construction of the president's house and a schoolroom with attached dormitories. By the fall of 1856, the school was nearly ready to open, and the Reverend John Pym Carter was selected as its first president.

Ashmun Institute was named after Jehudi Ashmun, who was born on April 21, 1794, in Champlain, New York. In 1820, four years after graduating from the University of Vermont, he took a job as the editor of *The African Intelligencer*, a magazine devoted to the movement for African emigration to Liberia promoted by the American Colonization Society, an African American organization. Through his involvement in the magazine, Ashmun learned that a conductor was needed for a trip to Liberia to help take slaves back to their homeland. After working for repatriation of African Americans, he died in 1828 after a long illness. In naming their school after him, the Dickeys memorialized Ashmun for his outstanding work. The first building of Ashmun Institute was dedicated on December 31, 1856, the fifth anniversary of the kidnapping of Rachel and Elizabeth Parker.

The First Students

Classes at Ashmun Institute began January 1, 1857, with two students, James Ralston Amos and his brother Thomas. The first decades of the institution's operation were rather difficult—funding continued to be a challenge, and the outbreak of the Civil War (1861-1865) emptied Ashmun Institute's classroom for a short time. There was concern that the institute would be raided as the war began, but no such instances were reported. After the war, there was a surge in enrollment, and the school began to expand.

Students at the four-year institute received instruction in geography, history, grammar, composition, elocution, and mathematics. They also received instruction in Greek, Hebrew, and Latin. In addition, the students learned church theology and history, as well as taking courses in prayer and pulpit exercises. Although scholarship was important, each term the students were also evaluated on their other qualities, including piety, talents, diligence, eloquence, prudence, economy, zeal, health, and influence. The curriculum changed and became even more diversified as the school became more established.

Creation of Lincoln University

On February 7, 1866, the board of the institute began the process to change the name of the institute to Lincoln University in honor of Abraham Lincoln, who had fought so vehemently for the rights of African Americans and who had helped to free them from slavery throughout the United States. The Pennsylvania legislature approved the change of name, and after April 4, 1866, Ashmun Institute was known as Lincoln University.

There were many notable presidents of the university as it continued to grow and become a respected institution. Isaac Norton Rendall, who was among the great contributors, was president from 1865 until 1905. In 1945, Horace Mann Bond became the first alumnus of Lincoln University to become its president, as well as the first African American to hold the position. He served in the position until 1957.

Lincoln University has remained a predominantly African American school and is proudly recognized as the oldest school with the purpose of educating African American youth. Among the list of graduates are several famous persons, including Langston Hughes, the famous poet and author, in 1929, and Thurgood Marshall, the first African American Supreme Court justice, in 1930.

Jeri Kurtzleben

Further Reading

Blassingame, John W., and John R. McKivigan, eds. *The Frederick Douglass Papers*. Series One. *Speeches, Debates, and Interviews*. Vol. 4, *1864-1880*. New Haven, Conn.: Yale University Press, 1991. Includes a speech in which Douglass discusses Lincoln University as an example; notes for the speech compares Lincoln University to other African American institutions.

Bond, Horace Mann. *Education for Freedom: A History of Lincoln University*. Princeton, N.J.: Princeton University Press, 1976. A major primary source that gives details of the university's beginning and growth. Written by a former president of Lincoln University.

Brown, M. Christopher, II, and Kassie Freeman, eds. *Black Colleges: New Perspectives on Policy and Practice*. Westport, Conn.: Praeger, 2004.

Drewry, Henry N., and Humphrey Doermann in collaboration with Susan H. Anderson. *Stand and Prosper: Private Black Colleges and Their Students*. Princeton, N.J.: Princeton University Press, 2001.

Hill, Leven, ed. *Black American Colleges and Universities*. Detroit, Mich.: Gale Research, 1994. Includes a brief university history, current statistics, and enrollment information.

Hornsby, Alton, Jr. *Chronology of African-American History*. Detroit, Mich.: Gale Research, 1991. Includes a short but descriptive history of Ashmun Institute at its beginning and as it changed to Lincoln University.

Ploski, Harry A., and James Williams, eds. *The African American Almanac: A Reference Work on the African American*. Detroit, Mich.: Gale Research, 1989. Places the founding of the institute among other the African American advances.

See also Atlanta Compromise; Education; National Council of Colored People; United Negro College Fund

Atlanta Compromise

The Event: Speech by Booker T. Washington offering an accommodation to white Americans
Date: September 18, 1895
Place: Atlanta, Georgia
Washington's controversial advocacy of accommodationism has a major influence on African American political and economic strategies.

Booker T. Washington, born a slave on a small Virginia plantation, gained his freedom at the end of the Civil War in 1865. He learned to read by studying spelling books and occasionally attending a school for African American children. In 1872, Washington enrolled at Hampton Institute in Virginia, a technical and agricultural school established for emancipated slaves. After graduation, he taught in Malden, West Virginia, then later returned to Hampton Institute.

In May, 1881, Washington received an invitation to join a group of educators from Tuskegee, Alabama, to help establish a technical and agricultural college for African American students. Tuskegee Institute opened on July 4, 1881, with Washington as its principal. Washington raised funds, acquired land, supervised the construction of buildings, and recruited talented faculty members. Within a decade, the school had gained a national reputation for providing outstanding technical and occupational training for African American students.

In the spring of 1895, Washington was invited to join a planning committee for the forthcoming Atlanta Cotton States and International Exposition, which would highlight the South's most recent developments in agricultural technology. Washington was asked to deliver one of the key addresses during the exposition's opening ceremonies, a speech that would focus on the role of African Americans in the South's agricultural economy.

The Address

Washington delivered his Atlanta Exposition address on September 18, 1895, to an audience of several thousand listeners. He opened by thanking the directors of the Atlanta Exposition for including African Americans in the event and expressing his hope that the exposition would do more to "cement the friendship of the two races than any occurrence since the dawn of our freedom."

Washington went on to predict that the exposition would awaken among both white and black southerners "a new era of industrial progress." He illustrated his point by telling a parable of a ship lost at sea whose crew members were desperate for fresh water. The captain of another ship, hearing the pleas for water by the captain of the distressed vessel, urged the lost sailors, "Cast down your bucket where you are." When the captain of the lost ship followed that advice, his crew members brought aboard sparkling fresh water from the Amazon River.

Washington then urged his African American listeners to cast down their buckets "in agriculture, mechanics, in commerce, in domestic service, and in the professions." He said that African Americans would prosper "in proportion as we learn to dignify and glorify common labour and put brains and skill into the common occupations of life." He added that "no race can prosper till it learns that there is as much dignity in tilling a field as in writing a poem."

Washington also told his white listeners to cast down their buckets among the South's African Americans, "who have, without strikes and labour wars, tilled your fields, cleared your forests, built your railroads and cities, and brought forth treasures from the bowels of the earth, and helped make possible this magnificent representation of the progress of the South." He encouraged white southerners to educate African Americans in "head, heart, and hand" so that they would remain "the most patient, faithful, law-abiding, and unresentful people that the world has seen." He asserted that in "all things purely social we can be as separate as the fingers, yet one as the hand in all things essential to mutual progress."

Washington concluded his speech by expressing his belief that the "wisest among my race understand that the agitation of questions of social equality is the extremest folly, and that progress in the enjoyment of all the privileges that will come to us must be the result of severe and constant struggle rather than of artificial

Booker T. Washington.
(Library of Congress)

forcing." He emphasized that African Americans must achieve economic self-reliance before they received "all the privileges of the law."

Washington's address was enthusiastically received by those present and the press. President Grover Cleveland wrote a congratulatory note. Washington received dozens of invitations to speak around the country and deliver his pragmatic message of economic self-reliance and political accommodationism.

Critics

Nevertheless, critics of Washington's philosophy soon surfaced, accusing Washington of making an unsatisfactory compromise by accepting an inferior social and political position for African Americans in exchange for economic opportunities. These critics argued that the tools for economic independence alone would not lead African Americans toward full citizenship and that the widespread segregation of and discrimination against African Americans in the United States, especially in the South, was proof of the flaws of Washington's reasoning.

Perhaps the most eloquent critic of Washington's message was W. E. B. Du Bois. In *The Souls of Black Folk* (1903), Du Bois, who would later found the National Association for the Advancement of Colored People (NAACP), asserted that Washington "represents in Negro thought the old attitude of adjustment and submission," that the ideas expressed in what he called Washington's "Atlanta Compromise" were merely "a gospel of Work and Money" that prompted African Americans to surrender political power, civil rights, and opportunities for higher education. In contrast to Washington, Du Bois advocated that African Americans receive the right to vote, civic equality, and opportunities for higher academic education, as opposed to the kind of occupational training offered at Tuskegee Institute.

James Tackach

Further Reading

Three biographies of Booker T. Washington that discuss the Atlanta address are Stephen Mansfield's *Then Darkness Fled: The Liberating Wisdom of Booker T. Washington* (Nashville, Tenn.: Cumberland House, 1999), Louis R. Harlan's *Booker T. Washington: The Making of a Black Leader, 1856-1901* (New York: Oxford University Press, 1972), and Arna Bontemps's *Young Booker: Booker T. Washington's Early Days* (New York: Dodd, Mead, 1972). Booker T. Washington's *Up from Slavery* (1901; reprint, New York: Bantam Books, 1970) contains the entire address and a discussion of the events surrounding it. In his *The Souls of Black Folk* (1903; reprint, New York: Penguin Books, 1989), W. E. B. Du Bois critiques the ideas expressed in Washington's Atlanta Exposition address.

See also Black colleges and universities; Education; National Association for the Advancement of Colored People; Niagara Movement; Talented Tenth; Universal Negro Improvement Association

Bakke case

The Case: U.S. Supreme Court ruling on affirmative action in education

Date: 1973-1978

In this ruling, the Supreme Court held that educational institutions may not use rigid quotas in their admissions policies but may take race into account in order to increase minority enrollment.

During the 1950's and 1960's, the United States made substantial progress in civil rights, aided by Supreme Court decisions that found state-sponsored segregation of the races to be unconstitutional. With its decision in *Brown v. Board of Education* (1954), the Court signaled that the equal protection clause of the Fourteenth Amendment to the Constitution could not be reconciled with public policy that discriminated on the basis of race. The Civil Rights Act of 1964 enacted this idea into legislation. The 1960's also heralded the beginning of a new effort to correct the wrongs of racial discrimination through the adoption of affirmative action programs.

Supporters of affirmative action contended that the removal of legal barriers was inadequate to ensure equality of the races. For example, President Lyndon B. Johnson argued that the effects of years of discrimination could not be erased by the dismantling of legal segregation and that affirmative action to aid those who had been the victims of that discrimination was necessary. Agencies throughout the federal bureaucracy adopted regulations requiring or encouraging the use of affirmative action programs by recipients of federal funds. In response to a regulation of this type from the Department of Health, Education, and Welfare, many colleges and universities throughout the country altered their admissions policies in order to recruit members of minorities more actively.

The University of California

The University of California at Davis Medical School (UCDMS) enrolled its first class in 1968. There were fifty students, three of whom were Asian and none of whom were African American,

Hispanic, or American Indian. Almost immediately, the school decided to create a special admissions program that would provide seats in each class for members of disadvantaged minorities. In 1970, eight seats were reserved for special admissions. In 1971, the total class size of the school was doubled to one hundred and the number of special admissions slots was doubled to sixteen. The admissions process became a two-track one, with applicants indicating whether they wanted to be considered as a disadvantaged minority. Persons found to qualify for special admissions competed against each other for the sixteen seats while all other applicants competed for the remaining seats. Applicants for special admissions did not have to meet the same requirements in terms of grade point averages and test scores as those competing in the general admissions process. Between 1968 and 1973, the year Allan Bakke first applied to Davis, the number of minority students enrolled in the medical school rose from three to thirty-one.

Allan Bakke was employed as an engineer with the National Aeronautics and Space Administration in California when he decided to apply to medical school in the fall of 1972. He had come to the decision that his true calling was in the practice of medicine. He applied to twelve medical schools that year and was rejected by all of them. Several of the schools cited Bakke's age, thirty-three, as the cause of the rejection. Bakke had an admissions interview at UCDMS and received high marks in the ranking of candidates for admission but, because of his late application, missed by a few points the cut-off score for the few seats left at that time. Bakke visited the school after being rejected and talked with an admissions officer who encouraged him to apply again the next year and to consider challenging the special admissions program. Bakke believed that he would have been admitted to the school in 1973 if sixteen places had not been set aside.

Reverse Discrimination

Bakke applied for the 1974 class and was again rejected. This time it appeared that his views on the special admissions program, which he had discussed with an administrator during his interview, had kept him from gaining admission. Bakke decided to sue the medical school, arguing that the special admissions program violated his equal protection rights because the sixteen-seat quota was allocated purely on the basis of race. Bakke's case brought to the limelight a new equal protection question: Can members of the white majority be the victims of racial discrimination? Bakke contended that affirmative action programs like the one at the medical school created "reverse discrimination" and were no less a violation of the equal protection clause because the victim was a member of the majority race instead of the minority.

UCDMS argued that it had compelling reasons for creating the racial classification. It sought to remedy past societal discrimination that had kept members of minorities from becoming doctors. Additionally, it believed that upon completion of their medical training, minority doctors would be more likely to return to their communities and provide much-needed medical care. Finally, the school contended that ethnic diversity was an important asset to the educational environment and that the special admissions program helped ensure a more diverse student body.

The question of "reverse discrimination" had been before the courts only once before. In 1971, Marco DeFunis had challenged a similar special admissions program at the University of Washington Law School which he believed had kept him from being accepted at that school. The trial court agreed with DeFunis's claim and ordered the school to admit him. The law school complied but appealed the decision against its program. At the appeals level the court sided with the school and the case reached the U.S. Supreme Court in 1974, the same year Bakke began his suit. The *DeFunis* case received considerable attention and clearly contributed to Bakke's decision to go ahead with his suit. In April of 1974 the Court decided to dismiss the *DeFunis* case as moot. DeFunis was about to graduate from the law school and the Court held that no true legal controversy existed any longer. This decision opened the way for Bakke's case to be the flag bearer for the reverse discrimination argument.

The Superior Court of California agreed with Bakke's position. It found that the special admissions program constituted a racial quota in violation of the constitutions of the nation and the state and the Civil Rights Act of 1964. It said that UCDMS could not take race into account in its admissions decisions. It refused, however, to order Bakke's admission to the school, finding no evidence that Bakke would have been admitted had there been no affirmative action program. Both Bakke and the medical school appealed the decision. In 1976, the Supreme Court of California ruled in Bakke's favor, holding that the special admissions program was a violation of the Equal Protection Clause of the Fourteenth Amendment and that Bakke must be admitted to the medical school. The medical school appealed this decision to the U.S. Supreme Court.

Bakke Case Resolved

At the end of its 1977-1978 term, the Supreme Court announced its decision. Four justices, led by John Paul Stevens, believed the program to be a violation of Title VI of the Civil Rights Act of 1964, which forbids discrimination on the basis of race in any program receiving federal funds. These justices believed that the Court should go no further than this in ruling on the case. Four other justices, led by William Brennan, argued that affirmative action programs were acceptable because they remedied the effects upon members of minorities of centuries of discrimination. These justices distinguished between invidious discrimination, which was forbidden by the Fourteenth Amendment, and what they saw as a benign discrimination, which was at the root of affirmative action programs. Some discrimination in favor of members of minorities was necessary if real equality instead of theoretical equality was the goal. Justice Harry Blackmun wrote, "In order to get beyond racism, we must first take account of race. . . . And in order to treat some persons equally, we must treat them differently."

Justice Lewis Powell wrote the decision that, because it allowed each of the other justices to join in at least part, became the ruling of the Court. Powell found that the UCDMS special admissions program was indeed unconstitutional. He argued that the equal protection clause prohibited policies based solely on racial factors unless there was some compelling state interest that could override the very high barrier to such classification. In examining the justifications offered by the medical school, he found only the academic interest in diversity convincing. He rejected the argument that past societal discrimination justified affirmative action. Reverse discrimination required a showing that the agency practicing it (in this case, UCDMS) had in the past discriminated. Since the school had opened in 1968 and begun its special admissions program in 1970, no such history of discrimination existed. Powell also rejected the argument that the program was justified because it served the medical needs of disadvantaged minority communities. The medical school could provide no evidence that special admissions doctors were any more likely than others to return to these communities to practice medicine. Powell held that the program could not stand. In this part of his opinion, he was joined by the four justices in the Stevens coalition, creating a majority to strike down the special admissions program and compel Bakke's admission.

Powell did not rule out all affirmative action programs as violations of equal protection. In the medical school's third justification, diversity, he found some legitimacy because of the traditional freedom granted to academic institutions to set their educational goals. Powell said that the desire for diversity justified some consideration of race as a factor in admissions decisions. The flaw in the UCDMS program was that race appeared to be the only factor shaping decisions for the sixteen seats. In this part of his decision, Powell was joined by the four justices in the Brennan coalition, thus creating a majority for the position that race may be considered as one factor among others in admissions decisions.

Impact

The landmark *Bakke* case provided something for both opponents and supporters of affirmative action. While it accepted the idea of "reverse discrimination" made by Allan Bakke and vindicated his rights, it refused to reject the concept of affirmative action altogether. For college admissions officers, it provided a roadmap for how to go about pursuing affirmative action in admissions decisions without violating the equal protection clause. For policymakers in general, it warned against the use of numerical quotas for accomplishing affirmative action ends. The division on the Court heralded an extended battle in the courts over which kinds of affirmative action programs would be found to be constitutional and which would not. In the years after *Bakke*, the courts struggled repeatedly, and contentiously, with questions regarding affirmative action in employment. *Bakke* raised more questions than it answered and brought to the forefront the breakdown of consensus on civil rights questions in the United States. When the issues of civil rights had been about the dismantling of legal barriers to equality, a broad consensus had existed about the justice of this course of action. It was generally agreed that the Constitution could not permit a legally segregated society. After the landmark desegregation decisions of the 1950's and 1960's, the questions became more complicated and the moral imperatives less clear. What kind of equality did the Constitution require? Once the legal requirements of segregation were removed, was there any further affirmative obligation for society to remedy the wrongs of the past? To what extent could individuals not responsible for past discrimination be made to bear the burden for the past? These were questions much more difficult to navigate in the murky waters of constitutional interpretation.

For Allan Bakke, the impact was more clear cut. He enrolled in the University of California at Davis Medical School in the fall of 1978. In the spring of 1982, he graduated to a loud round of applause from the audience. For thousands of minority students around the country, the *Bakke* decision provided new opportunities in higher education. The Court majority permitting race to be considered as one factor ensured that special admissions programs would continue. What can never be calculated is whether more or fewer of these students were provided educational opportunities because of the decision.

Katy Jean Harriger

Further Reading

Anderson, Terry H. *The Pursuit of Fairness: A History of Affirmative Action*. New York: Oxford University Press, 2004. Provides an excellent summary of the *Bakke* case.

Ball, Howard. *The Bakke Case: Race, Education, and Affirmative Action*. Lawrence: University Press of Kansas, 2000. An analysis of the law and politics that enveloped this case.

Dreyfuss, Joel, and Charles Lawrence III. *The Bakke Case: The Politics of Inequality*. New York: Harcourt Brace Jovanovich, 1979. Written by journalists in a readable narrative style that is sympathetic to arguments for affirmative action. Suggests that the focus of debate on qualifications obscured the underlying economic issues in affirmative action and signaled a fundamental change in race relations in the United States.

Eastland, Terry, and William J. Bennett. *Counting by Race: Equality from the Founding Fathers to Bakke and Weber*. New York: Basic Books, 1979. Presents an argument against pursuit of equality based on numerical quotas. Interesting historical discussion of different conceptions of equality in race relations in the United States.

Nieman, Donald G. *Promises to Keep: African-Americans and the Constitutional Order, 1776 to the Present*. New York: Oxford University Press, 1991. Readable historical essay with a good chapter at the end dealing with debate about affirmative action.

Schwartz, Bernard. *Behind Bakke: Affirmative Action and the Supreme Court*. New York: New York University Press, 1988. Provides behind the scenes insight into the decision-making process of the high court in this landmark case.

Sindler, Allan P. *Bakke, DeFunis, and Minority Admissions: The Quest for Equal Opportunity*. New York: Longman, 1978. Focuses on the issue of how to promote equal opportunity without engaging in reverse discrimination. Useful detailed study of underlying issues and court histories of Bakke and DeFunis cases.

Wilkinson, J. Harvie, III. *From Brown to Bakke: The Supreme Court and School Integration, 1954-1978*. New York: Oxford University Press, 1979. Chronicles role of Supreme Court in desegregation of education and argues that support for decisions breaks down as it moves from principle to imposing remedies of busing and affirmative action.

See also *Adarand Constructors v. Peña*; Affirmative action; Education; Equal Employment Opportunity Commission; *Sweatt v. Painter*; *United Steelworkers of America v. Weber*

Baptist Church

Identification: Protestant denomination that attracted many African American members

This denomination became an amalgamation of African and European forms of religious worship that found expression in the late eighteenth century.

The religious revivals collectively known as the first Great Awakening transformed the spiritual climate of British North America by the mid-eighteenth century. Church membership grew and evangelical religious ideas, which emphasized a person's own relationship with God, began to acquire hegemony over the religious values propagated by the established churches. Among those people who embraced evangelical ideals were African American slaves, who found attractive the notion of a personal God, the hope for salvation, and the less formal style of evangelical worship. This was especially true in the South, where African Americans benefited from a practice among some white evangelicals of allowing African Americans to preach to other African Americans and where African Americans were the targets of white missionary activity.

The Baptist Church

African Americans were particularly drawn to the Baptist faith, especially in the latter part of the eighteenth century. White Baptists, themselves often among the poorest in southern society, actively recruited African Americans. Furthermore, Baptists did not require formal education as part of ministerial training, and what learning they did encourage centered on mastering the contents of the Bible. Even African Americans held in bondage and denied opportunities for formal education could fulfill these expectations, and more than a few became ministers. African American slaves not only joined biracial Baptist churches but also fashioned their own fellowships, where they blended the traditional folk religions they brought from Africa with the evangelical nostrums of the Europeans, thus creating a hybrid African American religion.

In the Savannah River Valley, which connected the hinterlands around Augusta, Georgia, with the port city of Savannah, evangelical revivals among whites and African Americans bore organizational fruit among African Americans, who formed their own Baptist church at Silver Bluff, near Augusta, in 1773.

About that time, a slave named George Liele heard a sermon preached by the Reverend Matthew Moore, a white minister, and became convinced that he needed to respond to the gospel. Baptized by Moore, Liele became a preacher and began to exhort other slaves in the vicinity of Augusta to become Christians. Liele's master temporarily had to flee Georgia for his life and freed Liele. For the next several years, Liele and a colleague, David George, preached regularly at the Baptist church in Silver Bluff. George, who was born a slave in Virginia and had run away from a cruel master before coming to the Deep South as the slave of George Galphin, was converted after hearing sermons in the mid-1770's by several African American preachers, including Liele. George and Liele organized other churches, including the congregation at Yama Craw, outside Savannah, in 1777.

Among those who heard Liele preach at Yama Craw was Andrew Bryan, a South Carolina slave baptized by Liele in 1782. Bryan eventually purchased his freedom and devoted himself to his ministry. Although whites who feared an unshackled black man whipped Bryan twice and imprisoned him once, he continued to preach to ever-larger congregations, which often contained both black and white people. In 1788, his congregation constituted itself into the Savannah Georgia First Colored Church, commonly called the Savannah Church. At the time, it boasted 575 members, and it would grow to more than 800 by the time of Bryan's death.

A Fusion of Beliefs

The religious teachings of Liele, George, and Bryan fused the African concepts of a unitary universe where the sacred and pro-

Baptist churches, such as Birmingham's Sixteenth Street Baptist Church, were major organizational centers during the Civil Rights movement. (Library of Congress)

fane are not segregated, the European mythologies of Heaven, Hell, and redemption, and their present reality of slavery. God would help Africans through their travail of slavery and would one day lead them out of bondage. In this melding process, certain African religious practices were proscribed. The church covenant of Liele's Yama Craw Church specifically banned the consumption of blood and strangled meat of animals offered to idols, which had been a part of some West African religious rituals. Other African practices were given an important place, such as moaning as part of religious singing. This practice originated in ecstatic African religious rituals, and moaning and wailing have been preserved in southern gospel singing. This hybrid religious ritual did not confine itself to African American communities. The emotional shouts and ritual cadences of African worship affected the rhythms of white discourse as well, especially the sermon form, in which the preacher and congregation engage in something of a dialogue.

Both Liele and George eventually fled the South for the British Empire, seeking to continue their ministerial work without the specter of slavery hanging over them. Liele went to Jamaica, establishing the first Baptist churches there. George went to Canada, where he worked with both black and white people before organizing a Back-to-Africa movement, in which a thousand black Canadians went with George to Sierra Leone in 1792. Bryan, however, remained in the South, calling upon African Americans to lead better lives and, sometimes stealthily, urging whites to live out the Golden Rule in dealing with African Americans. By establishing churches that counseled patience while teaching a theology of ultimate deliverance, African American leaders like Liele, George, and Bryan helped African Americans survive slavery by encouraging them to expect freedom soon.

Edward R. Crowther

Further Reading

Black Church Beginnings: The Long-Hidden Realities of the First Years (Grand Rapids, Mich.: W. B. Eerdmans, 2004) by Henry H. Mitchell and Gayraud S. Wilmore's *Black Religion and Black Radicalism: An Interpretation of the Religious History of African Americans* (3d ed. rev. and enlarged. Maryknoll, N.Y.: Orbis Books, 1998) both provide information on the Baptist church. LeRoy Fitts's *A History of Black Baptists* (Nashville, Tenn.: Broadman Press, 1985) presents a sympathetic and readable account of black Baptist leaders and churches. C. Eric Lincoln and Lawrence H. Mamiya's *The Black Church in the African American Experience* (Durham, N.C.: Duke University Press, 1990) is a well-written survey of African American churches since their earliest times and their meaning in the African American struggle in the United States. Editor Gayraud S. Wilmore's *African American Religious Studies: An Interdisciplinary Anthology* (Durham, N.C.: Duke University Press, 1989) contains a series of essays that may help readers interpret the fragmentary documentary record of early African American religious life. Milton C. Sernett's *Afro-American Religious History: A Documentary Witness* (Durham, N.C.: Duke University Press, 1985) contains letters from Bryan and Liele and many other representative documents of the African American religious experience.

See also African Methodist Episcopal Church; African Methodist Episcopal Zion Churches; Black Christian Nationalist Movement; Black church; Church burnings; Free African Society; Slavery

Baseball's racial integration

The Event: Jackie Robinson's breaking of the color line in Major League Baseball
Date: 1947
Place: Brooklyn, New York
Until Jackie Robinson established himself as a major-league player, opening the way for other African Americans, professional baseball was rigidly segregated in North America.

In 1945, the United States was both triumphant and troubled. The most powerful nation in the world in the aftermath of World War II, the United States measured its strength not only in military and economic terms but also in the supposed moral superiority of American democracy. In 1945, however, segregation and racial exclusion remained the norms in American society. Even the U.S. armed forces were largely segregated. In the years following the war, Americans would have to come to terms with the gap between what their democracy was supposed to be and what it was. In this context, organized baseball extended an opportunity to African Americans and, in so doing, lost its status as a racist institution.

Background

The change did not come easily and might have been significantly delayed if not for Branch Rickey, the president of the Brooklyn Dodgers. The color line that excluded African Americans from organized baseball had its origins in the previous century and was solidly established. In 1923, it had been reinforced by an informal agreement among the major-league owners. This agreement was still very much in force in 1945, when Rickey decided to proceed with his plan to bring down baseball's color barrier.

Finding skilled African American players was not a problem. Although they were excluded from organized baseball, African Americans had not stopped playing the game. Barnstorming professional and semiprofessional teams and eventually entire "Negro" leagues arose, with the level of play comparable to that of the major and top minor leagues. Negro League teams often beat white all-star teams during the off-season. Separate, however, was not equal. African American players were paid much less and had to spend far more time traveling than white players. Nor did the Negro Leagues enjoy the stability of organized baseball. As a result, a pool of talented African American players was available to Rickey.

The integration of baseball had previously been advocated by African American sportswriters such as Sam Lacy of the *Baltimore Afro-America* and Wendell Smith of the *Pittsburgh Courier*. What Rickey brought to the issue was clout. He had the position and personality to do something about integrating baseball and to deal with any opposition that might arise. As with other civil rights advances of the 1940's, 1950's, and 1960's, there was stern opposition. Other major-league owners were opposed to Rickey's experiment. They argued that white fans and players were not ready for integration. Rickey believed that the time was right, and he pushed ahead.

Rickey's motivation has been the subject of considerable debate. He claimed to be acting on religious and moral grounds, but he undoubtedly was aware of the growing economic success of the Negro Leagues and the wealth of talent they might offer to the Dodgers. On the other hand, Rickey did not monopolize the best African American prospects, even recommending star outfielder Monte Irvin to the rival New York Giants. While motives are complex and difficult to discern, one thing is clear: Rickey had an unshakable belief in what he was doing.

Rickey's Choice

The question of who would shoulder the burden of breaking the color line was a difficult one. Rickey and other advocates of integration knew that the honor of being that person would be at least equaled by the ordeal, and that even a very strong individual might be broken by the twofold pressure of competing on the major-league level and being a crusader for racial justice. Because of the demanding job description, Rickey saw his choice to be one of awesome importance. It was Wendell Smith who recommended Jackie Robinson. Rickey had Robinson scouted and interviewed him. All the qualifications were there. Robinson was college educated and had played his college ball (three sports) on integrated teams. At twenty-six years of age, Robinson was mature but still in his prime. He also had demonstrated his dedication to the cause of racial equality, struggling against segregation while serving in the armed forces. Rickey saw in Robinson a man with fire in his belly, great self-control, and superb baseball skills. Robinson saw both an athletic and social challenge. With the support of his wife, Rachel, he decided to accept the challenge, signing a contract to play in the Dodger organization.

One obstacle had to be overcome before the Jackie Robinson experiment could begin. Rickey wanted Robinson to acclimate himself to organized baseball in the minor leagues for one year. In order for Robinson to be optioned to the Dodgers' minor league team in Montreal, the other major-league owners would have to approve. None of them did. Into this impasse stepped the new commissioner of baseball, Happy Chandler, a former Kentucky politician and veteran of public life. The previous commissioner, Judge Kenesaw Mountain Landis, had been an uncompromising opponent of integration. Indeed, it was Landis more than anyone who had engineered and maintained the 1923 agreement outlawing interracial play. Chandler had inherited Landis's autocratic power but not his attitude on the color line. Despite considerable pressure from the owners, Chandler overruled their fifteen-to-one vote against Rickey, allowing Robinson to begin his career in organized baseball in the spring of 1946. Later, Chandler claimed he made his decision because he did not wish to explain to his Creator that he had denied a fellow human being a chance to play baseball because of the color of his skin. Chandler's political sense was also astute. He correctly surveyed the political winds and realized that the criticism he took for allowing Robinson to play would have been dwarfed by the damage to his image if he had championed the cause of segregation. Americans were changing, not entirely or all at once, but enough to shift the tide on matters of race.

Then it was up to Robinson. He came through in every respect. He led Montreal to a league championship, winning the respect of International League players and fans alike. He proved that he could keep his mind on the game of baseball while putting up with verbal abuse and physical intimidation in the form of brushback pitches and high spikes. Playing half of his games in Montreal, a multicultural Canadian city, probably helped, but Robinson had clearly proved his mettle.

The following spring, Robinson made the Dodgers' roster, playing his first regular-season major-league game on April 15, 1947. Although Robinson got off to a slow start, he believed that his teammates were behind him. (This might not have been the case had Rickey not traded several Dodger players who refused to play with an African American.) Opposing teams were another matter. They rode Robinson unmercifully, as was the custom of the time with all rookies, often making race the focus of their comments. In living up to his agreement with Rickey, Robinson turned the other cheek to such comments to avoid jeopardizing his cause by touching off a feud or a brawl. Sympathetic reporters such as Walter Winchell tried to ease Robinson's burden by criticizing the worst offenders in their publications, a gesture for which Robinson later expressed gratitude. Soon Robinson began to play well, proving himself to be an excellent hitter and base runner as well as a versatile fielder.

Robinson on the Field

By the end of the year, Robinson had batted .297, won Rookie of the Year honors, and, quite literally, revolutionized baseball. The Dodgers won the National League pennant. With Robinson and many other African American players, they would win five more pennants in the next nine years, becoming a convincing testament to the possibilities of interracial cooperation. The other owners had been proved wrong. White players and fans overwhelmingly accepted integration, rejecting a past which most Americans were more than willing to forget.

The cost to Robinson was significant. His hair turned prematurely gray, and he spent many years recovering from the trauma of his groundbreaking achievement. He had made himself a target in order to rub out baseball's color line. For this Robinson suffered, but he never expressed regret.

Impact

The initial and most obvious impact of Jackie Robinson's triumph over the color line in baseball was to open up career opportunities for other African American players in organized baseball. Moved primarily by the need to stay competitive (the Dodgers dominated the National League for a decade with the help of African American players such as Robinson, Roy Campanella, Joe Black, Don Newcombe, and Jim Gilliam), and in the absence of the dire consequences they had predicted, other owners began to scout and sign talented African American players. There was still hesitancy on the part of some franchises, most notably the New York Yankees and Boston Red Sox, but by 1959 every major-league team had been integrated. Baseball had been successfully transformed into a symbol of racial equality and harmony rather than one of hypocrisy and frustrated dreams.

Jackie Robinson in 1951.
(National Baseball Library)

The indirect benefits of baseball's integration were also substantial. Understood not as a first cause, but as an important link in the chain of events, it facilitated later gains such as *Brown v. Board of Education* (1954), which desegregated schools, and the Civil Rights Acts of 1957, 1964, and 1965, which addressed other forms of segregation, job discrimination, and voting rights. The integration of baseball had rendered absurd the contention that the races were incapable of interacting fruitfully for common ends. Clearly, if athletes of different races could play together, people of different races could work and live together. Equal opportunity in baseball was clearly analogous to that throughout American society. Finally, baseball's integration fostered bonds between white fans and African American players. This made it less likely that white northerners would accept segregation and other forms of racial injustice passively, as they had in the past.

It is a mistake, however, to see Jackie Robinson's triumph over baseball's color line as a signal that racial justice and equality are no longer problematic issues in American society. While the player rosters of organized baseball teams became thoroughly integrated, African Americans remain clearly underrepresented in managerial, coaching, and front-office positions. There have, in addition, been charges of remaining discrimination on the field. Specifically, it has been alleged that players of marginal ability have better chances to make big-league rosters if they are white. Similarly, pockets of racial prejudice continued to exist among fans. Moreover, the existence of a pool of well-paid African American athletes is a misleading indicator of economic distribution according to race. African Americans continue to make up a disproportionate number of America's poor. Equality of opportunity and education remain goals of American society rather than accomplishments.

It has also been alleged that there were negative consequences to the integration of baseball. Obviously damaged by organized baseball's integration were the Negro Leagues, which had enjoyed their greatest success during the war years. While much of the profit from the Negro Leagues went into the hands of white promoters and agents, they still can be seen as an early enterprise in black capitalism, one for which Branch Rickey and Jackie Robinson did no good at all. It has also been argued that the integration of baseball hindered the development of alternative, separatist routes to true racial equality. Finally, because of the way he turned his cheek in response to various kinds of abuse from white players, Jackie Robinson has been seen as too passive a role model.

None of these limitations, allegations, or problems should diminish appreciation of Jackie Robinson. They simply encourage the acceptance of his character and accomplishments for what they were rather than the distortion of them for one purpose or another. Jackie Robinson did not manage to strike down racism with a single blow. Nor was he an "Uncle Tom" by any means. He was a fine athlete with highly developed social values and the courage to back them up. Perhaps most impressive was Robinson's refusal to become rigid in his thinking. As the terrain of race relations in the United States changed toward the end of his life, Robinson changed his political affiliation, citing the Republican Party's lack of commitment to the cause of racial equality. Recognizing the need for new initiatives rather than worship of the past, Robinson never presented his own experience as a reason for complacency. He saw clearly that the quest for racial justice was an ongoing struggle.

Ira Smolensky

Further Reading

Aaron, Hank. *I Had a Hammer.* New York: HarperCollins, 1991. Describes Aaron's early experience as one of relatively few African American players, his hall-of-fame career, and his subsequent frustration with the failure of baseball owners to integrate management and coaching staffs fully. Includes a chilling account of the hate mail Aaron received because of his race as he approached and ultimately surpassed Babe Ruth's record for lifetime home runs.

Frommer, Harvey. *Rickey and Robinson: The Men Who Broke Baseball's Color Barrier.* New York: Macmillan, 1982. Provides a rich portrait of the two figures central to the Jackie Robinson story.

Kahn, Roger. *The Boys of Summer.* New York: Harper & Row, 1972. A sport journalist's "then and now" portraits of Jackie Robinson and selected teammates on the Dodgers. Remarkable for its frankness and depth of feeling.

Myrdal, Gunnar. *An American Dilemma: The Negro Problem and American Democracy.* New York: Harper & Row, 1962. Originally published in 1945, Myrdal's book went into great detail and pulled no punches in its portrayal of American racism. A Swedish sociologist, Myrdal served the United States well in the role of social conscience, propelling Americans toward experiments in racial equality.

Peterson, Robert W. *Only the Ball Was White.* Englewood Cliffs, N.J.: Prentice-Hall, 1970. Describes life in the Negro Leagues. Also quotes from a 1923 agreement by white team owners that continued and formalized the exclusion of African American players.

Robinson, Jackie, with Wendell Smith. *Jackie Robinson: My Own Story.* New York: Greenberg Press, 1948. A straightforward account of Robinson's athletic career and experience breaking organized baseball's color line. Contains many photographs. Also notable is the participation of Smith, who wrote for the *Pittsburgh Courier,* an African American paper. It was Smith who recommended Robinson to Branch Rickey.

Simon, Scott. *Jackie Robinson and the Integration of Baseball.* Hoboken, N.J.: J. Wiley & Sons, 2002.

Tygiel, Jules. *Baseball's Great Experiment: Jackie Robinson and His Legacy.* New York: Oxford University Press, 1983. Written by a professional scholar, this work is a thoroughly researched social history. As such, it casts light not only on the personalities involved in the Jackie Robinson story but also on the broader social and historical context in which these individuals operated. Tygiel follows up the Robinson story by examining racial integration of all the major league teams and the subsequent issue of organized baseball's integration on the management level. He considers the Jackie Robinson "experiment" to be ongoing rather than successfully completed.

Voight, David Q. *America Through Baseball.* Chicago: Nelson-Hall, 1976. Chapter 8, "American Baseball and the American Dilemma," presents a thought-provoking critique of the so-called Jackie Robinson myth: the belief that Robinson's entry into baseball somehow fostered or signaled a golden age of racial equality.

Woodward, C. Vann. *The Strange Career of Jim Crow.* New York: Oxford University Press, 1957. A classic, highly readable account of segregation in the American South.

See also Journey of Reconciliation; Military desegregation; Segregation; Sports

Batson v. Kentucky

The Case: U.S. Supreme Court ruling on jury selection
Date: April 30, 1986

The Supreme Court ruled that the equal protection clause of the Fourteenth Amendment forbids a prosecutor from using peremptory challenges to remove potential jurors because of their race.

James Batson, an African American, was indicted for second-degree burglary. When the judge conducted a *voir dire* examination (preliminary check of suitability and qualifications) of the potential jurors, the prosecutor used his peremptory challenges to remove all four African Americans from the panel, resulting in an all-white jury. The Supreme Court had refused to disturb the same development in *Swain v. Alabama* (1965). After Batson's conviction, nevertheless, his lawyers asserted that the process of jury selection violated his rights to equal protection and to a jury drawn from a cross section of the community.

By a 7-2 majority, the Court accepted Batson's claim. Speaking for the majority, Justice Lewis F. Powell, Jr., remanded the case and instructed the trial court to require the prosecutor to justify the exclusion of members of the defendant's race from the jury. If the prosecutor were unable to give a racially neutral explanation, Batson's conviction would have to be reversed. Powell's opinion formulated a framework for future *voir dire* proceedings. The basic idea is that a pattern of exclusion based on race creates an inference of discrimination. Once such an inference is established, the prosecutor has the burden of showing that the peremptories are not discriminatory. Emphasizing that the Constitution does not guarantee a right to peremptory challenges, Powell wrote that potential jurors may not be eliminated simply because of the assumption that people of a particular race might be more sympathetic to a particular defendant. Thus, Powell's opinion requires color-conscious rather than color-blind procedures in jury selection, and it tends to encourage the use of racial quotas.

The *Batson* principles have been significantly expanded. In *Powers v. Ohio* (1991), the Court held that criminal defendants may object to race-based peremptory challenges even if the defendant and the excluded jurors do not belong to the same race. Later that year, in *Edmonson v. Leesville Concrete Company*, the Court applied the *Batson* framework to the selection of juries in civil trials. In *Georgia v. McCollum* (1992), the Court decided that the *Batson* ruling applies to defense attorneys. In *J. E. B. v. Alabama* (1994), moreover, the Court held that the equal protection clause prohibits discrimination in jury selection on the basis of gender.

Thomas Tandy Lewis

See also *Edmonson v. Leesville Concrete Company; Moore v. Dempsey; Norris v. Alabama; Powers v. Ohio; Strauder v. West Virginia; Williams v. Mississippi*

Birmingham March

The Event: Protest march against segregation
Date: April 4-May 7, 1963
Place: Birmingham, Alabama

A series of demonstrations in Birmingham, Alabama, sponsored by the Southern Christian Leadership Conference (SCLC), were designed to draw attention to the violent racism that underlay white southerners' defense of segregation.

A disappointing campaign in Albany, Georgia, in 1962, prompted the Southern Christian Leadership Conference to select Birmingham, Alabama, as its subsequent target for nonviolent demonstrations. Protests against segregation had failed in Albany because the city's chief of police, Laurie Pritchett, had held white mobs at bay and prevented the violent confrontations between police and protesters that would produce media coverage. Martin Luther King, Jr., and other SCLC leaders met in Savannah, Georgia, at the end of 1962 to plan a series of demonstrations in Birmingham, a city noted for its racial violence and uncompromising stand against the Civil Rights movement. The strategists hoped to gain national attention by provoking Birmingham officials into explicit displays of racial antagonism, thereby revealing the true face of southern segregation.

The March

Project C, the SCLC's code name for its assault on segregation in Birmingham, proceeded in three stages. First, on the morning of April 4, 1963, an economic boycott of downtown businesses went into effect, and small groups began staging sit-ins at downtown lunch counters. After Police Chief Eugene "Bull" Conner ordered arrests, the protest caught the attention of the media and the administration of President John F. Kennedy. Stage two began on April 6 with daily marches on city hall. As the protest leaders had expected, the Birmingham police arrested all of the demonstrators while flashbulbs popped and television cameras whirred.

King himself was arrested and during his incarceration penned his "Letter from Birmingham Jail," an eloquent statement of the motivations that guided the Civil Rights movement. Police began to respond to the daily marches with less and less restraint, and African Americans began turning out for the marches in ever-larger numbers and tightened the economic boycott. The sit-ins, protest marches, and police violence had riveted a national audience to their television sets by the time the third stage began on May 2.

That morning, more than one thousand African American children exited the Sixteenth Avenue Baptist Church as adult spectators cheered them on. The "children's crusade" sang and danced its way into the paddywagons waiting to take them to jail. Extensive criticism of the decision to use children rained down from both sides of the struggle, but King and the other leaders had little choice. Adults had become reluctant to march and serve jail time. More important, the protest leaders recognized that the sight of children being arrested would stir the heart of the nation. The police actions—beating and turning fire hoses on protesters—and their continued brutality were captured by the media as the marches and arrests continued until May 7.

The Senior Citizen's Committee, which had been organized by the Birmingham Chamber of Commerce to handle racial matters, feared that continued racial violence would drive away business and permanently damage the city's reputation. On the afternoon of May 7, they met in secret session and ordered their negotiators to open talks with the SCLC. After three days of negotiations, the two sides reached an agreement that called for the desegregation of public accommodations, nondiscrimination in the hiring and promoting of African American workers in Birmingham industries, and the formation of a biracial committee. Even though the SCLC compromised and allowed gradual rather than immediate implementation of these measures, the demonstrations in Birmingham were considered a significant victory for the movement.

Impact

Public reaction to the events in Birmingham, along with the easing of Cold War tensions, convinced President Kennedy that the time had come for federal action in defense of civil rights, and he asked Congress for civil rights legislation. The Civil Rights Act of 1964 was signed into law on July 2 by President Lyndon B. Johnson, Kennedy's successor. The act prohibited segregation of public accommodations, made discrimination by employers and unions illegal, and created the Equal Employment Opportunity Commission. The broader impact of the march was to change the tone of the Civil Rights movement from gradualism to immediacy; the African American community was no longer willing to wait for decent jobs, adequate housing, and a quality education. The march also marked the entry of poor and unemployed African Americans into the struggle.

Robert E. McFarland

Further Reading

Accounts of the Birmingham march can be found in Diane McWhorter's *Carry Me Home: Birmingham, Alabama, the Climactic*

Battle of the Civil Rights Revolution (New York: Simon & Schuster, 2001), S. Jonathan Bass's *Blessed Are the Peacemakers: Martin Luther King, Jr., Eight White Religious Leaders, and the "Letter from Birmingham Jail"* (Baton Rouge: Louisiana State University Press, 2001), Harvard Sitcoff's *The Struggle for Black Equality* (1993), and Taylor Branch's *Parting the Waters: America in the King Years, 1954-1963* (1988).

See also Civil Rights Act of 1964; Civil Rights movement; Million Man March; Million Woman March; Poor People's March on Washington; Selma-Montgomery march; Southern Christian Leadership Conference; Student Nonviolent Coordinating Committee

Black cabinet

Identification: Informal body of African American officials in the federal government
Date: Mid-1930's
The black cabinet had no dramatic impact on federal policies but made white New Dealers more responsive to African American problems.

The black cabinet was formed by more than a dozen African American men and women who had been appointed to federal positions by President Franklin D. Roosevelt by the year 1935. Known as the Federal Council on Negro Affairs after 1935, it was an informal gathering of African American advisers from various New Deal agencies led unofficially by Mary McLeod Bethune, the director of the National Youth Administration's Division of Negro Affairs. Its members included Robert Weaver, the Negro Affairs adviser in the Public Works Administration, and William Hastie, assistant solicitor in the Department of the Interior. Several other cabinet members later became nationally prominent. They usually met at the homes of Bethune and Weaver and informally had some impact on New Deal agencies. First Lady Eleanor Roosevelt often provided the impetus behind certain changes after meeting with Bethune.

The appointment of African Americans to federal positions symbolized the attempt by some New Dealers to eradicate racial injustice in the United States and influenced some African Americans to convert from the Republican to the Democratic Party. President Roosevelt, however, ultimately did not challenge the more intransigent elements of a still segregated society. Still, although the black cabinet did not dramatically alter federal government policies toward African Americans because the appointments were not at the highest levels and its membership was fluctuating, it made white New Dealers more responsive to African American problems.

David L. Porter

See also Politics and government; Summit Meeting of National Negro Leaders; Talented Tenth

Black Christian Nationalist Movement

Identification: Religious movement emphasizing the ethnic characteristics of African Americans
Date: Late 1960's
The movement correlated black Protestantism in the United States with African American heritage, culture, and political values.

African American Protestants have often had a sense of separation from other Christians in the United States, mostly because of slavery, segregation, and the formation of African American churches and denominations within the black community. This separation led to belief systems that stressed the history of oppression among African Americans and often likened them to the ancient Israelites living in slavery. This biblical analogy allowed African American Christians to interpret themselves as a religious people who were distinct, a people with their own national characteristics. The interpretation was supported in the 1960's and later by nationalistic political movements among African

Americans who were secular but dependent on the support of churches and religious organizations.

The movement termed Black Christian Nationalism is not one event but a series of occurrences including the establishment of congregations based on Black Christian Nationalist ideology, the publication of writings by major African American theologians, and the dissemination of the movement's ideas, which found varying levels of receptivity among religious African Americans. The most institutionalized example of Black Christian National-ism was the formation during the 1960's of churches called The Shrine of the Black Madonna in Detroit, Michigan, and some southern cities by the Reverend Albert Cleage. The foremost Afri-can American theologian promoting these ideas was Professor James Cone of Union Theological Seminary in New York City, au-thor of *Black Theology and Black Power* (1969) and *Black Theology of Liberation* (1970). These explicit examples, however, do not cap-ture the much broader dissemination of Black Christian National-ist ideas.

Younger, more formally educated pastors of African American Protestant congregations—denominations such as Methodists, Presbyterians, and Baptists—had been influenced by both bibli-cal analogies and current events of the 1960's. These pastors preached sermons comparing the plight of African Americans to the Israelites, stressing that African Americans in the United States were a separate nation that had been conquered by the larger surrounding white nation. They called for obedience to a God who was on the side of oppressed people, a Jesus who was dark skinned and non-European, and for identification with the nation of African Americans. The less-educated, more evangeli-cal holiness and Pentecostal ministers were less influenced by the ideas of Black Christian Nationalism. Some black Catholic priests interpreted Black Christians as a religious group for a separate "nation" of African Americans within the United States.

Impact

The somewhat disassociated congregations, writings, and dis-semination of ideas by young educated pastors that make up Black Christian Nationalism drew on two resources: an interpretation of the Bible associating African Americans with the enslaved people of God, the Israelites, and the Civil Rights and Black Power movements of the 1960's that clarified what constituted an oppressed nation within a nation. As Black Christian Nationalist views began to influence pastors and congregations, churches often abandoned the idea of the separation of church and state, and politics were considered a part of religious commitment. Being African American was identified as distinct from being any other sort of American, and religious organizations were perceived as the appropriate place to announce the religious-political ideology of Black Christian Nationalism.

William Osborne
Max C. E. Orezzoli

Further Reading

For Professor Cone's major ideas, see *God of the Oppressed* (1975). For a history of the subject see Gayroud Wilmore's *Black Religion and Black Radicalism* (1973). For a discussion of the relation between traditional Christianity and black nationalist feeling, see Major Jones's *Christian Ethics for Black Theology* (1974).

See also Black church; Black nationalism; Black Power movement; Church bombings; Nation of Islam; Republic of New Africa; Southern Christian Leadership Conference

Black church

Definition: Collective term for the many autonomous denominations of African American Christian churches

The black church evolved as a highly visible social institution in response to white racism in American society and racism in white-defined Christianity.

Although African American religious experience is diverse and social forms of religious life vary greatly, the black church has historically been the most visible religious institution in African American culture. As a visible institution controlled from within the black community, the black church has played a central role in African American social and political history. This history has evolved within the broader historical context of American racism and racial politics. The church, also evolving within that broader context, has been an important center for the development of African American Christian theology and for community identity.

The black church originated as a formal institution when African American religious leaders in Philadelphia were forcibly removed from worshiping on the main "whites only" floor of St. George's Methodist Episcopal Church. When Richard Allen and Absalom Jones were evicted from the church in 1787, they and their fellow black Christians concluded that the racism of white-defined Christianity precluded full Christian expression for African Americans in white-controlled congregations. Their formation of the Free African Society that year paved the way for the later creation of the fully autonomous African Methodist Episcopal (AME) Church, one of the earliest black churches in the United States. An institutionalized form of distinct African American Christian theology began to emerge.

Lincoln/Mamiya Model

In their expansive sociological study entitled *The Black Church in the African-American Experience* (1990), C. Eric Lincoln and Lawrence H. Mamiya propose a dynamic model for interpreting the sociology of black churches in their diversity and complexity. Lincoln and Mamiya identify the major black denominations as the AME Church, the AME Zion Church, the Christian Methodist Episcopal (CME) Church, the National Baptist Convention, U.S.A., Incorporated (NBCA), the Progressive National Baptist Convention (PNBC), and the Church of God in Christ (COGIC). These denominations, as well as many other smaller ones and local churches, provide institutional structure for the religious (and often political) life of millions of African American Christians.

Although sociologists and political historians debate the nature of the black church and its political role, Lincoln and Mamiya offer a "dialectical model of the black church" that encourages an open and ongoing analysis. The Lincoln/Mamiya model offers a

Black churches have played central roles in African American communities since the early nineteenth century, when they offered welcoming sanctuaries away from white oversight. (Library of Congress)

way of analyzing the ongoing tensions, both theological and political, within African American Christianity as those tensions are embodied in the structure of the black church. The model proposes the following six "dialectically related" pairs, or opposites. With these pairs the focus is on the ways that human experience shifts back and forth between the two opposites, sometimes tending more toward one idea, sometimes tending more toward the other.

For example, the first dialectic is that between "priestly" and "prophetic" functions of the church. In other words, it concerns how the church balances its role as the center for worship (priestly) in relation to its role as an agent for social change in the community (prophetic). Second, there is a dialectic tension in the black church between the "other-worldly" and the "this-worldly." Does the church focus on individual spiritual salvation for the "life to come" or does it focus on social justice in the here-and-now? The third dialectic proposed by Lincoln and Mamiya is between "universalism" and "particularism": how the black church negotiates its role in Christianity, broadly speaking, and its very particular role in African American history. The black church is part of a universal religious institution but is also a very particular response to white racism in American Christianity. A fourth dialectic is between the "communal" and the "privatistic": How does the church address individual spiritual life in the context of the social realities of African American experience? The fifth dialectic is especially important politically; it is between the "charismatic" and the "bureaucratic." This involves how the church uses the power of personalized and local leadership in relation to developing larger-scale institutional structure and national leadership as well as how it handles the tensions inherent in doing both. Finally, Lincoln and Mamiya join many African American historians and cultural critics when they identify the dialectical tension between "accommodation" and "resistance." Given the realities of white racism and African American history's origins in the experience of slavery, how has a primary social institution such as the black church moved between accommodating and resisting white mainstream culture in the United States?

Politics and the Church

It is in this final dialectic that much of the debate over the role of the black church in the twentieth century Civil Rights movement evolved. It is debated, for example, whether the church served as an accommodationist spiritual escape that diluted the intensity of its members, whether the church served as a fundamental source of activism and militancy, or whether the black church did both.

During the 1950's and the 1960's, the Civil Rights movement accelerated and moved to the center of the national political stage. Beginning with efforts to integrate schools following the Supreme Court's *Brown v. Board of Education* decision in 1954 and continuing through the Montgomery bus boycott (1955-1956), the formation of the Southern Christian Leadership Conference (1957), the Freedom Rides summer (1961), and the March on Washington (1963), hundreds of thousands of African Americans confronted American racism and fought for fulfillment of the stated U.S. commitment to freedom for all its people. The black church played a central role during these years, providing people and resources for grassroots organizing while cultivating leadership for the national movement.

During this period, tensions arose in the black community that illustrate the sociological complexity of the church as a social institution. From the perspective of the emerging Black Power movement, the church was suspect in its adherence to Christian principles of nonviolence in the face of white racial violence and was deluded in its emphasis on integration into mainstream American society. For black nationalists, this mainstream society remained white-dominated and white-controlled. Some nationalists argued that African American Christianity itself was flawed because of its origins as a religion of enslavement.

From another perspective, political and religious leaders such as Martin Luther King, Jr., proposed that African American Christianity provided both the spiritual and material bases for a militant liberation theology, one that posed a radical challenge to the white-supremacist status quo of the mid-twentieth century United States. King was a nationally recognized Christian leader, but with him were thousands of African American Christian women and men who argued that the black church provided the path of most, rather than least, resistance to white racism. As Lincoln and Mamiya point out, the fact that white racists bombed several hundred black churches during the civil rights period indicates that the threat posed to white supremacy by the black church was substantial.

A second debate that highlights some of the issues from the Lincoln/Mamiya model concerns the role of women in the black church. During the Civil Rights movement, women provided the "rank and file" of many organizing efforts, working together with men to form the core of the movement. In the church, however, men still maintained a monopoly in terms of formal congregational leadership. On the national level, this trend was even more pronounced; the nationally recognized black leadership of the Civil Rights movement was almost exclusively male. Women such as Rosa Parks, Fannie Lou Hamer, and Mamie Bradley (Emmett Till's mother) were recognized on a national level, but the political leadership of black women in many key political battles, especially on the local level, went unacknowledged both in the national media and in the formal leadership structure of the church.

Gender politics are significant because they highlight tensions within the church when issues that are often expressed in secular political terms (such as women's oppression) are also engaged in theological and spiritual terms. This can result in significant structural change within a social institution such as the black church. In the case of women and the church, the political becomes religious and the religious becomes political, bringing into play the dynamic tensions between the "this-worldly" and the "other-worldly," between the "priestly" and the "prophetic."

Sharon Carson

Further Reading

Black Church Beginnings: The Long-Hidden Realities of the First Years (Grand Rapids, Mich.: W. B. Eerdmans, 2004) by Henry H. Mitchell and *Black Religion and Black Radicalism: An Interpretation of the Religious History of African Americans* (3d ed. rev. and enlarged. Maryknoll, N.Y.: Orbis Books, 1998) by Gayraud S. Wilmore offer riveting information on the African American religious experience. E. Franklin Frazier and C. Eric Lincoln's *The Negro Church in America: The Black Church Since Frazier* (New York: Schocken Books, 1974) is an important sociological study that offers the comparative perspectives of two important scholars of the black church. C. Eric Lincoln and Lawrence H. Mamiya's *The Black Church in the African-American Experience* (Durham, N.C.: Duke University Press, 1990) covers theoretical and historical issues as well as providing in-depth denominational histories and useful statistical data. Peter J. Paris's *The Social Teaching of the Black Churches* (Philadelphia: Fortress Press, 1985) is a very good source for more detailed discussion of the ways that the black church, as a social institution, has participated in African American culture. *African American Religious Studies: An Interdisciplinary Anthology* edited by Gayraud S. Wilmore (Durham, N.C.: Duke University Press, 1989) offers both a wide range of readings in the subject of African American religion and an introduction to many important scholars in the field.

See also African Methodist Episcopal Church; African Methodist Episcopal Zion Churches; Baptist Church; Black Christian Nationalist Movement; Black nationalism; Church bombings; Church burnings; Civil Rights movement; Free African Society

Black codes

Definition: Post-Civil War state laws limiting the rights of newly freed African Americans

The black codes served to take away many of the freedoms that former slaves hoped to enjoy.

The months immediately following the end of the U.S. Civil War were a period of great uncertainty. Wartime president Abraham Lincoln had been assassinated, and his successor, Andrew Johnson, was wholly untested. No leadership could be expected from Capitol Hill, since Congress had gone into a long recess. In the southern states, a host of questions required immediate answers; foremost among these were questions relating to the place of the recently freed slaves in postwar southern society. Would the freed slaves continue to furnish an economical and reliable labor force for southern cotton planters? Would the former slaves exact subtle or blatant revenge upon their former masters? Should lawmakers grant African Americans the vote in the southern states? Should the U.S. government give them land? Should the states pay the cost of a basic education for them? What legal rights would these five million African Americans enjoy in the postbellum South?

Reconstruction Plans

President Johnson developed a lenient plan for Reconstruction, one that called on the southern states to quickly reorganize their state governments. His only major demands of these new governments were that they admit that no state had the right to leave the Union, and that they ratify the Thirteenth Amendment, which ended slavery. As the new southern state legislatures began to meet, their exclusively white members were most interested in passing laws that would answer some of the nagging questions about the future place of African Americans in southern society. Many legislators believed the freed slaves would not work unless forced to do so, and they feared the double specter of an economy without a labor supply and a huge mass of people who would live on charity or plunder. In earlier years, laws known as the "slave codes" had controlled the African American population; some lawmakers now called for a renewal of the slave codes to control the freed black population.

Mississippi's legislature was the first to take up the question of the rights of, or limitations on, African Americans. This body met in October, 1865, and quickly fell into arguments over what policies on racial matters should be enacted. Nearly half of the legislators favored laws that would, in almost every way, return African Americans to the position they had occupied in the time of slavery. Mississippi's governor, Benjamin G. Humphreys, intervened and urged lawmakers to ensure certain basic rights to the newly freed slaves. After Humphreys' intervention, the moderates in the Mississippi legislature had the upper hand and, on November 24, 1865, enacted a bill entitled "An Act to Confer Civil Rights on Freedmen."

As its title promised, Mississippi's new law did confer some basic rights on African Americans that they had not enjoyed as slaves. These rights included the right to sue and be sued, the right to swear out criminal complaints against others, the right to purchase or inherit land, the right to marry, and the right to draw up labor or other contracts. Although the law's title did speak of conferring civil rights, and a few new rights were indeed granted, this law—the first of the black codes of the southern states—was remarkable primarily for the rights it denied to African Americans. It did give African Americans the right to own land, but it denied them the right to rent rural land—thus the legislators sought to perpetuate large gangs of landless agricultural workers. The act recognized the right to marry, but it also provided that interracial marriage would be punished by life imprisonment for both parties. The right to testify in court was eroded by certain provisions that said the right to testify did not apply to cases in which both parties in a lawsuit or criminal case were white, nor to criminal cases in which the defendant was African American.

Labor Provisions

Most ominous was the provision that every black citizen in the state must sign a one-year labor contract by January 1 of each year and must honor that contract. Should the employee leave the employer before the end of the year, law enforcement officers were empowered to return the worker forcibly to his or her place of employment. In a provision reminiscent of the old laws that forbade giving help to runaway slaves, this new law made it a crime to give food, clothing, or shelter to any African American worker who had left his or her employer while still under contract. The punishment for helping a runaway was up to two months in jail; for those who helped the fugitive find work in a state other than Mississippi, the punishment was up to six months in jail. Once again, securing a stable labor supply for the state was at the forefront of lawmakers' goals.

After Mississippi passed this first black code, a flood of other laws soon followed in Mississippi and the other southern states. South Carolina's black codes forbade African Americans from pursuing any occupation other than agricultural work, unless the worker paid a prohibitively expensive fee. Black farmworkers there were required by law to work from sunup to sundown and forbidden from leaving the plantation without the permission of their employer. South Carolina and Mississippi both enacted severe vagrancy laws that called for the arrest of idle persons, drunkards, gamblers, wanderers, fighters, people who wasted their pay, circus hands, actors, and even jugglers. If these persons were African American, they were to be considered vagrants and fined up to one hundred dollars and imprisoned. If unable to pay their fine, their labor would be auctioned off to a white employer, and their wages used to satisfy the fine.

Differences Among the States

The black codes varied from state to state, but their northern opponents said they all had the common goal of returning the freed slaves to a system equivalent to bondage. In some southern states, African Americans were prohibited from owning guns. In other states, their assembly in groups was forbidden, or an evening curfew was imposed. President Johnson, himself a southerner, saw little objectionable in the black codes, but many northerners did. Occupying generals Daniel E. Sickles in South Carolina and Alfred H. Terry in Virginia overturned all or parts of the black codes in their areas, pending action in Congress. In Washington, Senator Lyman Trumbull wrote the Civil Rights Act of 1866, which declared that all persons born in the United States were U.S. citizens, and that all U.S. citizens enjoyed equality before the law. Congress passed this measure over the veto of President Johnson. By 1868, the Fourteenth Amendment brought this same promise of equality before the law into the Constitution itself.

The black codes were barely enforced. Overturned by the actions of occupying generals, and later by the U.S. courts, which found them in conflict with the Fourteenth Amendment, they were important chiefly for fueling a conflict in Washington between Johnson's lenient Reconstruction plan and Congress's insistence that the basic rights of African Americans be protected. These codes are also important for their role in bringing about passage of the Fourteenth Amendment. Although African Americans' rights generally were protected between 1866 and 1876, the southern states found many ways to draft laws that were color-blind on their face, but that could be enforced in a racially biased way. After Reconstruction, few southern elected officials, and few officeholders nationwide, were very interested in championing African American civil rights.

Stephen Cresswell

Further Reading

Cohen, William. "Negro Involuntary Servitude in the South, 1865-1940: A Preliminary Analysis." *Journal of Southern History* 42 (February, 1976): 35-50. Discusses the larger picture of black labor and its lack of freedoms, linking the black codes to peonage and to the South's convict labor system.

Foner, Eric. *Reconstruction: America's Unfinished Revolution.* New York: Harper & Row, 1988. This massive volume is the basic history of Reconstruction; chapter 5 covers the black codes and related events.

Harris, William C. *Presidential Reconstruction in Mississippi*. Baton Rouge: Louisiana State University Press, 1967. Discusses the drafting of Mississippi's black codes, which are especially important because they were a model for other southern state legislatures.

Litwack, Leon F. *Been in the Storm So Long: The Aftermath of Slavery*. New York: Alfred A. Knopf, 1979. Tells the Reconstruction story as much through the eyes of the freed slaves as from the point of view of white government officials.

Wallenstein, Peter. *Blue Laws and Black Codes: Conflict, Courts, and Change in Twentieth-Century Virginia*. Charlottesville: University of Virginia Press, 2004.

Wilson, Theodore B. *The Black Codes of the South*. Tuscaloosa: University of Alabama Press, 1965. The only book exclusively devoted to the black codes. Provides thoughtful analysis of the meaning of these laws in southern and African American history.

See also Civil Rights Act of 1866; Civil Rights Acts of 1866-1875; *Civil Rights* cases; Compromise of 1877; Disfranchisement laws in Mississippi; Fourteenth Amendment; Freedmen's Bureau; Jim Crow laws; Ku Klux Klan; *Plessy v. Ferguson*; Reconstruction; Segregation

Black colleges and universities

Definition: Historic institutions of higher education that have targeted African American students

Black colleges and universities have been a major education vehicle for African Americans, allowing them to become credentialed to interact with others at work and socially and have enhanced intergroup understanding and relations.

Lincoln University in Lincoln, Pennsylvania, established by Presbyterians in 1854, is the oldest black institution of its kind still in existence, and Wilberforce University in Ohio, established by Methodists two years later, is the second oldest. Both facilities have remained in their original locations. However, the first separate educational facilities for African Americans were private African schools established by free blacks after the Revolutionary War. Like later black colleges and universities, the early schools provided a strong sense of black identity as well as a way in which students could prepare for employment. Work opportunities, however, were often limited to manual labor or two professions that the larger society felt were less threatening: the ministry and teaching.

New Institutions

Many private and public historically black colleges and universities were established during the post-Civil War era and became the primary means by which African Americans could obtain a higher education in a society that restricted them from attending white institutions, either by law or by social norms. When they were created, many of these colleges were called "universities" or "colleges" but were actually secondary-school-level institutions. When studies that led to the professions of minister and teacher were incorporated into their curricula, these institutions rose to a post-high-school level. In most cases, the post-Civil War historically black colleges and universities included a theological purpose for all students: the instilling of what were considered Christian values.

By the early part of the twentieth century, American philanthropic organizations had started to help support black colleges and universities through financial gifts. In the North and West, these gifts were not considered problematic, but in the South, many whites insisted that fiscal support go to institutions that emphasized vocational and industrial training. Two major black academics of that era, Booker T. Washington of Tuskegee Institute in Alabama and W. E. B. Du Bois of Atlanta University in Georgia, debated the type of education that African Americans, especially in the South, should receive.

Washington emphasized the need for vocational and industrial training, while Du Bois focused on education that would lead to the professions. By the 1930's, however, the debate was moot: Most historically black colleges and universities had developed into full-fledged colleges that required a high school diploma for entrance, and many were increasing graduate studies. These developments began to be supported in the 1940's with the establishment of the United Negro College Fund, which pooled the fiscal resources of financially fragile private institutions. By the end of the twentieth century, enrollment at black colleges and universities had increased to its highest levels, which demonstrates that they retained their appeal to African Americans.

Demographics

Historically black colleges and universities are predominantly black academic institutions established before 1964 whose main purpose has historically been the educating of African Americans. Each must be state authorized to provide either a junior col-

Founded by the federal government in 1867, Howard University became one of the most prestigious black colleges in the nation. (Library of Congress)

lege education or a four-year bachelor's degree, and each must be accredited by an association recognized by the U.S. Department of Education or show progress toward achieving that accreditation.

There were 109 historically black colleges and universities in 1995. Fifty of these, or 46 percent of the total, were public institutions, and the remainder were private institutions. They were located in fourteen southern states, three northern states, and three midwestern states plus the District of Columbia and the U.S. Virgin Islands. The institutions offered more than 450 academic programs in the liberal arts, sciences, education, business administration, social work, law, medicine, dentistry, engineering, military science, theology, and other fields. Most of the institutions offered associate or bachelor's degrees. Thirty-eight of the schools offered master's degrees, and twelve offered doctorate degrees. Some offered professional degrees.

Enrollments in black colleges and universities represented about 3 percent of total higher educational institution enrollments in the United States in the mid-1990's. Black enrollments increased from the 1960's to 1980, decreased from 1981 to 1986, and then increased in the late 1980's and the 1990's. Generally, black male enrollment has slightly decreased over these periods, while black female enrollment has increased significantly. Historically black colleges and universities welcome nonblack students. In 1976, white enrollment in these institutions was more than 18,000; by 1989, this had increased to more than 26,000. Some institutions in gateway cities, such as Florida Memorial College in Miami, have had as much as one-third of their total student enrollments come from Hispanic communities. The majority of faculty and staff at these institutions are black, and the remainder are white, Latino, and nonblack foreign nationals. Although the institutions enroll just 20 percent of all African American undergraduates, they produce 30 percent of those who graduate.

Impact

American higher education has always been pluralistic; certain institutions were created primarily to serve students of a particular gender, race, ethnicity, or religion. Black colleges and universities fit this national pattern, even though their histories and original needs may have differed. The impact of these institutions on the African American communities of the United States has been significant: Many of the local and regional African American leaders—ministers, educators, politicians, businesspeople, writers, artists—throughout the latter part of the nineteenth and the entire twentieth century have been graduates of black colleges. One of the more famous graduates is civil rights leader Martin Luther King, Jr. Black colleges and universities, first established from necessity, have continued to be prominent in American educational life because they have a purpose that appeals to their majority clientele, the encouragement and credentialing of an ethnically aware population. At historically black colleges and universities, many black students thrive academically in an environment they consider supportive and socially acceptable.

William Osborne
Max C. E. Orezzoli

Further Reading
Two valuable resources on African American institutions of higher learning are *Black Colleges: New Perspectives on Policy and Practice* (Westport, Conn.: Praeger, 2004) edited by M. Christopher Brown II and Kassie Freeman and *Stand and Prosper: Private Black Colleges and Their Students* (Princeton, N.J.: Princeton University Press, 2001) by Henry N. Drewry and Humphrey Doermann in collaboration with Susan H. Anderson. *Historically Black Colleges and Universities: Their Place in American Higher Education*, by Julian Roebuck and Komanduri Murty (Westport, Conn.: Praeger, 1993), includes very specific data from studies of race relations among students on both black and white campuses. A fine, older anthology that considers many issues faced by black educational institutions is *Black Colleges in America: Challenge, Development, Survival*, edited by Charles Willie and Ronald Edmonds (New York: Teachers College Press, 1978). Many scholars have contributed to this volume, which includes discussions of the self-concept of the colleges, the role of the graduate, the interaction of black college faculty and students, and teaching in key

areas of the sciences and humanities. The United Negro College Fund has edited studies of black colleges and universities that provide continuing statistics and changing data, such as B. Quarles's "History of Black Education," in *United Negro College Fund Archives: A Guide and Index to the Microfiche* (New York: University Microfilms, 1985). The American Council on Education's Office of Minority Concerns publishes *Minorities in Higher Education: Annual Reports* (Washington, D.C., various years), an annual document full of data and statistics.

See also Atlanta Compromise; Education; School desegregation; Talented Tenth; United Negro College Fund

Black flight

Definition: Population shift from urban to suburban areas
Urban flight is often thought of as occurring primarily among whites. However, middle-class African Americans have also been leaving cities for suburbs, often settling in primarily black suburbs.

In the decades following World War II, the United States became an increasingly suburban nation as Americans left cities for suburbs. During the 1940's, the federal government began guaranteeing mortgage loans in order to encourage Americans to become homeowners. These mortgage guarantees went primarily to those buying homes in the suburbs, and they frequently underwrote home ownership in neighborhoods that intentionally excluded African Americans. At the same time, the growing use of private automobiles and the construction of the freeway network encouraged movement to the suburbs.

As white Americans became more suburban, African Americans became more urban. Early in the twentieth century, the African American population had been primarily rural. As agriculture became more mechanized, African Americans moved to urban areas. Black concentration in cities, like white concentration in suburbs, was encouraged by the federal government. The federal Public Housing Authority established public housing largely in central city areas and restricted residence in public housing to the most economically disadvantaged. Because African Americans were proportionately much more likely to be poor than whites were, the availability of public housing in cities combined with housing discrimination in the suburbs to bring black Americans into urban areas.

"White Flight"

By the 1970's, white movement from the cities to the suburbs had become known as "white flight." Many observers of current events believed that whites were fleeing the cities to get away from African Americans. The racial integration of schools, and especially the busing of children to achieve racial integration, may have contributed to the movement of whites out of the cities, although social scientists continue to debate this point.

Whites, however, were not the only ones to move to the suburbs. After the 1960's, the middle-class African American population grew rapidly, and suburban housing became more widely available for them. During the 1970's, the African American suburban population of the United States grew at an annual rate of 4 percent, while the white suburban population grew at a rate of only 1.5 percent. African American movement to the suburbs, labeled "black flight" by some social scientists, continued throughout the 1980's and 1990's. It was driven by many of the same factors that had been driving "white flight": the concentration of the poor in central city areas, the deteriorating condition of urban neighborhoods and schools, and the availability of suburban housing.

Black movement to the suburbs did not, however, lead to fully integrated neighborhoods across the United States. Instead, as authors Douglas S. Massey and Nancy A. Denton maintained in their influential book, *American Apartheid* (1993), African Americans tended to move into majority black suburban neighborhoods. Thus, "black flight" further concentrated minority poverty in the inner city by removing the middle class from inner city neighborhoods, while largely failing to integrate the American suburbs.

Carl L. Bankston III

See also Demographic trends; Economic trends; Employment; Great Migration

Black Is Beautiful movement

Identification: Movement which supported the study of African customs and history and celebrated the uniqueness of African American culture

Date: Mid-1960's-1970's

Part of a broader drive to change political, economic, and social conditions for African Americans, the Black Is Beautiful movement emphasized the importance of countering stereotyped representations.

The Black Is Beautiful movement, part of a broader drive to change political, economic, and social conditions for African Americans, emphasized the importance of countering stereotyped representations. Originating in the Black Power movement of 1965-1975, the phrase "black is beautiful" appealed to large segments of the black community not directly involved with movement organizations. Music and visual arts were central to this appeal: James Brown's "Say It Loud, I'm Black and I'm Proud" and Aretha Franklin's "Respect" signified the change in spirit from earlier integrationist phrases of the movement. Movement theorists, including Kwanza founder Ron (Maulana) Karenga, declared the necessity of an art connected with the African American community and committed to its well-being and proposed that black art should "praise the people" as well as "expose the enemy" and "support the revolution."

The Black Is Beautiful movement initiated sustained investigations of African traditions and history and celebrated the distinctiveness of African American culture. The success of evocations of "soul" in black music, food, speech, physical beauty, body language, and clothing inspired the creation of independent presses and bookstores and student demands for African American studies departments. Though the Black Power movement lost most of its impetus by 1975, the Black Is Beautiful ethos exerts a continuing influence on the struggles for multicultural, feminist, and homosexual self-definition.

Trudi D. Witonsky

See also African Liberation Day; Afrocentrism; Black nationalism; Black Power movement; Pan-Africanism; Stereotypes

Black Jews

Identification: African Americans who adhere to Judaism

There are no firm statistics for the number of African American Jews in the United States.

In its broadest sense the term "black Jews" includes all persons of African descent in the United States who claim to practice Judaism. Not all such African Americans call themselves Jews; believing that the word "Jew" implies whiteness, some prefer to label themselves "black Hebrews" or "Israelites." There are no authoritative figures on the number of black Jews in the United States. Estimates during the 1990's ranged from as few as 40,000 to as many as 500,000, but those estimates did not reveal how the numbers were established. One scholar, using the narrow definition of Jewishness accepted by Orthodox rabbis, put the number at no more than 5,000.

Accounts were occasionally printed in the nineteenth century of individual African Americans who attended Jewish congregational services, some of whom were said to have formally converted to Judaism. Not until the twentieth century were there reports of black Jewish congregations in the northern part of the United States. These were small synagogues or temples founded by African Americans and led by self-proclaimed black "rabbis." Many were trained and "ordained" by Wentworth Arthur Matthew, who founded the Commandment Keepers Ethiopian Hebrew Congregation in Harlem, New York, in 1919. Matthew was inspired by Marcus Garvey's Back-to-Africa movement and its celebration of the superiority of African civilization. Rejecting Christianity as a religion imposed on slaves by whites, he claimed to be reconstructing a proud African Jewish heritage, taken away from African Americans during slavery, that traced its roots through Ethiopia to the Jews of the Bible. Matthew was convinced that the ancient Hebrews were a black people, a belief also held by black Jews who asserted that they were descended from the lost tribes of Israel.

Religious Practices

Practices among black Jewish groups vary enormously. Congregations following the example of Rabbi Matthew attempt to observe Orthodox ritual traditions, though they might add their own dress and musical or liturgical forms. They eat only kosher foods, hold services on Fridays and Saturdays, and celebrate Jewish holidays, especially the Passover festival, which has particular resonance for African Americans. Others include Christian elements and symbols in their services. Some who call themselves black Hebrews or Israelites try to reconstruct the primitive Judeo-Christianity of the first century, asserting that Jesus is the Messiah of the Jews but rejecting most Christian theology.

Whether trying to reclaim a mythical African past or hoping to establish a new identity, African Americans were not welcomed by most white Jewish congregations. Some did become fully accepted members of regular Orthodox, Conservative, or Reform synagogues if they satisfied the Orthodox definition of Jewishness by being a child of a Jewish mother. Other African Americans became Jews through formal conversions, often entered into because they were a partner in a mixed marriage. With few exceptions, black synagogues and leaders have not been accepted as legitimate by the formal religious or secular American Jewish community nor been admitted into national denominational groups or local rabbinical councils. Most black groups have never applied for such membership, and those that have applied have had their applications ignored. Few black leaders have ever received official rabbinic ordination, although all heads of black synagogues call themselves rabbis, using their title in its original meaning, that of teacher.

Milton Berman

Further Reading

Chireau, Yvonne, and Nathaniel Deutsch, eds. *Black Zion: African American Religious Encounters with Judaism.* New York: Oxford University Press, 2000.

See also Crown Heights conflicts; Jews and African Americans

"Black Manifesto"

The Event: Call by militant black leaders for white Christian churches and Jewish synagogues to pay reparations to African Americans for the hardships of slavery

Date: April 26, 1969

Place: Detroit, Michigan

The initial reaction to the demands of the "Black Manifesto" was positive with promises of support coming from several denominations and groups, but soon the religious press across the spectrum attacked the manifesto and its strategies.

The "Black Manifesto" was presented by Student Nonviolent Co-ordinating Committee (SNCC) member James Forman to the National Black Economic Development Conference in Detroit, Michigan, and was adopted on April 26, 1969. The manifesto was a call to arms for African Americans to overthrow the current U.S. government, which it characterized as capitalist, racist, and imperialist, and to set up a black-led socialist government. The "Black Manifesto" demanded the payment of $500,000,000 in reparations to African Americans by white churches and Jewish synagogues to compensate for the hardships of slavery. Churches were specifically targeted because they were seen as agents of U.S. imperialism. The monies that were demanded in the manifesto were to be used to establish land banks, television studios, universities, and black presses. To pressure churches to pay the reparations, the manifesto advocated the disruption of church services and the seizure of church property.

The initial reaction to the demands of the "Black Manifesto" was positive with promises of support coming from several denominations and groups, but soon the religious press across the spectrum attacked the manifesto and its methods, which echoed Malcolm X's "by any means necessary" revolutionary strategies. The manifesto particularly alienated Jewish groups.

C. A. Wolski

Further Reading

For more information about the manifesto and its impact, see *Black Manifesto: Religion, Racism, and Reparations* (1969), edited by Robert S. Lecky and H. Elliott Wright.

See also Crown Heights conflicts; Nation of Islam; Student Nonviolent Coordinating Committee

Black nationalism

Definition: Identity movement that emphasizes the distinctiveness of black heritage and culture

Black nationalism is a revitalization movement that seeks to empower black communities so that they direct their own futures and have more control over their relations with other racial and ethnic groups.

Black nationalism, a historical movement that dates back to the sixteenth century, first appeared as protests by enslaved Africans who were being transported to the Americas and continued in the form of organized slave revolts that lasted until the Emancipation Proclamation. These protests could be termed nationalistic because the participants attempted to reclaim historic identities and rejected the power that whites had over them. One of the earliest, best-organized black nationalist movements was started by Paul Cuffe between 1811 and 1815. Cuffe was a black sea captain who transported several dozen black Americans to Africa in an attempt to establish a colony in Sierra Leone. Although black nationalism took various forms in the history of the United States, African Americans who emphasized their identity and power have always existed.

The International Aspect

Black nationalism has been most explicitly expressed and most broadly studied in the United States, but the movement is not limited to one nation. Black nationalists have asserted their distinctiveness and attempted to achieve self-empowerment in many postcolonial countries in the world, including Caribbean basin nations such as Jamaica, the Bahamas, Trinidad and Tobago, and, earlier in history, Haiti. Nationalistic feelings not only helped black people in these nations rid themselves of the European powers that had colonized them but also continue to affirm their distinctiveness. Black nationalist organizations have been active in Brazil, South Africa, and western Europe, particularly Great Britain. Many of the movements outside the United States have influenced African Americans, and American black nationalists have had an effect on black people in other countries, especially during the latter half of the twentieth century.

Black Nationalist Leaders

Throughout U.S. history, the black nationalist movement has been led by members of the clergy. In slave eras, some religious leaders would sing black spirituals that often had a political and social meaning in addition to their theological intent. Some of these songs, such as "Steal Away to Jesus," were used to gather plantation slaves who would escape to freedom. In postslave eras, African American ministers often became the major organizers of nationalistic movements because they were the primary leaders of black communities. In their sermons, ministers often drew analogies between the enslaved people of Israel in the Old Testament and disfranchised African Americans. Some black theologians such as Joseph Washington have suggested that black churches functioned as political organizations whose main goal was freedom from white oppression. In the early twentieth century, African American sociologist W. E. B. Du Bois advocated a dual-consciousness for African Americans that emphasized their distinctiveness while recognizing them as Americans. Eventually Du Bois became disenchanted with the limitations on black status in the United States and explicitly promoted a Pan-African movement that would coordinate freedom movements between

African Americans and Africa. Toward the end of his life, he considered Africa the national homeland for all black peoples and encouraged them to migrate there.

Marcus Garvey, a West Indian who had immigrated to the United States, was the creator of the largest mass movement of nationalistic black people in the history of the nation. Under the auspices of his Universal Negro Improvement Association (UNIA), millions of African Americans were recruited to one of the institutions and businesses he set up as alternatives to white-dominated facilities. These included black capitalist enterprises such as restaurants, grocery stores, hotels, and entertainment centers and a steamship line that served to transport black Americans wishing to migrate to Africa. Most important, he also established the African Orthodox Church, a religious denomination that symbolized the highest values of a people seeking freedom and empowerment. White hostility and organizational mismanagement diminished the UNIA's influence, but Garvey had demonstrated how separate institutions could help African Americans maintain their group identity and be empowered to express it.

Contemporary Black Nationalism

Many black movements followed in Garvey's footsteps, but one, in particular, has been successful in continuing parts of his legacy while rejecting any notion of moving back to Africa. The Nation of Islam, whose members are sometimes called Black Muslims, flourished under the leadership of Elijah Muhammad between the 1930's and the 1960's, reaching a peak membership of more than 100,000. The group's membership, however, does not reflect the many African Americans who did not join the organization but admired its tenets. The Nation of Islam shared Garvey's insistence that African Americans have their own separate organizations in a white-dominated nation and claimed that the black nation in the United States had a right to be an independent nation with its own land. The Nation of Islam claimed that black people were the original people of creation and, therefore, the pure race.

Black people were to remain separate from nonblacks because interacting with nonblacks could only make them less pure. The Nation of Islam emphasizes the central role of the man in the family, the importance of economic self-sufficiency, the necessity to abstain from degrading habits such as alcohol, drugs, and casual sex, and the worship of Allah, the creator. Their institutions are primarily mosques and religious houses of teaching and worship, but they also have agricultural areas in the South, small businesses in the North, and some educational facilities such as elementary schools in their headquarters, Chicago, Illinois.

The death of Elijah Muhammad and the division of his organization into several groups has not diminished the influence of some of his followers. Louis Farrakhan, the leader of the most important of these groups, has expanded membership, accepted some Latinos and members of other minorities into the Nation, and correlated the Nation of Islam's agenda with non-Muslim organizations including black Christian churches and black community-based political groups.

The Impact of Black Nationalism

The two major debates among black nationalists in the United States center on whether African Americans need to return to Africa or at least live separately and on what kind of alliances they should form with other organizations and people. Many people question whether a group can be seriously nationalistic without going back to Africa or establishing a separate territory within a previously white-dominated country. Malcolm X, who was Elijah Muhammad's primary spokesperson while he was a member of the Nation of Islam, first believed in setting up a separate nation within United States boundaries but later perceived nationalism as a commitment and act that did not require geographical separation.

Huey P. Newton and Bobby Seale, cofounders of the nationalistic Black Panther Party for Self-Defense, interpreted existing African American communities as unofficial black "places" that should be allowed self-determination and the expression of racial pride. Farrakhan has played down the notion of a separate land and instead emphasized the idea of separate thought. The second debate involves how closely black nationalists should ally themselves with either blacks who are not nationalistic or nonblacks. Malcolm X's organization, founded after he left the Nation of Is-

HERE AND NOW FOR BOBBY SEALE

We must save Bobby Seale because
we must save the Black Panther Party because
we must save the revolutionary spirit in America.

Poster issued by the Black Panther Party in support of its cofounder Bobby Seale when he was being tried for conspiracy to riot in 1968. (Library of Congress)

lam, Newton's Black Panther Party, and even Farrakhan's organization have worked with nonblacks, and all three have interacted with African American Christian clergy, who remain important black community spokespersons and organizers.

In the 1960's, when the U.S. Congress passed a series of desegregation laws, some people believed it would result in the demise of black nationalism. However, because the legal changes did not substantially affect discriminatory customs and attitudes, and African Americans remained the object of subtler forms of racism in their economic, political, and social lives, nationalism survived and grew. African Americans, even if they do not belong to a black nationalistic organization, continue to feel nationalistic pride and to attempt to empower themselves. As long as the United States is not a racially blind nation, it is likely that black nationalistic thinking and acts will affect American life. Black communal pride and black self-determination, the marks of identity and revitalization movements, remain relevant as long as the social implications of black "inferiority" persist.

William Osborne
Max C. E. Orezzoli

Further Reading

Rod Bush's *We Are Not What We Seem: Black Nationalism and Class Struggle in the American Century* (New York: New York University Press, 1999) is an important work in the study of this movement. *Modern Black Nationalism: From Marcus Garvey to Louis Farrakhan* (New York: New York University Press, 1997), an exceptional anthology, relates the major black power era leaders' ideas and discusses contemporary movements through the 1990's. The major academic proponent of black nationalism, W. E. B. Du Bois, traces his own evolving thinking and contradicts some of his earlier social ideas in *Dusk of Dawn: An Essay Toward an Autobiography of a Race Concept* (New York: Harcourt Brace, 1940). For interviews of major figures of the movement, see *The Negro Protest: James Baldwin, Malcolm X, Martin Luther King Talk with Kenneth B. Clark*, edited by Kenneth B. Clark (Boston: Beacon Press, 1963). An incisive interpretation of the changes in Malcolm X's life and thought appear in George Breitman's *Last Year of Malcolm X: The Evolution of a Revolutionary* (New York: Merit Publishers, 1967). One of the most important historical works on the Nation of Islam is C. Eric Lincoln's *The Black Muslims in America* (Boston: Beacon Press, 1961). The Black Panther Party's minister of information, Eldridge Cleaver, wrote the twentieth century classic autobiography evidencing black identity problems called *Soul on Ice* (New York: McGraw-Hill, 1968).

See also African Liberation Day; Afrocentrism; Black Christian Nationalist Movement; Black church; Black Is Beautiful movement; Black Panther Party; Black Power movement; Congressional Black Caucus; Million Man March; Nation of Islam; Pan-Africanism; Universal Negro Improvement Association

Black Panther Party

Identification: African American revolutionary organization often seen as the "vanguard" of the radical movement in the late 1960's
Date: Founded in October, 1966
Place: Oakland, California

The Black Panthers captured the imagination of both disaffected youth and the media by combining an urban paramilitary style with a program dedicated to "serving the people."

Founded in early October, 1966, at an antipoverty community center in North Oakland, California, the Black Panther Party for Self-Defense was the brainchild of Huey P. Newton, community organizer, law student, and street tough. Newton and the party's cofounder, Bobby G. Seale, an army veteran, sheetmetal worker, and aspiring comedian who also worked at the community center, had been active in black nationalist circles while they were students at Oakland's Merritt College during the early 1960's. Born in the South, they came of age in the urban ghetto, and although they were inspired by the Civil Rights movement, it was Malcolm X, not Martin Luther King, Jr., who fired their imaginations. After years of frustration with college-based African American militants who paid insufficient attention to Newton's "brothers on the block" and especially in the wake of the massive Watts riot in Los Angeles, which Newton and Seale saw as the beginning of a new era, the two formed their own organization dedicated to armed self-defense among the African American masses.

The idea for the name of the organization came from a Student Nonviolent Coordinating Committee (SNCC) project in Alabama that was spearheaded by Stokely Carmichael. This project, the Lowndes County Freedom Organization, used a black panther as its symbol. "The panther is a fierce animal," Newton explained later, "but he will not attack until he is backed into a corner; then he will strike out." Other groups also took the name, in Harlem and San Francisco in 1966 and in Los Angeles the following year, but only the Oakland group survived. Black Panther membership, at the height of the group's activity in the late 1960's, is disputed; estimates range from the high hundreds to the low thousands. By 1969, the group had chapters in most major northern cities and an international division.

Party Ideology

Part of the reason for the party's success in the late 1960's— and for its failure in the 1970's—may have been the nature and evolution of its ideology, which quickly proved to be class-conscious rather than race conscious. Newton and Seale drew eclectically from foreign revolutionaries and domestic militants in fashioning a program of black liberation predicated on the legitimacy of violence: They had read Mao Zedong, Frantz Fanon, and Che Guevara, who endorsed armed revolution; they were also familiar with the writings and activities of Robert F. Williams in North Carolina, the Deacons for Defense and Justice in Louisiana, and Malcolm X, all of whom advocated armed self-defense. However, as Newton explained in 1970, the Panthers became Marxist-Leninists who embraced dialectical materialism, which in four short years took them from black nationalism (liberation of the black "colony" in the United States), to revolutionary nationalism (nationalism plus socialism), to internationalism (solidarity with the oppressed peoples of the world), and finally to

This official propaganda poster of the Black Panther Party employs two of the organization's primary symbols: a gun and a book.
(Library of Congress)

"intercommunalism" (world revolution pitting oppressed communities against the U.S. "empire").

Newton later claimed to have undergone a slow transformation from black nationalism to socialism while he was in college in the early 1960's, based on his "life plus independent reading." Therefore, the party's original program called for full employment ("if the white American businessman will not give full employment, then the means of production should be taken from the businessmen and placed in the community"), decent housing ("if the white landlord will not give decent housing to our black community, then the housing and the land should be made into cooperatives"), an end to police brutality, exemption from military service, and release of all African Americans from prison.

Activities

Though one of their first campaigns was to force the city of Oakland to erect a traffic light at a dangerous intersection, initially the Panthers' political work consisted mainly of confronting law enforcement officials (whom they called an "occupying army"), especially while "patrolling the police." The activity involved groups of armed Panthers observing interactions between local residents and the police, advising the residents of their rights and, as a result, often engaging in tense confrontations with the officers. This direct attempt to confront white authority in the black community, which Newton later claimed was a way of exhausting all legal means to protect African Americans' rights in anticipation of revolutionary activity, was an enormous leap in the history of African American resistance in the United States. However, in the summer of 1967 when the California assembly passed legislation curbing the carrying of firearms, a bill aimed at the Panthers, the group stopped the patrols and dropped "for Self-Defense" from its name. As Black Panther chapters multiplied throughout the country, however, physical confrontations grew, with deaths on both sides. At the same time, the Panthers established what they called "survival programs," beginning with free breakfasts for schoolchildren and expanding into areas such as medical care, clothing, and education.

Before the California gun-control law was passed, Newton sent some thirty armed Panthers to protest at the state capitol in Sacramento. This dramatic demonstration generated some national publicity, but what set the stage for the Panthers' dramatic growth occurred early one morning in October, 1967, when the Oakland police stopped Newton after he had spent the night celebrating the end of his probation for assault. Gunfire followed, and the Panther leader was wounded, as was one policeman; another patrolman, Officer John Frey, died. Newton was charged with Frey's murder and faced possible execution. Charismatic ex-convict and writer Eldridge Cleaver, who edited the party newspaper, *The Black Panther*, and became its minister of information in 1967, orchestrated a national "Free Huey" campaign that made Newton a virtual icon.

Newton's celebrated 1968 trial ended in a manslaughter conviction, and the campaign to free him succeeded in 1970 when the conviction was overturned on appeal. Although these events earned for the Panthers national recognition, they also brought the attention of the authorities. The ensuing raids, prosecutions, and the promotion of internal dissension by the Federal Bureau of Investigation (FBI) wrecked the Black Panther Party. By 1970, much of the national and even regional leadership had gone underground or was awaiting trial, in jail, or in exile.

Impact

FBI director J. Edgar Hoover called the Black Panther Party the "greatest threat to the internal security of the country," and the U.S. government viewed them as a serious danger; however, the Panthers were more often ridiculed. According to Allen J. Matusow in his 1984 book, *The Unraveling of America: A History of Liberalism in the 1960's*, in one influential survey of the 1960's, the Panthers are described as a "handful of blacks with a mimeograph machine" who "existed mainly in the demented minds of white leftists." The group did attract the support of the leading militant African Americans, SNCC leaders Carmichael, H. Rap Brown, and James Forman, and even managed a short-lived alliance of sorts (the Panthers called it a "merger") with SNCC in 1968. In early 1969, the Students for a Democratic Society (SDS)—

at its height but soon to be destroyed by internal factionalism—endorsed the Panthers as the vanguard of the revolution in the United States. The Panthers also provided the model for other groups such as the Brown Berets, the Young Lords, the White Panther Party, the Red Guards, and the Gray Panthers; the group's ten-point platform and program (What We Want, What We Believe) became the blueprint for other 1960's groups. Finally, the Panthers changed the popular lexicon; for example, they introduced the epithet "pig," in reference primarily to police officers but also to government officials, and the rich.

Subsequent Events

Especially damaging was the public and bloody falling-out between Newton and Cleaver in early 1971, the climax of two years of internal splits and purges. The rift with Cleaver was a product of Newton's attempt to direct the group away from militant confrontation and to community organizing through the survival programs it had developed. Newton's continued run-ins with the law, however, resulted in his fleeing to Cuba, where he stayed from 1973 to 1977. The Black Panthers lived on in his absence and, after his return, remained a viable organization into the early 1980's, but it never regained its role as a leading revolutionary group.

Jama Lazerow

Further Reading

Liberation, Imagination, and the Black Panther Party: A New Look at the Panthers and Their Legacy (New York: Routledge, 2001) edited by Kathleen Cleaver and George Katsiaficas and *The Black Panther Party (Reconsidered)* edited by Charles E. Jones (Baltimore: Black Classic Press, 1998) both provide valuable insights into the Black Panther Party. *Off the Pigs!* (1976), edited by G. Louis Heath, provides a long historical introduction (based mostly on government sources and FBI informants), a sampling of primary documents, and an extensive bibliography. *The Black Panthers Speak* (1970), edited by Philip S. Foner, offers a good collection of writings and speeches. Important Panther autobiographies and memoirs include Seale's *Seize the Time* (1970) and Newton's *Revolu-*

tionary Suicide (1973). A sympathetic journalistic account can be found in Michael Newton's *Bitter Grain* (1980); a particularly negative treatment is presented in Hugh Pearson's *The Shadow of the Panther* (1994).

See also Black nationalism; Black Power movement; Black United Students; Hampton-Clark deaths; Republic of New Africa; Student Nonviolent Coordinating Committee

Black Power movement

Definition: Ideological shift away from integrationism and nonviolence and toward a radical black nationalism
This new way of thinking strongly influenced a wide range of movements and organizations in the 1960's.

Black nationalism as a tool for social, economic, and psychological empowerment has a long history, as seen, for instance, in the writings of Marcus Garvey (social activist and civil rights leader in the 1920's and 1930's) and Malcolm X (spokesperson for the Nation of Islam). After the February, 1965, assassination of Malcolm X, some civil rights activists turned toward a revolutionary nationalist philosophy that urged aggressive tactics and separatism and the abandonment of civil disobedience, legal cases, and other more reformist strategies.

The first use of "black power" as a slogan was during a 1966 march to Jackson, Mississippi, following the shooting of James H. Meredith, the first African American student to attend the University of Mississippi. Some in the Student Nonviolent Coordinating Committee (SNCC) felt nonviolent interracial action was ineffective and that SNCC should become an all-black organization. On June 16, several marchers were arrested and jailed in Greenwood, Mississippi, including SNCC chair Stokely Carmichael, who told supporters after he was released: "I ain't going to jail no more. What we gonna start saying now is 'black power.'" At the urging of SNCC activist Willie Ricks, who yelled, "What do you want? Black power!," the crowd of supporters picked up the chant. After national news coverage of Carmichael's release, the slogan rapidly spread across the nation.

The actual concept of black power remained contested and imprecise, although it divided the Civil Rights movement. Less radical organizations such as the National Association for the Advancement of Colored People and Martin Luther King, Jr.'s Southern Christian Leadership Conference opposed black power, while SNCC and the Congress of Racial Equality backed it. By the late 1960's, black power advocates were a diverse group that included businesspeople who used black power to push black capitalism, the paramilitary revolutionaries of the Black Panther Party who sought an end to capitalism, and the cultural nationalists of Ron Karenga's US organization. The advent of black power paralleled a geographic shift for the Civil Rights movement: In contrast to the nonviolent church-based southern civil rights struggle of the 1950's and early 1960's, African American "rebellions" had exploded in dozens of northern and western cities in 1964-1965, areas where civil rights organizing would continue through the late 1960's and 1970's.

Stokely Carmichael (center, pointing), the head of the Student Nonviolent Coordinating Committee, amid a demonstration in protest of Congress's attempts to deny Harlem representative Adam Clayton Powell his seat in 1967. (Library of Congress)

Impact

Black power resulted in greater racial pride and self-esteem for some African Americans. It also brought the interracialism of the early Civil Rights movement to a close, leading some white activists to shift their work to white communities and other causes. Others viewed black power as merely defiant symbolism that did not achieve real structural change. Nevertheless, its influence was widespread, spurring the creation of black studies programs in universities, the founding of the League of Revolutionary Black Workers within the labor movement, and the growth in the numbers of African Americans elected as representatives. Puerto Ricans, Chicanos, and Native American activists (who coined the phrase "red power" during the Alcatraz Island occupation), often stated that they were inspired by black power.

The extensive Federal Bureau of Investigation infiltration of black nationalist groups and subsequent state repression directed at these groups along with internal divisions (often along the lines of cultural versus revolutionary nationalism) led to the decline of many black power organizations by the mid-1970's. Black nationalism continued in various forms, including the popularity of Afrocentrism in the 1990's.

Vanessa Tait

Further Reading

Jeffrey O. G. Ogbar's *Black Power: Radical Politics and African American Identity* (Baltimore: Johns Hopkins University Press, 2004) is an informative analysis of the Black Power movement. Manning Marable's *Race, Reform, and Rebellion: The Second Reconstruction in Black America* (1991) chronicles the complex political transformations during the black power period. Clayborne Carson's *In Struggle: SNCC and the Black Awakening of the 1960's* (1981) examines how black power shaped a key civil rights organization. A documentary history of black power from 1791 to the late 1960's can be found in *The Black Power Revolt: A Collection of Essays* (1968), edited by Floyd Barbour.

See also Black Christian Nationalist Movement; Black Is Beautiful movement; Black nationalism; Black Panther Party; Civil

Rights movement; Congress of Racial Equality; Malcolm X assassination; Nation of Islam; Pan-Africanism; Republic of New Africa; Southern Christian Leadership Conference; Student Nonviolent Coordinating Committee

Black United Students

Identification: Militant organization of African American college students

Date: Founded during the late 1960's

These students, spurred by the Black Power movement, worked toward establishing black studies departments in colleges and universities.

In the latter half of the 1960's, African American college students, inspired by the Black Power movement, formed collectives in colleges and universities throughout the United States in order to improve the lives of African American students and institute black studies departments. The first record of students organizing as the Black United Students was at San Francisco State University in 1968. The group was organized by Professor Nathan Hare, who later denied his part in the student strike, and supported by the Third World Liberation Front, a coalition of minority groups.

In November, 1968, the Black United Students, with the encouragement of the Black Panther Party, called for a student strike at San Francisco State University. The group presented the campus administration with fifteen nonnegotiable demands relating to the creation of a black studies department and the improvement of black student life. In response to the students' protest, San Francisco State University created the first integrated black studies program in 1969. Previously, Meritt Junior College in nearby Oakland, California, had begun offering a few courses in black studies, primarily to appease some members of the Black Panther Party, such as Huey P. Newton, who were attending the junior college, but it did not create a complete black studies department.

In addition to their efforts toward establishing black studies departments, the Black United Students actively joined with other campus groups in antiwar, antiestablishment protests in the late 1960's and early 1970's. The most noteworthy of these protests occurred in 1970, when the Students for a Democratic Society (SDS) and the Black United Students cosponsored a demonstration at Kent State University in Ohio, where four young people were killed by the Ohio National Guard.

Impact

The efforts of the Black United Students and similar African American groups helped establish black studies departments in numerous colleges and universities in the late 1960's and the following decades. By the 1990's, approximately two hundred black studies programs had been created across the nation. These programs have evolved from the original 1960's programs, which were sometimes cursory and not very well thought out, into degree-granting, three-tiered programs. At the first level, these programs provide an introduction to African history and to the African experience in the Americas and in other parts of the world. At the second level, they begin to include more specific courses and examine current issues and research, delving into issues such as the place of African Americans in American society. At the third level, the programs offer an integrated look at African influences on and experiences of psychology, economics, political science, sociology, history, and literature.

In the late 1990's, a number of organizations calling themselves the Black United Students were located on campuses across the United States. These organizations act to further the interests of African American students.

Annita Marie Ward

Further Reading

Turmoil on the Campus (1970), edited by Edward J. Barder, discusses various issues raised by African American students in the 1960's.

See also Black Panther Party; Civil Rights movement; Education; Student Nonviolent Coordinating Committee

Bleeding Kansas

The Event: Territorial warfare between free-soil and proslavery
factions in Kansas
Date: Mid-1850's
Place: Kansas
The issues in the Bleeding Kansas conflict presaged the national Civil War.

With the opening of Kansas Territory to settlement in 1854 through
the Kansas-Nebraska Act, a contest began between groups supporting slavery (mainly persons from Missouri) and settlers from
the northwestern states who were Free-Soilers in practice, if not
ideology. The Missourians seized control of the territorial government and immediately enacted proslavery legislation. President
Franklin Pierce and his successor, James Buchanan of Pennsylvania, accepted the proslavery Kansas government and committed
the Democratic Party to the admission of Kansas as a slave state.

By September, 1855, enough Free-Soilers had entered the state
to enable them to repudiate the territorial legislature, organize a
Free State Party, and call for a constitutional convention to meet
in Topeka. A free-state constitution was written in October and
November, 1855, and in January, 1856, the party elected a governor and legislature. Kansas found itself with two governments—
one supporting slavery and considered legal by the Democratic
administration in Washington but resting upon a small minority
of the population, and the other representing majority opinion in
Kansas but condemned as an act of rebellion by President Pierce
and Senator Stephen A. Douglas of Illinois. Douglas, who had
drafted the Kansas-Nebraska Act of 1854, favored the theory of
popular sovereignty, letting the people decide the issue of slavery. That doctrine, however, was exposed—eventually by Abraham Lincoln in the Lincoln-Douglas debates—as unconstitutional:
The will of the people could not be held above constitutionally
protected rights.

Violence Begins

Although proslave and free-soil groups moved into Kansas,
actual bloodshed remained at a minimum through 1855; never-

theless, the territory quickly came to symbolize the sectional dispute. Violence became commonplace in Kansas through the spring and summer of 1856. Armed free-soil and proslavery parties skirmished along the Wakarusa River south of Lawrence as early as December, 1855; but it was the sack of Lawrence in May, 1856, by a large band of proslavery Border Ruffians from Missouri, that ignited the conflict. Retaliation was demanded: John Brown, the abolitionist crusader, his four sons, and three others struck at Pottawatomie, where they executed five settlers who were reputed to be proslavers. That act of terrorism sparked further retaliation.

Early in August, free-soil forces captured the slavery stronghold of Franklin; later that month, Free-Soilers, led by Brown, repelled an attack by a large party of proslavers at Osawatomie. Guerrilla warfare raged throughout the territory until September, when a temporary armistice was achieved by the arrival of federal troops and a new territorial governor, John W. Geary. However, a solution to the travail of Kansas could come only from Washington, D.C., and it would have to overcome the determination of the Democratic administration and its southern supporters to bring Kansas into the Union as a slave state. Meeting at Lecompton in January and February, 1857, the proslave territorial legislature called for an election of delegates to a constitutional convention. The measure passed over Governor Geary's veto.

Lecompton Constitution

The constitutional convention that met in Lecompton in September, 1857, hammered out a document to the electorate; the proslavery leadership would agree only to submit the document to the people with the choice of accepting it with or without the clause explicitly guaranteeing slavery. However, ample protection for slavery was woven into the fabric of the constitution. Opponents refused to go to the polls, and the proslavery Lecompton Constitution was approved in December, 1857.

The Free-Soil Party, meanwhile, had captured control of the territorial legislature and had successfully requested the new territorial governor, Frederick P. Stanton, to convene the legislature in order to call for another election. On January 4, 1858, the Lecompton Constitution met overwhelming defeat. Kansas was, by that time, free-soil in sentiment, but the Buchanan administration supported the Lecompton Constitution, which became a test of Democratic Party loyalty. Although Douglas came out against the administration's position, the Senate voted in March, 1858, to admit Kansas under the Lecompton Constitution. Public sentiment in the North opposed such a policy, and the House of Representatives voted to admit Kansas as a state only on the condition that the state constitution be submitted in its entirety to the voters at a carefully controlled election. That proviso was rejected by the Senate.

A House-Senate conference proposed the English Bill, a compromise measure that stipulated that the Lecompton Constitution should be submitted to the people of Kansas again: If the bill were approved, the new state would receive a federal land grant; if it were rejected, statehood would be postponed until the population of the territory reached ninety-three thousand. Although Congress passed the bill in May, the voters of Kansas rejected the Lecompton Constitution again, this time by a margin of six to one. In January, 1861, after several southern states announced secession, Kansas entered the Union as a free state under the Wyandotte Constitution.

John G. Clark
Updated by Larry Schweikart

Further Reading

Two valuable works on this era in history are Nicole Etcheson's *Bleeding Kansas: Contested Liberty in the Civil War Era* (Lawrence: University Press of Kansas, 2004) and Thomas Goodrich's *War to the Knife: Bleeding Kansas, 1854-1861* (Mechanicsburg, Pa.: Stackpole Books, 1998). Roy F. Nichols's *The Disruption of American Democracy* (New York: Macmillan, 1948) is a traditional, yet effective, analysis of the 1850's, emphasizing the destruction of the Democrats as the national party. William E. Gienapp's *The Origins of the Republican Party, 1852-1856* (New York: Oxford University Press, 1987) emphasizes the rise of the Republican Party as the crucial element in ending the earlier U.S. party system. Argues that the formation of the Republican Party represented a realignment that started with the demise of the Whigs, continued with the rise of the Know-Nothings, and culminated with the events in Kansas that galvanized the disparate elements.

See also Civil War; Compromise of 1850; Fugitive Slave Law of 1793; Fugitive Slave Law of 1850; Harpers Ferry raid; Kansas-Nebraska Act; Missouri Compromise; Proslavery argument

Bolling v. Sharpe

The Case: U.S. Supreme Court ruling on school desegregation
Date: May 17, 1954
This case had major theoretical implications, for it indicated that the Supreme Court continued to interpret the due process clauses as protecting substantive rights as well as procedures.

In *Bolling v. Sharpe*, a companion case to *Brown v. Board of Education*, the issue of segregated public schools in the nation's capital, a matter of congressional jurisdiction, was treated in an opinion separate from *Brown* because the Fourteenth Amendment did not apply to the federal government and because the applicable Fifth Amendment did not include an equal protection clause. From the perspective of practical politics, it would have been highly embarrassing for the Court to allow segregated schools in Washington, D.C., while ruling them unconstitutional in the rest of the country.

Speaking for a unanimous Supreme Court, Chief Justice Earl Warren first noted that the petitioners were African American minors who had been refused admission to a public school "solely because of their race." He then declared that the Court had long recognized that certain forms of governmental discrimination violated the constitutional mandate for due process of law. For precedents, he looked to an 1896 dictum by Joseph M. Harlan and to *Buchanan v. Warley*, a 1917 decision that had defended the equal right of citizens to own property based on a substantive due process reading of the Fourteenth Amendment. Also, Warren referred to obiter dicta in the Japanese American cases that acknowledged that racial classifications were inherently suspect, requiring that they be "scrutinized with particular care."

Warren gave an expansive interpretation of the "liberty" protected by the Fifth Amendment, explaining that it extended to the "full range of conduct which the individual is free to pursue." The government could restrict liberty only when justified by a "proper governmental objective," and racial segregation in education was not related to such an objective. Thus, the Washington, D.C., schools were imposing an "arbitrary deprivation" on the liberty of black children. In addition, Warren noted that it was "unthinkable" that the federal government might practice the kind of discrimination prohibited in the states.

Bolling v. Sharpe had major theoretical implications, for the case indicated that the Supreme Court continued to interpret the due process clauses as protecting substantive rights as well as procedures, although the substantive focus had shifted from property interests to liberty interests. Also, the decision affirmed that the ideas of liberty and equality are often overlapping and that constitutional due process of law prohibits government from practicing invidious discrimination.

Thomas Tandy Lewis

See also *Brown v. Board of Education*; *Buchanan v. Warley*; Little Rock school desegregation crisis; School desegregation; Segregation

Brotherhood of Sleeping Car Porters

Identification: Labor union of predominantly African American railroad workers

Date: Founded in 1925

This union won the wage and work-hour concessions it was demanding, thus becoming the first African American labor union to sign an agreement with a major U.S. corporation.

Poster for a 1930's production of Eugene O'Neill's 1920 play, The Emperor Jones, *about an American sleeping car porter who goes to a Caribbean island, where he makes himself a dictatorial ruler.* (Library of Congress)

A small group of men gathered in 1925 and organized the Brotherhood of Sleeping Car Porters in an effort to improve the Pullman Company's treatment of African American employees. Since the 1860's, black porters had been providing personalized service to rail passengers traveling in the finely furnished sleeping cars first introduced by George Pullman. Pullman cars, as they were known, were comparable to the nation's most luxurious hotels. The porters carried luggage, provided room service, made beds, and cleaned the cars. Despite their many duties, the porters were paid exceptionally low wages.

In the summer of 1925, with assistance from magazine publisher A. Philip Randolph, leaders of the New York branch of Pullman porters met to organize a union, the Brotherhood of Sleeping Car Porters. For twelve years, the union struggled to reach a compromise with the Pullman Company, nearly abandoning the effort on several occasions. Finally in 1937, the Brotherhood of Sleeping Car Porters won the wage and work-hour concessions it was demanding, thus becoming the first African American labor union to sign an agreement with a major U.S. corporation.

Donald C. Simmons, Jr.

Further Reading

Bates, Beth Tompkins. *Pullman Porters and the Rise of Protest Politics in Black America, 1925-1945*. Chapel Hill: University of North Carolina Press, 2001.

Tye, Larry. *Rising from the Rails: Pullman Porters and the Making of the Black Middle Class*. New York: Henry Holt, 2004.

See also Defense industry desegregation; Economic trends; Employment; Fair Employment Practices Committee; National Association for the Advancement of Colored People

Brown v. Board of Education

The Case: Landmark U.S. Supreme Court ruling on school desegregation

Date: May 17, 1954

The Supreme Court unanimously held that de jure (legally mandated) segregation of the public schools was prohibited by the equal protection clause of the Fourteenth Amendment.

Following the Civil War (1861-1865), racial segregation in public accommodations and education—through so-called "Jim Crow" laws—was one of the major tools of the southern states for maintaining a social system of white supremacy. In *Plessy v. Ferguson* (1896), the Supreme Court allowed state-mandated racial segregation based on the separate but equal doctrine. In *Cumming v. Richmond County Board of Education* (1899), the Court simply ignored the equal part of the doctrine when it allowed a community to maintain a public high school for white students without any similar institution for African Americans. In *Gong Lum v. Rice* (1927), the Court explicitly recognized the "right and power" of the states to require segregation in the public schools.

The Challenge Begins

In the 1930's the Legal Defense and Educational Fund of the National Association for the Advancement of Colored People (NAACP) began to mount a serious challenge to the constitutionality of Jim Crow laws in education. Rather than confronting *Plessy* directly, the NAACP first concentrated on equality of opportunity at publicly funded law schools. Decisions such as *Missouri ex rel. Gaines v. Canada* (1938) and *Sweatt v. Painter* (1950) indicated that the Court would insist on substantial equality of educational opportunity. In *McLaurin v. Oklahoma State Regents for Higher Education* (1950), the Court recognized that the policy of required separation was sometimes relevant to educational equality. With these victories, Thurgood Marshall and other NAACP lawyers decided that the time was ripe to question the constitutionality of segregation in elementary and secondary education.

Linda Carol Brown, an eight-year-old African American girl, was not allowed to attend the all-white school in her neighborhood of Topeka, Kansas. Her parents did not want her to be bused to the all-black school, which was far from home, and they filed a suit charging a violation of the Fourteenth Amendment. When the case was appealed to the Supreme Court, it was consolidated with similar cases from South Carolina, Virginia, Delaware, and Washington, D.C. The cases were listed in alphabetical order, so that the name *Brown v. Board of Education* appeared first. The cases were first argued in December, 1952. Marshall and other NAACP lawyers emphasized the psychological and sociological evidence of negative effects from mandated segregation. In defense of segregation, the school districts invoked *Plessy* and claimed that their all-black schools either had or would soon have equal funding for facilities and teachers' salaries.

The Court's Response

Because of the great opposition to school integration in the South, the justices recognized the desirability of presenting a united front in both the decision and the opinion. At least six of the justices agreed that *Plessy* should be reversed, but they strongly disagreed about how rapidly to proceed. One justice, Stanley F. Reed, argued on behalf of the continuation of *Plessy*, and another justice, Robert H. Jackson, wanted to move very cautiously and appeared determined to write a concurring opinion if the majority opinion were too critical of the Court's past approval of segregation. Deciding that it needed more information about the original intention of the framers and ratifiers of the Fourteenth Amendment, the Court scheduled a second argumentation of the cases for December, 1953. That summer, Chief Justice Fred M. Vinson, a moderate who was hesitant to order massive desegregation, unexpectedly died, and he was quickly replaced by the popular governor of California, Earl Warren. After Brown was reargued, Warren convinced his colleagues to defer the question of relief, and he skillfully consulted with the various justices in order to get a consensus. About a week before the decision was announced, Jackson decided not to issue a concurrence and Reed agreed not to dissent.

Warren's opinion for the Court, written in thirteen paragraphs of nontechnical language, declared that segregation in public education was "inherently unequal" and therefore unconstitutional. The public interpreted racial segregation of students "as denoting the inferiority of the Negro group," generating among African Americans "a feeling of inferiority as to their status in the community that may affect their hearts and minds in a way unlikely ever to be undone." Warren found that the historical evidence about the original intent of the Fourteenth Amendment was "inconclusive." Even if the framers and ratifiers had not intended to prohibit segregation in education, they had wanted to provide equal rights for public services, and the experiences of the twentieth century demonstrated that segregated schools were incompatible with the goal of equality. Formal education in the twentieth century, moreover, was much more important for a person's life chances than it had been when the Fourteenth Amendment was written.

Implementing Desegregation

The following year, in a decision commonly called *Brown II*, the Court addressed the issue of implementing desegregation. The NAACP wanted to proceed rapidly with firm deadlines, and the states warned that rapid desegregation would lead to withdrawal from the public schools and acts of violence. The Court settled on a cautious and ambiguous formula, requiring that segregation end "with all deliberate speed." The implementation of *Brown II*, which left much discretion to federal district judges, proceeded somewhat slowly for the first ten years. In *Alexander v. Holmes County* (1969), the Court abandoned the deliberate speed formula and ordered an immediate end to all remaining de jure segregation.

Brown is probably the most momentous and influential civil rights case of the twentieth century. In effect, the decision meant the eventual elimination of all state-sanctioned segregation. When *Brown* was announced, its implications were unclear in regard to the constitutionality of freedom of choice plans and de facto segregated schools based on housing patterns. The Court began to move beyond the issue of de jure segregation in *Green v. County School Board of New Kent County* (1968), ruling that previously segregated school districts had an "affirmative duty" to take the steps necessary to promote racially integrated schools.

Thomas Tandy Lewis

Further Reading

Bell, Derrick. *Silent Covenants: "Brown v. Board of Education" and the Unfulfilled Hopes for Racial Reform.* New York: Oxford University Press, 2004.

Clotfelter, Charles T. *After "Brown": The Rise and Retreat of School Desegregation.* Princeton, N.J.: Princeton University Press, 2004.

Kluger, Richard. *Simple Justice: The History of "Brown v. Board of Education" and Black America's Struggle for Equality.* New York: Alfred A. Knopf, 1976.

Martin, Waldo. *"Brown v. Board of Education": A Brief History with Documents.* Boston: Bedford/St. Martin's, 1998.

Ogletree, Charles J., Jr. *All Deliberate Speed: Reflections on the First Half Century of "Brown v. Board of Education."* New York: W. W. Norton & Co., 2004.

Patterson, James T. *"Brown v. Board of Education": A Civil Rights Milestone and Its Troubled Legacy.* New York: Oxford University Press, 2001.

Sarat, Austin, ed. *Race, Law, and Culture: Reflections on "Brown v. Board of Education."* New York: Oxford University Press, 1997.

Whitman, Mark, ed. *Removing a Badge of Slavery: The Record of "Brown v. Board of Education."* Princeton, N.J.: Markus Wiener, 1993.

See also *Alexander v. Holmes County Board of Education*; *Bolling v. Sharpe*; Civil Rights movement and children; *Cooper v. Aaron*; *Cumming v. Richmond County Board of Education*; Education; Fourteenth Amendment; *Green v. County School Board of New Kent County*; *Keyes v. Denver School District No. 1*; Little Rock school desegregation crisis; *McLaurin v. Oklahoma State Regents for Higher Education*; *Milliken v. Bradley*; National Association for the Advancement of Colored People; *Plessy v. Ferguson*; School desegregation; Separate but equal doctrine; Southern Manifesto; *Swann v. Charlotte-Mecklenberg Board of Education*; *Sweatt v. Painter*; White Citizens' Councils

Brown v. Mississippi

The Case: U.S. Supreme Court ruling on coerced confessions and defendants' rights

Date: February 17, 1936

The Supreme Court held that the due process clause of the Fourteenth Amendment prohibited states from using criminal confessions obtained by means "revolting to the sense of justice."

In the early 1930's, three African American tenant farmers in Mississippi were convicted of murdering a white planter. The main evidence was their confessions. At trial, police officers admitted that they had employed brutal whippings and threats of death to obtain the confessions. The defendants, nevertheless, were convicted and sentenced to be hanged. The Mississippi supreme court upheld the constitutionality of their trials and convictions.

By a 9-0 vote, the Supreme Court reversed the state court's ruling. Chief Justice Charles Evans Hughes's opinion held that coerced confessions violated a principle "so rooted in the traditions and conscience of our people as to be ranked as fundamental." At the same time, however, the Court reaffirmed that the self-incrimination clause of the Fifth Amendment was not binding on the states. Despite its modest requirements, *Brown* was the first in a line of cases requiring fundamental fairness for the use of confessions in state trials.

Thomas Tandy Lewis

See also *Edmonson v. Leesville Concrete Company*; Fourteenth Amendment; *Moore v. Dempsey*; *Norris v. Alabama*

Brownsville incident

The Event: Shooting incident that was unfairly blamed on a contingent of African American soldiers
Date: August 13, 1906
Place: Brownsville, Texas

The Brownsville incident illustrated the strong currents of racism that ran through early twentieth century America and the presumptions white Americans had about black behavior and the rights of African Americans in the military. The case was also one of the most serious lapses in the public record of President Theodore Roosevelt and a graphic example of the limits of his tolerance for black Americans during his presidency.

On August 13, 1906, a shooting incident occurred in Brownsville, Texas. White residents of the border town blamed a detachment of African American soldiers that had recently been stationed at nearby Fort Brown. According to local police reports, one person was killed and another wounded. Suspicion immediately fell on the black soldiers, and the officials in the U.S. Army concluded that the African American soldiers had been responsible for the incident. Physical evidence, however, showed that they had not been involved and the most probable explanation for the episode was that white citizens had staged the event to discredit the soldiers. The soldiers denied any knowledge of what had taken place.

The Army and President Theodore Roosevelt concluded that the men of the Twenty-fifth Infantry Regiment had been responsible for the shooting. Their failure to reveal what had taken place and their protestations of innocence were, in the minds of their white superior officials, proof of their guilt. The president ordered that all 167 black soldiers in the regiment should be dismissed from military service without trial and without pay. Shortly after the congressional elections of 1906, the soldiers were compelled to leave the Army.

The weakness of the government's case against the soldiers attracted the attention of conservative Republican senator Joseph B. Foraker of Ohio, who became a staunch defender of the soldiers and pressed for congressional probes into what had really happened. His opposition to Roosevelt on other issues had caused a rupture in his friendship with the president. Their disagreement over the Brownsville incident intensified their quarrel, and they clashed in public about the controversy in January, 1907. Roosevelt remained adamant that the accused men were guilty and used the full powers of the federal government to buttress his case. The War Department even hired private investigators to find damaging evidence against the soldiers, largely without success.

Despite congressional efforts to reduce the penalties that the black soldiers had suffered, these efforts produced few lasting results. Protests by African American groups in the North also failed to sway Roosevelt from his first hasty judgment about the men's guilt. Foraker left Congress in 1909 still convinced of the men's innocence.

The issue gradually faded from history and did not resurface until 1970, when John D. Weaver published *The Brownsville Raid*. His vigorous argument for the innocence of the men and the miscarriage of justice that they had suffered attracted public attention. Congressional pressure led the army to grant the men of the regiment honorable discharges more than six decades after their dismissal. Two aged surviving veterans of the unit received public recognition of what they had endured.

Lewis L. Gould

Further Reading
Weaver, John D. *The Brownsville Raid*. Foreword by Lewis L. Gould. College Station: Texas A&M University Press, 1992.
_____. *The Senator and the Sharecropper's Son: Exoneration of the Brownsville Soldiers*. College Station: Texas A&M University Press, 1997.

See also Buffalo soldiers; Military; Tuskegee Airmen; Tuskegee experiment

Buchanan v. Warley

The Case: U.S. Supreme Court ruling on housing discrimination
Date: November 5, 1917
Emphasizing property rights, the Supreme Court struck down state laws that mandated racial segregation in housing.

Early in the twentieth century, many southern cities enacted ordinances that mandated residential segregation. Louisville, Kentucky, prohibited both African Americans and European Americans from living on blocks where the majority of residents were persons of the other race. The National Association for the Advancement of Colored People arranged a sale of property to test the law. Although the Supreme Court had consistently sanctioned segregation, it ruled unanimously that the Louisville ordinance was unconstitutional. In his opinion for the Court, Justice William R. Day stated that the ordinance was an unreasonable restriction on the liberty of all people to buy and sell property, as protected by the due process clause of the Fourteenth Amendment. The decision showed that the protection of property rights and economic liberty could sometimes have the effect of promoting civil equality.

The *Buchanan* decision, however, was of limited impact for two reasons. First, it did not question the constitutionality of de jure racial segregation in areas such as education and transportation. Second, many private citizens began to enter into racially restrictive contracts, which were not rendered unenforceable until *Shelley v. Kraemer* (1948).

Thomas Tandy Lewis

See also *Bolling v. Sharpe*; *Patterson v. McLean Credit Union*; *Shelley v. Kraemer*

Buffalo soldiers

Definition: Respectful Indian nickname given to black soldiers in the U.S. Army during the nineteenth century

Regiments of buffalo soldiers served on the western frontier from 1866 until 1898. They played instrumental roles in helping the United States defeat the Apaches, as well as Mexican outlaws led by Pancho Villa. In addition to protecting settlers, installing telegraph lines, and building roads, buffalo soldiers escorted wagon trains and stagecoaches, built forts, and found sources of drinkable water. The name was retained by black units in the twentieth century, and many buffalo soldiers earned Medals of Honor for their valiant service in the U.S. military.

During early 1866, the first U.S. military units composed solely of African Americans, the Fifty-seventh and 125th United States Colored Infantry Regiments, were organized to provide protection for mainly white settlers in New Mexico. On July 28, 1866, the U.S. Congress approved the formation of six additional regiments of African American troops. The Ninth Cavalry regiment was activated on September 21, 1866 at Greenville, Louisiana. On the same day, the Tenth Cavalry regiment began duty at Fort Leavenworth, Kansas. Later in 1866, the Thirty-eighth, Thirty-ninth, Fortieth, and Forty-first infantry units composed of African Americans were assembled. Enlistment periods were for five years, with salaries of thirteen dollars per month, along with room, board, and clothing.

The members of these regiments fought many engagements against Plains Indians, who came to respect them greatly. Because the exceptional courage, dark skin, and curly hair of the African American soldiers resembled characteristics of the buffalo, the Indians dubbed members of the Ninth and Tenth Cavalry regiments "buffalo soldiers." The soldiers themselves were proud of the respect that the name conveyed. Before long, the title was applied to all African American soldiers.

The Ninth Cavalry served in Texas from 1867 until 1875, when they were transferred to the New Mexico District. There they participated in several military campaigns against the Apaches, who were led by such skilled leaders as Victorio, Geronimo, and the Apache Kid.

After serving for over eight years in Kansas and present-day Oklahoma, the Tenth Cavalry opened more than 300 miles of new

Troops of the 125th Colored Infantry Regiment on parade at Fort Randall in Dakota Territory. (Library of Congress)

roads and strung more than 200 miles of telegraph lines in Texas. In 1879-1880, the Tenth served in a key military campaign against Victorio and the Apaches whom the government regarded as "renegades."

During the Spanish-American War of 1898, buffalo soldiers fought in Cuba, and companies from the Ninth and Tenth Cavalries participated in Theodore Roosevelt's famous charge on San Juan Hill. In 1899, members of the Ninth and Tenth served in the Philippines to help control the Filipino nationalists. Buffalo soldiers also served in later conflicts in Malaysia, China, and Japan.

During World War I, buffalo soldiers patrolled the U.S.-Mexico border, while others served in the Philippines, Hawaii, and Europe. In 1941, the Ninth and Tenth Cavalry regiments were combined into the Fourth Cavalry Brigade, which was deactivated in 1944. During World War II, buffalo soldiers fought in Italy during the fall of Rome in 1944 and in breaking through the Gothic line in France in 1945.

In 1948, U.S. armed forces were officially desegregated, and buffalo soldiers were transferred to integrated military units.

Alvin K. Benson

Further Reading

Leckie, William H. *The Buffalo Soldiers: A Narrative of the Black Cavalry in the West.* Norman: University of Oklahoma Press, 2003.

Raabe, Emily. *Buffalo Soldiers and the Western Frontier.* Barrington, Ill.: Rigby, 2002.

Stovall, Taressa. *The Buffalo Soldiers.* New York: Chelsea House Publishers, 1997.

Willard, Tom. *Wings of Honor.* New York: Forge, 2000.

See also Military; Military desegregation; Tuskegee Airmen; World War II

Burton v. Wilmington Parking Authority

The Case: U.S. Supreme Court ruling on public accommodations
Date: April 17, 1961

The Supreme Court held that a state agency may not lease public property to a private restaurant on terms inconsistent with the equal protection clause of the Fourteenth Amendment.

In this case, the Supreme Court was asked to decide on the constitutionality of a segregated private restaurant located within a parking garage owned and operated by the city. William Burton, an African American, sued the city agency after he was denied service in the restaurant. By a 6-3 vote, the Court found that the city's association with the restaurant was sufficient to make it a party to the discrimination in violation of the Fourteenth Amendment. *Burton* illustrates the willingness of the Court under Chief Justice Earl Warren to expand the definition of state action in support of the Civil Rights movement. The public/private distinction became much less important after the Civil Rights Law of

1964 prohibited racial discrimination in private businesses open to the public. The doctrine of state action, nevertheless, continues to have significance in cases involving private clubs, as in *Moose Lodge v. Irvis* (1972).

Thomas Tandy Lewis

See also *Moose Lodge v. Irvis*; Segregation; *Shelley v. Kraemer*

Charleston race riots

The Event: Fighting between white Republicans and black Democrats during the months leading up to a presidential election
Date: September-November, 1876
Place: Charleston, South Carolina
Political corruption and intimidation characterized both sides in the conflict.

After the Civil War ended in 1865, South Carolina was controlled by northern-born whites and black southerners with support from the U.S. federal government. Southern whites who were allied with some black southerners attempted to regain control of the local government. By 1876, a tense atmosphere had developed between the two forces as a gubernatorial election approached between Republican Daniel H. Chamberlain, the incumbent and a Massachusetts-born former Union army officer, and Democrat Wade Hampton, a former slaveowner and Confederate lieutenant general.

Political corruption and intimidation characterized both sides. On September 6, black Democrats rallied in Charleston to support Hampton. A group of black Republicans attacked the black Democrats and their white escorts, and a riot ensued. The riot lasted for several days with black Republicans destroying property and attacking whites. One black man and one white man died, and about one hundred people were injured. Tensions remained high until the election on November 7, and the next day, as people were awaiting the election results, gunfire erupted in Charleston. Black police officers loyal to the Republicans began firing at the rioters. One black man and one white man were killed, and about a dozen other people were injured. Federal troops intervened and restored order. Both candidates claimed victory in the election, but by 1877, power had returned to white Democrats because of a political deal with the Republican presidential candidate.

Abraham D. Lavender

See also Civil War; Colfax massacre; Draft riots; Reconstruction

Chicago riots

The Event: Racially motivated civil disturbance
Date: July 25-September 24, 1967
Place: Chicago, Illinois

These riots combined with more extensive riots in more than thirty other U.S. cities during the summer, reflecting serious race relations problems throughout the United States.

Many African Americans from the southern United States began migrating to Chicago in the early twentieth century. Racism and mostly unsuccessful competition with whites over jobs and housing persisted for decades. As the summer of 1967 began, about 800,000 African Americans, many feeling frustrated and hopeless, lived in the city's crowded black ghettos.

On Tuesday night, July 25, African American youths began looting, smashing car windows, and throwing firebombs on Chicago's West Side. During the next week, vandalism, looting, and arson occurred on the South Side and the West Side. Police attributed the riots to reports of racial conflicts in other cities, and Mayor Richard Daley announced that live ammunition would be used against rioters. Police exchanged gunfire with youths firing from a building, and five Molotov cocktails were thrown into a store. About a hundred people were arrested. On August 1, an African American man was shot by a white man, and a firebomb was thrown. Fifty-two African Americans were arrested after they did not disperse, and more firebombs were thrown.

On August 3, the Reverend Jesse Jackson requested that Chicago be declared a disaster area. The situation calmed down, but on August 26, shots were fired while a blaze was being fought in the South Side, and nine African American youths were arrested. On September 14, an African American power rally sponsored by the Student Nonviolent Coordinating Committee (SNCC) charged police with brutality and fascism, and window smashing, rock throwing at cars, and scattered sniper fire was reported. Police, aided by leaders of African American street gangs, calmed the area. The next day, African American students boycotted classes to protest inadequate school conditions.

On September 22, in the suburb of Maywood, five hundred people pelted police cars with bottles because no African American students had been nominated for homecoming queen. Thirty people were arrested. The following day, after police shot and critically wounded a burglary suspect, about three hundred African Americans threw bricks and bottles through store windows, and police used tear gas. On September 24, ten African Americans and eleven whites were arrested in Maywood by police in an attempt to prevent a third night of violence. The Chicago riots were over for the summer of 1967.

The riots of 1967 were largely responsible for President Lyndon B. Johnson's appointing of the National Advisory Commission on Civil Disorders on July 27, 1967. The commission issued a report referred to as the Kerner Commission Report after its chairman, Governor Otto Kerner of Illinois. Although the commission did not select Chicago for one of its in-depth investigations, the conditions described in the report were also found in Chicago, and the Chicago riots were part of the unrest that led to the report.

Abraham D. Lavender

Further Reading

The *Report of the National Advisory Commission on Civil Disorders*, published by the Government Printing Office in 1968, gives the best understanding of the Chicago riot; Bantam Book's 1968 reprint of the report, entitled *The Kerner Report*, gives a good background.

See also Chicago sit-ins; Kerner Commission; New York riots; Newark riot; Race riots of 1967; Race riots of the twentieth century; Student Nonviolent Coordinating Committee; Washington, D.C., riots; Watts riot

Chicago sit-ins

The Event: Earliest sit-in demonstrations
Date: May-June, 1943
Place: Chicago, Illinois

These demonstrations were intended to change the attitudes of business owners and thus differed from the sit-ins of the later Civil Rights movement era; however, they set important precedents for the later sit-in movement.

Still in its first year when it launched the 1943 sit-ins in Chicago, the Congress of Racial Equity (CORE) had enthusiasm for nonviolent methods developed by Mohandas K. Gandhi in India's struggle for independence but had little experience with those methods. The Chicago Committee of Racial Equality that developed into CORE was founded in 1942, chiefly by James Farmer, Bernice Fisher, Homer Jack, George M. Houser, Joe Guinn, and James R. Robinson, all students in Chicago. This biracial group was headed by Farmer, one of two African Americans among the major founders. Farmer was a theology student whose father was a professor at Wiley College in Texas, and he was deeply interested in Christian pacifism. As a staff member of the Fellowship of Reconciliation (FOR), like Houser, Farmer wanted to apply Gandhian and Christian ideals to society with a view toward creating harmony and mutual respect among all races and classes.

This kind of social vision informed those who experimented with the sit-in technique in Chicago. In retrospect, Farmer has written, their early efforts there were idealistic. They hoped to change the minds of the restaurant owners and were "childishly literal-minded." They were not insistent that they be given access to public facilities on the basis of law but tried to convince their resisters that access would be good for business.

Preparations

The 1943 sit-ins were months in the making. CORE's earliest efforts to combat racial discrimination in Chicago were undertaken on a broad front: the university barber shop (which refused in November, 1942, to cut Bayard Rustin's hair), the medical school and the hospital, even the roller rink. By the end of 1942, CORE's attention was increasingly focused on restaurants that refused to serve African Americans. Two such restaurants were the Jack Spratt Restaurant near CORE Fellowship House and Stoner's Restaurant, a downtown establishment in the Loop that served chiefly an upper-middle-class clientele.

CORE first learned of racial discrimination at Stoner's in October, 1942, when three of its members (one of them black) were refused service by the owner himself. During the following five months, CORE gathered information at these two restaurants, attempting to comply with the Gandhian strategy that called for careful investigation to determine whether there was undeniable evidence of discrimination before proceeding to direct action. Interracial test groups were sent both to Stoner's and to Jack Spratt's. Sometimes the groups were served, but after a long period of waiting. On some occasions, they were served food that was overly salted or laced with broken eggshells. By December, 1942, CORE was sufficiently convinced of discrimination to spend a full week distributing to customers leaflets that pointed out the evidence and asked customers to protest against it as they paid their bills.

Some Chicago residents began to question CORE's pressure on Stoner's Restaurant, and as a result Houser and other CORE leaders decided to survey dozens of other Loop restaurants to determine whether Stoner's policy was typical or an exception to prevailing practices. The study showed that virtually all Loop eating establishments operated on a nondiscriminatory basis. CORE published the results in a pamphlet entitled "50 Loop Restaurants That Do Not Discriminate." CORE distributed this pamphlet to various groups, both white and black, and sent a copy to Stoner's management. Further efforts to desegregate the restaurant by test groups failed, and by January, 1943, Houser, Farmer, and other CORE officials were debating the possibility of direct action.

In March, 1943, CORE leaders considered staging what it called a sit-down, in which participants would occupy seats until served, at Stoner's. They decided against it after considering the logistical difficulties involved in a small group's efforts to gain meaningful attention in a two-hundred-seat restaurant. The project was delayed until June to coincide with CORE's first national convention, which would bring several direct action groups into Chicago and thus provide enough people to increase the chances of success. In May, however, CORE led a smaller sit-in operation at Jack Spratt's.

The sit-in at Jack Spratt's involved twenty-one CORE members, most of them white. The group entered the restaurant at the dinner hour on May 14, 1943, and refused to eat until the African Americans among them were served. Police officers were called, but they found they could do nothing to disperse the participants in the sit-in. Within two hours, the management of Jack Spratt's decided to serve all in the group, and in that sense the sit-in was a success. It was not clear whether such a demonstration would work at the larger Stoner's Restaurant, but the experience at Jack Spratt's encouraged CORE to follow through with the plans for a June sit-in there.

The sit-in at Stoner's Restaurant involved more than three times the number of participants. Some sixty-five people, sixteen of them African American, sat in at Stoner's during the evening meal on Saturday, June 5. Around 4:30 P.M. white demonstration participants entered the restaurant in groups of two, three, and four. They were readily seated. When the first of the two interracial groups entered shortly after 5:00 P.M., the six African Americans and two whites were ignored when they requested seats. After a half-hour wait, they were taken to a table and served. Houser reported that one of the white participants was kicked in the leg by the restaurant owner as the group passed.

As the first interracial group was seated, the second entered. Its nine African Americans and one white person were refused service and threatened, but they stood near the entrance for more than ninety minutes. The police were called three times but saw no cause for making arrests since the group was orderly.

After the third call, the police officers instructed the restaurant owner not to call again unless there was a compelling reason. Encouraged by expressions of sympathy from some of the restaurant staff, the interracial group stood quietly, refusing to budge. Other customers in the restaurant expressed support, and several of the black employees threatened to quit if the group was not served. CORE members pledged to stay all night if necessary.

Breaking the Impasse

Eventually, the deadlock was broken when an elderly white woman who was not involved with CORE invited one of the black women in the group to sit at her table. The white CORE participants who were already seated followed her example and invited the unseated group to join them. When only two were left standing, one of the hostesses approached them and invited them to follow her to a small table at the center of the restaurant. With that, applause broke out across Stoner's Restaurant. For several minutes, a spontaneous demonstration of support changed the tense atmosphere to one of relief.

Impact

The CORE-sponsored sit-ins of May and June, 1943, in Chicago, were less dramatic and received far less press coverage than the sit-ins of the early 1960's. Their historic significance has, however, been recognized. Considered the first sit-in of the modern Civil Rights movement in the United States they served as examples for later sit-ins conducted by the National Association for the Advancement of Colored People (NAACP) and for the massive wave of sit-ins triggered by an incident at Woolworth's lunch counter in Greensboro, North Carolina, in February, 1960.

To the leaders of the 1943 sit-ins, the results were gratifying. Almost no violence resulted, and the response from white people who observed the demonstration was generally very supportive. CORE leader Houser considered it a "well executed nonviolent demonstration for racial justice." The racial discrimination of Stoner's Restaurant continued unevenly throughout the war years, but by 1946 interracial groups were served without resistance.

For CORE, the experience confirmed the viability of the Gandhian methods to which it was committed. The Gandhian model called for investigation, early efforts at negotiation, firm expression of determination, personal spiritual preparation, and, if necessary, nonviolent direct action. CORE followed those steps meticulously in Chicago and was reinforced in its belief in the effectiveness of such an approach. James Farmer, the best known of the early CORE leaders, was convinced that the 1943 sit-ins strengthened CORE's resolve and heightened its influence. The sit-in at Stoner's coincided with CORE's first national convention, bringing groups from nine cities together; out of this convention grew the beginnings of national organizational affiliation known collectively as the Congress of Racial Equality (1944). The broadened organization's "Statement of Purpose and Action Discipline" clearly committed it to nonviolent direct action and the elimination of all racial discrimination and segregation. The Chicago experience was one of the specific examples of success to which the organization could point in future years and from which it could draw inspiration.

CORE soon began to sponsor training workshops to promulgate the principles of nonviolence and to train people in its techniques. Regional organizational subdivisions linked the national office with local affiliated committees. In that way, CORE retained a democratic structure while offering guidance and personnel for various campaigns. The Chicago experience continued to provide a point of reference demonstrating that collective nonviolent action could produce results.

Thomas R. Peake

Further Reading

Broderick, Francis L., and August Meier, eds. *Negro Protest Thought in the Twentieth Century*. Indianapolis: Bobbs-Merrill, 1965. This compendium of major documents on African American protest efforts includes valuable information on the founding of CORE and its early nonviolent direct action campaigns. James Farmer's philosophy of nonviolent social change is reflected, as are incidents at Stoner's Restaurant that led to the first CORE sit-in in 1943. Contains vivid summaries of the historical setting and an index.

Farmer, James. *Freedom, When?* New York: Random House, 1965. An insightful study by one of CORE's principal founders. Farmer's account is uniquely valuable for providing insight into the motivations, dreams, problems, and experiences of the mostly young activists who spearheaded racial desegregation in the United States. He describes conditions confronting African Americans before the Civil Rights movement of the 1960's and analyzes his own and others' goals, the emergence of black nationalism, and the continuing need for reform. Farmer avoids a sanguine or idealistic vision of the future, projecting instead a long struggle for freedom. Includes a table of contents.

Hentoff, Nat. *Peace Agitator.* New York: Macmillan, 1963. A. J. Muste was a ubiquitous influence on pacifism, nonviolence, and social reform movements in the United States for several decades. The value of Hentoff's study is its focus on Muste's outreach in shaping people such as James Farmer and eventually Martin Luther King, Jr.—to the extent that Muste's arguments against violence and war contributed to their nonviolent methods of social change. Scholarly in tone, the book is not documented but has numerous quotations and a detailed index.

Houser, George M. *Erasing the Color Line.* 3d rev. ed. New York: Fellowship Publications, 1951. Originally published in 1945, this personal account by Houser complements those of Farmer and James Peck. Beginning with descriptions of the problems confronting African Americans, he presents specific analyses of challenges faced in restaurants, service shops, swimming pools, housing situations, and prisons. Houser also discusses discrimination in employment and ends with his views on nonviolence. His accounts of racial discrimination include many tangible examples of nonviolent protest. This short booklet lacks notes or bibliography, but it has a table of contents and frequent chapter subdivisions to guide the reader.

Meier, August, and Elliott Rudwick. *CORE: A Study in the Civil Rights Movement*. New York: Oxford University Press, 1973. The most comprehensive and thoroughly researched of the books on CORE, this survey is a detailed account of its background, founding, and development. A scholarly book, it includes detailed references to primary and secondary material and analyzes objectively the successes and failures of CORE from its beginning in 1942 until the onset of its decline in the late 1960's. It is especially valuable for noting the Gandhian philosophy and techniques of CORE from 1942 to the 1960's. Contains elaborate notes, including a useful one on sources, and an index.

Peck, James. *Freedom Ride*. New York: Simon & Schuster, 1962. Although chiefly about the 1947 "Journey of Reconciliation" and the 1961 freedom rides, Peck's account is indispensable for an insider's perspective on the nature and distinctive challenges of CORE's early efforts to counter racism and segregation in the United States. Many accounts of jailings, beatings, and moments of hope and discouragement are included. His account is not scholarly in the conventional sense and contains no notes or bibliography.

Schmeidler, Emilie. *Shaping Ideas and Actions: CORE, SCLC, and SNCC in the Struggle for Equality, 1960-1966*. Ann Arbor, Mich.: University Microfilms International, 1983. An analytical study focusing on three of the major activist organizations of the Civil Rights movement. Lacking in sufficient historical detail on specific campaigns, it nevertheless provides useful analyses of the protest models of CORE and other civil rights organizations and helps the reader understand their differences and similarities. CORE's pre-1960 direct action campaign, including the Chicago sit-ins and the "Journey of Reconciliation," are seen as important to the organization's self-image and social effectiveness as a Gandhian direct action entity. Contains notes and table of contents.

See also Chicago riots; Civil Rights movement; Congress of Racial Equality; Greensboro sit-ins; Sit-ins

Chisholm's election to Congress

The Event: Election of the first black woman to the U.S. Congress
Date: November 5, 1968
Place: New York, New York

Shirley Chisholm was elected on a platform of opposition to all forms of discrimination and vigilant support for the interests of African Americans, women, children, Puerto Ricans, and members of other minorities.

The political education of Shirley Chisholm began in the Seventeenth Assembly District (AD) Club of Brooklyn and continued in the Bedford-Stuyvesant Political League. Decorating cigar boxes used to hold raffle tickets was one of Chisholm's first political jobs. Women did this work to raise money for the AD Club, but this work, according to Chisholm, was unsupported financially and unappreciated by the men of the club. She demanded money to pay the women and to cover the costs of supplies, tickets, and prizes, costs that the women had been paying. She got seven hundred dollars. In time, Chisholm became a member of the board of directors of the AD Club, and even though she was both a woman and African American, she became a vice president of the club while still in her twenties.

Preparing for a Political Career

Chisholm was introduced to Wesley McDonald (Mac) Holder during her senior year in college. Holder was to be the seminal political influence in Chisholm's life. She described him as the "shrewdest, toughest, and hardest-working black political animal in Brooklyn." In 1953, she joined Holder in a campaign to elect a black municipal court judge. The Bedford-Stuyvesant Political League grew out of that campaign. It was the Unity Club, of which she was a founding member, that was most important to her political future. Its goal was to gain political control of the Seventeenth District and end white rule there. Unity offered candidates for election in 1960, including its leader, Thomas R. Jones. Unity's campaign attracted the support of both Eleanor Roosevelt and Harry Belafonte, but its candidates lost. In preparation for 1962, Unity expanded its membership, held voter registration drives, and conducted political education seminars. It petitioned for the appointment of more African Americans and Puerto Ricans to city jobs and called for better health care; improved housing, transportation, and lighting; integrated schools; and expanded youth services. It demanded that both African Americans and Puerto Ricans be granted political representation equal to their numbers. Jones was elected, thereby ending white political rule in Bedford-Stuyvesant in 1962.

In 1964, Jones became a judge on the civil court in Brooklyn, opening the way for Chisholm to run for the New York legislature from the Seventeenth District with the support of Unity. With limited financial support, augmented by four thousand dollars of her own money, she won the Democratic nomination, then defeated Republican Charles Lewis, 18,151 to 1,893. She was neither the first black woman to seek office in Brooklyn—Maude B. Richardson had in 1946—nor the first black woman elected to the New York legislature—Bessie Buchanan had earlier represented Harlem. Chisholm's election in 1964 was the year after the Supreme Court handed down its decision in *Gray v. Sanders*, "one person, one vote." Reapportionment of districts that resulted from this decision aided in the election of eight African Americans to the New York legislature in 1964, six to the assembly and two to the senate.

Chisholm maintained that her years in the assembly were productive despite the fact that she was a political maverick. Legislation she introduced created the Search for Evaluation, Education, and Knowledge (SEEK) program that enabled African American and Puerto Rican students without adequate academic training to enter the state universities. She proposed legislation to promote day-care centers and provide unemployment insurance for domestic workers. Another measure protected female school teachers from losing tenure as a result of interruptions in employment related to pregnancy. She strongly opposed the use of state money for church-run schools because it would erode support for public education. Another bill she proposed would have required police officers to complete successfully courses in civil rights, minority problems, and race relations. The

Associated Press judged her to be one of the two most militant and effective black members of the assembly, along with Percy Sutton.

Chisholm Campaigns for Congress

Court-ordered reapportionment in 1968 created a new Twelfth District in Brooklyn. The new district was 80 percent Democratic and 70 percent black and Puerto Rican. Chisholm saw the district as ideal for her and announced her candidacy for Congress. Of eight AD leaders in the Twelfth District, only Thomas R. Fortune supported Chisholm; four supported William C. Thompson, an African American lawyer. Chisholm used that support to define Thompson as the candidate of the political bosses, adopting a campaign slogan of Fighting Shirley Chisholm—Unbought and Unbossed. The third candidate was Dollie Lowther Robinson, a lawyer and former labor leader and an official in the Kennedy administration's Labor Department.

A tenacious, outspoken campaigner, Chisholm enjoyed the support of the Unity Club and Mac Holder. With a sound truck, a caravan of cars, and a small army of volunteers, many of whom were women, she carried her campaign to the people—to housing projects, parks, churches, and even street corners. At each stop, Chisholm manned the sound truck while her volunteers fanned out in all directions, loaded with shopping bags stuffed with campaign literature. Her contact with Puerto Ricans was particularly effective because of her fluent Spanish (her college minor).

The political pundits predicted a Thompson victory in the Democratic primary, but the votes provided by the United Club in Bedford-Stuyvesant produced a victory by almost eight hundred votes. After the primary, Chisholm faced the Republican candidate, James Farmer, who actually lived in Manhattan. Both candidates stressed jobs, housing, and education, and both opposed the Vietnam War. Farmer's campaign suggested the need for a "strong male image" in Washington, an issue that unnecessarily raised the question of sex, in Chisholm's estimate. Actually, as Holder discovered, the district had more than twice as many female as male voters, making the issue of sex a liability for

Shirley Chisholm.
(Library of Congress)

Farmer. Chisholm found discrimination against women in politics particularly unjust. "Of course we have to help black men," she conceded, "but not at the expense of our own personalities as women. The black man must step forward, but that does not mean *we* have to step back."

Farmer failed to receive the support of the Brooklyn chapter of the Congress of Racial Equality. Some local Republicans, who resented the fact that he was an interloper, also withheld support. Furthermore, Farmer refused to support the Richard Nixon-Spiro Agnew presidential campaign (although he later accepted a position as assistant secretary of health, education, and welfare in the Nixon administration). Chisholm's strongest support came from the Puerto Rican community. She beat Farmer 34,885 to 13,777, with Conservative candidate Ralph J. Carrane receiving 3,771 votes. After her election in 1968, she was returned to the House of Representatives, with majorities in excess of 80 percent, in every election through 1980.

In the Ninety-first Congress, Chisholm requested a committee assignment consistent with her experience and education, preferably on the House Education and Labor Committee. Instead, she was appointed to the Agriculture Committee and its subcommittee on forestry and rural villages. She railed against the system as "petrified"; the seniority system, she said, should be called the "senility" system. Ultimately she took her case to the Democratic caucus. Even there, seniority prevailed and Chisholm was ignored. Finally, she simply walked down the aisle and stood in the well, waiting to be recognized. "For what purpose is the gentlewoman from New York standing in the well?" Wilbur Mills asked. Chisholm maintained that since there were only nine black congressmen (feminist terms such as "congresswoman" or "congressperson" were trivial in her opinion, especially given the problems of black women)—an underrepresentation relative to black population—the party was under a moral obligation to make the most effective use of them. Subsequently she was assigned to the Veterans' Affairs Committee, and in the Ninety-second Congress received appointment to the Education and Labor Committee.

Congressional Service

In her maiden speech in Congress, Chisholm responded to President Richard Nixon's reduction of funding for Head Start, an education program, in order to fund the antiballistic missile (ABM) program. She vowed to vote against any funding bill for the Department of Defense that came up in the House until the administration rethought its "distorted, unreal scale of priorities." Like the ABM program, however, the Vietnam War depleted national resources and energy needed to resolve domestic problems.

The legacy of the Civil Rights movement of the 1960's was little more than unenforced laws. More legislation was not the answer; proper enforcement was, she claimed. She was suspicious that integration was intent upon refashioning African Americans in the image of whites. The War on Poverty was a failure, too; it had been created by white middle-class intellectuals. She rejected the resort to violence that some militants advocated—even though she defined herself as a militant—because violence made African Americans victims of their own actions. The power structure of society resided with a few whites, she argued, so blacks, browns, yellows, reds, and even whites must unite in common cause, within the system, to secure justice.

In 1971, Chisholm joined members of the Congressional Black Caucus in presenting sixty demands to President Nixon. Earlier they had formed a shadow cabinet to oversee federal enforcement of civil rights laws. They asked the president to commit himself unequivocally to the goal of equality for all Americans, as had the National Advisory Commission on Civil Disorders appointed by President Lyndon B. Johnson in 1967. The government lacked both the will and the staff to address civil rights effectively and meaningfully, according to that commission's report. The pervasiveness of white racism, chronic discrimination, and segregation in employment, education, and housing had appalling effects on the ghetto life of African Americans, particularly youths, men, and the hard-core disadvantaged. The conscience of the whole nation needed to be aroused to oppose racism against African Americans and sexism against women, Chisholm contended.

Chisholm concluded that abortion had no relevancy to law, as no one should be forced to have or not have an abortion. She accepted the honorary presidency of the National Association for the Repeal of Abortion Laws, the goal of which was the repeal of all laws restricting abortion. She supported the Equal Rights Amendment in 1971; she had from the beginning in 1969 sponsored a House resolution calling for equal rights for men and women. Chisholm subscribed to the proposition that women were not inherently anything, only human. "In the end," she wrote, "antiblack, antifemale, and all forms of discrimination are equivalent to the same thing—antihumanism."

Presidential Candidate

Because black political strategists could not agree among themselves regarding the presidential election in 1972, Chisholm decided to seek the Democratic nomination, thereby becoming the first woman ever actively to seek the presidential nomination of a major political party. She could not win, but she could pioneer the way for others. She denied that she was the candidate of black Americans, even though she was black and proud of it, or the candidate of women, even though she was a woman and equally proud of that. "I am the candidate of the people," she said. Only two members of the Congressional Black Caucus, Ronald Dellums and Parren Mitchell, were at her side when she announced her candidacy on January 25, 1972. The National Organization for Women did not endorse her because it would have lost its tax-exempt status, but feminists Betty Friedan and Gloria Steinem ran as Chisholm delegates for the Democratic convention in Manhattan. They lost. Militant Gay Liberation members joined her campaign in Boston. She defended their rights, too. She welcomed the support of Bobby Seale and the Black Panthers, to the chagrin of some of her advisers. An extraordinary cross-section of Americans supported her campaign, but most conspicuous in the absence of their support were black male politicians—not all, but most.

The use of busing to correct racial imbalances in public schools was one of the most controversial issues of the campaign. For Chisholm, open housing was the real solution to the problem, but lacking that, busing was an expedient alternative.

With only 151 delegate votes at the convention, Chisholm was obviously unable to influence its deliberations on behalf of the issues of importance to African Americans and members of other minorities, women, children, and the less fortunate. In that she failed, but in Congress she had championed the cause of job training, child welfare programs, open housing, urban development, and consumer affairs. Her work on behalf of educational opportunity programs was exemplary. She helped abolish the House Committee on Un-American Activities. She called for a national holiday in honor of Martin Luther King, Jr., and for a study commission on Afro-American history and culture. Her voice was heard across the land, and the courage of her conscience served to remind the nation of its birthright of equality and justice for all.

Jimmie F. Gross

Further Reading

Brownmiller, Susan. "This Is Fighting Shirley Chisholm." *The New York Times Magazine* (April 13, 1969): 32-102. Based on an interview with Chisholm. Contains information relating the congressional candidates in 1968 to the presidential candidates.

Chisholm, Shirley. *The Good Fight.* New York: Harper & Row, 1973. Essentially an account of the presidential campaign in 1972. To some degree, it relates the campaign to the other candidates, but it is primarily focused on the issues and conficts in the state primaries. Limited scope is given to the machinations of the convention. A number of position papers are included in the appendix.

_____. *Unbought and Unbossed.* Boston: Houghton Mifflin, 1970. An autobiography that begins with her Barbadian background, of which she is particularly proud. The focus is on her election to Congress in 1968 and her opinions on a number of issues, including the Vietnam War, coalition politics, abortion, and black politicians.

Duffy, Susan, comp. *Shirley Chisholm: A Bibliography of Writings by and About Her.* Metuchen, N.J.: Scarecrow Press, 1988. An extensive compilation of sources, indispensable to the serious student. Many of the citations are widely available.

Kuriansky, Joan, and Catherine Smith. *Shirley Chisholm, Democratic Representative from New York.* Washington, D.C.: Grossman, 1972. Emphasis on Chisholm's congressional actions, with some analysis of her voting record and with comments by Chisholm.

Romero, Patricia W., ed. *In Black America 1968: The Year of Awakening.* New York: Publisher's Company, 1969. Of general value, it provides the broad racial and political setting for understanding the context within which Chisholm launched her congressional career.

See also Congressional Black Caucus; Jackson's run for the presidency; King assassination; Politics and government; Poor People's March on Washington; Voting Rights Act of 1965; Washington, D.C., riots; Wilder's election to Virginia governorship

Church bombings

The Events: Racially motivated hate crimes directed against African American churches

Date: 1960's

Places: Southern states

The bombings of African American churches in the South generated international interest. White segregationists in the 1960's expressed their rage at civil rights groups by destroying the churches that served as a focal point for African American activities.

In the 1950's, the slow desegregation of public facilities began in the United States. The era was symbolized by the Montgomery, Alabama, bus boycott led by ministers of African American churches including Martin Luther King, Jr. Activists, often initially African American college students, challenged public places that required separate facilities such as transportation agencies, retail outlets, and medical centers. As the Civil Rights movement developed, a broader spectrum of the African American populace and some whites participated. As more African Americans demonstrated resistance to segregation, the reaction to that resistance increased. Although the protesters were largely peaceful, the reaction to them was often violent.

Bombings of African American buildings—churches, private homes, businesses, and schools—was fairly widespread by the early 1960's. By 1963, racially motivated bombings had been reported in Alabama, Arkansas, Florida, Georgia, Louisiana, Mississippi, South Carolina, and Virginia. However, some incidents went unreported because some victims were too afraid; other incidents were not publicized by local law-enforcement personnel who were often suspected of having condoned or having taken part in the bombings. The exact numbers of bombings of African American structures in the 1960's cannot be calculated, but it certainly far exceeds the few widely publicized incidents that eventually drew national and international attention.

Homes and Churches

Besides churches, the homes of civil rights activists were a prime target. In Birmingham, Alabama, the home of the brother of Martin Luther King, Jr., was nearly demolished by a bomb. A firebomb was used to partially destroy the home of an African American congressman in Clarksdale, Mississippi, and in Jackson, Mississippi, a bomb exploded in the carport of Medgar Evers, the state's leader of the National Association for the Advancement of Colored People, who was later murdered. Bombs exploded at the University of Alabama at Tuscaloosa, where an African American woman was enrolled, and at the integrated University of Mississippi at Oxford. Black-owned businesses in Birmingham, the Mississippi towns of Greenwood and Gulfport, and Charleston, South Carolina, were also targeted. In many cases, the homeowners or business employees and clientele inside the structures were injured. In most cases, the targeted people and institutions were somehow associated with desegregation events. Often, the bombings were not fully investigated, no one was charged, and perpetrators, if identified, were unrestrained. In cases where indictments were sought, penalties were sometimes modest.

African American churches became a focal point of the bombings. White segregationists correctly understood how significant the churches were in the 1960's struggles for civil rights. First, the church was the most important community organization among African American people. A majority of African Americans were either members of a church or viewed it as a center of black life in the towns and cities in which they resided; no other institution was as widespread or as symbolic of African American values. Second, the churches had historically produced communal leadership. Ministers were not only spiritual leaders, they helped educate people, provided social services to the needy, and became important political leaders. Third, civil rights activists held their major meetings as well as strategy sessions in African American churches. Often, the churches were the only sites where African Americans could gather under black leadership without interruption by whites. The churches encouraged the development of leadership that was not dependent on the larger community, and this group of ministerial and lay leaders was interpreted as a threat by whites attempting to preserve segregation.

African American churches in the South had been vandalized and terrorized before the 1960's, sometimes by individual whites and sometimes by groups of whites expressing racist feelings. The bombings of the 1960's differed in that far more organization was behind the acts. Often the major white supremacist organizations, such as the Ku Klux Klan and the White Citizens Councils, planned and executed these events. Giving covert support to these organizations were white community leaders who would explicitly state their segregationist views but would not personally commit any violent acts, preferring to let the members of the supremacist organizations act on their behalf. These community leaders included governors and congressmen.

Arkansas and Birmingham

The most-publicized African American church bombings that took place in the 1960's occurred in Pine Bluff and Gillet, Arkansas, and in Birmingham. In Gillet, no reason was ever given for the dynamiting of a rural African American church. In Pine Bluff, the bomb that set an African Methodist Episcopal church on fire was perceived to be a reaction to the pastor's activities: He had been an adviser to African American students who were attempting to desegregate lunch counters in the city.

The bombings of churches in Birmingham were part of forthright resistance to segregation in the 1950's and 1960's that included the use of fire hoses and police dogs against unarmed, peaceful civil rights protesters. By 1963, Bethel Baptist Church, an African American congregation, had been bombed twice, with devices strong enough to damage homes in the area. In the latter part of 1963, the Sixteenth Street Baptist Church was shattered by a bomb, and that event became an international symbol of the danger for African Americans struggling to desegregate the South. The church, a centrally located, large, and prestigious edifice, was the main meeting place for activists, until September 15, 1963, when a bomb not only injured worshipers but also killed four young girls aged ten to fourteen. They died in their Sunday

Thousands of people attended the funeral of fourteen-year-old Carol Robertson, one of the girls killed in the 1963 bombing of Birmingham's Sixteenth Street Baptist Church. (Library of Congress)

school classrooms, and their bodies were mutilated by the force of the blast.

Photos of the destruction accompanied by pictures of the victims when they were alive appeared in newspapers and on television screens around the world. For many, Birmingham symbolized the depth of racism in the United States, and the four dead girls and twenty-three wounded parishioners were martyrs in a struggle for social justice. The Sixteenth Street Baptist Church was no longer safe to use for further rallies; the bombers had accomplished their immediate goal in destroying the facility. King wired Alabama governor George Wallace that the blood of the victims was on Wallace's hands. The governor disclaimed any association with the bombers and any responsibility for establishing a social climate that would lead to such acts.

Impact

The response to the church bombings varied. White southern politicians who favored segregation did not admit any responsibility for the bombings, and very few clearly stated their opposition to the violence and the groups believed responsible for it. Some politicians made no comment, and others claimed that civil rights activists associated with the churches had indirectly encouraged the violence. Northern and western politicians and the international press evidenced concern and some alarm, especially following the bombing of the Sixteenth Street Baptist Church in Birmingham. This concern, along with other factors, later resulted in some national policy changes: The passage of the Civil Rights Act of 1964 was clearly influenced by the overt violence against religious organizations and especially by the deaths of the four children attending Sunday school in Birmingham. The image of innocent girls dying in a house of worship evoked both an emotional response and a practical one on a national and international level. However, although northern and western politicians decried the bombings, they did not relate these events to the more subtle racism that existed in their own districts.

The impact of the church bombings on the African American community was quite different from the intimidation that the bombers had intended. Some researchers think that the bombings and the resulting injuries and deaths were a major factor in causing many African Americans to turn away from nonviolent protest and become more attracted to organizations that emphasized self-defense and separation of the races. Integration became less attractive; black power became more inviting. Nonviolent protest organizations such as King's Southern Christian Leadership Conference (SCLC) were considered by some to be ineffectual in such circumstances, while the relatively militant Black Panther Party and the Nation of Islam, with its spokesperson Malcolm X, grew increasingly influential. The bombers of African American churches may have achieved their immediate goals, but they did not prevent desegregation or the empowering of African Americans. Rather, they further discredited the segregationist cause and encouraged many African Americans to move toward a more militant ideology.

William Osborne
Max C. E. Orezzoli

Further Reading

The bombings of churches and other buildings in the South is examined in Francis M. Wilhoit's *The Politics of Massive Resistance* (1973) and *Racial Violence in the United States* (1969), edited by Allen Grimshaw.

See also Black Christian Nationalist Movement; Black church; Church burnings; Civil Rights movement; Ku Klux Klan; *R.A.V. v. City of St. Paul*; Southern Christian Leadership Conference

Church burnings

The Events: Many African American churches were targets of arsonists who committed copycat crimes during the 1990's
Date: June 6, 1996
Place: Charlotte, North Carolina
An arsonist burned the sanctuary of the Matthews-Murkland Presbyterian Church, prompting the federal government to intensify efforts to stop church arson in the 1990's.

Church arson occurred frequently in the twentieth century. Many African American churches in the South were targets of racial violence during the Civil Rights movement in the 1950's and 1960's. Some supporters of segregation expressed their anger at legal decisions that initiated integration of public facilities by vandalizing African American churches. Arsonists often burned churches in which civil rights activists met in an attempt to intimidate them. Perhaps the best-known incident was the 1963 firebombing of the Sixteenth Street Baptist Church in Birmingham, Alabama, in which four girls died.

By the 1990's, many arsonists were not motivated by racial intolerance but rather were thrill seekers or copycats. According to Morris Dees, civil rights activist and cofounder of the Southern Poverty Law Center, some arsonists burned vulnerable churches as acts of meanness rather than to achieve any political agenda. Many arsonists set fires to feel superior and powerful, to collect insurance money, or because of peer pressure. The National Fire

Protection Association estimated that two thousand church fires occurred annually at churches with congregations consisting of various races and sects. One-fourth of these fires were arson.

Because so many African American churches were burned in the mid-1990's, black pastors testified at congressional hearings. They alleged that federal investigators did not consider the matter seriously enough. The pastors emphasized that African American communities valued churches as peaceful refuges from external conflicts.

Churches heightened security, especially at night when many of the fires occurred. Nationally, businesses offered rewards for information about church arson, and newspapers reported on each fire, speculating that there was a pattern or conspiracy. The National Church Arson Task Force, consisting of federal agents affiliated with the Bureau of Alcohol, Tobacco and Firearms (ATF) and the Federal Bureau of Investigation (FBI), and state and local personnel, coordinated efforts to solve the crimes. Federal grants were created to rebuild burned churches.

Matthews-Murkland Presbyterian Church

An hour before midnight on Thursday, June 6, 1996, flames engulfed the sanctuary of the Matthews-Murkland Presbyterian Church. Built around 1903, the sanctuary had been replaced by a newer building and was no longer used for worship when it burned. The church was historically significant because it had been built by former slaves and belonged to the first all-black Presbytery in the United States. Located in an affluent southeast Charlotte neighborhood, the church had a congregation of mostly African Americans.

Witnesses saw the fire and alerted emergency personnel to extinguish the blaze. Local broadcast journalists arrived on the scene in time to film the fire. This was the first church arson recorded on videotape. Footage of the church fire was broadcast internationally on the Cable News Network (CNN).

No people were injured in the blaze; however, the sanctuary was destroyed with damages totaling approximately $200,000. The ATF and FBI surveyed the scene with city and state law enforcement and fire investigators. They declared the fire an arson.

North Carolina governor Jim Hunt promised a $10,000 reward for information leading to the arrest of the arsonist.

Two days after the fire, a thirteen-year-old white girl confessed that she had set the blaze as part of a Satanic ritual. She also expressed antiblack opinions but admitted that she did not know that the Matthews-Murkland Presbyterian Church was an African American church.

Law enforcement officers arrested and charged the girl, whose name was not released, with arson. They found lighter fluid and other incriminating evidence in her room. During a medical evaluation, health professionals decided that she was emotionally disturbed. Based on this examination, investigators determined that the fire she set was not connected to any others. She pleaded guilty in juvenile court on July 1, 1996, and her family sent her to a mental health facility. Three months later, she was sentenced to twelve months of probation and two hundred hours of community service.

Consequences

On the Saturday after the fire, President Bill Clinton devoted his weekly radio address to outlining how the federal government would expand its efforts to end church burnings. He identified the Matthews-Murkland Presbyterian Church as the thirtieth southern black church razed within an eighteen-month period. Clinton accorded church arson investigation a higher priority and pledged his support for legislation that eased efforts to prosecute federally people who assaulted religious structures.

At the Sunday service at Matthews-Murkland Presbyterian Church following the fire, the Reverend Larry Hill preached a sermon about forgiveness. About two hundred people, including members of Congress and prominent civil rights leaders, gathered near the sanctuary's remains. Hill later expressed concern for the young arsonist and hope for her rehabilitation.

After the girl's confession revealed that the fire was not racially motivated, President Clinton canceled a speaking engagement at the North Carolina church. Church leaders chose to use donations to build a community center for at-risk children instead of rebuilding the sanctuary.

Most people still believed that the church fires were set by white supremacists to express their racist beliefs. Reporter Gary Fields of *USA Today* investigated the church fires and determined that many journalists had incorrectly concluded that each fire fit into a larger pattern. Although some arsonists did specifically target black churches, many other arsonists acted individually for racially unrelated reasons. Both whites and African Americans were arsonists, and white churches and synagogues had also been damaged. The Charlotte arson reinforced his findings.

Arsonists set fire to three North Carolina churches within one month of the Charlotte fire. The National Church Arson Task Force increased its efforts to educate people about arson and to implement preventive measures. More Americans became aware of church arson as a result of the media's coverage of the Matthews-Murkland fire. That fire caused politicians to focus on arson. Both federal and state officials announced plans to implement stricter penalties for church arsonists.

Elizabeth D. Schafer

Further Reading

Pinn, Anthony B. *The Black Church in the Post-Civil Rights Era.* Maryknoll, N.Y.: Orbis Books, 2002.

See also Baptist Church; Black church; Church bombings; Congressional Black Caucus; *R.A.V. v. City of St. Paul*

Civil Rights Act of 1866

The Law: Federal legislation guaranteeing certain civil rights to former slaves

Date: Passed by Congress on April 9, 1866

This law was the first major attempt by Congress to protect the rights of former slaves.

At the end of the Civil War lay the long road of Reconstruction. As early as 1863, President Abraham Lincoln had expressed a plan for Reconstruction after the Civil War. These plans required a loyalty oath and acceptance of emancipation from southern states desiring readmission to the Union. It was not until after Lincoln's assassination that Reconstruction began in earnest.

Andrew Johnson, the seventeenth president of the United States, was vice president at the time of Lincoln's death in 1865. He inherited the problems of rebuilding the country after a lengthy civil war, which had ended in April, 1865. Johnson believed that the responsibility for developing Reconstruction policy should be handled by the president. Johnson's Reconstruction policy provided for a loyalty oath by citizens of states seeking readmission, revocation of the act of secession, abolition of slavery, and repudiation of the Confederate war debt. Several states—including Arkansas, Louisiana, and Tennessee—were readmitted in early 1865 without congressional approval. By the end of 1865, all states had been readmitted except Texas. This Reconstruction plan, however, failed to address the issues associated with the former slaves and their rights.

Debt Owed to Former Slaves

Congress believed that a debt was owed to the former slaves. The Freedmen's Bureau was created in 1865 as a temporary assistance program to address some of this debt. Food, medicine, schools, and land were made available to freedmen. Early in 1866, Congress passed a new Freedmen's Bureau Act and the first federal Civil Rights Act. Both were vetoed by President Johnson, because he feared that the legislation would extend to people of other races. He asked, "Was it sound to make all these colored people citizens?" Congress succeeded in quickly overturning these vetoes. In the Senate, J. W. Forney reported that the Senate agreed to pass the vetoed legislation with a two-thirds majority on April 6, 1866. The House of Representatives followed suit on April 9, 1866, the anniversary of the Confederacy's surrender.

During this same time, less positive events were impacting the freed blacks. The year 1866 brought the founding of the Ku Klux Klan. African Americans were subjected to killings, beatings, and torture. This often occurred to keep them out of the political arena, which offered opportunities for power. Perhaps more detrimental to African Americans was the institutionalized racism of the black codes. Black codes, or black laws, were legal enactments developed to regulate the actions and behaviors of freedmen in the South. These codes allowed legal marriage between African Americans, limited rights to testify in court, and limited rights to sue others. The codes also supervised the movements of African Americans in the South, restricted the assembly of unsupervised groups of African Americans, forbade intermarriage between people of color and whites, banned African Americans from carrying weapons, restricted African American children to apprenticeships that were nearly slavery, and forced African Americans into employment contracts that carried criminal penalties if abandoned. Violation of these codes often resulted in stiffer criminal punishment for African Americans than similar violations did for whites. Southern politicians reinstated by Andrew Johnson's Reconstruction policy were responsible for passage of these codes. It was in this environment that Congress found it necessary to develop legislation to combat the antiblack sentiment.

The Civil Rights Act of 1866 was the first federal law to protect the civil rights of African Americans. Section 1 of this provision established the right of citizenship to all persons born in the United States, without regard to previous servitude. As citizens, African Americans were granted the right to enter into and enforce contracts; inherit, lease, sell, hold, and convey property; give evidence in courts; benefit equally from all laws and ordinances; and be subject to punishments that were the same as given to whites for similar crimes. Section 2 provided for misdemeanor penalties for anyone who deprived another of the rights afforded in section 1. Additional sections dealt with those who were granted the authority to prosecute and enforce this legislation. In order to ensure that this legislation would be enforced, Congress further established acts that were referred to as enforcement acts. Additionally, Congress drafted the Fourteenth Amendment to the Constitution of the United States to protect the freedmen's status.

Constitutional Guarantees

Historically, the Constitution had been the source of civil liberties for the United States. The first eight amendments to the Constitution provided for a variety of freedoms. The First Amendment granted the freedoms of speech, religion, and assembly, as well as the right to petition the government for the redress of grievances. The Second, Third, and Fourth Amendments provided for a federal militia, the right to own private property, and the right to be protected from unreasonable seizures and searches of private property. The Fifth Amendment provided for the right of due process, ensured that one need not present evidence against oneself, and prevented double jeopardy in court (that is, one cannot be tried for the same offense twice). The Sixth through Eighth Amendments provided for further fair and equitable treatment by the judicial system. The purpose of various civil rights acts has been to extend these rights to all people, particularly those groups for whom these rights were originally withheld, and provide for their enforcement.

Several civil rights acts have been passed in the United States since 1866. The Civil Rights Act of 1871 made it a crime to deny equal protection under the law through duress or force. Civil rights legislation passed in 1875, which guaranteed African Americans the right to use public accommodations, was ruled unconstitutional eight years after it was passed. This continued a downhill turn in the rights of African Americans, eventually leading to the Supreme Court's "separate but equal" decision in *Plessy v. Ferguson* (1896). This was the rule until 1954, when the Supreme Court determined that separate but equal was inherently unequal, in *Brown v. Board of Education of Topeka, Kansas.* It was not until 1964, and again in 1968, that any additional civil rights legislation was enacted at the national level. The 1964 and 1968 acts prohibited discrimination in employment, in use of public accommodations such as hotels, and in housing and real estate.

President Johnson's Veto

When President Andrew Johnson vetoed civil rights legislation aimed at granting rights to freed blacks, he began a two-year campaign that would end with an impeachment trial. Congressmen became increasingly concerned with Johnson's apparent plan to subvert and sabotage Reconstruction. His appointment of former Confederate leaders who had not vowed allegiance to the

Union, his lack of tact in dealing with those with whom he disagreed, his efforts to circumvent Congress and extend presidential powers, and his veto of important civil rights legislation resulted in a special meeting of the House of Representatives on March 2, 1867. Two measures were passed at this special session. One deprived Johnson of his responsibilities as commander in chief of the military; the second deprived him of the right to remove those with whom he disagreed from their cabinet positions. Finally, a resolution was passed to impeach Johnson for alleged violations of these measures. The senate failed to convict Johnson by one vote. However, Johnson was more compliant in the Reconstruction process after this trial.

Sharon L. Larson

Further Reading

Abernathy, M. Glenn. *Civil Liberties Under the Constitution.* 5th ed. Columbia: University of South Carolina Press, 1989. Discusses the Bill of Rights and the historical relevance of civil rights legislation.

Asch, Sidney H. *Civil Rights and Responsibilities Under the Constitution.* New York: Arco, 1968. Analysis of amendments, such as the right-to-vote amendment, in the light of ethical questions of the day.

Bardolph, Richard, ed. *The Civil Rights Record: Black Americans and the Law, 1849-1870.* New York: Thomas Crowell, 1970. Presents legal documentation of the African American move toward legal equality.

Blaustein, Albert P., and Robert L. Zangrando, eds. *Civil Rights and the American Negro: A Documentary History.* New York: Trident Press, 1968. Discusses the civil rights legislation that has been passed specifically in relation to the end of slavery.

Chalmers, David M. *Hooded Americanism: The First Century of the Ku Klux Klan.* 3d ed. Durham, N.C.: Duke University Press, 1987. A historical and political examination of the Ku Klux Klan. Lends validity to the discussion of the civil rights and emancipation legislation of the post-Civil War era.

Franklin, John Hope. *From Slavery to Freedom: A History of Negro Americans.* 3d ed. New York: Alfred A. Knopf, 1967. Explores the progress of African Americans through slavery, emancipation, Reconstruction, and the early 1960's Civil Rights movement.

McKissack, Patricia, and Frederick McKissack. *The Civil Rights Movement in America, from 1865-Present.* 2d ed. Chicago: Children's Press, 1991. A discussion of the progress in civil rights since the end of the Civil War and slavery in the United States.

Weinstein, Allen, and Frank Otto Gatell. *Freedom and Crisis: An American History.* 2 vols. New York: Random House, 1978. Volume 2, chapter 24 discusses the dramatic events surrounding Lincoln's assassination, Johnson's impeachment trial, and congressional reconstruction.

See also Black codes; Civil Rights Act of 1964; Emancipation Proclamation; Fourteenth Amendment; Freedmen's Bureau; Reconstruction; Thirteenth Amendment

Civil Rights Act of 1957

The Law: First federal civil rights legislation since 1875
Date: 1957
The law created the U.S. Commission on Civil Rights, to investigate complaints of violations of civil rights, along with other measures.

During the mid-1950's, the Civil Rights movement gathered momentum as it challenged racial segregation and discrimination in many areas of southern life. One area where progress proved slow was voting rights. Intimidation and irregular registration procedures limited electoral participation by African Americans. By 1957, support for legislation to protect voting rights was growing among northern Republicans and Democrats in Congress. Yet Congress had not passed a civil rights bill since 1875, and there was strong southern opposition to any change in the status quo. It was, however, Senator Lyndon B. Johnson of Texas, the Senate majority leader, who took the lead. Not known at this point in his career as an advocate of civil rights, Johnson used his considerable legislative ability to shepherd the new bill through Congress.

It passed just as the Little Rock school desegregation crisis was breaking.

The bill had several major provisions. It created a new body, the Civil Rights Commission, to investigate complaints of violations of civil rights. It raised the Civil Rights Section of the Department of Justice to the status of a division, to be headed by an assistant attorney general. It also made it a federal crime to harass those attempting to vote and allowed the attorney general to initiate proceedings against those violating the law.

The law's short-term effects were modest. Though the number of African American voters did grow, many impediments to voting remained, especially in the rural South. Many criticized the act's weak enforcement procedures: The Civil Rights Commission could gather information and investigate complaints, but it could take no action to protect those trying to vote. Not until the Voting Rights Act of 1965 would effective machinery for ensuring voting rights be established.

On the other hand, in the early 1960's, the administration of President John F. Kennedy did use the act's provisions (which were strengthened by the 1960 Civil Rights Act) to proceed against some of the worst cases of harassment. Also the act broke a psychological barrier by putting the first national civil rights law in eighty-two years on the books. It also highlighted the importance of voting rights to the overall civil rights struggle.

William C. Lowe

See also Civil Rights Act of 1960; Civil Rights Act of 1964; Civil Rights Act of 1968; Civil Rights Act of 1991; Civil Rights Acts of 1866-1875; *Civil Rights* cases; Little Rock school desegregation crisis; United States Commission on Civil Rights

Civil Rights Act of 1960

The Law: Federal legislation extending voting rights protections
Date: May 6, 1960
The law proved unable to cope with many problems confronting African Americans in the South.

The Fifteenth Amendment to the Constitution, passed in 1870, was designed to protect the right of African Americans to vote. The amendment simply says: "The right of citizens of the United States to vote shall not be denied or abridged by the United States or by any State on account of race, color, or previous condition of servitude." Officials in the southern states, however, found numerous ways to disfranchise black voters without violating the Fifteenth Amendment, such as the literacy test, poll tax, grandfather clause, and white primary. As a result of these voting barriers, most African Americans were eliminated as voters, in spite of what the Fifteenth Amendment was designed to do.

Enforcing the Fifteenth Amendment

The civil rights bills of the late 1950's and the 1960's were designed to make the Fifteenth Amendment enforceable. Since the end of Reconstruction, Congress had passed only one civil rights bill, in 1957. The 1957 law sought to empower the federal government to protect voting rights by seeking injunctions against voting rights violations. In reality, the 1957 law was so weak that

President Dwight D. Eisenhower signing the Civil Rights Act of 1960.
(Library of Congress)

only a few suits were brought by the Department of Justice against the illegal practices of voting officials. The 1957 Civil Rights Act established the U.S. Commission on Civil Rights, which was given the authority to investigate civil rights abuses. The commission could draw national attention to civil rights problems and recommend legislation to Congress, but it had no enforcement powers. African Americans and civil rights supporters realized that something substantial was needed to protect black voting rights.

In 1959, President Dwight D. Eisenhower introduced a seven-point civil rights program. Three parts of the bill dealt with education and school desegregation, the most significant provision being the attempt to make it a crime to interfere with court-ordered desegregation. The bill requested a two-year extension of the Civil Rights Commission and contained several other provisions to combat economic discrimination. The only section of the law that involved voting rights was the provision that states must preserve voting records for three years. This provision was needed to prove whether there was a pattern or practice of discrimination in voting.

Conspicuously missing from the Eisenhower bill was a request that Congress authorize the attorney general to bring civil proceedings to protect voting rights. This provision, known as Title III, had been the heart of the administration's 1957 Civil Rights Act. Title III would have allowed the federal government to prevent interference with civil rights instead of only being able to punish such interference after the fact. Intense southern opposition to Title III forced the administration to abandon the provision in the 1957 Civil Rights Act, as Eisenhower believed that Congress was not ready to incorporate Title III in the administration's new bill.

The House judiciary subcommittee, comprising mostly northern civil rights supporters, strengthened the Eisenhower bill and restored Title III. The full Judiciary Committee, containing many southern opponents of civil rights, quickly gutted most of the stronger sections passed by the subcommittee. The weakened bill was passed by the Judiciary Committee and forwarded to the important Rules Committee. The Rules Committee, chaired by

Howard Smith, a Virginia segregationist, did not act on the bill until civil rights supporters threatened to discharge the bill from the Rules Committee's jurisdiction. The Democratic Study Group, a newly formed organization consisting of liberal Democrats, led the movement to free the bill from the Rules Committee. The Rules Committee finally sent the civil rights bill to the floor of the House for consideration by the entire House.

Southern Opposition

Southern Democrats led much of the opposition to the bill. Opponents contended that the bill went too far in protecting voting rights and encroached on the rights of states to control the election process. Representative William Colmer, a Democrat from Mississippi, said that "even in the darkest days of Reconstruction, the Congress never went as far as the proponents of this legislation, in this 1960 election year, propose to go." After defeating numerous southern amendments to weaken an already weak bill, the House voted 311 to 109 to approve the civil rights bill and send it to the Senate.

The United States Senate has often been the burial ground of civil rights laws, especially during the 1940's, 1950's, and 1960's. This was primarily the result of two factors. First, southern Democrats, by virtue of their seniority, controlled many key committees, including the Judiciary Committee, to which civil rights legislation, by jurisdiction, must be referred. Second, southern senators were skillful in the use of legislative tactics, such as the filibuster, to kill legislation.

The Eisenhower bill was sent to the Senate Judiciary Committee, chaired by Democratic senator James Eastland of Mississippi. Eastland, a staunch segregationist, refused to act on the bill. Only as a result of a parliamentary maneuver undertaken by Majority Leader Lyndon Johnson and Minority Leader Everett Dirksen was the bill brought to the floor of the Senate for debate.

Southern senators, led by Democrat Richard Russell of Georgia, organized a filibuster. All southern senators participated in the filibuster, with the exception of the two senators from Tennessee and the two senators from Texas. Supporters of the civil rights bill attempted to end the lengthy filibuster by invoking cloture, which required two-thirds of the Senate to vote to stop the filibuster. When the cloture vote took place, only forty-two of the one hundred senators voted to stop the filibuster. The civil rights supporters not only failed to get the two-thirds vote required but also failed to muster a simple majority.

Passage

The defeat of cloture meant that the southern Democratic senators had won and could dictate the terms of the final bill. The final, watered-down version of the bill contained little that would protect the voting rights of African Americans. The most significant provision authorized federal judges to appoint federal referees to assist African Americans in registering and voting if a pattern or practice of discrimination was found. The Senate passed the weakened bill by seventy-one to eighteen, and President Eisenhower signed the bill into law on May 6, 1960. The fact that only two other individuals were present when Eisenhower signed the bill into law testifies to its legislative insignificance.

Perhaps the weakness of the 1960 Civil Rights Act was its main legacy. The law proved to be unable to cope with many problems confronting African Americans in the South. Many African Americans who attempted to register or vote lost their jobs, were subjected to violence, or were victimized by double standards or outright fraud on the part of voting officials. The impotence of the 1960 Civil Rights Act to deal with these issues, combined with the lack of progress in increasing the number of African American voters in the South, forced Congress to pass the powerful Voting Rights Act in 1965. This legislation would forever transform the political landscape of the South, and its consequences have continued to be felt.

Darryl Paulson

Further Reading

Abernathy, Charles F. *Civil Rights and Constitutional Litigation: Cases and Materials.* 2d ed. St. Paul, Minn.: West, 1992. Somewhat technical, but an interesting approach to the interplay between congressional and judicial sources of civil rights.

Berman, Daniel M. *A Bill Becomes a Law: Congress Enacts Civil Rights Legislation*. New York: Macmillan, 1966. Case study of the passage of the 1960 Civil Rights Act.

Black, Earl, and Merle Black. *The Vital South: How Presidents Are Elected*. Cambridge, Mass.: Harvard University Press, 1992. Examines how presidential politics changed in the South, primarily as a result of the passage of civil rights laws.

Lawson, Steven F. *In Pursuit of Power: Southern Blacks and Electoral Politics, 1965-1982*. New York: Columbia University Press, 1985. Investigates how civil rights and voting rights laws have impacted Southern politics of blacks and whites.

Tate, Katherine. *From Protest to Politics: The New Black Voters in American Elections*. Cambridge, Mass.: Harvard University Press, 1994. Demonstrates how U.S. politics in the 1990's was influenced by the policies of prior decades.

Whalen, Charles, and Barbara Whalen. *The Longest Debate: A Legislative History of the 1964 Civil Rights Act*. Washington, D.C.: Seven Locks Press, 1985. A former member of Congress provides an inside view of the politics surrounding the 1964 Civil Rights Act.

See also Civil Rights Act of 1957; Civil Rights Act of 1964; Civil Rights Act of 1968; Civil Rights Act of 1991; Civil Rights Acts of 1866-1875; Congress of Racial Equality; "I Have a Dream" speech; *Katzenbach v. McClung*; *Smith v. Allwright*; Twenty-fourth Amendment; United States Commission on Civil Rights; Voting Rights Act of 1965

Civil Rights Act of 1964

The Law: Landmark federal legislation that expanded voting rights protections and established new protections against employment discrimination and discrimination in public accommodations

Date: July 2, 1964

Responding to a vigorous activist movement, Congress passes the most far-reaching civil rights legislation since Reconstruction.

The road to the passage of the Civil Rights Act of 1964 was long and tortuous. In June, 1963, President John F. Kennedy had addressed the nation and appealed to the American people to cooperate to meet the crisis in race relations. On June 19, he urged Congress to enact an omnibus bill to meet the demands of African Americans for racial equality. The bill he proposed included titles dealing with public accommodations, employment, federally assisted programs, and education.

Background

The bill was reported by the House committee in November, just two days before the assassination of President Kennedy (November 22, 1963) in Dallas. As the stunned nation recovered, there was an outpouring of emotion for the late president. President Lyndon B. Johnson addressed the Congress and urged it to honor President Kennedy's memory with the passage of the omnibus civil rights bill. Johnson, who had been viewed as a part of the conservative establishment opposed to civil rights when he was Senate majority leader, now became its most vigorous champion. Whether this transformation came from a change in conscience, a change in position, or a desire to be seen as a national leader cannot be known, but Johnson made a firm commitment to civil rights in his state of the union address. He challenged the new Congress to become known as the one that had done more for civil rights than any in one hundred years.

Martin Luther King, Jr., who had been at the forefront of a decade of struggle by African Americans for equality, gave his support to President Johnson at the time. However, he announced plans to resume demonstrations, which had been suspended since the assassination of President Kennedy, to make it clear to Congress and the country that the time to pass a civil rights bill had come. Together with the lobbying of civil rights groups and the efforts of activists and leaders, in cooperation with labor and religious leaders, King's actions forced the passage of the bill in the House. Despite the favorable action in the House, success in the Senate was difficult because of a filibuster. Senator Hubert H. Humphrey, who was a coordinator for the civil rights effort in the Senate, worked to gain the cooperation of Senator

Everett M. Dirksen, the Senate minority leader. After compromise language was worked out with Senator Dirksen, a bipartisan vote ended the filibuster, and the Civil Rights Act of 1964 was passed on July 2.

The passage of the 1964 Civil Rights Act was largely in response to protests and demonstrations initiated by civil rights activists and African American leaders. In the 1950's, African Americans had mobilized a social movement to eradicate the social injustices they faced throughout the United States. The mass effort to end legal segregation in public accommodations in the South had been sparked by Rosa Parks, an African American woman who, in 1955, had disobeyed the law by refusing to relinquish her seat to a white man on a crowded bus in Montgomery, Alabama. The subsequent Montgomery bus boycott heralded a new Civil Rights movement, which ended the Jim Crow laws that had forbidden African Americans from using the same public accommodations—transportation, hotels, restaurants, schools, and other public facilities—along with whites. Leaders such as Malcolm X—who encouraged African Americans to challenge unfair practices and laws by teaching black nationalism and racial pride—also played a major role in the passage of the 1964 Civil Rights Act.

Provisions of the Act

The act contained provisions designed to eliminate discrimination in public accommodations and in other areas such as voting, employment, federally funded programs, and education. Although laws had been passed in 1957 and 1960 to eliminate voting discrimination, unfairly administered literacy tests were still used to discriminate against African Americans. The 1964 act prohibited local officials from applying different standards to African Americans and whites when literacy tests were administered in federal elections. Completion of the sixth grade in an English-language school created a presumption of literacy.

Voting was viewed as a local issue, and there was general concern by those who opposed the Civil Rights Act that it would permit undue intervention of the federal government into local affairs. This argument was significant in determining the authority

President Lyndon B. Johnson signing the Civil Rights Act of 1964, as other government officials and civil rights leaders look on. (Library of Congress)

of the attorney general to bring suits concerning voting discrimination. The issue was resolved by providing that the attorney general could bring action if it were determined that a pattern of discrimination existed to prevent citizens from voting. This limited the possible federal intervention in local affairs, because litigation could not be initiated for an isolated incident of discrimination against one citizen. The act provided for a three-judge federal district court to hear cases of voter discrimination, which then could be appealed directly to the Supreme Court. One problem with the 1957 and 1960 acts had been the great length of time required to bring suit and process an appeal. The voting provisions of the 1964 act brought little change, and a major voting rights bill was passed the following year.

The results of the public accommodations provisions of the 1964 act were more impressive. Hotels, restaurants, service stations, places of amusement, and government-owned public facilities were forbidden to discriminate because of race, color, religion, or national origin. Although the attorney general could intervene only in cases of general public importance, discriminatory practices in public accommodations changed dramatically, and in a short time, the rigid separation of the races in places of public accommodation ended.

Ending discrimination in public accommodations proved to be much easier than desegregating schools or eliminating employment discrimination. The U.S. Supreme Court had decided in 1954 in *Brown v. Board of Education* that maintaining separate schools for African Americans and whites was unconstitutional, because African Americans were being deprived of their right to equal protection, as guaranteed by the Fourteenth Amendment. The Court held that in the sphere of public education, the doctrine of separate but equal was impracticable and that school desegregation should occur with all deliberate speed. However, schools were slow to comply with the Court's decision. A strong stand by Congress was important, because the courts had borne the entire burden of school desegregation, and they were vulnerable to the charge of usurping the power of Congress to make law. In cases of school discrimination, the attorney general was given greater latitude in bringing suits than in other civil rights areas, having only to determine that a complaint was valid and that the complainant was unable to maintain a suit before court action could be initiated. Although the attorney general's power in this area was more extensive than in other civil rights matters, Congress made clear that the goal was *desegregation* only; the 1964 act did not give any official or court the power to order racial *balance*.

Guidelines issued by the Office of Education were important in reducing segregation in schools. These guidelines also stipulated that there could be no discrimination in programs funded by the federal government. Because the federal government funds a great variety of programs, such as housing and urban development, the potential for this provision as a weapon against discrimination is great.

Preventing discrimination in employment was another major goal of the Civil Rights Act. Employers were forbidden to discriminate on the basis of race, color, religion, national origin, and (unlike the other parts of the 1964 act) sex. The act covers employers' practices in hiring, paying, promoting, and dismissing employees; referral by employment agencies; and trade unions' admission of members. Employers with as few as twenty-five employees ultimately would be covered, but this figure would be reached over three years. Employers were required to keep records, which have been useful in determining practices of discrimination.

Equal Employment Opportunity Commission

An Equal Employment Opportunity Commission was established but, until a 1972 amendment, did not have power to bring suit against an employer. The commission could only try to persuade the employer; if that failed, the case could be referred to the attorney general with a recommendation that a suit be instituted. The attorney general had the power to bring suit not only upon the recommendation of the Equal Employment Opportunity Commission but also if there was a pattern or practice of discrimination. If a suit were brought and there was a finding of discrimination, the court had a wide range of remedies: It could enjoin the employer from further discriminatory practice, order reinstatement of an employee with back pay, or order the hiring of an employee. However, the act specifically stated that an employer is not required to grant preferential treatment because of an imbalance in the races of employees.

The act, at that time revolutionary in its coverage, would nevertheless encounter obstacles to its effectiveness. These limitations included the large caseloads of enforcement agencies, such as the Equal Employment Opportunity Commission, delaying timely investigations; the great length of time required to litigate cases; difficulty in retaining attorneys; the high costs of litigation; problems in identifying coworkers willing to be witnesses; and reverse discrimination lawsuits arguing that employer policies to ensure the civil rights of protected classes violate the civil rights of others. Many of these conditions would hinder the effectiveness of the 1964 Civil Rights Act, its provisions, and enforcement agencies. Thus, although the 1964 Civil Rights Act has remained the foundation of a series of civil rights acts passed since the 1960's, the goal of equal opportunity for all citizens of the United States has continued to be a worthwhile and necessary pursuit.

Doris F. Pierce
Updated by K. Sue Jewell

Further Reading

Abraham, Henry J. *Freedom and the Court: Civil Rights and Liberties in the United States.* New York: Oxford University Press, 1967. Focuses on civil rights and liberties in the United States.

Bell, Derrick. *Faces at the Bottom of the Well: The Permanence of Racism.* New York: Basic Books, 1992. Employs literary models in addressing how African Americans experience injustice in the judicial system.

_____. *Race, Racism, and American Law.* 2d ed. Boston: Little, Brown, 1977. A comprehensive analysis of U.S. law that reveals how racial inequality is integrated into the legislative and judicial systems.

Harvey, James C. *Black Civil Rights During the Johnson Administration.* Jackson: University and College Press of Mississippi, 1973. An analysis of the political influences and compromises at the birth of the civil rights laws of the Lyndon Johnson administration.

Jewell, K. Sue. *From Mammy to Miss America and Beyond: Cultural Images and the Shaping of U.S. Social Policy.* New York: Routledge, 1993. Discusses how institutional policies and practices in the United States contribute to social inequality for African Americans in general, and African American women in particular.

_____. *Survival of the Black Family: The Institutional Impact of U.S. Social Policy.* New York: Praeger, 1988. Examines how societal institutions, including the legal system, affect the stability of the African American family.

Kotz, Nick. *Judgment Days: Lyndon Baines Johnson, Martin Luther King, Jr., and the Laws That Changed America.* Boston: Houghton Mifflin, 2005. An examination of two of the most prominent men behind the 1964 act.

Schwartz, Bernard, ed. *Civil Rights.* Vol. 2 in *Statutory History of the United States.* New York: Chelsea House, 1970. Contains the actual texts of the acts together with debates and commentaries.

See also Civil Rights Act of 1866; Civil Rights Act of 1957; Civil Rights Act of 1960; Civil Rights Act of 1968; Civil Rights Act of 1991; Civil Rights Acts of 1866-1875; *Civil Rights* cases; Civil

Rights movement; Civil Rights Restoration Act; *Cooper v. Aaron*; Equal Employment Opportunity Act of 1972; Equal Employment Opportunity Commission; Fair Employment Practices Committee; Fair Housing Act; Fourteenth Amendment; *Fullilove v. Klutznick*; *Griggs v. Duke Power Company*; *Katzenbach v. McClung*; National Association for the Advancement of Colored People; Southern Christian Leadership Conference; Twenty-fourth Amendment; United States Commission on Civil Rights; Voting Rights Act of 1965

Civil Rights Act of 1968

The Law: Federal legislation prohibiting housing discrimination
Date: April 11, 1968
The Civil Rights Act of 1968 banned racial discrimination in the sale or rental of most types of housing.

After 1965, the Civil Rights movement devoted increasing attention to conditions in the North. It found much segregation there, a condition that was rooted in residential patterns rather than in Jim Crow laws. The prevalence of segregated housing determined the composition of schools and other aspects of urban life. Martin Luther King, Jr.'s Chicago campaign in 1966 focused national attention on the housing issue. His lack of success showed that white resistance to opening neighborhoods to minority residents was strong and would be difficult to overcome. Urban riots in northern and western cities provoked a "white backlash," as many northern whites ceased their support for further civil rights reform. In 1966 and 1967, President Lyndon B. Johnson tried and failed to persuade Congress to pass civil rights bills outlawing discrimination in housing.

Passing the Act

In 1968, liberal Democrats in the Senate brought forward a new civil rights bill containing a fair housing provision. Heavy lobbying by Clarence Mitchell, of the National Association for the Advancement of Colored People (NAACP), helped to marshal a majority of senators in support of the bill. As with earlier civil rights measures, southern senators attempted to talk the bill to death with a filibuster. However, in return for some relatively minor modifications in the bill, the leader of the Republican minority, Senator Everett Dirksen of Illinois, agreed to support an attempt to cut off the filibuster. This succeeded, and the bill passed the Senate on March 11, 1968.

In the House of Representatives, passage was far from sure. The assassination of Martin Luther King, Jr., on April 4, however, shocked the country and dramatically altered the political landscape. Support for the bill grew; it passed easily and was signed by President Johnson on April 11.

Fair Housing

The main thrust of the 1968 Civil Rights Act was to outlaw discrimination on the basis of race, religion, or national origin in the sale and rental of most forms of housing in the United States, as well as in the advertising, listing, and financing of housing. Exempted from the act's coverage were single-family houses not listed with real estate agents and small apartment buildings lived in by the owner. (About a month after the act became law, the Supreme Court ruled, in the case of *Jones v. Alfred H. Mayer Company*, that the Civil Rights Act of 1866 prohibited racial discrimination in housing and other property transactions.) Two other provisions of the act also grew out of the racial turmoil of the 1960's. One enumerated specific civil rights whose violations were punishable under federal law. Another sought to make the act more acceptable to the growing number of Americans concerned about urban riots by specifying stiff penalties for inciting or engaging in riots.

As a housing measure, the act proved disappointing. Its enforcement provisions were weak. Those with complaints of discrimination were directed to file them with the Department of Housing and Urban Development (HUD), which would then attempt to negotiate a voluntary settlement. If this failed, complainants would have to file their own lawsuits; the federal government would intervene only in cases where there was a clear pattern of past discrimination. In addition, white resentment at attempts to integrate neighborhoods remained high. Banks often found ways to avoid the law's provisions, making it difficult for many African American families to secure necessary financing. By the late twentieth century, it was clear that the act had not ended the country's dominant pattern of racial segregation in housing.

The Indian Bill of Rights

The Civil Rights Act of 1968 contained another provision unrelated to concerns over fair housing: the Indian Bill of Rights. This was grounded in the fact that Indians on reservations, as members of tribal communities, were not considered to be covered by the Bill of Rights. In 1896, the Supreme Court had ruled, in the case of *Talton v. Mayes*, that the Bill of Rights did not apply to Indian tribes or to their courts. In 1961, Senator Sam Ervin, a North Carolina Democrat, was surprised to discover the fact. Over the next several years, he held hearings on the subject. In 1968, he was able to amend the civil rights bill moving through the Senate to include coverage of Indian rights.

The Indian Bill of Rights extended a variety of constitutional protections to Native Americans with regard to the authority of their tribal governments. Among these were freedom of speech and religion, as well as protections for those suspected or accused of crimes. In fact, all or part of the First, Fourth, Fifth, Six, and Eighth Amendments were held to apply to reservation Indians, as was the Fourteenth Amendment's guarantee of due process. Some parts of the Bill of Rights were not included, however; the First Amendment's ban of religious establishments was not included, in deference to tribal customs, nor were the Second Amendment's right to bear arms or the Third's prohibition against the quartering of troops. Most important to most Indians was a provision that required tribal permission before states could further extend jurisdiction over tribal land.

William C. Lowe

Further Reading

Useful views of the 1968 Civil Rights Act may be found in James A. Kushner's *Fair Housing: Discrimination in Real Estate, Community Development, and Revitalization* (New York: McGraw-

Hill, 1983), Lyndon B. Johnson's *The Vantage Point: Perspectives of the Presidency 1963-1969* (New York: Holt, Rinehart and Winston, 1971), Donald G. Nieman's *Promises to Keep: African-Americans and the Constitutional Order, 1776 to the Present* (New York: Oxford University Press, 1991), and John R. Wunder's *"Retained by the People": A History of the American Indians and the Bill of Rights* (New York: Oxford University Press, 1994).

See also Civil Rights Act of 1957; Civil Rights Act of 1960; Civil Rights Act of 1964; Civil Rights Act of 1991; Civil Rights Acts of 1866-1875; Civil Rights movement; *Jones v. Alfred H. Mayer Company*; *Katzenbach v. McClung*; *Shelley v. Kraemer*; United States Commission on Civil Rights

Civil Rights Act of 1991

The Law: Federal legislation prohibiting employment discrimination

Date: November 21, 1991

The 1991 Civil Rights Act made it easier for those who considered themselves victims of various types of discrimination to bring their cases to court.

To many supporters of the Civil Rights movement, the 1980's was a decade of disappointment, when earlier gains seemed threatened by unsympathetic presidents and a conservative political atmosphere. Especially troubling from this viewpoint was the direction taken by the U.S. Supreme Court. In 1989, the Court issued a number of decisions that seemed to endanger past protections against employment discrimination by making the position of voluntary affirmative action programs less secure (*Richmond v. J. A. Croson Company*), making it more difficult for women and members of minorities to sue for job discrimination (*Wards Cove Packing Company v. Atonio*), and reducing protection against racial harassment on the job (*Patterson v. McLean Credit Union*).

Reaction against these decisions, especially the last two, made it easier for liberal Democrats to create a bipartisan coalition in

Congress in support of an effort to pass a new civil rights bill. Though the administration of President George Bush did not initially support the bill, the president did sign the bill when it finally passed after two years of congressional consideration and debate.

The Civil Rights Act of 1991 took the form of a series of amendments to Title VII of the Civil Rights Act of 1964. Among its many sections were three important provisions. One sought to overturn the *Wards Cove* decision, which had required those claiming employment discrimination to prove that a specific employer practice had created a discriminatory effect and allowed employers to justify such a practice as a "business necessity." The act eliminated the latter claim as a defense against a charge of intentional discrimination. Another provision counteracted the *Patterson* decision by extending the 1875 Civil Rights Act's ban on racial discrimination in contracts to cover protection from harassment on the job. Finally, the act allowed victims of discrimination to sue for larger monetary damages in cases brought under the 1964 Civil Rights Act and the 1990 Americans with Disabilities Act.

Though rather technical and legalistic in character, the 1991 Civil Rights Act did make it easier for those who considered themselves victims of various types of discrimination to bring their cases to court.

William C. Lowe

See also Civil Rights Act of 1957; Civil Rights Act of 1960; Civil Rights Act of 1964; Civil Rights Act of 1968; Civil Rights Acts of 1866-1875; Equal Employment Opportunity Commission; *Griggs v. Duke Power Company*; *Runyon v. McCrary*; United States Commission on Civil Rights

Civil Rights Acts of 1866-1875

The Laws: Federal legislation granting citizenship rights to African Americans and outlawing racial discrimination in public accommodations

Dates: April 9, 1866 and March 1, 1875

Although the Civil Rights Acts of the Reconstruction era failed to secure any long-lasting equality for African Americans, they did provide points of reference for the Civil Rights movement of the 1950's and 1960's.

After the Thirteenth Amendment abolished slavery throughout the United States in 1865, almost all freed blacks were without property or education, and most white southerners bitterly opposed any fundamental improvement in their political and social status. In 1865-1866, southern legislatures enacted the highly discriminatory black codes, and proponents of racial equality responded by calling for new federal laws.

Congress, using its new authority under the Thirteenth Amendment, overrode President Andrew Johnson's veto to pass the first Civil Rights Act on April 9, 1866. This law conferred citizenship on African Americans, a measure necessitated by the Supreme Court's Dred Scott decision (*Scott v. Sandford*, 1857). The law included a list of enumerated rights, including the right to make and enforce contracts, to sue and give evidence in court, and to purchase and inherit all forms of property. It also punished

One of the provisions of the Civil Rights Act of 1875 banned racial segregation on public transportation, but the Supreme Court overturned the act eight years later. (Library of Congress)

public officials if they used their legal powers to deny equality to African Americans. Since the law's constitutionality was questionable, many of its major provisions were incorporated into the Fourteenth Amendment.

On July 16, 1866, Congress again overrode President Johnson's veto, this time to enlarge the scope of the Freedmen's Bureau. Among other items, this law authorized the bureau to use military commissions to try persons accused of violating the civil rights of freedmen.

Again voting to override a presidential veto on March 2, 1867, Congress passed the First Reconstruction Act. Dividing the South into five military districts, the act required southern states to call new constitutional conventions elected by universal manhood suffrage and to ratify the Fourteenth Amendment. Under the act, 703,000 African Americans and 627,000 whites were registered as voters, with black majorities in five states.

As the Ku Klux Klan conducted a wave of terrorism against African Americans and Republicans in the South, Congress responded with the Ku Klux Klan Acts of 1870 and 1871, which provided police protection to enforce the rights guaranteed in the Fourteenth and Fifteenth Amendments. In several decisions, such as *United States v. Cruikshank* (1876), the Supreme Court ruled that key parts of the statutes exceeded the constitutional powers of Congress.

Finally, on March 1, 1875, President Ulysses S. Grant signed into law the Civil Rights Act of 1875. This far-reaching act, largely the work of Senator Charles Sumner, outlawed discrimination based on race in public accommodations (inns, businesses, theaters, and the like) and made it illegal to exclude African Americans from jury trials. In the *Civil Rights* cases (1883), however, the Supreme Court struck down most of the 1875 law, holding that the Fourteenth Amendment did not authorize Congress to prohibit discrimination by private individuals. This decision ended almost all federal attempts to protect African Americans from private discrimination until the passage of the Civil Rights Act of 1964.

Although the Civil Rights Acts of the Reconstruction era failed to guarantee any long-lasting equality for African Americans, they did provide points of reference for the Civil Rights movement of the 1950's and 1960's. The Civil Rights Act of 1866 was resurrected in *Jones v. Alfred H. Mayer Company* (1968), when the Supreme Court upheld its use to outlaw private racial discrimination in economic transactions as a "badge of slavery."

Thomas Tandy Lewis

See also Black codes; Civil Rights Act of 1957; Civil Rights Act of 1960; Civil Rights Act of 1964; Civil Rights Act of 1968; Civil Rights Act of 1991; *Civil Rights* cases; Civil War; Disfranchisement laws in Mississippi; Fourteenth Amendment; Freedmen's Bureau; Grandfather clauses; *Jones v. Alfred H. Mayer Company*; Ku Klux Klan; Race riots of 1866; Reconstruction; *Runyon v. McCrary*; *Scott v. Sandford*; Thirteenth Amendment; United States Commission on Civil Rights; *United States v. Cruikshank*

Civil Rights cases

The Cases: U.S. Supreme Court rulings in five cases pertaining to Thirteenth and Fourteenth Amendments

Date: October 15, 1883

The Court ruled that Congress could not outlaw discrimination by private parties under the authority of the Civil War Amendments, and Congress was prevented from legislating against private discrimination in public accommodations for nearly one hundred years.

In the aftermath of the Civil War, the U.S. Constitution was amended three times in five years. The three amendments, taken as a whole, were designed not only to end slavery but also to eliminate its "badges and incidents." Each of the amendments contained a clause empowering Congress to pass implementing legislation. In 1875, Congress passed a Civil Rights Act that made it illegal for anyone to deny access to places of public accommodation—including inns, public transportation, and theaters—on account of race, color, or previous condition of servitude. Five cases claiming violations of the public accommodations provisions were consolidated for decision by the Supreme Court.

The Court vs. Congress

The Court ruled that Congress did not have the authority to prohibit discrimination by private individuals. Justice Joseph P. Bradley's majority opinion analyzed the congressional authority granted by two of the Civil War Amendments. The Fourteenth Amendment, he said, gave Congress authority to provide relief from state action which interfered with a person's rights to due process of law and to equal protection of the laws. The amendment did not allow Congress to legislate against an invasion of rights by private individuals. Such power belonged to the state alone. Since the Civil Rights Act purported to provide a remedy for private discrimination, it exercised a congressional power not granted by the Constitution.

In regard to the Thirteenth Amendment, the Supreme Court conceded that Congress had been empowered to abolish "all badges and incidents of slavery"; however, the "badges and incidents" included only legal disabilities, such as the inability to make contracts, hold property, and have standing in court. They did not include the "social rights of men and races in the community." The Court concluded that it was time for the former slave to "take the rank of a mere citizen, and cease to be the special favorite of the laws."

In his dissent, Justice John Marshall Harlan argued that since state governments established and maintained the roads, highways, and harbors used by public conveyances, and since the states licensed theaters, inns, and other places of public accommodation, state tolerance of discrimination amounted to state action that furthered discrimination in violation of the Fourteenth Amendment.

The significance of the *Civil Rights* cases is twofold. First, the Court ruled that Congress could not outlaw discrimination by private parties under the authority of the Civil War Amendments. Therefore, the victims of racial discrimination could expect relief only from state governments, which, in the South, had by 1883 reverted to the control of white supremacists. Second, the *Civil Rights* cases prevented Congress from legislating against private discrimination in public accommodations for nearly one hundred years. In 1964, Congress passed a Civil Rights Act that drew its authority not from the Civil War Amendments but from the "commerce clause" in the U.S. Constitution.

William H. Coogan

See also Black codes; Civil Rights Act of 1957; Civil Rights Act of 1964; Civil Rights Acts of 1866-1875; Disfranchisement laws in Mississippi; Fourteenth Amendment; Jim Crow laws; *Jones v. Alfred H. Mayer Company*; *Moose Lodge v. Irvis*; *Plessy v. Ferguson*; Race riots of 1866; Thirteenth Amendment; *United States v. Cruikshank*

Civil Rights movement

The Event: Mass movement led by African Americans during the mid-twentieth century

Date: mid-1950's to late 1960's

The modern Civil Rights movement broke down many racial barriers, forced legislative changes, and transformed American politics and society.

Although the modern Civil Rights movement began with the Montgomery bus boycott in 1955, the struggle for civil rights has been an ongoing battle. The founding of the National Association for the Advancement of Colored People (NAACP) in 1909 was one of the first attempts to organize in the pursuit of civil rights. With the exception of some legal victories under the leadership of the NAACP, there was little progress in the field of civil rights until the end of World War II.

Voting Rights and a Legacy of Discrimination

With the end of Reconstruction after the Civil War, all the southern states developed devices to eliminate black voters. Each of the southern states adopted new state constitutions between 1890 and 1910 and employed devices such as the grandfather clause, the white primary, the poll tax, and the literacy test to strip African Americans of their right to vote. These devices were enormously successful. There were more than 130,000 black voters in Louisiana in 1896. By 1900, only two years after Louisiana adopted a new constitution containing many discriminating features, there were only 5,320 black voters left on the rolls.

For several reasons, African Americans made securing the right to vote their number-one objective. First, the U.S. Constitution, particularly the Fifteenth Amendment, contains specific guarantees against voter discrimination. Second, African Americans believed there was less social stigma involved in granting the right to vote than in integration. Integration meant race mixing, which was feared by white southerners. Giving African Americans the right to vote did not mean that whites would have to intermingle with African Americans. Finally, African Americans believed that securing the right to vote would bring about other changes. Black voting would result in the election of black politicians, and it would force white politicians to moderate their racial views.

The grandfather clause was the first major barrier to fall. Grandfather clauses said that if a person had a relative who voted before the Civil War (before 1861), then the person was exempt from other voter qualifications. Because African Americans were not allowed to vote before the Civil War, they had to meet voter qualifications such as poll taxes and literacy tests. The U.S. Supreme Court unanimously struck down grandfather clauses in *Guinn v. United States* (1915).

The next major barrier to fall was the white primary election. As the term implies, only whites were permitted to vote in primaries. Since southern politics was dominated by the Democratic Party, whoever won the Democratic primary would win the general election. If African Americans could not participate in the primary selection process, then they had no real input into the selection of political candidates.

In 1924, the Texas legislature passed a law prohibiting African Americans from participating in that state's primary election. A unanimous U.S. Supreme Court struck down the Texas law in *Nixon v. Herndon* (1927). Immediately, the Texas legislature passed another law delegating authority to the executive committee of each party to determine who could participate in the primaries. As expected, they excluded African Americans from

A longtime civil rights activist, Ella Jo Baker, helped found the Student Nonviolent Coordinating Committee, and was one of many women who played prominent roles in the Civil Rights movement. (Schomburg Center for Research in Black Culture, New York Public Library)

participation. In a 5-4 decision, the U.S. Supreme Court once again threw out Texas's white primary in *Nixon v. Condon* (1932). Undaunted, Texas made a third effort to ban African Americans from the primaries. In 1932, the state convention of the Texas Democratic Party, without any authorization from the state legislature, limited primaries to white voters. A unanimous U.S. Supreme Court, in *Grovey v. Townsend* (1935), upheld the action of the state convention, concluding that there was no state discrimination involved. Political parties were voluntary associations that had the right to determine their membership. It was not until *Smith v. Allwright* (1944), some twenty years after the first Texas white primary law was passed, that the U.S. Supreme Court finally declared white primaries to be unconstitutional. The NAACP had brought most of the white primary cases, including the *Smith* case, to the U.S. Supreme Court.

The third major voting barrier to fall was the poll tax, which was the payment of a fee in order to vote. African Americans were less able to afford the tax, and poor whites could always find someone to pay or waive their tax. Opponents of the poll tax tried to get Congress to abolish the fee. Five times the House of Representatives passed legislation to ban poll taxes, but each time the legislation was filibustered by southern senators. In 1964, the Twenty-fourth Amendment, which eliminated poll taxes in federal elections, was approved. Two years later, in *Harper v. Virginia Board of Elections*, the U.S. Supreme Court abolished poll taxes in state and local elections.

The last barrier to fall was also the most significant barrier in keeping African Americans from voting: the literacy test. Most literacy tests required the voter to be able to read, write, and understand sections of the state or federal constitution. Although many African Americans could pass the reading and writing portion of the test, almost all failed the understanding portion, primarily because white voter registrars had the sole authority to determine if a person understood a section of the constitution.

Attempts to get the courts to ban literacy tests were unsuccessful. The U.S. Congress passed the Voting Rights Act of 1965, which prohibited literacy tests in areas that were covered by the law. In 1970, an amendment to the Voting Rights Act banned literacy tests in all fifty states, and another amendment in 1975 permanently banned literacy tests.

School Desegregation

Before the Civil War, most states prohibited African Americans from getting an education. After the Civil War, schools were established for black education, but on a segregated basis. In many areas, education for African Americans ended at the sixth grade. High schools, vocational schools, and colleges and universities were often unavailable for black students.

In 1890, the Louisiana legislature passed a Jim Crow law requiring "separate but equal" accommodations for white and black passengers on the railroads. The railroads backed a challenge to the law because of the additional expense they would encounter. Homer Plessy, one-eighth black, was selected to test the law; he sat in the whites-only coach and was arrested. In *Plessy v. Ferguson* (1896), in a 7-1 decision, the U.S. Supreme Court upheld the Louisiana law. The Court found no violation of the "equal protection clause" of the Fourteenth Amendment because whites were as separated from blacks as blacks were from whites. Although the *Plessy* decision had nothing to do with education, the doctrine of "separate but equal" was quickly adopted to justify segregated schools.

The NAACP led the legal attack against segregated schools. The first strategy of the organization was not to seek to overturn *Plessy* but, on the contrary, to seek enforcement of *Plessy*. African American schools were indeed "separate," but were they "equal"? Black schools received far fewer dollars per student to operate, and black teachers were paid a fraction of what white teachers received. Black schools had a limited curriculum, few textbooks, no transportation for students, and often the buildings were no more than one-room shacks. In a series of Supreme Court cases involving higher education in the South, the NAACP time and again demonstrated that black schools were not equal. In fact, in many of the cases, there were no law schools or professional schools available to African Americans. The Supreme Court consistently ordered the enrollment of black students where "separate but equal" was not being met.

Challenging "Separate but Equal"

By the late 1940's, the NAACP was ready to mount a direct challenge to *Plessy v. Ferguson*. Cases were brought in South Carolina, Delaware, Virginia, Kansas, and the District of Columbia. In 1954 the U.S. Supreme Court overturned *Plessy* and the "separate but equal" doctrine in *Brown v. Board of Education*. Chief Justice Earl Warren, speaking for a unanimous Court, wrote: "We conclude that in the field of public education the doctrine of 'separate but equal' has no place. Separate educational facilities are inherently unequal."

Many southern states invoked the doctrine of states' rights and argued that the federal government was usurping the power of states to control education. Massive resistance to the court's decision became the standard policy throughout the South. Some school districts closed their schools rather than integrate, while other communities exploded in violence. When a large, unruly mob prevented the integration of Central High School in Little Rock, Arkansas, President Dwight D. Eisenhower was forced to send in federal troops to protect the nine black students.

Token integration was the policy during the 1960's, but in 1969 the U.S. Supreme Court finally declared that the time for delay was over. Fifteen years after *Brown*, the Court declared that school districts were ordered to comply "at once" with the *Brown* decision. School districts increasingly relied upon busing as the means to desegregate the schools, and opponents of busing in both the North and South argued that it was leading to the destruction of neighborhood schools.

Direct Action

On December 1, 1955, a racial incident in Montgomery, Alabama, transformed the face of the Civil Rights movement. On that day, Rosa Parks, a black seamstress, refused to give up her seat on a Montgomery bus to a white passenger. Parks was arrested, and her arrest ushered in the Civil Rights movement. African Americans, led by a new resident to the community, the Reverend Martin Luther King, Jr., organized one of the most effective mass movements and boycotts in the nation's history, a boycott of the city's bus system. Almost a year after the boycott began, Montgomery officials reluctantly desegregated the bus system after a decision from the Supreme Court.

King emerged from the bus boycott as a national political figure, and in 1957, he and his supporters established the Southern Christian Leadership Conference (SCLC). Combining his Christian beliefs with the precepts of nonviolent resistance, King led several mass protest movements against what he perceived to be the moral injustices of a segregated society. In 1963, King wrote his famous "Letter from Birmingham Jail," in which he outlined his views on just and unjust laws. That same year, King led more than 200,000 civil rights supporters on a March on Washington, D.C. In 1965, King led one of the last major protests of the Civil Rights movement when he and his supporters marched from Selma to Montgomery, Alabama, to pressure Congress to pass a voting rights bill.

Another significant phase of the Civil Rights movement was characterized by "sit-ins." Triggered by four black college students seeking service at the "white" lunch counter of the local Woolworth's in Greensboro, North Carolina, within days similar sit-ins took place in more than sixty communities. Two months after the sit-in started in Greensboro, the lunch counters were integrated.

Many of the student leaders in the sit-in movement came together in 1960 and established the Student Nonviolent Coordinating Committee (SNCC). SNCC played a major role in voter registration drives throughout the South. By the mid-1960's, tired of the violence against them and the slow pace of change, SNCC became one of the most militant of the civil rights organizations and a key exponent of "black power."

In 1960, the Congress of Racial Equality (CORE) initiated the "Freedom Rides." Thirteen riders—some white, some black—boarded buses in Washington, D.C., on a trip through the heart of the deep South. Attacked and viciously beaten by white mobs outside Anniston, Alabama, and in Birmingham, the Freedom Riders focused the attention of the nation on the failure of southern states to protect passengers in interstate travel.

Realizing the difficulties African Americans experienced in seeking service in public accommodations such as hotels, restaurants, and theaters, Congress passed the landmark Civil Rights Act of 1964, which made it illegal to discriminate in public accommodations on grounds of "race, color, religion or national origin." Another section of the law banned discrimination in employment and established the Equal Employment Opportunity Commission (EEOC) to enforce the law. The section on employment discrimination established "affirmative action," an approach that has been blamed by some for eroding white support for the Civil Rights movement.

The Collapse of the Civil Rights Movement

After 1965, the Civil Rights movement fell into disarray and decline. There were numerous reasons for the decline of the movement. To begin with, the broad base of public support for civil rights began to erode. Many Americans believed that Congress had passed enough legislation to deal with the problem of discrimination (most notably the sweeping 1964 Civil Rights Act) and that now it was time to let those laws work. Another factor was the nationalization of the push for civil rights. Until the mid-1960's the civil rights issue was widely viewed as a southern problem. When the movement moved northward, some white northerners withdrew their support. With the institution of busing for school desegregation and the attempt to integrate housing, many white Americans in the North felt threatened.

The controversy over affirmative action policies also divided support for the movement. To many Americans, affirmative action meant quotas and programs that unfairly threatened their own job security. Another factor was the diffusion of the movement as it was broadened to include discrimination based on age, gender, physical disability, and sexual orientation. Fewer Americans were willing to support what they viewed as special privileges for women, people with disabilities, and homosexuals than to support civil rights, particularly voting rights, for African Americans.

The urban riots of the 1960's shattered white support for civil rights. White voters and politicians—President Lyndon B. Johnson among them—felt betrayed by the riots. They thought that the nation was trying to deal with the problems of racism and discrimination. Congress had passed three civil rights laws and one voting rights law within an eight-year period. When the Watts

One of the most dramatic moments in the Civil Rights movement was the August, 1963, March on Washington. (Library of Congress)

riot in Los Angeles broke out within a week after passage of the Voting Rights Act of 1965, the "white backlash" against civil rights essentially brought the movement to a halt. The riots represented the chasm that still existed between black and white, and they frightened many whites into thinking of "law and order" first and civil rights gains second. On the national scene, the escalating war in Vietnam drew attention away from the Civil Rights movement. When Martin Luther King, Jr., openly opposed the war, he was widely criticized by many civil rights leaders, as well as by President Johnson. In the late 1960's, the Vietnam War displaced the issue of civil rights.

Ideological disputes among black leaders of the movement also led to its collapse. Major disputes arose among civil rights organizations such as the NAACP, SCLC, CORE, and SNCC with respect to tactics and objectives. Younger African Americans, particularly those in SNCC, were dismayed by the slow pace of change and, as a result, favored more militant tactics. The emergence of the Black Power movement in 1966, led by young leaders such as Stokely Carmichael of SNCC, was a direct assault on the approach of King and other moderates.

Accomplishments

The Civil Rights movement forever altered the political landscape of the United States. Perhaps the greatest accomplishment of the movement can be seen in the thousands of African Americans who hold elective office. The number of black members of Congress was at a record high in the mid-1990's. African Americans have been elected to virtually every political office in all areas of the country. The Civil Rights movement also ended the humiliating practice of segregation and abolished the laws which attempted to create two classes of citizens. Finally, the Civil Rights movement created a sense of pride and self-esteem among those who participated in the movement.

Darryl Paulson

Further Reading

Good overviews of the Civil Rights movement include Michael J. Klarman's *From Jim Crow to Civil Rights: The Supreme Court and the Struggle for Racial Equality* (New York: Oxford University Press, 2004), Fred Powledge's *Free at Last? The Civil Rights Movement and the People Who Made It* (Boston: Little, Brown, 1991), and Robert Weisbrot's *Freedom Bound: A History of America's Civil Rights Movement* (New York: Plume, 1991). An excellent source on the major barriers to black voting and the struggle to overturn those barriers is Steven Lawson's *Black Ballots: Voting Rights in the South, 1944-1969* (New York: Columbia University Press, 1976). On school desegregation, the best single source is Richard Kluger's *Simple Justice: The History of Brown v. Board of Education and Black America's Struggle for Equality* (New York: Alfred A. Knopf, 1976). The legislative battle over the Civil Rights Act of 1964 is splendidly told in Charles and Barbara Whalen's *The Longest Debate* (Washington, D.C.: Seven Locks Press, 1985). The major civil rights organizations are described in Clayborne Carson's *In Struggle: SNCC and the Black Awakening of the 1960's* (Cambridge, Mass.: Harvard University Press, 1981) and Taylor Branch's *Parting the Waters: America in the King Years, 1954-63* (New York: Simon & Schuster, 1988). A definitive biography of a key figure in the Civil Rights movement is Barbara Ransby's *Ella Baker and the Black Freedom Movement: A Radical Democratic Vision* (Chapel Hill: University of North Carolina Press, 2003).

See also Birmingham March; Black church; Black Power movement; Chicago sit-ins; Church bombings; Civil Rights movement and children; Civil rights worker murders; Congress of Racial Equality; Freedom Rides; Greensboro sit-ins; "I Have a Dream" speech; Jews and African Americans; King assassination; Little Rock school desegregation crisis; Mississippi Freedom Democratic Party; Montgomery bus boycott; National Association for the Advancement of Colored People; National Urban League; Rainbow Coalition; School desegregation; Sit-ins; Southern Christian Leadership Conference; Southern Manifesto; Student Nonviolent Coordinating Committee; Summit Meeting of National Negro Leaders; United States Commission on Civil Rights; University of Mississippi desegregation; Voting Rights Act of 1965; White Citizens' Councils

Civil Rights movement and children

In the course of the struggle to obtain civil rights, African American children were beaten, clubbed, gassed, threatened by lynch mobs, attacked by police dogs, blasted by high-power water hoses, arrested, jailed, and even killed.

Many African American children—from the very young to teenagers—were involved in the Civil Rights movement of the 1950's and 1960's in the United States. They participated in marches, demonstrations, boycotts, pickets, sit-ins, desegregation of schools, voter registration campaigns, and freedom rides. Some children accompanied their activist parents to organizing meetings, which were often held in black churches and conducted by members of the National Association for the Advancement of Colored People (NAACP), the Student Nonviolent Coordinating Committee (SNCC), the Southern Christian Leadership Conference (SCLC), the Council of Federated Organizations (COFO), and other civil rights organizations.

The children were primarily involved in the movement in the South, especially Mississippi, Alabama, Georgia, Tennessee, Arkansas, and Florida, where both de jure (by law) and de facto (by custom) segregation existed. Although the movement was nonviolent, it elicited violent acts from angry white mobs who gathered around protests, local authorities trying to break up demonstrations and arrest protesters, and racist groups who bombed churches and attacked African Americans in an effort to intimidate them. In the course of the struggle to obtain civil rights, African American children were beaten, clubbed, gassed, threatened by lynch mobs, attacked by police dogs, blasted by high-power water hoses, arrested, jailed, and even killed.

In May of 1963, in Birmingham, Alabama, thousands of children marched for civil rights as part of the Children's Crusade. Birmingham police commissioner Eugene "Bull" Connor, a staunch segregationist, gave the order for police to attack the children with nightsticks, police dogs, and high-power water hoses. The police arrested the children, filling the city jails and then imprisoning children in a makeshift jail at the fairgrounds. In September, 1963, a bomb exploded in the Sixteenth Street Baptist Church in Birmingham, killing four young girls who had been attending Sunday school. The church had been selected as a target because civil rights activists gathered there and organized protests.

Children also played an important, and difficult, role in school desegregation. Their parents filed lawsuits on their behalf, but it was the children who attended these schools who bore the brunt of racially motivated attacks, verbal and physical abuse, and social isolation. Two of the nationally publicized cases occurred in Topeka, Kansas, and Little Rock, Arkansas. Topeka operated eighteen public elementary schools for white children only and four schools for black children. The Reverend Oliver Brown, on behalf of his daughter Linda Carol Brown, and twelve other black plaintiffs, on behalf of their children, filed a lawsuit to protest this segregation. After much expert testimony, the U.S. Supreme Court in 1954 issued a landmark decision that ended segregation of children in public schools solely on the basis of race, because segregation deprived minority children of equal educational opportunities. In 1957, nine black youths (known as "the Little Rock Nine"), led by Daisy Bates, desegregated Little Rock's Central High School. President Dwight D. Eisenhower had to use state troopers to protect the children from physical violence by armed white adults opposed to desegregation.

Bernice McNair Barnett

See also *Brown v. Board of Education*; Civil Rights movement; Little Rock school desegregation crisis; School desegregation; Segregation

Civil Rights Restoration Act

The Law: Federal legislation devised to clarify earlier mandates regarding the funding of educational institutions
Date: March 22, 1988

Congress required recipients of federal financial assistance to uphold nondiscriminatory requirements of the 1964 and subsequent civil rights legislation in all respects, not merely in activity aided by federal funds.

Title VI of the Civil Rights Act of 1964 mandated that federal funds could not be used to support segregation or discrimination based on race, color, or national origin. The law did not affect a number of other civil rights problems, however. At Cornell University's School of Agriculture, for example, women could not gain admission unless their entrance exam scores were 30 percent to 40 percent higher than those of male applicants. Epileptics were often barred from employment, and persons in their fifties were often told that they were qualified for a job but too old. To rectify these problems, Congress extended the scope of unlawful discrimination in federally assisted schools in Title IX of the Education Amendments Act of 1972 to cover gender; the Rehabilitation Act of 1973 expanded the same coverage to people with disabilities; and the Age Discrimination Act of 1975 added age as a protected class.

Enforcement of the statute regarding education was initially assigned to the Office for Civil Rights (OCR) of the U.S. Department of Health, Education, and Welfare, which later became the U.S. Department of Education. OCR ruled that the statute outlawed not only discrimination in the particular program supported by federal funds but also discrimination in programs supported by nonfederal funds. All recipients of federal financial assistance were asked to sign an assurance of compliance with OCR as a condition of receiving a federal grant.

Grove City College

From 1974 to 1984, Grove City College in western Pennsylvania received $1.8 million in tuition grants and guaranteed student loans but refused to sign an assurance of compliance. The college argued that the funds were for students, not the college, but OCR insisted that the financial aid was administered as a part of the college's financial aid program and, therefore, the college must pledge as a whole not to discriminate on the basis of race, color, national origin, or gender. OCR instituted enforcement proceedings against Grove City College, and an administrative law judge ruled in 1978 that the college could no longer receive federal student loan moneys.

Grove City College and four students desiring financial aid then sued. In 1980, when the case was first tried, the federal district court ruled in favor of Grove City College on the grounds that no sex discrimination had actually occurred. On appeal, the court of appeals reversed the lower court's decision, and the matter was taken up by the Supreme Court of the United States, this time with Terrel H. Bell, head of the newly created federal Department of Education, as the defendant.

In *Grove City College v. Bell* (1984), Justice Byron R. White delivered the majority opinion of the Court, which held that OCR did not have sufficient congressional authority to withhold funds from Grove City College for failure to sign the assurance of compliance. Moreover, according to the Court, violations of Title VI could occur only in the specific program or activity supported directly with federal funds, a judgment that went beyond the question raised by the case. Justices William J. Brennan, Jr., and Thurgood Marshall dissented.

A New Bill

Shortly after the Supreme Court ruling, OCR dropped some seven hundred pending enforcement actions, resulting in an outcry from civil rights groups over the decision. Representative Augustus F. Hawkins authored the Civil Rights Restoration Act in the House, and Senator Ted Kennedy sponsored the bill in the Senate. Their aim was to amend all the affected statutes—Title VI of the Civil Rights Act of 1964, Title IX of the Education Amendments Act of 1972, the Rehabilitation Act of 1973, and the Age Discrimination Act of 1975. According to the bill, any agency or private firm that wanted to receive federal financial assistance would have to comply with the nondiscrimination requirement as a whole, even if the aid went to only one subunit of that agency or firm.

Although Hawkins's version quickly passed in the House of Representatives, the measure was caught up in the politics of abortion, and the bill died in the Senate. Opponents advanced more than one thousand amendments over a period of four years, and representatives of the administration of President Ronald Reagan testified against passage of the law. A group known as the Moral Majority broadcast warnings that the bill would protect alcoholics, drug addicts, and homosexuals from discrimination, although there were no such provisions in the proposal.

More crucially, the Catholic Conference of Bishops, which was traditionally aligned with the Civil Rights movement, wanted two amendments to the bill. One proposed amendment, which was unsuccessful, would have exempted institutions affiliated with religious institutions from complying with the law if religious views would be compromised thereby. The other proposed amendment, which was opposed by the National Organization for Women, was an assurance that no federal funds would be spent on abortion. Congress delayed finding a compromise.

In 1987, leaving out references to abortion, Congress finally adopted the Civil Rights Restoration Act. By vetoing the measure, Reagan became the first president to veto a civil rights bill since Andrew Johnson. Supporters of the act sought to override the presidential veto. Opponents in the Senate tried to destroy the bill by various amendments in debate on the floor of the Senate on January 28, 1988. Senator John C. Danforth proposed an amendment that would disallow federal payments for abortion. This amendment passed. With the passage of the act by the Senate on March 22, 1988, Congress overrode Reagan's veto, and the law went into effect immediately.

Michael Haas

Further Reading

The law is explained and analyzed in Veronica M. Gillespie and Gregory L. McClinton's "The Civil Rights Restoration Act of 1987: A Defeat for Judicial Conservatism" in *National Black Law Journal* (12, Spring, 1990), Robert K. Robinson, Billie Morgan Allen, and Geralyn McClure Franklin's "The Civil Rights Restoration Act of 1987: Broadening the Scope of Civil Rights Legislation" in *Labor Law Journal* (40, January, 1989), and Robert Watson's "Effects of the Civil Rights Restoration Act of 1987 upon Private Organizations and Religious Institutions" in *Capital University Law Review* (18, Spring, 1989). Mark Willen's "Congress Overrides Reagan's Grove City Veto" in *Congressional Quarterly Weekly Review* (46, March 26, 1988) explains the parliamentary maneuvers required to get the law passed.

See also Affirmative action; Civil Rights Act of 1964; Education

Civil rights worker murders

The Event: A group of white supremacists attacked and murdered three civil rights workers
Date: June-July, 1964
Place: Nashoba County, Mississippi
The murders brought profound changes to the Deep South generally and to Nashoba County, specifically. Eventually, those directly involved were tried and convicted, and the cause for which the three men died, black enfranchisement, became a reality.

The struggle for black equality reached its crest in the two years after the August, 1963, March on Washington. During that period, the last elements of legal segregation died. More important, black disfranchisement, the key to maintaining the old, dual system of life in the South, also ended. The registration and enfranchisement of African Americans came, however, at a heavy cost: Three young civil rights workers were killed for their efforts to give the right to vote to those who had been denied it since the end of Reconstruction in the 1870's. The murders of James Earl Chaney, Andrew Goodman, and Michael Henry Schwerner focused international attention on the Civil Rights movement and brought a commitment from the federal government to bring to justice those responsible for the crime.

After judicial decisions had ended the tradition of separate schools and facilities in the South, civil rights organizations turned their attention to registering African Americans as voters. Believing that access to the ballot box was the key to empowering the dispossessed, organizations such as the Student Nonviolent Coordinating Committee (SNCC) and the Congress of Racial Equality (CORE) sought to organize massive voter registration drives in the Deep South.

Mississippi

In particular, leaders targeted the state of Mississippi, the poorest and least literate in the nation. During the winter of 1963-1964, the Council of Federated Organizations (COFO), a confederation of civil rights organizations, planned for the Mississippi Freedom Summer, which had as its goal the registration of as many African Americans as possible. More than one thousand white college students volunteered to spend their summer organizing community centers and teaching reading, writing, and civics to rural African Americans who wanted to become voters. In the area of Nashoba County, Mississippi, COFO's plans were unpopular with most white citizens. For the first time since the end of Reconstruction, the national Ku Klux Klan organized local klaverns in the area.

Michael Schwerner, a graduate of Cornell University, and his wife had moved to Meridian, Mississippi, during the winter to begin the preparations for the Freedom Summer. A committed believer in racial equality, Schwerner quickly became a target for the white supremacists of Nashoba County. Various plans to eliminate him were discussed in Klan meetings. James Chaney was a native of the area and had become a paid COFO staff member a few months before he was murdered. Andrew Goodman was one of the Freedom Summer volunteers who was scheduled to work in Nashoba County. He arrived in the area on June 20 and was killed one day later.

Background to the Murders

The events surrounding the murder of the three civil rights workers began on June 16, when a group of armed white men beat the lay leaders of the Mount Zion Methodist Church in Longdale, a small, all-black community in Nashoba County. Later that night, several of the whites returned and set fire to the church, which was to have housed one of the Freedom Schools. On June 21, Chaney, Goodman, and Schwerner drove to Longdale from Meridian to examine the church's remains. On their return from Nashoba County, Deputy Sheriff Cecil Ray Price stopped their car for speeding. After arresting Chaney for driving sixty-five miles per hour in a thirty-five mile per hour zone, Price arrested Goodman and Schwerner for suspicion of arson in the Mount Zion church fire. He then placed the three in the Nashoba County jail, where they remained for more than five hours.

At about the time that the three were placed in jail, COFO was activating its procedures for locating field workers who had not returned or phoned by 4:00 P.M. In addition to telephoning all of the area hospitals, COFO staff placed calls to all the jails. When the Nashoba County jail was called by the Meridian COFO office, however, the person who answered the phone flatly denied having seen any of the three. While Chaney, Goodman, and Schwerner were in the jail, Price, a member of the White Knights of the Ku Klux Klan, notified his Klan superiors and made arrangements for the elimination of the troublemakers. Specifically, leaders of the local klavern located a bulldozer operator and arranged for him to dispose of the three men's bodies even before they were released from jail. Several years later, it became known that the murder plan was finalized before the three were released from the jail that evening.

The Murders

Sometime after 10:00 P.M., Deputy Price allowed Chaney to pay a twenty dollar fine for speeding and prepared to release all three men. None was permitted to make a phone call, and all three knew that a release after dark was dangerous. Price escorted the three to their car and directed them to leave Nashoba County. On the drive back toward Meridian, a high-speed car chase began as Chaney, Goodman, and Schwerner raced for the county line. They did not make it. Price stopped their car again and ordered the three into his car as the rest of the Klan posse arrived. The three cars—Price's, the posse's, and the COFO car, driven by a Klansman—proceeded to a deserted dirt road. Once off the main road, Schwerner and Goodman were pulled from the car and shot through the heart at point-blank range. Before Chaney was killed, he was beaten severely with a blackjack. He was shot three times, with the third shot fired into his brain. The bodies of the three were carried to a remote farm, where a cattle pond was under construction. The bodies were dumped into a prepared hole in the fresh earthen dam, and the COFO station wagon was driven in the opposite direction and burned.

Reactions to the Murders

The reaction to the disappearance of the three was swift. On June 22, U.S. Attorney General Robert Kennedy ordered a full-scale inquiry by the Federal Bureau of Investigation (FBI). Following the discovery of the burned car on June 23, President Lyndon B. Johnson authorized the use of two hundred men from the Meridian naval air station to aid in the search. Within Nashoba County, popular belief held that the three were hiding in an attempt to arouse northern sympathy for their work. Some even argued that COFO was responsible for the arson at the Mount Zion church, using it to complete the hoax effect. J. Edgar Hoover, director of the FBI, flew to the area on July 10, at the president's request, to investigate the disappearances personally. At a press conference in Jackson, Mississippi, Hoover disclosed that the FBI force in the state had been increased to 153 agents—more than ten times the normal number—to protect civil rights workers.

On August 5, the bodies of Chaney, Goodman, and Schwerner were unearthed from the new dam. Despite autopsies that unequivocally showed that Goodman and Schwerner had been shot to death and that Chaney had suffered an "inhuman beating" before dying from three gunshot wounds, a Nashoba County coroner's jury ruled on August 25 that it was unable to determine the cause of death for any of the three.

On December 4, Hoover announced the arrests of nineteen men on federal conspiracy charges in connection with the murders, including Price and his superior, the Nashoba County sheriff. The FBI focused on the role of the Klan in the deaths, and more than 60 agents infiltrated the Mississippi Klan to obtain evidence. More than 1,000 Mississippians, including 480 Klan members, were interviewed during the investigation.

Impact

The murders of James Chaney, Andrew Goodman, and Michael Schwerner brought profound changes to the Deep South generally and to Nashoba County, Mississippi, specifically. Eventually, those directly involved were tried and convicted, and the cause for which the three men died, black enfranchisement, became a reality.

When the 1964 Nashoba County Fair opened six days after the bodies had been recovered, the mood was subdued and tense. Arizona senator Barry Goldwater, the Republican nominee for president, canceled a planned appearance at the event, even though it had been an obligatory stop for politicians in the past. The discovery of the corpses also ended most of the discussions of a COFO-arranged hoax. Instead, the FBI used the discovery as a lever to secure information from Klansmen who mistrusted each other and feared arrest in the case. Since the FBI learned the precise location of the bodies, it was clear that agents were receiving very reliable information. A number of those involved suspected that more than just the burial location had been passed to the federal government, and the Klan's code of silence was broken as several sought to save themselves by cooperating with the investigation.

Using laws passed as part of the Civil Rights Act of 1870, the federal government obtained grand jury indictments charging those involved with conspiracy to deny Chaney, Goodman, and Schwerner their civil rights. No substantive local investigation of the crime ever took place, and no murder charges were ever filed by the state of Mississippi. On October 20, 1967, a federal jury in Meridian convicted Cecil Ray Price and six co-defendants of the charges, marking the first successful prosecution in Mississippi history of white officials and Klansmen for crimes against African Americans or civil rights workers. After unsuccessful appeals, all the defendants entered federal custody on March 19, 1970, five and one-half years after the three murders.

The impact on the fight for civil rights was less clear. On July 2, 1964, Congress enacted the Civil Rights Act of 1964, which prohibited discrimination in public accommodations, publicly owned facilities, federally funded programs, and union membership. It also created the Equal Employment Opportunity Commission to end discrimination in employment. In November, 1964, Lyndon Johnson won a landslide reelection, capturing 61 percent of the popular vote and 94 percent of the African American vote. Two million more African Americans voted in that election than had in 1960.

Following the discovery of the bodies and the revelation that Chaney had been beaten before his murder, unlike Schwerner and Goodman, the trend toward self-segregation within the Civil Rights movement came to the fore. Some African Americans had come to believe that they needed to lead their own fight and that whites could not be part of it. As the 1960's progressed, these differences of opinion within the Civil Rights movement became more acute, and the movement became more diffuse as a result. Some, like Martin Luther King, Jr., rejected the idea of a movement for racial equality practicing segregation within itself. Others, like the leadership of SNCC, assumed a more radical position and eventually expelled all nonblacks from its projects. By then, enfranchisement for all was no longer a dream but instead a reality, and the Civil Rights movement was a success in ending legal segregation.

E. A. Reed

Further Reading

Branch, Taylor. *Pillar of Fire: America in the King Years, 1963-65.* New York: Simon & Schuster, 1998.

Cagin, Seth, and Philip Dray. *We Are Not Afraid.* New York: Macmillan, 1988. This is the best one-volume work on the Mississippi murders, the result of research into oral histories, court transcripts, and investigators' files. Annotated, with a complete index.

Grimshaw, Allen D., ed. *Racial Violence in the United States.* Chicago: Aldine, 1969. One of the most comprehensive anthologies on racial violence. Covers American history beginning with seventeenth century slave revolts and running through the riots of the 1960's. Contains a complete bibliography and index.

Leuchtenburg, William F. *A Troubled Feast: American Society Since 1945*. Boston: Little, Brown, 1973. A valuable, brief volume that provides a balanced introduction to recent American history. The Civil Rights movement is discussed within the context of broader social movements of the era. Contains a list of suggested readings and an index.

Lewis, Anthony. *Portrait of a Decade: The Second American Revolution*. New York: Random House, 1964. One of the seminal books on American race relations in the 1950's and early 1960's, this single volume examines the origins and manifestations of the disagreements over civil rights through analyses and excerpts from both the popular and the scholarly press. Contains an index.

McClymer, John F., ed. *Mississippi Freedom Summer*. Belmont, Calif.: Thomson/Wadsworth, 2003. New study of the summer in which the Civil Rights movement achieved its greatest triumphs.

Mars, Florence. *Witness in Philadelphia*. Baton Rouge: Louisiana State University Press, 1977. This first-person account of the events in Nashoba County, as told by a white woman, provides valuable insight into life before, during, and after the murders, the investigation, and the federal prosecution. Although not scholarly, it yields a textured view of the events that is valuable for those who want to understand better how such an event could have happened. Contains annotations, an index, and photographs.

Marsh, Charles. *God's Long Summer: Stories of Faith and Civil Rights*. Princeton, N.J.: Princeton University Press, 1997.

Sitkoff, Harvard. *The Struggle for Black Equality, 1954-1980*. New York: Hill & Wang, 1981. One of the best books for an overview of the American Civil Rights movement. This volume places the various elements of the movement into an understandable context for nonspecialists. Biographical essay and index.

See also Civil Rights movement; Freedom Summer; Harlins murder; Hawkins murder; King assassination; Malcolm X assassination; Student Nonviolent Coordinating Committee; Till lynching

Civil War

The Event: War between Northern and Southern states that established the primacy of the federal government over the states in the administration of justice and elevated the ethical system of free-labor capitalism as the national standard

Date: 1861-1865

The war's most profound effects on race relations in the United States resulted from its ending of slavery and emancipation of enslaved African Americans.

The Civil War redefined relationships both between the U.S. government and the individual and between the federal and state governments. During the course of the conflict, the Union and Confederate governments pursued aggressively nationalistic policies that undermined states' rights, civil liberties, and property rights.

The Slavery Issue

By the mid-nineteenth century, the free-labor ideal had taken hold in the states of the North. It was believed that economic opportunity should be open to all. To many in the North, the slave system in the South appeared to be the antithesis of the free-labor ideal. Northerners believed that slavery was inefficient, that it degraded labor as a whole, and that it created economic stagnation. Though most were willing to tolerate slavery where it existed, they wanted the western territories reserved for free white labor. They interpreted the Constitution as a document that made freedom national and slavery local.

Southerners shared a belief in the positive benefits of economic opportunity, but they identified it with the acquisition of land and slaves. Southerners dreamed of extending the slave system into the territories, arguing that the territories were the common property of all Americans; to prohibit slavery within them deprived southern people of their right to share in the nation's bounty.

The Republican victory in 1860 brought to power an administration pledged to restrict slavery in the territories. Fearing that the new administration would undermine slavery, seven southern states asserted their right to secede from the federal union and form a new government. Abraham Lincoln's administration denied the right of secession and refused to relinquish federal property in the South to the new Confederacy. When the state of South Carolina fired on a federal fort in Charleston harbor, President Lincoln called upon the states to supply troops to suppress the rebellion and preserve the federal union. Four additional states believed Lincoln's action to be an unjust usurpation of federal power and joined the Confederacy.

For the Lincoln administration, the highest good was the preservation of the Union. All issues of justice were considered in relation to that objective. The Confederacy was dedicated to the proposition that human property was an unalienable right and must be preserved. For the first year of fighting, the Lincoln administration took no action to destroy slavery. It enforced the provisions

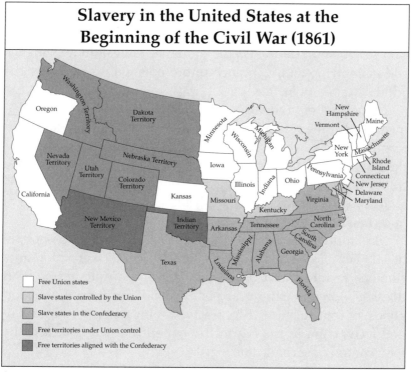

Slavery in the United States at the Beginning of the Civil War (1861)

- Free Union states
- Slave states controlled by the Union
- Slave states in the Confederacy
- Free territories under Union control
- Free territories aligned with the Confederacy

Source: Adapted from Eric Foner and John A. Garraty, eds., *The Reader's Companion to American History.* Boston: Houghton Mifflin, 1991.

of the Fugitive Slave Law, and Lincoln rebuked Union general John C. Frémont when he issued a proclamation freeing the slaves of Confederate sympathizers in Missouri. Lincoln's Emancipation Proclamation did not take effect until January 1, 1863. When he issued the proclamation, Lincoln justified his action in terms of military necessity. The proclamation freed only the slaves behind Confederate lines, but after the Emancipation Proclamation was issued, the Union army became a force for liberation.

Civil Liberties

Both the Union and Confederate governments restricted traditional civil liberties during the conflict. In early 1862, the Confederate Congress authorized Confederate president Jefferson Davis to suspend the writ of *habeas corpus* and to declare martial law in areas in danger of attack. That same year, President Davis ordered the first military draft in North America and established a Conscription Bureau to carry it out. Even more striking, the Confederacy never established a Supreme Court and allowed their attorney general to judge the constitutionality of laws. That omission seriously undermined the notion of judicial independence and gave the executive branch unprecedented powers over the administration of justice.

Thousands of civilians were arrested by the Union government during the war, and many were tried by military courts. In response to civil disturbances in Baltimore, Lincoln suspended the privilege of *habeas corpus* on April 27, 1861, along the rail line from Philadelphia to Washington. The suspension was later extended to other areas of the North and gradually became general in certain types of cases.

Most military arrested by the Union government were not political. The vast majority of civilian prisoners were blockade-runners, residents of Confederate states, army deserters, draft dodgers, foreign nationals, people who dealt in contraband goods, or fraudulent war contractors. A loyal opposition continued to function in the North throughout the war and actually won control of several state legislatures.

Among those arrested early in the war was John Merryman. Merryman was a member of a pro-Confederate Maryland cavalry unit that had damaged railroad bridges in April, 1861. Merryman's attorney successfully petitioned a federal circuit court for a writ of *habeas corpus* to show just cause for his arrest. The commander of Fort McHenry, where Merryman was being held, refused to honor the writ on the grounds that President Lincoln had suspended the privilege in Maryland. Judge Roger B. Taney responded by issuing a circuit court ruling stating that only the Congress had the power to exercise such a suspension (*Ex parte Merryman*, 1861). In spite of the ruling, Lincoln continued to maintain his right to suspend the writ as an essential power necessary to suppress the rebellion.

For purposes of election propaganda, unscrupulous Republican politicians and military officers attempted to exploit fears that traitorous secret organizations existed in the Midwest. Recent scholarship has demonstrated that the major "Copperhead" societies, such as the Knights of the Golden Circle and the Sons of Liberty, were little more than paper tigers. In the wake of Democratic victories in the state elections of 1862, Republican newspaper editors frequently printed tales of treasonable Democratic activities.

When Ohio Democrat Clement L. Vallandigham declared that the war was being fought to free blacks and enslave whites, General Ambrose Burnside ordered his arrest. A military commission convicted Vallandigham of attempting to hamper the government's efforts to suppress the rebellion and recommended imprisonment. President Lincoln altered the sentence to banishment, and Vallandigham was escorted to Confederate lines. Lincoln justified his action by arguing that it made no sense to shoot a simple-minded deserter and do nothing to the man who induced him to desert.

Later in the war, Democratic activist H. H. Dodd of Indiana organized the Sons of Liberty to protect the civil liberties of those opposed to the Republican administration. Acting on rumors that the Sons of Liberty had aided Confederates, Union general Henry Carrington arrested Indiana Democrats linked to the Sons of Liberty, including editor Lambdin Milligan. A military commission sentenced three of the defendants to death. Others received prison terms. The death sentences were never carried out, but it is clear that the men were tried on questionable evidence by military commissions in areas where civil courts were functioning. After the war, the Supreme Court ruled in *Ex parte Milligan* (1866) that such trials were illegal.

Treatment of Black Troops

When the conflict began, neither the Union nor Confederate governments would sanction the use of African American soldiers. As the Union government moved toward an acceptance of emancipation, however, it also began to organize African American regiments.

In spite of the large-scale recruitment of black soldiers during the last two years of the war, the Union army discriminated against African Americans in a wide variety of ways including pay, chance of promotion, and the amount of fatigue duty black units were expected to perform. Although a few African Americans did receive commissions, the vast majority of officers in the United States Colored Troops (USCT) were white combat veter-

After the Union army abandoned its opposition to using black troops in combat, the Fifty-fourth Massachusetts Colored Regiment became one of the most distinguished units of the Civil War. (Library of Congress)

ans. The men of the USCT proved their courage at the battles of Port Hudson, Milliken's Bend, and Fort Wagner, where they took heavy casualties. Generally, however, the prejudice of many commanding officers led to the use of USCT regiments for fatigue or guard duty while saving white units for combat.

The Confederacy reacted harshly to the use of black troops by the Union army. President Davis approved of the execution of black prisoners of war in South Carolina in November, 1862. Later, Davis ordered that all former slaves captured while serving in the Union army be returned to the states for trial. The massacre of black prisoners by Confederate troops on several occasions forced Union authorities to threaten retaliation in order to stem the injustice.

The use of large numbers of black troops by the Union war effort helped pave the way for universal emancipation. Throughout his political career, Lincoln consistently asserted that slavery was morally wrong. Though emancipation began as a military tactic, it became a war aim. The courage of black soldiers allowed Lincoln to secure passage of the Thirteenth Amendment, providing for an end to slavery throughout the country.

Military Justice

The system of military justice employed within the army was seriously flawed. At least 267 soldiers were executed by the Union army during the Civil War era. More than half of those executed were either foreigners or African Americans. A number of black soldiers were convicted of mutiny for protesting unequal pay in the Union army. Racial tensions accelerated during the final months of the conflict. A high number of black soldiers were executed for alleged sexual offenses against white women. The Confederacy had an incomplete record of military justice. Since many southern officers had received their training in the prewar U.S. Army, the procedural flaws of courts-martial were similar in both armies.

The Civil War moved the United States toward a more perfect application of its ideals of equality and justice. The United States entered the war as a federal union with contrasting standards of justice, one based on free-labor ideals, the other on the slave sys-

Members of the Fourth U.S. Colored Troops at Fort Lincoln, Maryland, at the conclusion of the Civil War. (Library of Congress)

tem of the southern states. Property rights took precedent over human rights, and equal justice was denied African Americans in virtually every section of the country. The Union government, through its policy of emancipation and the enlistment of African Americans into its armed forces, transformed the war from a crusade to preserve the Union into a war of liberation. In doing so, it expanded the nation's concept of justice to include equality for African Americans.

Thomas D. Matijasic

Further Reading

David W. Blight's *Race and Reunion: The Civil War in American Memory* (Cambridge, Mass.: Belknap Press of Harvard University Press, 2001) and Jeffrey Rogers Hummel's *Emancipating Slaves, Enslaving Free Men: A History of the American Civil War.* (Chicago: Open Court, 1996) are valuable additions to the literature on the Civil War. The most comprehensive source for military records on the Civil War is the U.S. War Department's *The War of the Rebellion: A Compilation of the Official Records of the Union and Confederate Armies* (130 vols., Washington, D.C.: U.S. Government Printing Office, 1880-1901). An excellent overview of all aspects of the war condensed into readable form is James M. McPherson's *Battle Cry of Freedom: The Civil War Era* (New York: Oxford University Press, 1988). Robert I. Alotta's *Civil War Justice: Union Army Executions Under Lincoln* (Shippensburg, Pa.: White Mane, 1989) argues that the military justice system was hopelessly flawed. Joseph T. Glatthaar's *Forged in Battle: The Civil War Alliance of Black Soldiers and White Officers* (New York: The Free Press, 1990) chronicles discrimination within the Union army. Frank L. Klement's *Dark Lanterns: Secret Political Societies, Conspiracies, and Treason Trials in the Civil War* (Baton Rouge: Louisiana State University Press, 1984) explodes the myth of vast treasonable societies operating in the North during the war. Mark E. Neely, Jr.'s *The Fate of Liberty: Abraham Lincoln and Civil Liberties* (New York: Oxford University Press, 1991) defends Lincoln's record on civil liberties and disputes the notion that arbitrary arrests were common. James G. Randall's *Constitutional Problems Under Lincoln* (rev. ed. Urbana: University of Illinois Press, 1951) blames Lincoln's subordinates for violations of civil liberties. Emory M. Thomas's *The Confederate Nation: 1861-1865* (New York: Harper & Row, 1979) is a brief, readable overview of the functioning of the Confederate government.

See also Bleeding Kansas; Charleston race riots; Civil Rights Acts of 1866-1875; Colfax massacre; Compromise of 1850; Confiscation Acts of 1861 and 1862; Draft riots; Emancipation Proclamation; Fifteenth Amendment; Fourteenth Amendment; Harpers Ferry raid; Kansas-Nebraska Act; Military; Missouri Compromise; Reconstruction; *Scott v. Sandford*; Thirteenth Amendment; Vietnam War

Clinton massacre

The Event: Killing of more than twenty African Americans by angry white mobs
Date: September 4-6, 1875
Place: Clinton, Mississippi
The Clinton massacre served as the impetus that inspired white Mississippi "redeemers," as they were called, to do whatever was necessary to take control away from the Republicans and force black submission.

In 1875, widespread resentment of congressional Reconstruction (the effort to rebuild and rehabilitate the South after the Civil War) mounted among whites in Mississippi. White Democrats began coordinating efforts to carry the fall statewide elections. The dominant issue for Democrats in the 1875 electoral campaign was the threat or fear of race war. Several race riots had already occurred throughout Mississippi during the summer. Democratic political solidarity was still in question, however, until the Clinton massacre of September 4-6. Clinton, a town in Hinds County, was the site of a political rally to which both Democratic and Republican speakers were invited. The rally was disrupted by gunfire, and both black and white people were killed and wounded. Confusion followed.

News of the incident quickly spread throughout the state. Bands of armed whites converged on Clinton, and a reign of terror followed. Officials estimated that twenty to fifty African Americans were killed by the angry white mobs. Many African Americans fled to other towns, and some sought refuge in the woods. The Republican governor of Mississippi, unable to convince the president to send troops, watched helplessly as an undeclared race war waged throughout the state. Freedmen were denied access to the polls or were forced to vote for Democratic candidates. The Clinton massacre had served as the spark that inspired white Mississippi "redeemers," as they were called, to do whatever was necessary to take control away from the Republicans and force black submission.

Donald C. Simmons, Jr.

See also Colfax massacre; Disfranchisement laws in Mississippi; Dyer antilynching bill; Lynching; Race riots of 1866; Race riots of 1943; Race riots of the twentieth century; Reconstruction

Clotilde capture

The Event: Capture of the last ship to deliver slaves to the United States
Date: July, 1859
Place: Mobile Bay, Alabama

The arrest and prosecution of the Clotilde *finally ended the illegal slave trade to the United States and brought a symbolic end to slavery.*

There are contradictory reports about slavers—ships especially built to transport slaves—during the period from 1858 to 1861. Historians, however, have managed to piece together an accurate account of the *Clotilde*, the last U.S. slave ship, which smuggled more than a hundred Africans into Alabama.

The slave trade was outlawed by Congress in 1808. This brutal business continued without serious interference, however, until the early 1820's, when federal officials began capturing slavers and freeing their prisoners. Public sentiment, even in the South, did not favor revival of the trade. To annoy northern antislavery and abolitionist advocates, numerous rumors were spread by slave traders and sympathizers about slavers landing on the southeastern coast. For example, the *New York Daily Tribune* received many letters reporting landings of slavers in Florida and the Carolinas. There were even rumors in the 1860's of a prosperous underground slave-trading company operating in New Orleans. The *Clotilde*'s history, however, has been confirmed by eyewitness accounts and careful reconstruction of events by historians.

Congress had revived laws against slave trading and declared that anyone convicted would be hanged. The United States had been later than almost every other civilized nation in the world in abolishing slave trading. Even New York City, bastion of abolitionists, became a refuge for eighty-five slave ships, many of them built and sent to Africa from that city. Much profit could be made in the $17,000,000-per-year business. According to one account, 15,000 Africans were smuggled to the United States in 1859 alone, the last 117 of whom were brought by the *Clotilde*. In contrast, the British government, after issuing its injunction against the slave trade in the eighteenth century, seized and destroyed 625 slave ships and freed their forty thousand prisoners. In the United States, only the abolitionists consistently confronted the government for its apathy toward slave smuggling.

The Meagher Brothers' Scheme

Timothy Meagher, with brothers Jim and Byrns, masterminded the *Clotilde* project. An imposing Irishman known for his adventurous character, Timothy Meagher was a plantation owner and captain of the steamboat *Roger B. Taney*, which carried passengers, cargo, and mail to and from Montgomery on the Alabama River. Apparently in a lighthearted argument with some passengers on his steamboat, Meagher made a thousand-dollar bet that within a year or two he would bring a ship full of slaves to Mobile Bay without being apprehended by federal officials. Meagher had many years' experience in cruising the Alabama River. He knew his way around every hidden bayou, swamp, canebrake, and sandbar better than anyone else in the South. For his operation, he needed a slave ship. He purchased a lumber schooner called the *Clotilde* for thirty-five thousand dollars in late 1858 and rebuilt it as a 327-ton slaver. He hired his friend Bill Foster, who was experienced in constructing and sailing the old slavers, as skipper.

Foster was to sail to the west coast of Africa and seek the Dahomey kingdom's assistance in procuring two hundred young slaves. The *Clotilde* was equipped with a crew, guns, and cutlasses. To control the prisoners, Meagher supplied the ship with iron manacles, rings, and chains. Foster hired his crew from all over the South, enticing them with liquor, money, and promises of adventure. In the dead of night, massive quantities of food, mainly yams and rice, and drinking water were transported to the ship from Meagher's plantation. To give the ship the look of a lumber schooner, some piles of lumber were placed on the deck. Captain Foster hired the infamous King Dahomey and his drunken thugs to raid villages and capture two hundred young, healthy men and women. The attacks must have taken place early one summer morning in May or early June of 1859. King Dahomey's band raided the two peaceful villages of Whinney and Ataka. They burned huts, injured women and children, and tied up more than 170 young Africans by their necks. The captives were forced into the hold of the *Clotilde*.

The return trip was an awful scene of helpless people, racked with convulsions, crammed into dark, damp quarters, lacking adequate food and water. Foster had as many as thirty-nine bodies thrown overboard before arriving back in the United States. The ship returned in July, 1859, and waited in front of Biloxi in the Mississippi Sound. Foster hired a friend's tugboat and in the dead of night, pulled the *Clotilde*, undetected by government vessels present in Mobile Bay, to a prearranged location in the swamps of the Tombigbee River. Meagher was the best man to maneuver the craft in the treacherous bayous. The sick, exhausted Africans were moved quietly to an out-of-the-way plantation belonging to Meagher's friend, John M. Dabney, who hid them in the canebrakes. From there, Meagher took charge of his steamer, the *Roger B. Taney*, and kept Foster and the *Clotilde* crew members hidden aboard her until they reached Montgomery, where they were paid off and whisked to New York City for dispersal.

The slaver *Clotilde* was promptly burned at water's edge as soon as its African cargo had been removed. Meagher made elaborate preparations to throw townsfolk and government officials off the track. The Department of Justice was informed, however, and Meagher was arrested at his plantation and placed on trial in short order. Meagher's trial was a sham. He was released on bond for lack of evidence. His efforts to conceal all signs of the ship and its cargo had paid off, but he had to spend close to $100,000 in lawyers' fees and bribes. The prosecution was delayed, and the secessionists came to his rescue. News of the *Clotilde*'s landing and Meagher's trial was drowned by the presidential campaign and widespread talk of civil war.

Government officials finally learned where the Africans were hidden. They commissioned the steamer *Eclipse* for finding and transferring the Africans to Mobile. Meagher, learning of the government's decision, got the *Eclipse* crew and government passengers drunk, giving him and his men time to move the prisoners to a friend's plantation two hundred miles up the Alabama River.

Disaster and Aftermath

Meagher's slave-smuggling venture was a financial disaster. He bought the Africans from Dahomey for $8,460 in gold plus ninety casks of rum and some cases of yard goods. He was able to sell only twenty-five slaves; it is not clear exactly what happened to the rest. There were reports that Meagher later transferred the others to his plantation near Mobile. Some ended up marrying and living with local black people in the vicinity. Some were reported to have died of disease. Many others settled in cabins behind the Meagher plantation house, which was burned in 1905.

In 1906, a journalistic account of the *Clotilde* episode appeared in *Harper's Monthly* magazine. The author, H. M. Byers, had found several soft-spoken Africans who told of having been smuggled aboard the *Clotilde*. They still maintained some of their own culture and language, along with their African gentleness of demeanor. Most of their children were married to local black residents of Mobile and neighboring areas. Byers conducted extensive interviews with two who had endured the journey from Africa to Alabama: an old man named Gossalow, who had a tribal tattoo on his breast, and an old woman named Abaky, who had intricate tribal tattoos on both cheeks. Gossalow and his wife had been stolen from the village of Whinney, and Abaky from the town of Ataka, near King Dahomey's land. They had kept many of their old traditions in their original form with little modification. For example, they still buried their dead in graves filled with oak leaves. They spoke nostalgically of their peaceful West African farms, planted with abundant yams and rice.

Chogollah Maroufi

Further Reading

Byers, H. M. "The Last Slave Ship." *Harper's Monthly Magazine* 53 (1906): 742-746. A sensationalized journalistic version of the episode, but filled with valuable and accurate details. Especially valuable are the author's interviews with two surviving Africans who were smuggled into the United States aboard the *Clotilde*.

Howard, Warren S. "The Elusive Smuggled Slave." In *American Slavers and the Federal Law: 1837-1862*. Berkeley: University of California Press, 1963. Provides various accounts of the *Clotilde*.

Klein, Herbert S. *The Atlantic Slave Trade*. New York: Cambridge University Press, 1999.

Sellers, James Benson. *Slavery in Alabama*. Birmingham: University of Alabama Press, 1950. Conveys the historical and social mood of that period and gives some details of the *Clotilde's* smuggling operation.

Spear, John R. *The American Slave Trade: An Account of Its Origins, Growth, and Suppression*. Williamstown, Mass.: Corner House, 1978. A well-researched and thoroughly documented book about the slave trade in general. Chapter 19 provides an account of the *Clotilde* voyage and its aftermath.

Thomas, Hugh. *The Slave Trade: The Story of the Atlantic Slave Trade, 1440-1870*. New York: Simon & Schuster, 1997.

Wish, Harvey. "The Revival of the African Slave Trade in the United States, 1859-1860." *Mississippi Valley Historical Review* 27 (1940-1941): 569-588. A comprehensive account of various smuggling operations just before the Civil War.

See also Abolition; *Amistad* slave revolt; Slavery

Colfax massacre

The Event: Killing of more than sixty African Americans by a white terrorist organization
Date: April 13, 1873
Place: Colfax, Louisiana

Fighting for political rights, more than sixty African Americans died in what was the bloodiest single case of racial violence during the Reconstruction. Afterward, President Ulysses S. Grant ignored pleas for justice on behalf of the slain.

The terrorist group known as the White League formed across Louisiana during the Reconstruction (1866-1877) to keep African Americans out of the political arena. The league's activities led to the Colfax massacre, the bloodiest single instance of racial violence in the Reconstruction period in all the United States. Disputes over the 1872 election results had produced dual governments at all levels of politics in Louisiana. Fearful that local Democrats would seize power, former slaves under the command of African American Civil War veterans and militia officers took over Colfax, the seat of Grant Parish, Louisiana.

On Easter Sunday, April 13, 1873, a series of brutal acts were carried out by the White League in Colfax, resulting in the deaths of more than sixty African Americans. After the African American men had laid down their weapons and surrendered, many were flogged, mutilated, and murdered, and African American women were also raped and murdered. A pile of more than twenty bodies was found half-buried in the woods. Monroe Lewis, an elderly black gentleman, was dragged from his bed, forced to say his prayers, and then shot. After being forced to cook food for a party of more than ninety white men, Charles Green was executed. Petitions to President Ulysses S. Grant requesting that justice be rendered were ignored.

Alvin K. Benson

See also Charleston race riots; Civil War; Clinton massacre; Lynching; Orangeburg massacre; Reconstruction

Colored Women's League

Identification: Group composed of African American women crusading for better conditions for African Americans
Date: Founded in June, 1892
Place: Washington, D.C.
This organization joined with another organization to form the National Association of Colored Women to promote self-protection, self-advancement, and social interaction.

The Colored Women's League (CWL), also known as the National League of Colored Women and the Washington Colored Woman's League, emerged in Washington, D.C., when black women active in education, benevolent, and literary societies joined together in June, 1892, in an effort to improve conditions for African Americans.

Helen A. Cook, wife of John T. Cook, served as president, and the recording secretary was Charlotte Forten Grimké, a teacher from Port Royal, South Carolina. Other founders included

Coralie Franklin Cook, wife of a Howard University administrator; teachers Anna J. Cooper, Mary Jane Patterson, Mary Church Terrell, and Anna E. Murray from M Street School; and Josephine B. Bruce, the first black teacher in the Cleveland schools, who later married Senator Blanche K. Bruce.

As Chicago prepared to host the World Columbian Exposition of 1893, the Board of Lady Managers rejected the petitions of these Washington women to participate in the planning process because they did not represent a national organization. In response, the Washington Colored Woman's League issued an invitation to black women throughout the country to affiliate as a national league. Women's clubs responded from the state of South Carolina and from the cities of Philadelphia, Kansas City, Denver, and Norfolk, Virginia.

In January, 1894, the organization incorporated, becoming the Colored Women's League. In October, the CWL received an invitation for membership in the National Council of Women (NCW). Its members accepted and sought to expand representation for the NCW convention in the spring of 1895. Instead, the competition between women's clubs in New York and in Boston resulted in the creation of a second national organization, the National Federation of Afro-American Women. The two national organizations merged in July, 1896, to form the National Association of Colored Women (NACW) to further self-protection, self-advancement, and social interaction. In 1896, Terrell became the first president of the NACW.

Dorothy C. Salem

See also Combahee River Collective; Million Woman March; National Association of Colored Women; National Black Women's Political Leadership Caucus; National Council of Negro Women

Combahee River Collective

Identification: Group consisting of black feminists and lesbians
Date: Founded in 1974
Place: Boston, Massachusetts

*This group of black feminists challenges multiple sources of oppression,
including racial, sexual, heterosexual, and class oppression.*

The Combahee River Collective, consisting of black feminists and
lesbians, was first organized in 1974 and took its name from Harriet Tubman's 1863 military campaign to free slaves. The members of this Boston-based group are committed to combating multiple systems of oppression and to enacting revolutionary social
and political changes.

Many black feminists of the twentieth century saw themselves
as continuing the "herstory" of African American women, including such early activists as Sojourner Truth, Harriet Tubman,
and Mary Church Terrell. They located their contemporary roots
in both the black liberation movements (including the Civil Rights
and Black Nationalist movements) and the American women's
movement. By necessity, however, they also found themselves
challenging the sexism in predominantly male-centered liberation groups, as well as the elitism and racism of white feminism.
Thus, beginning in the late 1960's, black feminists and other feminists of color took part in the second wave of the American
women's movement, in which many women of color challenged
the racist and elitist blind spots in the American feminist movement. By 1973, some New York-based black feminists felt the
need to form an independent coalition that came to be known as
the National Black Feminist Organization (NBFO).

Some members of the NBFO, unhappy with what they perceived to be the organization's "bourgeois-feminist stance" and
"lack of a clear political focus," left to form the Combahee River
Collective. Although they suffered from internal disagreements
influenced by differences related to class, politics, and sexuality,
by 1976 the remaining group had decided to function as a study
group, committed to publishing black feminist writings and working on specific social and political projects. While editing *Capitalist Patriarchy and the Case for Socialist Feminism* (1978), Zillah
Eisenstein asked the Combahee River Collective to contribute to
her anthology. In response, three members of the group—Demita
Frazier, Beverly Smith, and Barbara Smith—drafted the *Combahee
River Collective Statement* in April, 1977.

Subsequently, the statement was published in several other anthologies, and in 1986, it was finally published as a pamphlet by Kitchen Table: Women of Color Press. The statement focuses on four major areas: the general development of black feminism; the collective's statement of beliefs; a history of the Combahee River Collective, highlighting the problems of organizing black feminists; and a brief outline of the issues and projects of black feminism.

In the *Combahee River Collective Statement*, the members of the collective noted that although they are dedicated to advancing the struggle of black women, they do not support a philosophy of feminist/lesbian separatism, and they believe in forming coalitions with other progressive liberation groups. As politically committed socialists, they believe in the liberation of all oppressed people and believe that racial, sexual, heterosexual, and class oppression are often enacted simultaneously. Thus, in their brief pamphlet, the Combahee River Collective articulated an important concept concerning black feminist history, theory, and practice.

See also Colored Women's League; Million Woman March; National Association of Colored Women; National Black Women's Political Leadership Caucus; National Council of Negro Women

Compromise of 1850

The Laws: Agreement among sectional factions, worked out in five separate congressional bills, that permitted California to join the Union as a free state
Date: September 20, 1850
The Compromise of 1850 may be seen as a last national attempt to resolve the question of slavery in the territories, as the United States moved closer to civil war.

The U.S. Constitution, while creating a mechanism for the addition of states and acknowledging the right of each state to permit and even encourage slavery within its boundaries, made no mention of slavery's status in future states. Congress, when it admitted a state, could impose any condition it wished. The national government had first addressed the issue of slavery in territories and new states when the Confederation Congress passed the Northwest Ordinance of 1787. This ordinance excluded slavery from the unsettled area north of the Ohio River to the Mississippi River's eastern bank, the edge of U.S. holdings.

The Missouri Question

The issue reemerged in 1817, when Missouri, where between two thousand and three thousand slaves lived, applied to join the United States as a slave state. The question came before the Congress in 1819, and sectional tensions erupted. The U.S. Senate had eleven states each from the free North and the slave-owning South, but the North's growing population gave it a decisive advantage in the House of Representatives, so proslave forces committed themselves, at the minimum, to maintaining a balance between the regions in the Senate.

A temporary solution emerged in 1820, when Senator Henry Clay of Kentucky brokered a solution to the crisis. The Missouri Compromise stipulated that Missouri would be admitted to the Union as a slave state, while Maine, which had petitioned for statehood in late 1819, was admitted as a free state. The compromise also prohibited slavery from the remainder of the Louisiana Purchase in the area north of 36 north latitude, while permitting it south of that line. Between 1820 and 1848, this solution maintained national peace, and the Senate remained balanced.

The Southwest and California

The Mexican War disrupted the relative peace. The United States received millions of acres of land spanning the area from the Continental Divide west to the Pacific Ocean and south from the forty-ninth parallel to Mexico. Before the war ended, David Wilmot, a member of the House of Representatives from Pennsylvania, attached an amendment to an appropriations bill stipulating that any territory acquired from Mexico must exclude slavery in perpetuity. Although the bill failed to win passage, the Wilmot Proviso fueled the smoldering fires of sectionalism, as many assumed that any additional western lands would be governed by the Missouri Compromise.

In 1849, just a year after the discovery of gold in California, the young California Republic petitioned the Senate for admission to the Union. Besides disrupting the balance between slave and free states, California straddled the 1820 compromise's line and threw the prior agreements into chaos. In both houses of Congress, the question of slavery became paramount: southerners rejected any attempt to exclude the practice from the West by nearly unanimous margins, while Free-Soilers from the North rejected the possibility of losing equal economic competition by similar percentages. Left in the middle were some elements of the national Whig Party, which struggled to preserve the Union while remaining a

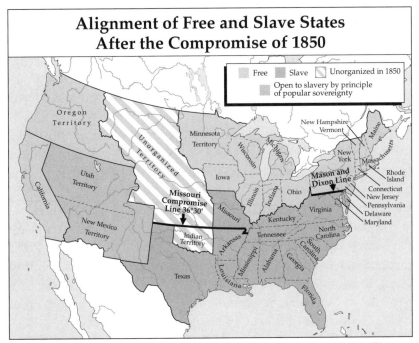

Alignment of Free and Slave States After the Compromise of 1850

After the Mexican War, the United States acquired vast western tracts. The new land and the California gold rush prompted western migration, raising the issue of slavery in the territories once again, thirty years after the Missouri Compromise. The Compromise of 1850 admitted California as a free state; created the territories of Utah and New Mexico with no restrictions on slavery; fixed the modern Texas boundary; paid Texas for ceding lands for the New Mexico territory; prohibited slave trading in Washington, D.C.; and enacted the Fugitive Slave Act of 1850.

national party. The idea of disunion grew. Senator John C. Calhoun of South Carolina, long a firebrand for states' rights, proposed the formation of a sectional party to guarantee the practice of slavery. William Seward, an abolitionist representative from New York, also rejected the possibility of a compromise, citing the immorality of slavery. President Zachary Taylor, a hero of the Mexican War and a southerner, supported California's admission as a free state while rejecting the extreme position of persons such as Calhoun.

Five Resolutions

The first concrete proposal for compromise came from Senator Clay on January 29, 1850. Clay proposed a series of five resolutions: that the California Republic join the United States as a free state; that the rest of the territory acquired in the Mexican Cession be organized without any decision on slavery; that Texas receive monetary compensation in exchange for giving up its claims to parts of contemporary New Mexico; that the slave trade within the District of Columbia be abolished (although the actual practice of slavery would not be affected); and that a more rigorous fugitive slave law be enacted.

On February 5 and 6, Clay presented his resolutions and spoke for the Union's preservation. One week later, Mississippi senator Jefferson Davis rejected Clay's proposals, using bitter language that also attacked northern intentions. On March 4, the ailing Calhoun, in a speech delivered by Virginia's James Mason, rejected compromise on the principle of slavery in the territories. On March 7, Daniel Webster acknowledged that both sides had just grievances and urged support for Clay's whole plan, calming some tensions with his eloquent plea that the Union be preserved. On March 11, Seward stated the abolitionist's opposition to the compromise because of the immorality of slavery.

In April, the Senate referred Clay's resolutions to a select committee. The committee reported back to the full Senate an omnibus bill that contained the substance of the five original resolutions and sparked another four months of debate. Two major stumbling blocks to the compromise disappeared in July, when President Taylor and Calhoun both died. Millard Fillmore, who supported the compromise's ideas, replaced Taylor, who had bitterly opposed the omnibus bill. While Clay was vacationing, Stephen A. Douglas broke the omnibus bill into five parts and steered them through the Senate, and the House of Representatives followed suit. By September 20, Congress had adopted the five bills that made up the Compromise of 1850.

In 1854, the attempts at balancing the competing interests of the Free-Soil North with the proslave South ended when Senator Douglas proposed that the Kansas and Nebraska areas be organized using the concept of popular sovereignty. Congress adopted the Kansas-Nebraska Act that year, triggering the formation of a national political party dedicated to the idea of an exclusively free-soil policy in the West. The new Republican Party immediately became a force on the national political landscape, and its candidate, John C. Frémont, came within four states of being elected president in 1856. Ultimately, the election of Abraham Lincoln in 1860, a man committed to both the preservation of the Union and the free-soil doctrine, drove the South to secession.

John G. Clark
Updated by E. A. Reed

Further Reading

Works that examine the forces and events preceding the Civil War include John C. Waugh's *On the Brink of Civil War: The Compromise of 1850 and How It Changed the Course of American History* (Wilmington, Del.: Scholarly Resources, 2003), Bruce Collins's *The Origins of America's Civil War* (New York: Holmes & Meier, 1981), editor Eric Foner's *Politics and Ideology in the Age of the Civil War* (New York: Oxford University Press, 1980), Hamilton Holman's *Prologue to Conflict: The Crisis and Compromise of 1850* (New York: W. W. Norton, 1966), David Potter's *The Impending Crisis, 1848-1861* (New York: Harper & Row, 1976), and editor Kenneth Stampp's *The Causes of the Civil War* (rev. ed., Englewood Cliffs, N.J.: Prentice-Hall, 1974).

See also Bleeding Kansas; Civil War; Fugitive Slave Law of 1793; Fugitive Slave Law of 1850; Harpers Ferry raid; Kansas-Nebraska Act; Missouri Compromise; Northwest Ordinance; Proslavery argument; Thirteenth Amendment

Compromise of 1877

The Event: Political resolution of the disputed presidential election of 1876 that put Republican Rutherford B. Hayes in office

Date: January, 1877

To get its candidate into the presidency, the price that the Republic Party paid in the Compromise of 1877 was ending Reconstruction in the South.

The Compromise of 1877 represents the attempt toward equality that failed during Reconstruction when newly elected President Rutherford B. Hayes ended efforts to establish a biracial democracy in the South. During his presidential campaign, Hayes favored "home rule" for the South as he campaigned against New York governor Samuel J. Tilden, a Democratic reformer. Although Tilden won the popular vote, Hayes claimed victory in South Carolina, Florida, and Louisiana. Republican Reconstruction governments still controlled these states, and it was doubtful that a former Union general could carry them by any other means than fraud.

After ending Reconstruction in the southern states, newly elected president Rutherford B. Hayes forgot his pledge to protect the rights of African Americans in the South. (Library of Congress)

Many southern Democrats, particularly scalawags, accepted Hayes's election, particularly if he would leave the South alone after taking office. Ohio Republicans and southern Democrats met in a Washington, D.C., hotel and reached an agreement that if Hayes could assume the presidency, he would remove federal troops from South Carolina and Louisiana so that Democrats could regain control. Hayes consented after being sworn in. Race relations worsened because the Democrats ignored their promises to treat black southerners fairly and Hayes forgot his pledge to ensure the rights of freedmen. Reconstruction had allowed African Americans to reconstitute their families, participate in government, and enjoy equality in dealing with whites, but the 1877 Compromise engendered a hatred of reform throughout the South for nearly one hundred years. African Americans would suffer social restrictions until the 1960's.

Douglas W. Richmond

See also Black codes; Disfranchisement laws in Mississippi; Gerrymandering; Politics and government; Reconstruction; *Slaughterhouse Cases*

Confiscation Acts of 1861 and 1862

The Laws: The first act confiscated all property, including slaves used in the Confederate war effort, but did not clearly free the slaves. The second act stated that slaves would not be returned and would be set free after a certain period of time

Dates: August, 1861, and July, 1862

The difference between the first and second acts showed the growing resolve in the Union to end slavery and set the stage for the Emancipation Proclamation.

In August, 1861, the U.S. Congress passed a law confiscating all property, including slaves, used in the Confederate war effort. The law required judicial proceedings before any property could be appropriated, and it left unclear whether any confiscated slaves would be freed. The following July, Congress passed the

Second Confiscation Act. The 1862 law, which also required a judicial hearing, declared that rebels were traitors whose property could be seized for the lifetime of the owner. The only property that would not be returned to the rebels' heirs was slaves, who were regarded as captives of war and set free after a period of sixty days. President Abraham Lincoln doubted that Congress possessed the constitutional authority to free slaves in the states. When he signed the bill into law, he included a statement of objections to its provisions. Although the power to confiscate rebel property was rarely used during or after the war, the difference between the first and second acts revealed the growing determination in the Union to end slavery and set the stage for the Emancipation Proclamation, which Lincoln issued in January, 1863.

Thomas Clarkin

See also Civil War; Emancipation Proclamation; Slavery

Congress of Racial Equality

Identification: African American civil rights organization
Date: Founded in June, 1942
Place: Chicago, Illinois

Better known as "CORE," the Congress of Racial Equality helped to eradicate discrimination in interstate travel on buses and trains and to end discrimination in both the public and private sectors of society, especially in housing and employment.

The "Big Five" civil rights organizations in America—the National Association for the Advancement of Colored People (NAACP), the Urban League, the Student Nonviolent Coordinating Committee (SNCC), the Southern Christian Leadership Conference (SCLC), and the Congress of Racial Equality (CORE)—utilized different approaches in their quest for racial equality. The NAACP excelled in both litigation and lobbying, while the Urban League focused on economic development. SNCC, SCLC, and CORE all utilized techniques of nonviolent direct action. Although the SCLC was the best known of these groups due to the

Elected national director of CORE in 1968, Roy Innis continued in that office into the twenty-first century, overseeing many shifts in the organization's philosophy. (Library of Congress)

media savvy of its leader, the Reverend Martin Luther King, Jr., CORE pioneered the technique and was using it for two decades before the SCLC and SNCC were created.

Founded in Chicago in 1942, CORE attempted to apply the nonviolent techniques of Mohandas K. Gandhi to the racial problems in America. Skeptical of the approaches of the NAACP and the Urban League, CORE members believed that discrimination had to be confronted directly, without hatred and violence but also without compromise. All CORE members were required to read Krishnalal Shridharani's book *War Without Violence* (1939), which described Gandhi's philosophy and methods.

Growing out of the religious radicalism of the 1930's, CORE was dominated by Methodist leaders in its early years. Many were socialists, and most were pacifists. Three of the six individuals most responsible for the formation of CORE either spent time in jail or served in Civilian Public Service camps because they were conscientious objectors to military service. CORE leaders were admirers of the industrial unions and copied their "sit-down" strikes. In fact, the first CORE "sit-ins" were actually called sit-downs.

The belief in nonviolence was for both religious and practical reasons. Since many of the early members were ministers or divinity students, nonviolence was merely an extension of their Christian beliefs blended with the Hindu philosophy of Mohandas Gandhi. Pragmatically, nonviolence was viewed as the only appropriate approach to resolving racial problems. A minority group utilizing violence would likely be assisting in their own demise. CORE leaders expressed concerns about movements of black militancy and retaliation and believed that nonviolent direct action was the most reasonable approach to furthering racial equality.

CORE was founded as an interracial organization; four of its founders were white and two were black. James Farmer, a charismatic leader with a divinity degree from Howard University, was CORE's first national chairman and later served as national director from 1961 to 1966. The first major project that CORE undertook was to help black students obtain housing in neighborhoods surrounding the University of Chicago. White members of CORE secured property with restrictive covenants attached to the property. These covenants prevented African Americans from renting or buying the property. The white CORE members then leased the property to African Americans, and integrated housing was established.

Campaign Strategy

During its first two decades of operation, CORE concentrated on integration of public accommodations. A 1946 project, the Journey of Reconciliation, captured national attention for CORE. In order to test compliance with a recent Supreme Court decision outlawing segregation in interstate travel, CORE decided to take a two-week interracial trip into the South. Eight black and eight white CORE members rode Trailways and Greyhound buses into Virginia, North Carolina, and Kentucky. CORE challenged the segregated seating on the buses but did not challenge segregation in bus stations, restrooms, or restaurants. Twelve arrests were made. The Journey of Reconciliation served as a forerunner to the better-known Freedom Rides in 1961.

During the 1940's and 1950's, CORE's membership was small, mostly non-southern, and usually located in university towns.

Efforts to establish chapters in the South failed due to fears of economic reprisals or violence. While CORE had twenty chapters in 1950, the number of chapters dropped to a half dozen by the mid-1950's. There were several reasons for CORE's membership problems. Since most chapters were on college campuses, members would graduate and leave. The McCarthyism of the early 1950's, which brought any political leftist organization under suspicion, helped to suppress membership. CORE also lacked a strong national organization and a staff to help recruit and retain membership. A final problem, and a common one in most interracial groups, was the complaint that whites dominated the leadership structure. Membership became such a problem for CORE that only seven individuals attended the organization's 1957 national convention.

CORE in the Civil Rights Movement

With the advent of the sit-in movement in Greensboro, North Carolina, on February 1, 1960, CORE found an issue to rejuvenate its membership and become a leading force in the Civil Rights movement. With the return of James Farmer as national director of CORE in 1961, CORE decided to take on its most challenging project. Farmer and CORE decided to launch the Freedom Rides of 1961.

In 1960, the U.S. Supreme Court, in *Boynton v. Virginia*, extended the prohibition against segregation in interstate travel to cover terminal accommodations as well as trains and buses. Thirteen CORE members, seven African Americans and six whites, boarded Trailways and Greyhound buses in Washington, D.C., and headed into the Deep South. James Farmer and John Lewis were among the riders. (Lewis would soon become chairman of the Student Nonviolent Coordinating Committee and later serve as a member of Congress from Georgia.) It did not take long for arrests and violence to occur. The first arrest took place in Charlotte, North Carolina, and the first extensive violence occurred in Anniston, Alabama. A white mob with chains, sticks, and rocks broke bus windows and slashed tires. The Greyhound bus was fire-bombed, while the Trailways bus was boarded by a white mob who severely beat the Freedom Riders.

One CORE member suffered permanent brain damage from his beating.

The buses were attacked again in Montgomery, Alabama. Most of the original Freedom Riders were either in jail or in hospitals, so new riders were recruited in Montgomery. Members of CORE, SNCC, and the SCLC continued the ride to Jackson, Mississippi, where 360 were arrested. In September of 1961 the Interstate Commerce Commission issued a rule banning segregated facilities in interstate travel. Although ignored in many parts of the Deep South, CORE had won a major moral victory.

The success of the Freedom Rides revitalized the southern Civil Rights movement and elevated CORE to the forefront of civil rights organizations. Farmer was thrust into national prominence, and CORE chapters sprang up all over the nation. CORE members felt vindicated that their philosophy of nonviolent direct action had produced a major victory and mobilized thousands of black and white people to work together in seeking racial justice.

Other Direct-Action Campaigns

After the Freedom Rides, CORE continued to participate in direct action campaigns throughout the Deep South, but the organization was never able to match the success of the Freedom Rides. As CORE efforts continued to be met with violence, many members began to reexamine the organization's philosophy. The murders of CORE workers Michael Schwerner, Andrew Goodman, and James Chaney in Mississippi in 1964 caused many members to abandon the group's nonviolent philosophy. Black members also questioned the value of interracial membership, with many coming to the conclusion that only African Americans should remain members.

In 1965, CORE was so fundamentally different from what it had been when it was established that Farmer decided to resign. In 1968, Roy Innis took over as national director. In 1978, Washington journalist Jack Anderson accused Innis of ordering the shooting of a former colleague and the beating of another. Also in 1978, former CORE leader James Farmer unsuccessfully tried to oust Innis as CORE director. Farmer charged that Innis had fraudulently raised millions of dollars using CORE's name and that Innis had made himself into a "permanently installed dictator." Innis attacked Farmer for leaving the organization in a shambles and contended that Innes had raised millions of dollars for inner-city community development projects.

Darryl Paulson

Further Reading

Chong, Dennis. *Collective Action and the Civil Rights Movement.* Chicago: University of Chicago Press, 1991. A theoretical study of the dynamics of collective action within the Civil Rights movement.

Farmer, James. *Freedom—When?* New York: Random House, 1965. The national director of CORE describes the dilemmas confronting CORE and other civil rights groups.

_____. *Lay Bare the Heart: The Autobiography of the Civil Rights Movement.* New York: New American Library, 1985. An eyewitness account of the Freedom Rides and other civil rights events. Highlights the strengths and weaknesses of the movement.

Meier, August, and Elliott Rudwick. *CORE: A Study in the Civil Rights Movement, 1942-1968.* New York: Oxford University Press, 1973. The most thorough account of the founding and philosophy of CORE.

Morris, Alden. *The Origins of the Civil Rights Movement.* New York: Free Press, 1984. Describes the interrelationships of leading civil rights groups, both tensions and cooperation.

See also Black Power movement; *Brown v. Board of Education*; Chicago sit-ins; Civil Rights Act of 1960; Civil Rights Act of 1964; Civil Rights movement; Freedom Rides; Freedom Summer; Greensboro sit-ins; National Association for the Advancement of Colored People; Southern Christian Leadership Conference; Student Nonviolent Coordinating Committee

Congressional Black Caucus

Identification: Group comprising African American members of Congress formed to advance the concerns of African Americans and other members of minority groups

Date: 1970

The caucus also strove to ensure that the government assisted others in need, including children, the elderly, and the physically and mentally ill.

The Congressional Black Caucus, a group comprising African American members of the U.S. Congress, was established in 1970 by thirteen members of the House of Representatives who joined together "to promote the public welfare through legislation designed to meet the needs of millions of neglected citizens." Before that year, the House had never had so many African Americans among its 435 members, yet thirteen was still a small minority. The founders of the Congressional Black Caucus hoped that they could gain more visibility and power working together than they could acting alone.

In 1971, the Congressional Black Caucus was granted a meeting with President Richard M. Nixon, during which its members presented a document describing sixty actions the government should take on domestic and international issues. The president promised to promote desegregation by seeing that civil rights laws were more stringently enforced (later, caucus members came to believe that he did not work hard enough to fulfill his promise). Media coverage of the meeting helped the group gain recognition. Over the next quarter-century, members of the caucus built and strengthened ties with other influential members of the black community, including educators, community and religious leaders, and local and state legislators, which enabled the group to influence public policy at all levels of government.

Although originally formed to promote the concerns of African Americans and other members of minority groups, the caucus also worked to ensure that the government assisted others in need, including children, the elderly, and the physically and mentally ill. The group asserts that it is possible and desirable to develop a national African American position on matters of federal policy, and it has sought to direct that effort. Since its founding, the group has introduced and supported legislation concerning domestic issues such as employment, welfare and health care reform, education reform, small business development, urban revitalization, and federal disaster relief.

In 1981, members of the caucus spoke out against the budget proposed by President Jimmy Carter, believing that it devoted too much funding to the military and too little to social programs. At House Judiciary Committee hearings in 1996, following a rash of firebombings of black churches across the South, the caucus criticized the federal government's apparent failure to prosecute those guilty of the crimes. Many of the group's positions have been unpopular, even among some African Americans; in the late 1990's, for example, the caucus strongly endorsed the work of the controversial leader of the Nation of Islam Louis Farrakhan, who was accused by many of teaching anti-Semitism.

As the visibility and influence of the caucus increased, the group called for action on international issues of special concern to African Americans, including human rights. It was one

Members of the Congressional Black Caucus seen during a meeting with President Richard M. Nixon in 1971. (Library of Congress)

of the earliest and strongest voices urging that the United States use pressure against apartheid in South Africa and to call for increased attention and aid to other African nations.

Cynthia A. Bily

See also Black nationalism; Chisholm's election to Congress; Church burnings; Politics and government; Summit Meeting of National Negro Leaders

Cooper v. Aaron

The Case: U.S. Supreme Court ruling on school desegregation
Date: September 12, 1958

The Supreme Court held that fear of violence did not provide justification for postponing school desegregation, and it also affirmed that its constitutional interpretations were legally binding on governors and state legislators.

In *Brown v. Board of Education* (1954) the Supreme Court ordered an end to segregated schools and overturned the "separate but equal" doctrine established in *Plessy v. Ferguson* (1896). The ambiguity about how to implement school desegregation, however, created the opportunity for school boards to delay and defy the Court's order.

After the *Brown* decision, the Little Rock, Arkansas, school board approved a plan calling for the desegregation of grades ten through twelve in 1957, to be followed by the desegregation of junior high schools and, finally, the elementary schools. The plan was to be completed by the 1963 school year.

Nine black students, carefully selected by the National Association for the Advancement of Colored People (NAACP), were to begin integration of Central High School on September 3, 1957. The day before desegregation was to begin, Governor Orval Faubus ordered the Arkansas National Guard to prevent the black students from enrolling. Governor Faubus claimed that he acted to prevent violence from occurring. After three weeks, a federal court injunction forced the National Guard to withdraw.

On September 23, the nine black students entered Central High School and were met by an unruly mob. President Dwight D. Eisenhower was forced to dispatch federal troops to Little Rock to enforce the Court's desegregation order. In the face of the civil unrest, the school board asked for and received a two-and-a-half-year delay in their desegregation plan. The NAACP appealed the delay in *Cooper v. Aaron*.

Basic Issues

Two primary issues confronted the U.S. Supreme Court. First, could the desegregation plan be postponed because of the fear of civil unrest? On September 12, 1958, a unanimous Supreme Court emphatically said no: "The law and order are not here to be preserved by depriving the Negro children of their constitutional rights." Second, were the governor and legislature bound by decisions of the federal Court? Invoking the supremacy clause of the Constitution, the Court said: "No state legislative, executive or judicial officer can War against the Constitution without violating his undertaking to support it."

Although Governor Faubus lost the legal battle, he became a political folk hero in Arkansas and was elected to six consecutive terms (1955-1967). President Eisenhower was both praised and condemned for his actions. He was praised for sending in federal troops to enforce the Court's decision and condemned for failing to endorse personally the *Brown* decision and lend the weight and prestige of the White House to the Court's ruling. The *Cooper* case was the first legal confrontation over the enforcement of *Brown v. Board of Education*. The courts stood alone in this enforcement effort until Congress passed the 1964 Civil Rights Act. The Civil Rights Act endorsed the *Brown* decision and cut off federal funds to school districts refusing to comply with the Court's desegregation decision.

Darryl Paulson

See also *Brown v. Board of Education*; Civil Rights Act of 1964; Little Rock school desegregation crisis; *Plessy v. Ferguson*; Segregation

Council of Federated Organizations

Identification: Unique coalition of the major civil rights groups operating in Mississippi

Date: 1962-1965

Place: Mississippi

Through its massive Mississippi voter-registration project, the Council of Federated Organizations (COFO) played an important role in the struggle of Mississippi's African American population to achieve voting rights.

During the 1960's Civil Rights movement, Mississippi was perhaps the most difficult and dangerous arena in which activists worked. Essentially a closed society on racial issues, white Mississippi fought tenaciously, often violently, to maintain a way of life based on white supremacy. While some civil rights groups sought to eliminate the state's dual society by pushing to desegregate schools and public accommodations, others worked to open up Mississippi through black political enfranchisement. One organization that played an important role in this effort was the Council of Federated Organizations (COFO).

Makeup of COFO

COFO was a unique coalition of the major civil rights groups operating in Mississippi. The council included the Student Nonviolent Coordinating Committee (SNCC), the Congress of Racial Equality (CORE), the National Association for the Advancement of Colored People (NAACP), and the Southern Christian Leadership Conference (SCLC). Initially formed in 1961 to assist jailed freedom riders in Jackson, COFO was revitalized in 1962 to increase the number of black registered voters. An additional purpose was to eliminate interorganizational competition over the distribution of foundation funds administered through the Voter Education Project (VEP).

Neither the NAACP nor the SCLC played significant roles in COFO, although Mississippi NAACP head Aaron Henry served as its president. SNCC, which supplied COFO with most of its staff and much of its operating funds, dominated the coalition.

Robert Moses, a soft-spoken Harvard graduate student and able veteran SNCC community organizer, served as voter project director; he was assisted by CORE's David Dennis, another activist skilled in grassroots voter-registration projects.

Few informed COFO staffers were unaware of Mississippi's history on black voting issues. This history had clearly indicated little white support for black political involvement. The first southern state to disfranchise its black electorate constitutionally, Mississippi had bolstered its legal impediments with extralegal efforts whenever it felt the status quo sufficiently threatened. Years of disfranchisement had combined with economic dependence, grinding poverty, rigid segregation, and educational deprivation to trap black Mississippians in an oppressive condition that often worked against direct challenges to white domination.

Significant challenges occurred. Influenced by the landmark *Brown v. Board of Education* Supreme Court decision (1954), in 1955 black Mississippians launched a major voter-registration drive. It ended in failure. Economic reprisals took their toll on many applicants, but the physical violence targeted against the leadership proved more effective. The year 1955 was especially bloody. Black Mississippi was convulsed by the murder of the city of Belzoni's NAACP president and voting-rights champion, George Lee, the near-assassination of his activist friend Gus Court, and the daylight murder of Brookhaven farmer and civil rights supporter Lamar Smith. Operating in such a repressive atmosphere, COFO's task would be difficult at best.

Voter Registration

In 1960, African Americans constituted 42 percent of Mississippi's population; when COFO began its registration campaign, however, only 5.3 percent of the eligible black population had surmounted the discriminatory laws to qualify as voters. Primarily involved in registering rural African Americans, particularly in the share-cropping delta counties, the organization encountered stiff white resistance and considerable black apprehension. Election officials devised ingenious harassment and delaying tactics against applicants. When such maneuvers or economic intimidation failed to dissuade black interest, violence again came into play. It raged in 1963 in key locations in the delta registration drive. Moses himself barely escaped being assassinated in Greenwood; however, he remained undaunted in his efforts.

Coalition leaders believed that only with federal intervention could any reasonable amount of success be expected, but little help or encouragement came from Washington. COFO did achieve greater success in disproving white myths about black voting indifference. The highlight of the organization's 1963 activities was its registration of black voters for its so-called Freedom Election. Eighty mostly white college students from Yale and Stanford Universities were recruited by veteran activist Allard Lowenstein to assist COFO staffers in the campaign. They helped to register eighty-two thousand persons for a mock election that coincided with the regularly scheduled gubernatorial election. Voters could cast ballots for the official candidates or the representatives of a "freedom slate," consisting of gubernatorial candidate Aaron Henry and his running mate, the Reverend Edwin King, a white Tougaloo College clergyman. Mississippi officials took little interest in the symbolic Henry/King victory, but the election demonstrated that black Mississippians were clearly interested in acquiring equal political rights and representation.

Freedom Summer

Moses and COFO organizers were encouraged by the Freedom Election. Its outcome added importance to a campaign announced by Dennis for a massive 1964 voter-organizing project dubbed "Freedom Summer." The project called for a large influx of mostly white college students to assist COFO staffers in registering black voters, establishing community centers, and organizing freedom schools to teach educationally deprived youths basic subjects and to teach adults voting techniques. Project plans also included the establishment of a new political organization, the Mississippi Freedom Democratic Party (MFDP). The party was to serve as an effective alternative to the all-white state Democratic Party and to challenge its delegation in the 1964 national convention.

Freedom Summer clearly bore the influence of Moses, who insisted that whites not be excluded from participating. Dennis agreed. The two leaders reasoned that exposing the children of prominent and affluent whites to the daily terror experienced by African Americans would dramatize effectively the need for federal protection and intervention in the Mississippi movement. It was a calculated motive upon which many SNCC staffers frowned, but one which later circumstances partially justified.

After a week of orientation and training in an Oxford, Ohio, women's college, hundreds of idealistic youth came to Mississippi to work in the summer project. Mississippi hastily mobilized to combat this "invasion," increasing the size of the highway patrol and enacting legislation designed to curb the project. Jackson's enlarged police force heavily armed itself and even purchased an armored tank. The Ku Klux Klan and similar extremist groups grew in numbers and influence.

The reality of conducting civil rights activity in the South's most racially oppressive state quickly confronted the volunteers. Numerous workers were falsely arrested, assaulted, or shot at; the homes and churches of many COFO partisans were bombed and burned; and election officials redoubled their efforts not to make concessions in administering Mississippi's discriminatory registration laws. The reign of terror struck fear in the hearts of workers and prospective black registrants.

Clearly, the greatest disruptive event of the summer project was the tragic disappearance of COFO workers James Chaney, Andrew Goodman, and Michael Schwerner. An intensive manhunt uncovered their bodies in Neshoba County on August 5, six weeks after the search began, in an earthen dam on a remote farm. Their kidnapping and assassination by Klansmen shocked the nation, partially bringing to reality COFO leaders' cynical prediction of government intervention if white youths became murder victims.

That intervention did not occur to the extent desired or expected by COFO workers. Still generally unprotected, the volunteers persisted in their activities, although their registration efforts remained largely ineffective. Throughout the rest of 1964, COFO's energies centered primarily on MFDP affairs, particularly on seeking the party's recognition as a vital political force. By the beginning of 1965, the coalition and the registration drive had essentially ended; COFO officially disbanded in 1966.

Confronting Violence

Nothing affected COFO's registration activities as much as the increased violence they provoked. The repercussions were widespread, affecting staff members and registrants, Mississippians and non-Mississippians alike. Violence had always been used by racial extremists against those who sought to undermine Mississippi's white supremacy, but at the height of the registration campaign its usage became more tenacious and its results more deadly. During Freedom Summer alone, in addition to the well-publicized Neshoba County lynchings, at least four other deaths occurred that were related to the state's accelerated civil rights activities. Slightly less grave were the more than one thousand arrests, thirty-five shootings, and eighty beatings, and the bombing or burning of sixty-five homes, churches, and other buildings.

The ever-present terror and the reluctance of the federal government to protect project workers and black registrants influenced the effectiveness of COFO in achieving its objectives. For working-class African Americans, the fear of physical reprisal often interacted with the reality of economic reprisal, creating a high price to pay for registering to vote. When added to the force of the state's discriminatory registration procedures, the results were discouraging. In the two years from 1962 to 1964, when COFO was functioning at its highest level, black voter registration increased by only 1.4 percent. Mississippi's 1964 registration rate of 6.7 percent for African Americans was the lowest in the nation. This lack of significant progress in Mississippi caused the Voter Education Project in late 1963 to divert its financial contributions from COFO to more promising voter projects.

Still, COFO persisted. The various campaign obstacles had a sobering effect on all involved, but the project also produced positive signs. The 1963 Freedom Election was convincing evidence of black voting aspirations, and it helped to stimulate interest across the state. This expanded interest continued into the summer project. Despite the summer's terrorism, some seventeen thousand African Americans were convinced to seek registration in their county courthouses, although only sixteen hundred actually succeeded. Additionally, the motivation translated into real grassroots political action in the form of the MFDP. The party did not gain recognition as the legitimate representative of Mississippi Democrats. Through the efforts of such personable and magnetic individuals as Fannie Lou Hamer, however, black Mississippians' political plight received further national exposure.

Legacy

Perhaps COFO's greatest contribution in the voting-rights struggle was its role in dramatizing the inhumanity of Mississippi's resistance to black political involvement. In so doing, it aided immeasurably the national call for a greater federal role in southern voting practices. COFO's project eventually thus achieved one of its deeper aims. Martin Luther King, Jr.'s Selma voting-rights campaign clearly influenced congressional passage of the 1965 Voting Rights Act, but COFO's Mississippi project was also significant.

Ultimately, COFO aided in opening Mississippi society and shaping its participatory political culture. In 1991, Mississippi had more black elected officials than any other state in the nation. With the country's largest percentage of African Americans in its population, Mississippi had achieved the meaningful political empowerment that many COFO idealists envisioned.

Robert L. Jenkins

Further Reading

Belfrage, Sally. *Freedom Summer.* New York: Viking Press, 1965. One of the best personal accounts to come out of the 1964 Freedom Summer project. Belfrage's book covers her training and orientation in Ohio and the ordeal of the white resistance in Mississippi.

Branch, Taylor. *Pillar of Fire: America in the King Years, 1963-65.* New York: Simon & Schuster, 1998.

Cagin, Seth, and Philip Dray. *We Are Not Afraid: The Story of Goodman, Schwerner, and Chaney and the Civil Rights Campaign in Mississippi.* New York: Macmillan, 1988. A detailed account of the murders of the three civil rights workers and the COFO Freedom Summer project. The authors do much to correct the often-repeated suggestion that the Federal Bureau of Investigation played a significant role in protecting the volunteers.

Carson, Clayborne. *In Struggle: SNCC and the Black Awakening of the 1960's*. Cambridge, Mass.: Harvard University Press, 1981. One of the best civil rights organizational histories available. Comprehensively treats the student group, its difficulties and successes, and its evolution from nonviolence to militancy in the mid-1960's. The coverage of Mississippi voting rights and COFO matters is especially good. Notes and index.

Dittmer, John. "The Politics of the Mississippi Movement, 1954-1964." In *The Civil Rights Movement in America*, edited by Charles W. Eagles. Jackson: University Press of Mississippi, 1986. A good analysis of the black Mississippi struggle. Dittmer understandably focuses much attention on the COFO project. Notes.

Holt, Len. *The Summer That Didn't End*. New York: William Morrow, 1965. The personal account of a black Washington, D.C., lawyer who came to Mississippi to work in the 1964 Freedom Summer project. Holt focuses on the civil rights worker murders and the individual COFO projects. Appendix and index.

Lawson, Steven F. *Black Ballots: Voting Rights in the South, 1944-1969*. New York: Columbia University Press, 1976. A comprehensive study of the black voting-rights struggle.

McAdam, Doug. *Freedom Summer*. New York: Oxford University Press, 1988. A sociohistorical study of the COFO volunteers and what influenced them. McAdam claims that the project forever changed these liberal whites, radicalizing them in ways that appeared in their post-1964 summer reform efforts. Appendix, notes, bibliography, and index.

McClymer, John F., ed. *Mississippi Freedom Summer*. Belmont, Calif.: Thomson/Wadsworth, 2004.

Meier, August, and Elliot Rudwick. *CORE: A Study in the Civil Rights Movement, 1942-1968*. New York: Oxford University Press, 1973. The most comprehensive and scholarly treatment of the Congress of Racial Equality. Includes much discussion of CORE's involvement in the Mississippi voting-rights struggle. References, notes, and index.

Silver, James W. *Mississippi: The Closed Society*. New York: Harcourt, Brace & World, 1964. The classic indictment of Mississippi and its reluctance to address change in its racial order. The book's genesis was primarily the violent white reaction to the integration of the University of Mississippi.

Zinn, Howard. *SNCC: The New Abolitionists*. Cambridge, Mass.: South End Press, 2002. Although not a formal history, this book is a penetrating analysis of SNCC by one of its first historians, who was also its adviser. Although dated, it remains essential reading for understanding this organization, which formed the largest part of the COFO coalition.

See also Disfranchisement laws in Mississippi; Gerrymandering; Mississippi Freedom Democratic Party; University of Mississippi desegregation; *Williams v. Mississippi*

Cowboys

Definition: African Americans who worked as ranch hands on the Western frontier

The contribution of the African American cowboy to the westward movement and the settlement of the western United States is undeniable.

Despite the predominantly white images in television and film Westerns, many cowboys were African American. Attracted by the high wages and the pull of the open range, the cowboys were a diverse lot that included former Civil War soldiers, former African American slaves, Mexicans, and American Indians. Evidence suggests that perhaps as many as 25 percent of cowboys were African American. Most of these African Americans were unable to read or write, so few records of their daily life exist, but like their peers, they spent as many as four straight months in the saddle, working the long drives. The cowboy's job was dangerous, hard, and lonely.

Because cowboys had to work together to herd cattle on trails, segregation was impractical, but African American cowboys were constantly reminded of the inequalities of the time. Pay for African American cowboys was frequently less than for their

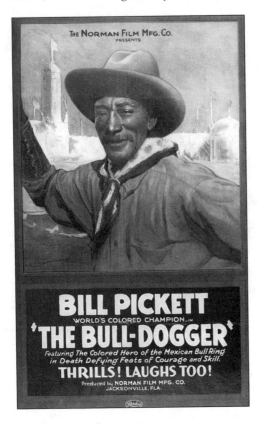

Although black contributions to opening the West were ignored by the white-dominated Hollywood film industry, a parallel black film industry celebrated its own Western heroes. A real cowboy of African and Native American descent, Bill Pickett (1870-1932) competed successfully in rodeos until banned because of his African heritage and had a twenty-six-year career in Wild West shows and films. He died from a kick in the head by a horse while working on a ranch. (Library of Congress)

white counterparts, and segregation was common in cattle towns along the trail. Despite the discrimination they faced, however, the contribution of the African American cowboy to the westward movement and the settlement of the western United States is indisputable.

Donald C. Simmons, Jr.

See also Film history; Segregation on the frontier; Stereotypes

Crown Heights conflicts

The Event: Racial unrest between Hasidic Jews and their immigrant neighbors
Date: August, 1991
Place: Brooklyn, New York

*The disturbances led to investigations at both the state and national lev-
els. The Justice Department also conducted investigations of possible
civil rights violations.*

Crown Heights, a racially mixed section of Brooklyn, New York,
began to experience civil unrest in the late 1980's. Many of the residents are poor black immigrants from Caribbean countries and
Lubavitchers. The latter are Orthodox (Hasidic) Jews who maintain a strong religious identity that is reflected in their dress and
their insularity. These groups had been subjected to stereotyping
and victimized by discrimination, from both within and without the Crown Heights community. African American leaders
charged that the Lubavitchers received better treatment from local authorities than that accorded black residents, and Hasidic
leaders countered that black anti-Semitism made Lubavitchers
victims of street crimes and subject to continual harassment.

Triggering the Violence
     The racial unrest erupted into full-scale rioting in the summer
of 1991, on the heels of the accidental killing of a seven-year-old
Guyanese American youth named Gavin Cato. On the evening of
August 19, a car carrying the Lubavitcher Grand Rebbe and
Menachem Schneerson, a Hasidic spiritual leader, ran a red light
at the intersection of President Street and Utica Avenue, striking
and killing Cato and injuring his cousin, Angela. As a crowd
gathered at the scene, a private Jewish ambulance whisked away
the Hasidic driver, Yosef Lifsh, and his two passengers. Their de-
parture spurred an angry reaction, leading, three hours later,
to the fatal stabbing of Yankel Rosenbaum, a visiting Hasidic
professor from Australia, and the arrest of his alleged attacker, a
sixteen-year-old Trinidadian American and Brooklyn resident,
Lemrick Nelson, Jr.
     In the predawn hours of August 20, after Rosenbaum's death
at Kings County Hospital, protests escalated into mob violence,
with African Americans and Hasidic Jews fighting with words,
stones, and bottles, ignoring police efforts to stop the rioting. The
violence continued through the next two days, fed by the rumor
(later shown to be true) that the Hasidic driver, Lifsh, had left on a

plane bound for Israel. Black leaders, including the Reverend Al Sharpton and Alton Maddox, demanded the arrest and return of Lifsh, and their followers rebuffed the efforts of New York mayor David Dinkins and police commissioner Lee Brown to restore peace, especially after learning that Nelson had been charged with second-degree murder in Rosenbaum's death. By August 24, rioting finally gave way to protest marches and an uneasy peace maintained by auxiliary police units that had been sent into Crown Heights to restore order.

In the months following the demonstrations, both groups complained that the police and city officials did little to solve the community's problems. In September, the Brooklyn grand jury refused to indict Lifsh in the death of Cato, angering the black citizens and their leaders. More unrest followed in October, 1992, when Nelson was acquitted of all charges in Rosenbaum's death. The Hasidic Jews protested and within a month filed a class-action suit against the city government on the grounds of unfair treatment in the 1991 riots.

The disturbances led to investigations at both the state and national levels. One major New York report issued in July, 1993, by Richard Girgenti, state director of criminal justice, was highly critical of both Mayor Dinkins and Commissioner Brown. The report, forwarded to the U.S. Attorney General, also led to ongoing Justice Department investigations of possible civil rights violations.

John W. Fiero

See also Black Jews; "Black Manifesto"; Hawkins murder; Jews and African Americans

Cubans and African Americans

The tension that arose between African Americans and post-1959 Cuban refugees in the Miami area of Florida (Dade County) represents an illuminating case study of the effects of immigration on urban racial and ethnic relations in the late twentieth century.

In the late twentieth century, the attitude of African Americans and their organizations to immigration was one of ambivalence. As a minority group, African Americans could not consistently oppose immigration as a threat to some imagined American cultural or ethnic purity. Yet many African Americans, struggling against discrimination and disadvantage, feared immigrants as competitors for scarce jobs and public services. In Dade County, Florida, unrestricted immigration from Cuba after Fidel Castro took power in 1959 fed the anxieties of black Miami residents about economic displacement and political disempowerment. The black riots that erupted in Miami in 1980, 1982, and 1989, although ostensibly sparked by police brutality, were widely ascribed by contemporary commentators to resentment against Cuban refugees.

Cuban Refugees

Tensions between African Americans and black immigrants from Jamaica and Haiti have been mitigated somewhat by a shared African heritage; with the refugee flow from Cuba, however, this factor did not come into play as much. When Castro took power in Cuba in 1959, people of full or partial African descent constituted nearly 40 percent of the total population of Cuba; yet 90 percent or more of the Cuban refugees of the 1960's and early 1970's were white. It was not until the Mariel boatlift of May to September, 1980, that the proportion of Afro-Cubans in the refugee flow came to approximate that of the island's population.

By the beginning of 1980, many of the Cuban refugees of the 1960's and early 1970's, who had arrived nearly penniless, had grown prosperous. Such success was due to the relatively high proportion of professionals and entrepreneurs among the earliest refugees, the refugees' hard work, and the generous assistance (about $2.6 billion between 1972 and 1976) that the refugees, as defectors from a communist regime, received from the federal government to help defray the costs of vocational training and retraining, transportation, and resettlement. African Americans complained that the refugees received more assistance than either other immigrants or poor native-born Americans did. The

Mariel boatlift refugees of May to September, 1980, and refugees who arrived after that year did not, however, receive as much government help as the earlier waves of immigrants.

African Americans also complained about the way refugees benefited from federal programs not specifically targeted at refugees. When affirmative action policies were implemented in the late 1960's to provide set-asides for minority businesses, Hispanics were considered to be a minority and Cubans were Hispanics; hence, refugee-owned businesses were judged to qualify as minority-owned businesses. Local African Americans resented what they saw as poaching by white newcomers on an entitlement originally intended for African Americans.

Immigration Status of Cubans as Bone of Contention

From 1959 to 1980, hardly any Cuban reaching U.S. shores was deported. The Cuban Adjustment Act of 1966 enabled all Cuban refugees to change their status to that of permanent resident after one year of living in the United States; other immigrants did not enjoy this privilege. After 1972, more and more Haitians, like Cubans, tried to reach the United States. Cubans fleeing by boat were always welcomed. In contrast, Haitians fleeing by boat were unceremoniously sent back to Haiti if intercepted at sea, detained in prison if they reached Florida, and often deported. Although the official justification for the disparity in treatment was ideological (Cuba was communist; Haiti was not), many Miami black activists perceived racism. Many Cuban escapees were white; almost all Haitian escapees were black. In May, 1995, U.S. president Bill Clinton officially ended the privileged status of Cuban refugees. When the first Cuban escapees were sent back to Cuba, on May 10, Miami Cubans staged a four-day action of civil disobedience; Miami's native-born African Americans stayed away from the protest.

Between 1968 and 1989, there were several episodes of rioting by black Miamians, the bloodiest of which took place in 1980. The riots of 1980, 1982, and 1989 were widely attributed by journalists and scholars to the resentment of black Miami residents against Cuban refugees, although this was only one reason. All the riots stemmed from responses to alleged police misuse of force. In 1982 and 1989, the officers who used force were Hispanic, and Cubans did tend to rally around Hispanic police officers accused of brutality. Yet conflict between blacks and police officers had existed even before the mass arrival of Cuban refugees.

Although one victim of black violence in the 1980 riot was a Cuban refugee, other victims were non-Hispanic whites: The mob was as much antiwhite as anti-Cuban. Nor were native-born African Americans the only ones to complain about police brutality. In 1992, an incident of police violence against a Haitian in a Cuban-owned store aroused protest; and in 1990, Miami's Puerto Ricans also rioted against an alleged police abuse of force.

Job Displacement and Conflict in Local Politics

Whether Cuban refugees gained occupationally at the expense of Miami's African Americans is a controversial issue, although local black leaders lodged complaints about such displacement as early as the early 1960's. Allegations that Cubans ousted African Americans from service jobs in hotels and restaurants were met by counterallegations that African Americans were themselves leaving such jobs voluntarily and that the percentage of Miami African Americans in white-collar jobs had increased by 1980. By founding many new businesses, Cuban refugees created jobs; many such jobs, however, went to fellow refugees rather than to African Americans. As the Hispanic population grew and trade links with Latin America expanded, native-born African Americans were hurt by the job requirement of fluency in Spanish. Although the Miami area economic pie grew during the 1960's and 1970's, the African American slice of that pie, scholars concede, was stagnant; compared with pre-1980 Cuban refugees, they suffered in 1980 from greater poverty and unemployment and had a lower rate of entrepreneurship.

From 1960 to 1990, the Hispanic percentage of Dade County's population (most, but not all of it, Cuban) rose from barely 10 percent to 49 percent; the black percentage of the county's population never rose above 20 percent. By the late 1970's, more and more Cuban refugees were becoming naturalized U.S. citizens, gaining both the right to vote and a decisive weight in local politics. In 1983, the Puerto Rican-born mayor dismissed the black city manager, replacing him with a Cuban. Cuban American candidates defeated African American candidates for the posts of mayor of Miami in 1985, Dade County Schools superintendent in 1990, Dade County district attorney in 1993, and mayor of Dade County in 1996. The Cuban influx into elective politics prevented a black takeover of city hall (as had taken place in Atlanta, Georgia, and Detroit, Michigan), thereby reducing the chances for black businesspeople to benefit from municipal contracts. Yet African Americans' powerlessness was relative: They could vote and affect the outcome of elections.

The Nelson Mandela Affair and the Miami Boycott

In spring of 1990, Mayor Xavier Suar persuaded the Miami city government to withdraw its official welcome to Nelson Mandela, the leader of the black liberation struggle in South Africa, who was then touring the United States. Mandela, in a television interview, had praised Castro. Partly in response to this slap at Mandela, a Miami black civil rights leader, H. T. Smith, called for a nationwide boycott by black organizations of Miami-area hotels; this boycott was remarkably effective. It was ended in 1993 with an agreement promising greater efforts to employ African Americans in Miami's hospitality industry.

Dade County's politics were not simply a Cuban-African American struggle. Sometimes African Americans saw non-Hispanic whites as allies against the Cubans: In his losing bid for Congress against a Cuban American in 1989, the non-Hispanic white candidate won most of the black votes. Sometimes African Americans saw both Cubans and non-Hispanic whites as oppressors of African Americans. In a lawsuit that met with success in 1992, African Americans and Cubans cooperated in an effort to make the Dade County Commission more representative of ethnic minorities.

African Americans did not always form a united front against the Cubans: In a 1980 referendum ending the provision of Spanish-language documents and services by the Dade County government, black voters split, 44 percent for the proposition and 56 percent against. (Bilingualism was restored in 1993.) Haitians and native-born African Americans did not agree on all issues; among non-Hispanic whites, white ethnic migrants from the North did not always agree with white Anglo-Saxon Protestants of southern background; and some of Miami's non-Cuban Hispanics resented Cuban predominance.

In other major U.S. cities, Cubans were, if present at all, a smaller part of the larger Hispanic group. Only in Miami did Hispanics build up a powerful political machine; hence, black resentment of Hispanic political power played little role in race relations elsewhere. The police brutality issue also operated differently: in Compton, California, Washington, D.C., and Detroit, Michigan, for example, there were complaints, in the early 1990's, about alleged brutality by black police officers against Hispanics.

Paul D. Mageli

Further Reading

Ruth Reitan's *The Rise and Decline of an Alliance: Cuba and African American Leaders in the 1960's* (East Lansing: Michigan State University Press, 1999) is a valuable contribution to the study of Cuban and African American relations. *Between Race and Empire: African-Americans and Cubans Before the Cuban Revolution* (Philadelphia, Pa.: Temple University Press, 1998) edited by Lisa Brock and Digna Castañeda Fuertes is an illuminating study of early relations between the two groups. In *Imagining Miami* (Charlottesville: University Press of Virginia, 1997), the best introductory study, Sheila Croucher attacks the notion that either the black or the Cuban community is a monolith. Her analysis of the Mandela affair and the subsequent boycott is especially enlightening. Marvin Dunn's *Black Miami in the Twentieth Century* (Tallahassee: University of Florida Press, 1997) is informative on the riots. On the politics of bilingualism, consult Max Castro's essay in Guillermo J. Grenier and Alexis Stepick's *Miami Now!* (Tallahassee: University Press of Florida, 1992). The displacement thesis is presented most clearly in historian Raymond A. Mohl's "On the Edge: Blacks and Hispanics in Metropolitan Miami Since 1959," *Florida Historical Quarterly* (vol. 69, no. 1, July, 1990). For rebuttals of this thesis, consult chapter 3 of Alex Stepick and Alejandro

Portes's *City on the Edge: The Transformation of Miami* (Berkeley: University of California Press, 1993) and Alex Stepick and Guillermo Grenier's "Cubans in Miami," in *In the Barrios: Latinos and the Underclass Debate*, edited by Joan Moore and Raquel Pinderhughes (New York: Russell Sage Foundation, 1993). *City on the Edge* is also informative on Miami's Haitians.

See also Haitians; Irish and African Americans; Jamaicans; Miami riots; West Indians

Cumming v. Richmond County Board of Education

The Case: U.S. Supreme Court ruling on separate but equal doctrine

Date: December 18, 1899

The Supreme Court refused to enforce the equal stipulation in the separate but equal doctrine governing segregated schools that had been established in its landmark 1896 decision.

Just three years after announcing the separate but equal doctrine in *Plessy v. Ferguson* (1896), the Supreme Court unanimously refused to take action in a case in which school facilities for black and white people were definitely unequal. *Cumming*, which amounted to the Court's first approval of racially segregated public schools, was never overturned. John Marshall Harlan, who wrote the opinion for the Court, had dissented vigorously in *Plessy* but was unable to find a clear, unmistakable disregard of equality in *Cumming*.

In 1879 the Augusta, Georgia, school board had established the first African American public high school in the state. The board closed the school in 1897, claiming that the money was needed for black primary school education. Because a Georgia statute explicitly provided for separate but equal facilities, the local judge did not bother to consider the U.S. Constitution in overturning the board's judgment. Still, the Georgia supreme court, without offering any significant reasons, overturned the local judge's opinion.

African Americans argued that under the Fourteenth Amendment's equal protection clause, they were entitled to a high school if one was provided for white students. However, Harlan asserted that the African American plaintiffs had to prove the board decision was motivated exclusively by hostility toward African Americans, which was impossible to prove. To reach his decision, Harlan ignored several lower court precedents that went in the opposite direction.

Richard L. Wilson

See also *Brown v. Board of Education*; Fourteenth Amendment; *Plessy v. Ferguson*

Defense industry desegregation

The Event: President Franklin D. Roosevelt's issuing of Executive Order 8802, which prohibited discrimination of race or color in the defense industry and armed forces
Date: June 25, 1941

The 1941 desegregation of the U.S. defense industry was a major step in the advancement of African American civil rights and black-white relations.

Ever since the Revolutionary War, the United States had experienced difficulty in bringing African Americans into its military. Although one of the victims of the Boston massacre, Crispus Attucks, was an African American, and black soldiers were with George Washington when he made his famous 1776 Christmas crossing of the Delaware River to attack the Hessians at Trenton and Princeton, it was not until the Civil War (1861-1865) that African American troops were recruited officially into the United States Army. Even then, however, a rigid policy of segregation was maintained. In the two wars that followed, the Spanish-American War (1898) and World War I (1914-1919), both the Army and Navy had black troops, but largely in supporting roles, and always as separate, segregated units. In addition, black troop strength was kept deliberately low, partly to avoid offending white soldiers and partly because the military establishment had a low opinion of the abilities of African American troops.

Roosevelt's Role

During the 1930's, however, under the presidency of Franklin D. Roosevelt, these prejudiced traditions began to change. Roosevelt's New Deal, which had been put into place to fight the ravages of the Great Depression, also addressed a number of social conditions, including civil rights. Although civil rights were never at the forefront of Roosevelt's agenda, his administration was more committed to them than any previous presidency had been, and his wife, the redoubtable Eleanor Roosevelt, was an especially strong and capable advocate for racial equality and justice. In addition, the shrewdly realistic president, who foresaw the coming struggle with Nazi Germany, realized that the U.S. military needed every capable citizen, of whatever color or background. The policy of "Jim Crowism," or rigid segregation of black and white people, remained largely in place, however.

Correctly estimating the extent and depth of prejudice against African American participation in the military, especially in positions of responsibility, Roosevelt moved cautiously. He had been assistant secretary of the Navy under President Woodrow Wilson during World War I, and he now prodded and encouraged the Navy high command to enlist additional African Americans and to place them in positions of greater responsibility than stewards or mess servers.

Gradually and slowly, the Navy responded. A similar broadening took place in the Army in 1935, when the president insisted that African American medical officers and chaplains be called up from the reserves. On October 9, 1940, Roosevelt announced a revised racial policy for the armed forces; its intent was to bring more African Americans into the military and to place them in positions of trust and responsibility. At a glacial but perceptible pace, the United States military was becoming more receptive to African Americans.

Despite President Franklin D. Roosevelt's order to desegregate the defense in-dustries, African American women were not permitted to serve in the U.S. Navy's Women Accepted for Voluntary Emergency Service (WAVES) until 1944. (National Archives)

Slow Progress

The progress was not sufficiently rapid for many African Americans, among them A. Philip Randolph, president of the Brotherhood of Sleeping Car Porters, one of the strongest and most effective African American unions in the country. Randolph, who well understood that black voters had become an essential part of the Democratic Party's electoral base, calculated that Roosevelt would need to respond to African American demands, especially as the 1940 presidential elections approached. Randolph's logic and timing were correct.

In 1940, Roosevelt ran for an unprecedented third term as president. Randolph, along with former Republican city councilman Grant Reynolds of New York City, began a campaign against the Jim Crow practices still prevalent in the United States military. Randolph and Reynolds also called for greater opportunities for African American workers in the rapidly growing defense industries, which had arisen as the United States rearmed against the threat from Nazi Germany and imperialist Japan. As the campaign intensified, Roosevelt faced a difficult situation that threatened his southern, conservative support at the same time that it endangered his urban, liberal allies. When Randolph announced plans for a march on Washington, scheduled for July 1, 1941, Roosevelt knew he must act. His determination was steeled by the resolve of his wife, Eleanor, who had long been a champion of equal rights for African Americans, and whose contacts with the black community were strong and deep.

Executive Order 8802

On June 25, 1941, Roosevelt issued Executive Order 8802, which enunciated a broad policy of racial equality in the armed forces and the defense industry. The order was clear and sweeping in its intent:

> In offering the policy of full participation in the defense program by all persons regardless of color, race, creed, or national origin, and directing certain action in furtherance of said policy . . . all departments of the government, including the Armed Forces, shall lead the way in erasing discrimination over color or race.

President Roosevelt backed up the policy by establishing the Fair Employment Practices Committee, which was charged with monitoring and enforcing compliance among civilian contractors. It is estimated that Roosevelt's executive order, combined with the work of the commission, helped to bring fifty-three thousand African American civilians into defense industry jobs they otherwise would not have held.

The timing of the policy was impeccable. Randolph and the other campaign leaders, satisfied that the Roosevelt administration was sincere in its commitment to civil rights, called off the march on Washington. Political conservatives, who otherwise might have challenged the president's order, had to admit that it would not be proper to expect African Americans to serve in the military without allowing them to hold responsible positions and achieve corresponding rank. Black voters responded enthusiastically to the Roosevelt reelection campaign, helping him to sweep to victory in the November balloting.

Inevitably, there were racial tensions and outbreaks of violence, especially in lower- and middle-class northern neighborhoods. In 1943, for example, tension between black and white workers led to open violence at a park on Belle Isle near Detroit; in the end, federal troops had to be called in to restore order, and twenty-five African Americans and nine whites had been killed. Similar, if less bloody, events took place in other cities. Still, the transition to a more equitable situation continued in both civilian and military life.

However, the traditional segregation remained. During World War II, black units still were kept separate and apart from white troops, and were generally reserved for support and logistical duties rather than combat. When the difficulties and emergencies of battle required it, African American units were brought into the fighting line; generally, they acquitted themselves well. By the end of the war, African Americans had distinguished themselves as ground soldiers, sailors, and pilots in both combat and noncombat situations. After the surrender of the Axis Powers in 1945, there was a sense of inevitable change ahead for the United States military. The question of whether it would be a peaceful, productive change remained.

After World War II

Harry S. Truman, who assumed the presidency in 1945 after the death of Franklin D. Roosevelt, was determined to make the change in a proper fashion. He assembled a special Civil Rights Committee which, on October 30, 1947, issued its report, *To Secure These Rights*. Clearly and unhesitatingly, the report called for the elimination of segregation in the United States military.

As the 1948 presidential elections approached, the issue of African Americans in the military affected the political atmosphere. Truman and the national Democratic Party, as heirs of the Roosevelt New Deal, had strong connections with the Civil Rights movement and its leaders; at the same time, much of the traditional Democratic strength was in the South, where civil rights issues were strongly opposed by the entrenched establishment. Southern politicians, such as Strom Thurmond of South Carolina, threatened to bolt the party if the Democrats adopted a strong civil rights platform at their convention; however, inspired by the passionate appeal of Mayor Hubert H. Humphrey of Minneapolis, the Democrats did indeed adopt a positive plank on civil rights. The southerners stormed out, nominating Thurmond to run on the "Dixiecrat" ticket, and Truman went on to win a come-from-behind victory in November.

One element of that victory was Truman's own Executive Order 9981, issued on July 26, 1948, just after the Democratic Party convention. Truman's order was similar to but stronger than Roosevelt's: It required equal opportunity in the armed forces of the United States, regardless of race, and called upon the military services to move immediately to implement the directive. The Air Force reacted promptly and soon achieved remarkable integration of black and white troops; the Navy and Marines were more hesitant in their acceptance. In the end, however, all branches of the armed forces responded, making them among the most egalitarian and equitable of U.S. institutions.

Michael Witkoski

Further Reading

Richard Dalifiume's *Desegregation of the U.S. Armed Forces: Fighting on Two Fronts, 1939-1953* (Columbia: University of Missouri Press, 1969) emphasizes the role of African Americans as soldiers, sailors, and airmen and sheds additional light on Roosevelt's order and its impact. Bernard C. Nalty's *Strength for the Fight: A History of Black Americans in the Military* (New York: Free Press, 1986) provides a comprehensive narrative of the relationship between African Americans and the U.S. armed forces. Richard Stillman's *Integration of the Negro in the U.S. Armed Forces* (New York: Frederick A. Praeger, 1968) provides an especially good discussion of the Roosevelt and Truman policies regarding blacks in the military. The U.S. Department of Defense's *Black Americans in Defense of Our Nation* (Washington, D.C.: Government Printing Office, 1991) is a pictorial documentary that covers all branches of the armed forces and includes defense- and military-related occupations as well. C. Vann Woodward's *The Strange Career of Jim Crow* (2d rev. ed., New York: Oxford University Press, 1966) has remained a definitive work on legal and official segregation in American life.

See also Brotherhood of Sleeping Car Porters; Fair Employment Practices Committee; Integration; Military; Military desegregation; President's Committee on Civil Rights; Race riots of 1943; World War II

Demographic trends

Definition: Historical changes in the size, composition, characteristics, and geographical distribution of African Americans

During their long history in North America, African Americans have constituted one of the largest population groups in the Western Hemisphere, and their demographic history is a major part of American history. Since the first Africans arrived in North America during the early seventeenth century, the African American population has grown to reach a total of thirty-six million people—a number greater than the populations of about 158 members of the 191 countries in the United Nations in the year 2005.

The first African slaves arrived in Virginia in 1619. Through the following years, more people from Africa began appearing throughout the new colonies established by Europeans on the eastern coast of North America. The first slaves came to the Dutch lands in the northeast in 1626. The Dutch colonial city of New Amsterdam, later New York, had 100 African slaves in 1640, nearly one-third of the settlement's total population. By the time the English conquered the Dutch colony in 1664, an estimated 1,500 people were living in New Amsterdam, 300 of whom were slaves of African origin.

The Slave Population
With the growth of plantation economies in Virginia and surrounding areas from the late seventeenth century onward, the South became the main destination for people from Africa. During the 1680's, slave traders transported 2,000 Africans into Vir-

African American Population Growth, 1790-2000, with Projections Through 2050

Year	Total African Americans	Percentage of total population
1790	757,208	19.3
1800	1,002,037	18.9
1810	1,377,808	19.0
1820	1,771,656	18.4
1830	2,328,642	18.1
1840	2,873,648	16.8
1850	3,638,808	15.7
1860	4,441,830	14.1
1870	5,392,172	13.5
1880	6,580,973	13.1
1890	7,488,676	11.9
1900	8,833,994	11.6
1910	9,797,763	10.7
1920	10,463,131	9.9
1930	11,891,843	9.7
1940	12,865,518	9.8
1950	15,042,286	10.0
1960	18,871,831	10.5
1970	22,580,000	11.0
1980	26,945,025	11.7
1990	29,986,060	12.1
2000	35,818,000	12.7
2010	40,454,000	13.1
2020	45,365,000	13.5
2030	50,442,000	13.9
2040	55,876,000	14.3
2050	61,361,000	14.6

Source: U.S. Bureau of the Census, Census of Population and Housing, 2000; U.S. Interim Projections by Age, Race, and Hispanic Origin, 2004.

ginia, and this number increased to about 4,000 in the following decade. Arrivals from Africa doubled again, to an estimated 8,000 in the first decade of the eighteenth century.

In South Carolina and Georgia, the slave trade led to so rapid an increase in the African population in the early eighteenth century, that there were about twice as many people of African descent as whites in this part of the South by the 1720's, when arrivals from Africa had risen to 2,000 per year.

Spanish-held Florida also contained large numbers of free blacks, as well as slaves, at that time, and one-fourth of the 1,500 people in the Florida city of St. Augustine were of African ancestry in 1746. At the mouth of the Mississippi River, African slaves had arrived in Louisiana with French settlers in the early eighteenth century, but their numbers increased slowly until the Spanish took control of Louisiana in 1769. Under the Spanish and then after the return to French possession, Louisiana rapidly developed an economy based on plantation slave labor.

Post-Eighteenth Century Trends

The numbers of African Americans have increased steadily over the course of American history. At the same time, the total American population has also grown. African Americans made up a much larger percentage of Americans at the beginning of the nation's history than at any time since. By the time of the first U.S. Census in 1790, the African origin population had grown to a reported 757,208 people—a figure that represented nearly one-fifth of the new nation's entire population.

Before the mid-twentieth century, African Americans were highly concentrated in the South, where they made up an estimated one-third of the population from 1790 until the Civil War (1861-1865). Although the numbers of African Americans grew steadily through the first half of the nineteenth century, the European population—thanks to increased immigration—grew even more rapidly, so that the proportion of African Americans decreased through that period. By 1840, people of African descent made up slightly under 17 percent of the total population. This figure fell to slightly under 16 percent in 1850 and 14 percent in 1860.

Part of the slower growth of African Americans, compared to Europeans, was due to the fact that the U.S. Constitution had officially ended the importation of slaves from Africa in 1808. Although some slaves continued to be smuggled into the country after that date, the end of the legal shipment of slaves from across the Atlantic did slow down African American population growth.

The United States has always had a free black population, but most African Americans were held in slavery until the end of the Civil War. Of the 757,208 people of African ancestry in the country in 1790, less than 8 percent (59,406) were free. In 1850, 434,495 "free colored" people (the term used by the census that year) lived in the United States. This meant that slightly under 89 percent of all African Americans remained slaves in the middle of the nineteenth century.

Immediately after the Civil War ended in 1865, the Thirteenth Amendment abolished slavery throughout the United States. Immigration from Europe then increased greatly, with virtually no immigration from Africa. This disparity resulted in a steady decline in the African American proportion of the nation. By 1920, African Americans made up less than one-tenth of all Americans. After World War II ended in 1945, the African American proportion of the national population began to rise once again. By the beginning of the twenty-first century, slightly under 13 percent of Americans were of African ancestry, and that proportion was expected to continue to increase slowly until the middle of the new century.

Geographical Distribution

By the time of the American Revolution, slavery was concentrated in the plantation-farming regions of the South. Virginia, with an economy based on tobacco production, was one of the African American population centers. Rice and sugarcane in South Carolina and Louisiana were tended by slaves. With the invention of the cotton gin during the 1790's, cotton became a highly profitable plantation crop and its cultivation rapidly spread throughout the South. The concentration of slave labor in the South meant that African Americans were also concentrated

Geographical Distribution
of African Americans, 1870-2002

Year	Northeast	Midwest	South	West
1870	4.4	4.8	90.6	<0.1%
1880	3.4	5.4	91.2	<0.1%
1890	3.6	5.8	90.3	<0.1%
1900	5.1	5.7	88.8	0.3
1910	5.3	5.9	88.1	0.8
1920	6.9	7.2	85.2	0.6
1930	9.6	10.6	78.7	1.0
1940	10.3	11.3	76.9	1.5
1950	12.8	13.5	70.2	3.5
1960	16.1	18.2	60.6	5.1
1970	19.7	19.3	54.1	6.9
1980	18.0	20.4	53.4	8.2
1990	15.5	16.2	58.7	9.6
2000	17.6	18.8	54.8	8.9
2002	18.1	18.1	55.3	8.6

Source: Steven Ruggles et al., *Integrated Public Use Microdata Series: Version 3.0* (Minneapolis: Minnesota Population Center, 2004); Jesse McKinnon, *The Black Population in the United States* (U.S. Census Bureau, Current Population Reports, March 2002).

there. In 1800, 92.7 percent of all people classified as "black" by the U.S. Census in that year lived in southern states.

Some southern states had fairly large free black populations. In 1850, Maryland, which is considered a "border" southern state, had 74,723 free blacks—the largest number of any state at that time. Virginia, with a free black population of 54,333, had the second largest number. A few northern states also had significant numbers of free black residents. Pennsylvania's 53,626 free blacks in 1850 made it home to the third-largest free black population in the country. During that same year, New York, with 49,069 "free colored" people had the fourth-largest group.

After the Civil War, African Americans were no longer slaves, but they remained overwhelmingly concentrated in the South. In 1870, more than nine of every ten African Americans still lived in the South, and this continued to be true throughout the nineteenth century. The first "Great Migration" from the South to northern cities took place during the early twentieth century, particularly during and just after World War I.

One of the primary northern destinations of black southerners was the city of Chicago. In part, the popularity of Chicago was a result of the work of Robert S. Abbott, a businessman and publisher of the widely read newspaper the *Chicago Defender*. On May 15, 1917, Abbott began promoting what he called "The Great Northern Drive," a campaign urging the oppressed people of the South to move north. Chicago's African American population more than doubled during the second decade of the twentieth century: from 44,000 in 1910 to 109,000 in 1920. Over the following ten years, it more than doubled again, to 234,000.

Movement to northern cities such as Chicago transformed the national distribution of African Americans. By 1930, few than 79 percent of African Americans were still living in the South. About one out of every ten lived in the Northeast, and one out of every ten lived in the Midwest. During the 1930's, the northward migration began to slow. Plantation owners resisted the loss of sharecroppers and other laborers. As northern jobs grew scarce during the Depression years, the attraction of Chicago and other northern cities diminished.

The next great shift in the distribution of African Americans occurred during World War II and the years following it. Between 1940 and 1970, an estimated 5,000,000 African Americans left the southern countryside for the cities of the North. In 1940, nearly 77 percent of all African Americans still lived in the South; by 1950, this figure had dropped slightly more than 70 percent and by 1960 to slightly more than 60 percent. By 1970, 1 in 5 African Americans lived in the Northeast and 1 in 5 lived in the Midwest. The West showed an even higher rate of increase. Before World War II, slightly fewer than 2 percent of the entire African American population lived in the West; by 1990, nearly 10 percent lived there.

Despite these changes, by the early years of the twenty-first century, a majority of African Americans still lived in the South. Even within the South, however, there had been a great change in where people lived. African Americans began the twentieth century living primarily in the southern countryside; they began the twenty-first century residing mostly in city centers.

From the Country to the City

Before 1920, most Americans of all races lived in rural areas. African Americans, however, were even more likely than others to live in the countryside. In 1870, nearly 87 percent of African Americans were rural residents, compared to about 72 percent of white Americans. The 1920 census was the first to show a majority of Americans living in or around cities. In that year, close to two-thirds of African Americans still lived in rural areas, though.

Until World War II, African Americans remained more likely than whites to live in the country, and a majority of African Americans were rural residents. After the war, both tendencies began to change rapidly. From 1940 to 2000, the proportion of African Americans living in rural areas went steadily down, from just above 50 percent to only about 10 percent. The proportion of white rural residents were 38-39 percent in 1940 and 1950, and that proportion fluctuated around 25 percent from 1960 to 2000.

The disappearance of agricultural jobs encouraged the movement of African Americans to cities. By the 1960's, the sharecropper system, under which landless farmers paid landowners for the use of land with a large share of harvests, had virtually disappeared in most of the South. Mechanization had reduced the need for human labor. In 1967, the U.S. government included agricultural workers under its minimum wage law. As a result, farmworkers immediately became much more expensive for southern planters, who became even more dependent on machines and used more chemical herbicides, instead of field workers, to combat weeds. After centuries of heavy African American concentration in agriculture, agricultural jobs were finally disappearing.

African Americans went through a dramatic demographic change, from an almost entirely rural group at the beginning of the twentieth century to an almost entirely urban group at the

Percentages of African Americans and White Americans Living in Central Cities, 1870-2002

Year	African American	White
1870	4.7	13.7
1880	5.8	15.8
1890	NA	NA
1900	11.0	23.9
1910	15.5	28.1
1920	21.3	31.9
1930	NA	NA
1940	27.5	28.6
1950	33.2	26.4
1960	47.1	26.2
1970	NA	NA
1980	57.2	23.9
1990	54.9	22.4
2000	52.7	21.3
2002	51.5	21.1

Source: Steven Ruggles et al., *Integrated Public Use Microdata Series: Version 3.0* (Minneapolis: Minnesota Population Center, 2004); Jesse McKinnon, *The Black Population in the United States* (U.S. Census Bureau, Current Population Reports, March 2002).

century's end. Moreover, African Americans became concentrated in the central areas of cities. In the late nineteenth century, about 1 in 20 African Americans lived in a central city. Until 1950, fewer African Americans than whites lived in central city areas. By the beginning of the twenty-first century, however, more than half of all African Americans not only lived in urban areas, but lived in the centers of urban areas. This contrasts with a figure of only about 20 percent for white urban residents. This concentration of African Americans in urban cores and the residences of whites in suburbs meant that white and black American residents of the same cities often lived in completely separate neighborhoods.

By the end of the twentieth century in 2000, African Americans constituted majorities in many large cities. With an 84-percent African American population, Gary, Indiana, led the nation. Other cities with black majorities included Detroit, Michigan (82 percent); Birmingham, Alabama (74 percent); Jackson, Mississippi (71 percent); New Orleans, Louisiana (67 percent); Baltimore, Maryland (64 percent); Atlanta, Georgia (61 percent); Memphis, Tennessee (61 percent); Washington, D.C. (60 percent); and Richmond, Virginia (57 percent).

Age, Family Size, and Family Structure

During the twentieth century, the average age of all Americans rose. This was true for African Americans, as well as others, but African Americans have tended to be slightly younger than the majority white population. In the year 1900, the median age of African Americans was 19 years, meaning that the numbers of people above and below that age were equal. At that same time, the median age of whites was 23.

During the second half of the twentieth century, the aging of the population was briefly reversed by the so-called post-World War II "baby boom," which lasted until the early 1960's. As the baby boomers themselves aged, however, the average age of Americans again rose. In 1970, the median age of African Americans was 21 and that of whites was 28. By the year 2000, the median age of white Americans was 38 and that of African Americans was 30.

One reason that African Americans have tended to be somewhat younger than other Americans is that they have generally had somewhat larger family sizes. In 1900, the average African American family contained 5.41 members, while the average white family contained 5.13. By 2000, these figures had dropped to 3.32 for African Americans and 3.02 for whites.

Despite the fact that African Americans have continued to have larger families than the majority population, these families actually contained fewer adult members. In 1900, nearly 90 percent of white children and nearly 78 percent of African American children lived in families containing both mothers and fathers. During the 1960's, however, family structures in American society began to change rapidly, particularly among African Americans. By 2000, only 41 percent of African American children lived in two-parent families. The largest proportion, 47 percent, lived in families with only a mother. Another 6 percent lived in families with only a father and 6 percent (mostly older teenagers) lived in households with no parents present.

Educational Attainment and Income

In 1870, five years after the end of slavery in the United States, only about 1 in 4 African Americans could read and write, and only about 1 of every 10 African American children between the ages of 6 and 12 was attending school. By 1920, 3 out of every 4 African Americans could both read and write, and nearly 80 percent of elementary school-age children were attending school.

Despite the rapid historical advancement in education, however, African Americans have continued to be at a disadvantage in educational attainment. In 2000, only 13 percent of African American men above age 25 had college degrees, while 15 percent of African American women over 25 had finished bachelors or advanced degrees. These figures indicate that large numbers of African Americans attained high levels of formal education; however, their proportions remained substantially below those of the white population. More than one-fourth (26 percent) of white men and nearly one-fourth (23 percent) of white women over 25 completed college educations.

A lower average level of education was one of the reasons African Americans received less income than other Americans, although some social scientists argue that continuing racial discrimination was a more important factor. In 2000, the median family income of all Americans exceeded $50,000, but the figure for African American families was only $33,255. African American family incomes represented about 62 percent of white family incomes. However, comparisons of only families containing two married partners narrowed the gap considerably, with African

American families bringing home a median income of $50,690, compared to $59,199 for white families.

Future Trends

In the year 2005, the size of the African American population was expected to continue to grow. However, other segments of the American population are also expected to grow, so that the African American proportion of the total population should not change dramatically. Projections by the U.S. Bureau of the Census estimate that African Americans will number about 61 million, just under 15 percent of the total population in the year 2050. Much of the future population growth is expected to be the result of more rapid growth of other nonwhite groups, especially Latinos and Asians, who were the most numerous immigrants to the United States during the late twentieth and early twenty-first centuries.

Although some movement to the suburbs may be expected in years to come, especially as the size of the African American middle class grows, African Americans will probably continue to be more likely than the majority of the U.S. population to live in the central parts of cities. Those in the central cities are likely to face continuing economic problems and difficulties in finding jobs.

Carl L. Bankston III

Further Reading

Berlin, Ira. *Generations of Captivity: A History of African American Slaves.* Cambridge, Mass.: Harvard University Press, 2003. Provides an examination of the factors shaping the growth of the African American population during the years of slavery.

McKinnon, Jesse. *The Black Population: 2000.* Washington, D.C.: U.S. Census Bureau, 2001. The U.S. Census Bureau is the main source of demographic information on the United States, and McKinnon's book is the best place to begin an examination of the African American population. This short publication can be found in most libraries that contain census materials. It is also freely available online at the bureau's Web site.

Massey, Douglas S., and Nancy A. Denton. *American Apartheid: Segregation and the Making of an Underclass.* Cambridge, Mass.:

Harvard University Press, 1993. Covers the growth of segregation and its impact on African American employment, housing, and incomes during the twentieth century.

Patillo-McCoy, Mary. *Black Picket Fences: Privilege and Peril Among the Black Middle Class.* Chicago: University of Chicago Press, 1999. Interesting and well-written examination of the lives of members of the African American middle class.

See also Agriculture; Black flight; Economic trends; Great Migration; One-drop rule; Slavery

Disfranchisement laws in Mississippi

The Law: Laws to disfranchise African Americans had a number of components, the most important of which were a literacy test and a poll tax

Date: August, 1890

In August, 1890, the Mississippi legislature passed laws that effectively eliminated the black vote in the state.

At the end of the nineteenth century, Mississippi and South Carolina had the largest black populations in the United States. In 1890, fifty-seven of every hundred Mississippians were black. The Fifteenth Amendment to the U.S. Constitution (ratified in 1870) provided that no state could deny the right to vote on account of race; thus, Mississippi had a large black electorate. During the early 1870's, Mississippi voters elected hundreds of black officeholders, including members of Congress, state legislators, sheriffs, county clerks, and justices of the peace. In the mid-1870's, white Democrats launched a counteroffensive, using threats, violence, and fraud to neutralize the African American vote. After 1875, very few African Americans held office in Mississippi.

By 1890, many politicians in Mississippi were calling for a convention to write a new constitution for the state. They complained that although only a small number of African Americans were voting, this small number could prove decisive in close elections. Many white leaders feared that black votes could decide close elections and worked toward a new constitution with provisions that effectively would disfranchise black voters. It would be difficult to draft such provisions, however, without running afoul of the Fifteenth Amendment.

The state's two senators illustrated the divisions of opinion that were so widespread among white Mississippians. Senator Edward C. Walthall argued against a constitutional convention, warning that it would only excite political passions for no good purpose. He felt certain there was no way to eliminate black political participation without violating the Fifteenth Amendment, and that if Mississippi made such an attempt, the U.S. government would show new interest in enforcing African American voting rights. On the other hand, Senator James George attacked the old constitution, claiming that it had been drafted by carpetbaggers and ignorant former slaves. George urged that the "best citizens" should now take the opportunity to draft a new state constitution. He warned that black voting could revive unless the state took measures to reduce the black electorate by provisions of the state's highest law.

A bill calling a constitutional convention passed both houses of the state legislature in 1888, but Governor Robert Lowry vetoed it, warning that it was better to accept the state's existing problems than to run the risk of creating new ones by tampering with the state's constitution. Two years later, a similar bill passed both houses of the legislature, and the new governor, John M. Stone, signed the law. Election of delegates was set for July 29, 1890. The voters would elect 134 delegates, 14 of them from the state at large and the rest apportioned among the counties.

The state's weak Republican Party (to which many African Americans adhered as the party that had freed them from slavery) decided not to field a slate of candidates for at-large delegates. In heavily black Bolivar County, Republicans did offer a local delegate slate with one black and one white candidate. In Jasper County, the white Republican candidate for delegate, F. M. B. "Marsh" Cook, was assassinated while riding alone on a country road. In two black-majority counties, the Democrats allowed white conservative Republicans onto their candidate slates. In several counties, Democrats split into two factions and offered the voters a choice of two Democratic tickets. As it turned out, the constitutional convention was made up almost exclusively of white Democrats. The membership included only three Republicans, three delegates elected as independents, and one member of an agrarian third party. Only one of the 134 delegates was black: Isaiah T. Montgomery of Bolivar County.

The Mississippi Plan

Delegates elected the conservative lawyer Solomon S. Calhoon as president of the convention and immediately set about their work. Convention members had no shortage of ideas on how to limit the suffrage almost exclusively to whites without violating the Fifteenth Amendment. Some suggested that voters must own land, which few African Americans in Mississippi did. Others favored educational tests, since African Americans, only a generation removed from slavery, had had fewer educational opportunities than whites and therefore were often illiterate.

As finally devised, the Mississippi plan for disfranchisement had a number of parts, the most important of which were a literacy test and a poll tax. Under the literacy test, the would-be voter must either be able to read or to explain a part of the state constitution when it was read to him. This latter provision, the so-called "understanding clause," was included as a loophole for illiterate whites. Delegates knew that voting registrars could give easy questions to white applicants and exceedingly difficult ones to African Americans. The poll tax provision stated that a person must pay a poll tax of at least two dollars per year, for at least two years in succession, in order to qualify to vote. The voter would have to pay these taxes well in advance of the election and keep the receipt. The tax was quite burdensome in a state where tenant farmers often earned less than fifty dollars in cash per year. Because Mississippi's African Americans were often tenant farmers, poorer than their white counterparts, it was thought they would give up the right to vote rather than pay this new tax.

The Effect

In a notable speech, the black Republican delegate, Isaiah T. Montgomery, announced that he would vote for these new suffrage provisions. He noted that race relations in the state had grown tense and that black political participation in the state had often led whites to react violently. His hope now, Montgomery explained, was that black disfranchisement would improve race relations and as the years passed, perhaps more African Americans would be permitted to vote. The new constitution passed the convention with only eight dissenting votes; it was not submitted to the voters for their ratification.

The new suffrage provisions went into effect just before the 1892 elections. The new voter registration requirements disfranchised the great majority of African Americans in the state; they also resulted in the disfranchisement of about fifty-two thousand whites. The new registration resulted in a list of seventy thousand white voters and only nine thousand African American voters. The predominantly black state Republican Party had won 26 percent of the vote for its presidential candidate in 1888; after the new registration, in 1892, the Republican standard-bearer won less than 3 percent.

Under the Constitution of 1890, Mississippi had an almost exclusively white electorate for three-quarters of a century. This constitution served as a model for other southern states, which eagerly copied the literacy test, the understanding clause, and the poll tax into their state constitutions. Only after passage of new laws by the U.S. Congress in 1964 and 1965 would African American voters again make their strength felt in southern elections.

Stephen Cresswell

Further Reading

Stephen Cresswell's *Multiparty Politics in Mississippi, 1877-1902* (Jackson: University Press of Mississippi, 1995) discusses the drafting of the 1890 constitution and its role in limiting the success of the Republican and Populist Parties. Albert D. Kirwan's *Revolt of the Rednecks: Mississippi Politics, 1876-1925* (Lexington: University Press of Kentucky, 1951) remains the basic political history for the period before, during, and after the state's 1890 constitutional convention. J. Morgan Kousser's *The Shaping of Southern Politics: Suffrage Restriction and the Establishment of the One-Party South, 1880-1910* (New Haven, Conn.: Yale University

Press, 1974) is a detailed explanation of how new constitutions in Mississippi and other southern states led to a homogeneous electorate, essentially a small clique of middle-class whites.

See also Black codes; Civil Rights Acts of 1866-1875; *Civil Rights* cases; Clinton massacre; Compromise of 1877; Council of Federated Organizations; Fourteenth Amendment; Freedmen's Bureau; Gerrymandering; Ku Klux Klan; *Plessy v. Ferguson*; Reconstruction; *Smith v. Allwright*; Thirteenth Amendment

Draft riots

The Event: Wide-scale racial disturbances in New York City prompted by the federal government's first conscription act
Date: July, 1863
Place: New York, New York

Estimates of the casualties in the violence range up to more than one thousand. In spite of the violence, the federal government was determined to enforce the draft with even more vigor.

The firing on Fort Sumter on April 12, 1861, at the beginning of the Civil War, came at a time when the regular U.S. Army numbered only about 16,000 officers and troops. The traditional method of increasing the size of the army was to expand the state militias and to form a volunteer emergency national army recruited through the states. The immediate response of President Abraham Lincoln to the firing on Fort Sumter was to call for 75,000 militia volunteers for three months' service. This call was exceeded, and some volunteers were turned away because the expectation was that a show of force would be sufficient to defeat the South. Congress and the president subsequently found it necessary, however, to call for more volunteers. Repeated defeats of the Union army and the resultant loss of men caused President Lincoln to call for 300,000 volunteers in the summer of 1862.

The difficulty of obtaining volunteers was soon apparent; bounties were increased, and the threat of the draft was invoked. Congress passed the Militia Act of July, 1862, which allowed the states to draft men into the militia and encouraged enlistments. President Lincoln called for another 300,000 men to be enrolled into the militia. Although the Militia Act of 1862 gave the federal government power to enroll men in situations where the state machinery was inadequate, the short-term (nine-month maximum) nature of the militia draft and the inequities of the system made it less than satisfactory.

Conscription Begins

Spurred by the loss of 75,000 men, by news of a conscription law passed by the Confederacy, and by the failure of the states to provide men promptly for the various calls, Congress passed its own Conscription Act on March 3, 1863. Henry Wilson, chairman of the Senate Committee on Military Affairs, was responsible for the introduction of a bill that eventually was passed and labeled "An Act for Enrolling and Calling Out the National Forces and for Other Purposes." This act was the first national draft law in the history of the nation. It called for the creation of the "national forces," which were to consist of all able-bodied male citizens and alien declarants between twenty and forty-five years of age, including African Americans. White opposition to African Americans in federal army uniforms noticeably lessened as a result of the draft. In all, more than 168,000 African American recruits were drafted. Certain high officials, medically unfit persons, and hardship cases were exempted. Exemption could also be obtained by paying three hundred dollars or by securing a substitute.

The system was operated by the War Department under the direction of Colonel James B. Fry, provost-marshal-general. Provost-marshals were appointed in districts similar to the congressional districts and enrollments began. Quotas were established, and credit was given for enlistments. If the quotas were not met, drawings were held to determine who should be drafted. Small cards were placed in sealed envelopes in a large trunk, and the names were drawn in public by a trustworthy citizen wearing a blindfold. The system of paying three hundred dollars for exemption from service subsequently was abolished, but the privilege of hiring a substitute was continued. The names of more than three million men were gathered, but only about 170,000 were drafted, and 120,000 of those produced substitutes. The primary intent for passage of the law was to speed up voluntary enlistment, and more than one million men enlisted. The chief motivation for these enlistments was probably the threat of the draft.

Opposition

The draft brought President Lincoln and Secretary of War Edwin McMasters Stanton into conflict with state governors. Those governors who were unenthusiastic about the conduct of the war openly criticized the president and the draft, while governors who favored a more vigorous prosecution of the war often complained that their states had not been given full credit for previous enlistments. Lincoln and Stanton often temporized with the governors by granting postponements or additional credits as the end of the war drew near.

There was considerable resistance to the draft. Pennsylvania, Illinois, Indiana, and Kentucky had problems with enrollment, and draft offices and officers were attacked in those states. The Irish in New York and New Jersey were particularly incensed by the draft, many viewing the conflicts as a rich man's war and a poor man's fight. With fifty-one categories of diseases qualifying men for medical exemption, the system was fraught with medical resistance problems. Surgeons administering medical qualifying exams were confronted by faked hernias (the most widespread cause of exemption), eye problems caused by applying eye irritants, and pretended deafness. Giving incorrect birth dates, claiming false dependents, and even the enrollment of dead people were other methods of noncompliance. Finally, there were the runaways. Given time to settle their affairs before departing for camp, a considerable number of draftees either relocated or fled to Canada.

With the public generally hostile to the draft, the best way for a community to avoid it was to fill the quota with volunteers. Consequently, bounty taxes were implemented to raise revenues to attract foreigners, new immigrants, and the poverty-stricken to enlist. The paying of bounties corrupted the draft system. It produced bounty jumpers who, attracted by lump-sum payments, were willing to jump off trains or boats to escape conscription.

Riots

Notorious resistance to the draft instigated the draft riots in New York City. Governor Horatio Seymour's speech of July 4, 1863, attacking the Lincoln administration for violations of individual liberty, did nothing to decrease the hostility of the New York Irish toward African Americans and the abolitionists. Antidraft rioting, which took place between July 13 and 15, destroyed property and physically harmed many African Americans. Some New York militia units that had been engaged at Gettysburg were hastily ordered back to New York to stop the rioting. Estimates of the casualties in the violence range up to more than one thousand. In spite of the violence, the federal government was determined to enforce the draft with even more fervor.

Confederacy and Conscription

The Confederacy's calls for volunteers and its national conscription law antedated those of the Union. Jefferson Davis's call for 100,000 volunteers came before the firing on Fort Sumter, and the Conscription Act was passed on April 16, 1862, almost a year before similar legislation was passed by the United States. The Confederate act conscripted men from eighteen to thirty-five years of age; later the same year, it was extended to include those between seventeen and fifty years of age. The Confederate law included a substitute system and a controversial list of exempted persons held to be essential at home. The category that caused the most discussion was that which exempted one slave owner or overseer for each twenty slaves. The Confederate draft was also controversial because it was a national levy; it made no concession to the doctrine of states' rights for which most southerners claimed to be fighting.

It appears that the Confederacy's early use of a conscription law enabled General Robert E. Lee's armies to continue their general success in the Civil War well into 1863. It was only after the North also began drafting men that President Lincoln could be confident of victory. The North, with a much larger population, was able to sustain its losses and to continue the war indefinitely; the Confederacy could not. Continuance of the draft underscored Northern determination to continue the war to its conclusion. The result was Lee's surrender at Appomattox and the restoration of the Union.

Mark A. Plummer
Updated by Irwin Halfond

Further Reading

Iver Charles Bernstein's *The New York City Draft Riots: Their Significance for American Society and Politics in the Age of the Civil War* (New York: Oxford University Press, 1990) is a detailed, highly readable study of the Civil War's worst draft riot. James W. Geary's *We Need Men: The Union Draft in the Civil War* (Dekalb: Illinois University Press, 1991) is an extensively footnoted study of the draft law's origins, operation, and effects. Stephen M. Kohn's *Jailed for Peace: The History of American Draft Law Violation, 1658-1985* (New York: Praeger, 1987) is a thorough study of resistance to compulsory conscription from colonial to recent times.

See also Charleston race riots; Civil War; Emancipation Proclamation; Race riots of 1866

Dyer antilynching bill

The Law: Bill seeking to make lynching a national crime subject to federal prosecution and penalty
Date: January, 1922
The bill languished in the Senate and ultimately failed as did two subsequent antilynching bills.

After World War I, the National Association for the Advancement of Colored People (NAACP) sought congressional sponsors for federal antilynching legislation. More than three thousand people, mostly African Americans, had been lynched between 1889 and 1918. Of sixty-nine lynchings in 1921, 92 percent targeted African Americans. In April, 1921, President Warren Harding re-

Do Not Look at The Victim
His Earthly Problems Are Ended
Instead Look at The Seven Children Who
Gaze at This Gruesome Spectacle

This Victim Suffered Physical Torture
For A Few Short Hours. But What
Psychological Havoc is Being Wrought
in The Minds of The Children?
Into What Kind of Citizens Will They Grow Up?

Poster created by the National Association for the Advancement of Colored People in its campaign to get federal legislation to outlaw lynching. (Association for the Study of African American Life and History)

quested that Congress pass antilynching legislation. Representative L. C. Dyer of Missouri introduced a bill that made lynching a national crime subject to federal prosecution and penalty. The House in January, 1922, easily adopted the Dyer bill, 220 to 119.

The Dyer bill languished in the Senate Judiciary Committee. Southern senators opposed the federal government's interference with the police powers of the states. The Dyer bill finally reached the Senate floor at a special session on the ship subsidy bill in November, 1922. The NAACP intensified its efforts to secure passage of the Dyer measure, sending senators a memo, signed by numerous professionals, urging adoption. Southern and border senators, led by Oscar Underwood of Alabama and Pat Harrison of Mississippi, filibustered the Dyer bill for a week. Republican senators at a December caucus abandoned their efforts to secure approval of the Dyer bill, clearing the way for Senate consideration of the ship subsidy bill. Other antilynching bills, including the Costigan-Wagner bill of 1935 and the Wagner-Gavagan bill of 1940, likewise failed.

David L. Porter

See also Clinton massacre; Ku Klux Klan; Lynching; Till lynching; *United States v. Cruikshank*

Economic trends

Burdened by being held in involuntary servitude throughout most of their long history in North America, African Americans have been at the bottom of the income scale; however, since the mid-twentieth century, their economic condition has steadily improved, helping them to close the gap with the rest of the population

In the year 1860—the last before the Civil War—the U.S. Census counted a population of 4,441,830 African Americans in the United States. At that time, 9 of every 10 of those people were considered to be the property of others. Legally, they were slaves. Most people held in slavery worked in agriculture, but a small number in urban areas worked in trades or as laborers.

Slavery

Slaves tended many of the country's most important export crops. Tobacco, one of the earliest cash crops in Virginia and the surrounding regions, depended heavily on slave labor. Later, rice, grown in parts of South Carolina and other states, and sugarcane, grown chiefly in Louisiana, became important cash crops grown by slaves. With the development of the cotton gin at the end of the eighteenth century, cotton became the most profitable agricultural export of the entire United States. Even in the nonslaveholding North, much of the profit that made industrialization possible came from trade in crops produced by slaves.

The slave trade itself was a significant part of the early American economy. In 1807, the U.S. Congress pass legislation banning the importation of slaves from abroad, beginning the following year. From that date, American involvement in the international slave trade dropped substantially. However, the internal trade in slaves continued. As the United States spread westward and as the cotton industry grew in the deeper South, the sale of slaves from older, upper South states to Deep South states became a major economic activity.

The relatively small number of African Americans who were not slaves—the so-called free blacks—occupied positions that were mostly at the bottom of the economic ladder. The 1860 census counted 488,070 "free colored" people in the United States, a little more than one-third of whom were of mixed race, according to census data. More than 70 percent of the free blacks worked in only four occupations: as laborers, domestic household and laundry workers, salaried farmworkers, and independent farmers. The most common category, accounting for 26 percent of all workers, was "laborer." Only about 7 percent of all free black workers in the United States were owners or tenant farmers, compared to one-third of all whites.

The small number of free African Americans also owned relatively little property just before the Civil War. Among free African American men over twenty-one years of age, 83 percent owned no real estate, such as a house or land, and 63 percent owned no personal property of recordable value. By comparison, just under 58 percent of adult white men owned no real estate and just under 37 percent had no personal property. The small number of free African Americans who did own possessions of substantial value had only a fraction of the wealth of whites. Among those the census referred to as "free colored" adult men who owned some real property, the median value of the property was $500, compared to $1,500 for white men. The median value of personal property of free men of color with property was just $100, compared to $370 for whites.

On the eve of the Civil War, then, slave labor was a key part of the developing American economy. Only about 10 of every 100 African Americans were part of the free labor force, though. Moreover, those who were free worked mostly in menial occupations and received little of the nation's wealth.

Reconstruction

Reconstruction was the period just after the Civil War when the southern states were occupied by northern military forces, as the U.S. government attempted to bring about some political and social change in the South. After the U.S. Congress took control of Reconstruction policies away from President Andrew Johnson in 1867, the federal government made efforts to include African Americans in public life. During the late 1860's and 1870's, African Americans were elected to public offices throughout the South. The Bureau of Refugees, Freedmen, and Abandoned Lands (known as the Freedmen's Bureau) tried to improve the economic situation of former slaves by negotiating labor contracts for them with plantation owners and by setting up schools. While Reconstruction did bring about some political participation for African Americans, it brought about little real economic change for them. Most African Americans remained at the bottom of the job market and worked on farms owned by other people.

In 1870, just over half of the working African Americans in the United States (52 percent) were farm laborers. The next most common occupation was in domestic service, as private

In 1900 Booker T. Washington (seated, second from left) and T. Thomas Fortune founded the National Negro Business League to promote black enterprise. (Library of Congress)

household workers (13 percent), followed by unclassified laborers (12 percent). Another 11 percent were farm owners or tenants working farms belonging to others. By 1880, the percentage of farmers had almost doubled, to 19 percent. However, many of these farmers were sharecroppers, participants in a farming system that began to evolve in the wake of slavery. Sharecroppers worked lands belonging to others, generally white owners, handing over large portions of their crops to the owners after each harvest. The most common occupation for African Americans in 1880 was still that of farm laborer (36 percent), the percentage of general laborers had gone up to 20 percent. Another 14 percent of African Americans were in domestic service after the end of Reconstruction.

The United States was primarily an agricultural society during the years following the Civil War. During the 1870's and 1880's, about 43 percent of white Americans were in agriculture. However, African Americans were even more heavily concentrated in this industry, since 64 percent in 1870 and 65 percent in 1880 were in agriculture. The only other industry containing many African Americans was that of private household service, which contained about 14 percent of African American workers in 1870 and 19 percent in 1880. Well over three-quarters of the African American workers toiled in either low-level farmwork or domestic service during and after the years of Reconstruction

Jim Crow Era

Reconstruction ended with the withdrawal of federal troops from the southern states in 1877. Afterward, the U.S. economy began a period of rapid expansion and industrialization. The growth of the railroads, manufacturing, mining, and banking propelled the nation toward an urban, factory-based economy. Much of the new workforce for this industrializing nation came from immigration, though, not from African Americans, who continued to be concentrated in agriculture in the South. By 1910, nearly 90 percent of African Americans still lived in the South and a majority of all African Americans were still employed in agriculture, although only about one-third of all Americans and one-fourth to one-third of white Americans worked in agriculture. Most African Americans continued to work on land belonging to others. Of those who worked in agriculture in 1910, 70 percent were farm laborers and wage workers, working for land owners for pay or a share of the harvest. Many of these were sharecroppers, who had no money to rent land.

The sharecropping system emerged during and after Reconstruction. Most African Americans in the South were landless and had neither tools nor money. Landowners often could not afford to hire workers, or they found it more profitable to make use of workers they would not have to pay. Agricultural laborers moved onto land on which the owners provided small houses and tools. In return, the workers were obligated to turn over portions of their crops—usually from 20 to 50 percent—to the owners. Meanwhile, the owners extended credit for seed and living expenses until the harvests. Because the landowners kept the records of debts, sharecroppers were often overcharged when the harvest times arrived and lost even greater portions of the crops than originally agreed. Although there were also many white sharecroppers, African Americans were particularly concentrated in this kind of work.

Among the African American workers who were not in agriculture in 1910, over one-third (mostly women) were doing laundry in private homes or working as domestic servants. Another one-fourth of those outside agriculture were laborers. The concentration of African Americans in low-paying, manual labor was the economic side of the "Jim Crow" system in the United States. This was a name given to the system of maintaining racial inequality through laws requiring racial segregation, through limiting the rights of African Americans to vote and participate in government at all levels, and through occupational and housing discrimination.

The First Great Migration

The movement of African Americans from the rural South to the industrial North is often called the Great Migration. That migration actually unfolded in two great waves. The first took place during and after World War I and the second during and after World War II. World War I began to break the hold of the rural

South on African Americans and to offer economic opportunities in places where they would have greater freedom from the Jim Crow system.

As many men entered the military during the war and industries began hiring in greater numbers to meet the needs of the war-driven economy, new opportunities for employment for relatively unskilled workers opened up in the North. Although plantation owners in the South often resisted the loss of their workers, the lure of job opportunities and freedom from oppression drew many people northward.

One of the primary northern destinations of southern African Americans was the city of Chicago. In part, the popularity of Chicago was partly a result of the work of Robert S. Abbott, a businessman and publisher of the widely read newspaper the *Chicago Defender*. Abbott began "The Great Northern Drive" on May 15, 1917, urging the oppressed people of the South to move North. The African American population of Chicago more than doubled during the second decade of the twentieth century: from 44,000 in 1910 to 109,000 in 1920. Over the following ten years, it more than doubled again, to 234,000. By 1930, over 1 in 5 African Americans lived in the Northeast or Midwest.

Despite the Great Migration, most African Americans continued to live in the South, and agriculture continued to be a major economic activity for them. Nevertheless, by 1920 the majority of African Americans no longer worked in agriculture. However, even outside the South, they continued to hold positions at the bottom of the occupational ladder. One in 4 African Americans worked as laborers in 1920, compared to less than 1 of every 10 whites.

During this period, portering jobs in hotels, on trains, and in other places emerged as a major occupational opportunity for African Americans. In 1920, 3 percent of all African American men and about 10 percent of African American men outside the South worked as porters. Sleeping car porter positions on trains became prestigious and valued jobs for people who were shut out of most other jobs in American society, and they attracted some of the best-educated men in African American society. The Brotherhood of Sleeping Car Porters became one of the most active and effective black labor unions, and it was an early leader in the struggle for civil rights.

The Second Great Migration

During the 1930's, the movement northward began to slow. Plantation owners in the South resisted the loss of sharecroppers and other laborers. As northern jobs grew scarce during the Depression years, the attraction of northern cities such as Chicago diminished. After World War II, though, the Great Migration began again, at a much greater level. Between 1940 and 1970, an estimated five million African Americans left the southern countryside for the cities of the North.

The northward migration led to a steady growth of African Americans living in the Northeast and the northern part of the Midwest. While over three-quarters of African Americans (77 percent) lived in the South in 1940, just over one-half (54 percent) lived in the South in 1970. At the same time, both the movement north and a movement to cities in the South transformed African Americans from a predominantly rural population to an urban population. This affected their positions in the American economy, since it placed them in cities at the moment when urban manufacturing jobs were beginning to decline as part of the American economy.

The Postindustrial Economy

By the 1960's, the sharecropper system had virtually disappeared in most of the South. Mechanization had reduced the need for human labor in agriculture. In 1967, the U.S. government included agricultural workers under its minimum wage law. As a result, farmworkers immediately became much more expensive for southern planters, who relied even more on machines and began substituting chemicals for human laborers to eliminate weeds. After centuries of heavy concentration in agriculture, jobs as agricultural workers had finally become largely unavailable for African Americans. This did mean that they were no longer locked in to the kinds of rural labor that had held so many of their ancestors through the centuries of slavery and the decades of segregation following slavery. At the same time, however, the entire national economy was changing. After around 1970, factories located in cities became less important parts of American economic life, so that even factory jobs were becoming less available. As the old jobs in agriculture declined and African Americans were becoming an urban population, jobs in the cities also declined.

One of the consequences of the postindustrial transformation of the American economy, in which jobs in manufacturing decreased, was that the gap between the unemployment rates of African Americans and whites grew even wider. In 1940, as the Depression of the 1930's drew to an end, African Americans had an unemployment rate of just over 10 percent, while the rate for white Americans was just under 10 percent. By 1970, the overall level of unemployment had gone down, but African Americans had a much higher unemployment rate than whites: over 7 percent for the former and under 3 percent for the latter. As unemployment rates increased through the rest of the twentieth century, unemployment among African Americans grew worse. Their unemployment rates were more than double those of whites through the rest of the century, and African American unemployment rates were consistently higher than they were in the difficult economy of 1940.

People are classified as "unemployed" if they are looking for work but do not have jobs. Those who give up looking for work are considered outside the labor force. During the postindustrial period of the American economy, African Americans were much more likely than others to give up looking for work completely. In 1970, 16 percent of African American men between the ages of 25 and 64 who were not in school were out of the labor force, compared to less than 8 percent of white men in the same age range. Rates of labor force nonparticipation went up steadily throughout the twentieth century, so that by the year 2000 one-third of African American men and 15 percent of white men who were not enrolled in school and between 25 years of age and retirement age were outside the labor force. Joblessness had become a serious problem for African Americans.

The Black Middle Class and the Underclass

Until the 1960's, widespread social and economic discrimination prevented the growth of a large black middle class. Although there were always black business owners and professionals, those people made up only a small part of the African American workforce, who tended to be heavily concentrated in low-income, low-status jobs. In 1960, for example, only 14.4 percent of all African Americans lived in households that enjoyed incomes two times higher than the poverty level, compared to 48 percent of whites. Using a slightly different definition of middle class, author Bart Landry, in his influential book *The New Black Middle Class* (1987) found that only 13.4 percent of African Americans could be found in middle-class jobs. Even those who were members of the black middle class often had difficulty passing their economic status on to their children.

From the early 1960's, the black middle class began to expand rapidly. By 2000, about half the people of African ancestry in the United States lived in households with incomes twice the poverty level. Although the proportion of whites at this income level had also increased rapidly over the previous four decades, to nearly three-fourths, the economic trend had been one of remarkable upward mobility for a minority group that had earlier had few economic opportunities.

A number of researchers have pointed out that government employment is particularly important to the black middle class. In 2000, more than 1 of every 5 employed African Americans worked for federal, state, or local governments, compared to only 14 percent of employed whites. This meant that middle-class African Americans were particularly vulnerable to government cutbacks, and that they had less access to private sector employment, which frequently offered better salaries than public sector jobs.

At the same time that the black middle class was growing, many African Americans continued to live in poverty. The percentage of African Americans with household incomes below the official poverty level declined steadily between 1960 and 2000. Nevertheless, nearly 1 African American of every 4 was living in poverty in the year 2000. Even more disturbing, more than 1 in 10 African Americans lived in extreme poverty, with household incomes that were one-half the poverty level or below, at the turn of the twenty-first century.

Low-income African Americans were heavily concentrated in cities, where employment was often either unavailable or offered few opportunities for advancement. With high rates of unemployment among men in these urban communities, single-parent households headed by women became a common pattern. The urban, economically disadvantaged segment of the African American population was described as the "underclass" by some scholars and journalists.

Carl L. Bankston III

Further Reading

Berlin, Ira. *Generations of Captivity: A History of African American Slaves.* Cambridge, Mass.: Harvard University Press, 2003. Provides an examination of the factors shaping the growth of the African American population during the years of slavery and gives a good view of slavery as an economic and social institution.

Foner, Eric. *Reconstruction, 1863-1877.* New York: Harper & Row, 1988. Looks at efforts of former slaves to be economically self-supporting and at how the failure of the American government to meet the economic needs of its newly freed citizens produced years of continuing racial inequality.

Landry, Bart. *The New Black Middle Class.* Berkeley: University of California Press, 1987. Path-breaking study of the grim economic realities of African American efforts to achieve middle-class status.

McKinnon, Jesse. *The Black Population: 2000.* Washington, D.C.: U.S. Census Bureau, 2001. The U.S. Census Bureau is the main source of demographic information on the United States, and McKinnon's book is the best place to begin an examination of the African American population. This short publication can be found in most libraries that contain census materials. It is also freely available online at the bureau's Web site.

Massey, Douglas S., and Nancy A. Denton. *American Apartheid: Segregation and the Making of an Underclass.* Cambridge, Mass.: Harvard University Press, 1993. Covers the growth of segregation and its impact on African American employment, housing, and incomes during the twentieth century.

Patillo-McCoy, Mary. *Black Picket Fences: Privilege and Peril Among the Black Middle Class*. Chicago: University of Chicago Press, 1999. Interesting and well-written examination of the lives of members of the African American middle class.

Waldinger, Roger. *Still the Promised City? African-Americans and New Immigrants in Postindustrial New York*. Cambridge, Mass.: Harvard University Press, 1996. Examines why African Americans had difficulty finding even unskilled jobs in large cities in the years following World War II.

See also Agriculture; Brotherhood of Sleeping Car Porters; Demographic trends; Education; Employment; Equal Employment Opportunity Act of 1972; Equal Employment Opportunity Commission; Fair Employment Practices Committee; Great Migration; Irish and African Americans; Poor People's March on Washington; Sharecropping

Edmonson v. Leesville Concrete Company

The Case: U.S. Supreme Court ruling on jury composition
Date: June 3, 1991

The Supreme Court extended its ruling that potential jurors could not be peremptorily excluded on the basis of race from criminal trials to include civil trials.

Thaddeus Edmonson, an African American construction worker, sued his employer, the Leesville Concrete Company, in 1988, claiming compensation for injuries suffered in a workplace accident. Edmonson invoked his right to a trial by jury. During the pretrial examination of potential jurors, the company's lawyers used their peremptory challenges to excuse two of the three black members of the panel. Edmonson asked the district court to require the company to provide a race-neutral explanation of the dismissals of the black panelists. Under *Batson v. Kentucky* (1986), racial motivation for juror challenges was held unconstitutional in criminal cases. In *Batson*, the U.S. Supreme Court had reasoned that the use of race as a criterion in jury challenges by the prosecution violates the equal protection clause of the U.S. Constitution. Edmonson's case presented the issue of whether such dismissals are improper in civil cases. The trial court denied Edmonson's request and, after conflicting decisions in the court of appeals, he appealed to the Supreme Court.

In 1991, Justice Anthony Kennedy wrote for the Court in a 6-3 decision holding that racially based juror challenges are unconstitutional even in civil cases. Because the juror challenges use the power of the government to select jury members, the discrimination becomes "state action" even though invoked by a private litigant. All state action must be consistent with constitutional rules forbidding racial discrimination.

Justice Sandra Day O'Connor dissented, arguing that only governmental discrimination is forbidden by the equal protection clause and that the act of Leesville Concrete's counsel was not state action.

Robert Jacobs

See also *Batson v. Kentucky; Moore v. Dempsey; Norris v. Alabama; Powers v. Ohio; Strauder v. West Virginia; Williams v. Mississippi*

Education

Since the emancipation of the slaves in 1863, the debate has raged over the role of education and educational institutions in the African American community in the United States. After the Civil Rights movement of the 1950's and 1960's, the importance of an equal education and performance on standardized testing led the educational community to reevaluate the impact of education and its significance for African American students.

The Civil War (1861-1865), Reconstruction (1863-1877), and the Thirteenth Amendment (1865) ended slavery. Although free African Americans had attended schools in some northern states long before the Civil War, southern states had prohibited the teaching of either slave or free African American children. Emancipation in 1863 brought with it the challenge of providing educational opportunities for the freed men and women and their children, particularly in the former Confederate states.

The Legacy of Slavery

In 1865, Congress created the Freedmen's Bureau to help former slaves adjust to freedom. The bureau continued to function until 1872 and, under the leadership of General O. O. Howard, established schools throughout the South. At their peak in 1869, these schools had about 114,000 students enrolled. The schools taught reading, writing, grammar, geography, arithmetic, and music through a curriculum based on the New England school model. A small number of African American teachers were trained in these schools, but the schools were usually staffed by northern schoolteachers, who brought with them their values, their educational ideas, and their methods. These white educators from northern states promoted the stereotypical idea of the kind of education African Americans should receive. Samuel C. Armstrong and many like-minded educators stressed industrial training and social control over self-determination. Many believe this philosophy was designed to keep African Americans in a subordinate position.

From Washington to Du Bois

Booker T. Washington was the leading educational spokesperson for African Americans after the Civil War. Washington, who was born a slave, experienced the hectic years of Reconstruction and, in a speech delivered at the Atlanta Exposition in 1895, articulated the outlines of a compromise with the white power structure, a policy later known as accommodationism. A student of Armstrong, Washington believed that industrial education was an important force in building character and economic competence for African Americans. He believed in moral "uplift" through hard work. At the Tuskegee Institute, which he helped establish in 1881, Washington shaped his ideas into a curriculum that focused on basic academic, agricultural, and occupational skills and emphasized the values of hard work and the dignity of labor. He encouraged his students to become elementary school-teachers, farmers, and artisans, emphasizing these occupations over the professions of medicine, law, and politics.

Although revered initially, Washington has become an increasingly controversial figure. Some people say he made the best of a bad situation and that, although he compromised on racial issues, he can be viewed as a leader who preserved and slowly advanced the educational opportunities of African Americans. Critics of Washington see him as an opportunist whose compromises restricted African American progress.

W. E. B. Du Bois was a sociological and educational pioneer who challenged the established system of education. Du Bois, an opponent of Washington's educational philosophies, believed the African American community needed more determined and activist leadership. He helped organize the Niagara Movement in 1905, which led to the founding in 1909 of the National Association for the Advancement of Colored People (NAACP). Du Bois was a strong opponent of racial segregation in the schools. Unlike Washington, Du Bois did not believe in slow, evolutionary change; he instead demanded immediate change. Du Bois sup-

Facilities such as this southern schoolhouse for African Americans in 1939 made a mockery of the "separate-but-equal" doctrine in education. (Library of Congress)

ported the NAACP position that all American children, including African American children, should be granted an equal educational opportunity. It was through the efforts of the NAACP that the monumental U.S. Supreme Court case *Brown v. Board of Education* (1954) outlawed segregation in U.S. public schools. Du Bois believed in educated leadership for the African American community and developed the concept of the Talented Tenth, the notion that 10 percent of the African American population would receive a traditional college education in preparation for leadership.

Post-Civil Rights Era

Du Bois's educational and political philosophies had a significant influence on the Civil Rights movement of the 1950's and 1960's. Out of the effects of public school desegregation during the 1950's and 1960's and the Black Power movement of the 1970's grew a new perspective on the education of African Americans. Inspired by historians such as Cheikh Anta Diop and Basil Davidson, educational philosophers such as Molefi Kete Asante formed the Afrocentric school of education. Asante and his followers maintain that a curriculum centered on the perspective of African Americans is more effective in reaching African American youth than the Eurocentric curriculum to which most students are exposed. Low test scores and historically poor academic records could be the result, according to Afrocentrists, of a curriculum that does not apply to African American students.

Statistics

According to *The African American Education Data Book* (published in 1997 by the Research Institute of the College Fund/ United Negro College Fund), in 1994, approximately 43.5 million students were enrolled in public elementary and secondary schools, and nearly 5 million students were enrolled in private elementary and secondary schools. African Americans represented 16.5 percent of all public school enrollments. African Americans were underrepresented at private elementary and secondary schools, where they constituted only 9.3 percent of all enrollments. The number of African Americans enrolled in public schools declined as grade level increased, a finding that supports the evidence that African Americans leave school at higher rates than children of the same age in other racial groups. African Americans represented only 12.5 percent of those who received regular high school diplomas in 1994.

In schools made up primarily of African American students and located mainly in economically depressed urban centers, nearly a quarter of all students participated in remedial reading programs, and 22 percent participated in remedial math. By comparison, schools with less than 50 percent African American students had 14.8 percent of students enrolled in remedial reading and 12 percent enrolled in remedial math. Furthermore, only 87 percent of African American high school seniors graduate on time compared with 93 percent of non-African American seniors.

Test Scores

African American students have historically scored far below whites in geography, writing, reading, and math. The National Educational Longitudinal Study of 1988 reported that the average seventeen-year-old African American student had a reading score only slightly higher than that of the average white thirteen-year-old. Compared with whites, African American Scholastic Aptitude Test (SAT) takers had lower high school grade-point averages, fewer years of academic study, and fewer honors courses. Data collected by the National Assessment of Educational Progress, however, reveal that African Americans had registered gains in reading, math, and other subjects between the 1970's and the 1990's. Despite these gains, African Americans are underrepresented among high school seniors applying for college and represented only 9 percent of the college population in the 1990's (a decrease from 10 percent in the 1970's).

It is not surprising that many African Americans see no value in postsecondary education. Regardless of socioeconomic status or whether they had received a high school diploma, a higher percentage of African Americans who were eighth-graders in 1988 were unemployed and not in college than their white counterparts in 1993, a year after their scheduled high school graduation. Despite affirmative action legislation, African Americans still are less likely to be hired for a job when competing against equally qualified white applicants.

Socioeconomic Status

In both 1980 and 1990, African American high school sophomores were concentrated in the lowest two socioeconomic status quartiles. The proportion of African Americans in the lowest socioeconomic status quartile declined from 48 percent in 1980 to 39 percent in 1990. In both 1980 and 1990, African Americans were underrepresented in the upper two socioeconomic status quartiles. In addition, African Americans often attend schools with fewer resources in poorer neighborhoods of large, urban areas. Fifteen percent of schools that have primarily African American students have no magnet or honors programming, as opposed to only 1.6 percent of schools with a majority of white students. Also, a higher percentage of schools with a majority of African American students participated in the National School Lunch Program. The poverty level in the African American community is one of the factors believed to be responsible for consistently low scores on standardized testing. Along with poverty, the African American community has also experienced a greater amount of violence and delinquency among high-school-age youths. The homicide rate among African American men increased by more than two-thirds in the late 1980's, according to a study by Joe Schwartz and Thomas Exter (1990).

Parental Attitudes

Although much of the effort of public policymakers goes into integrating schools and creating more diversity in inner-city schools, African American parents seem more interested in developing a stronger academic program in their children's schools. A survey taken in 1998 by Public Agenda, a nonpartisan public-opinion research firm, showed that 80 percent of African American parents favored raising academic standards and achievement levels in primarily African American schools over emphasizing integration. Eleven percent of the parents polled said they would like to see the schools both integrated and improved. Of the white parents polled, 60 percent expressed a fear that discipline and safety problems, low reading scores, and social problems would result if African American students were transferred to a mostly white school. The Public Agenda survey demonstrates the differences in opinions on education based on racial background. For example, nearly 50 percent of African American parents felt that teachers demanded too little of their children because of the children's race. Despite the difference in opinion on these public issues, both African American and white parents expressed a great interest in their children's school success and the quality of their children's education.

Jason Pasch

Further Reading

A good introduction to the topic can be found in *The Encyclopedia of African American Education* (Westport, Conn.: Greenwood Press, 1996), edited by Faustine C. Jones-Wilson. *Issues in African American Education* (Nashville, Tenn.: One Horn Press, 1991), by Walter Gill, provides good background on the issues surrounding education. Booker T. Washington's *Up from Slavery* (New York: Doubleday, 1938) is a classic text on Washington's educational philosophy and life story. W. E. B. Du Bois's ideas can be found in *The Philadelphia Negro: A Social Study* (Philadelphia: University of Pennsylvania Press, 1899) and *Dusk of Dawn: An Essay Toward an Autobiography of a Race Concept* (New York: Harcourt, Brace & World, 1940). The Afrocentric philosophy is described in Molefi Kete Asante's *Kemet, Afrocentricity, and Knowledge* (Trenton, N.J.: Africa World Press, 1990). Statistics covering every aspect of African American education can be found in *The African American Education Data Book* (Research Institute of the College Fund/UNCF, 1997), by Frederick D. Patterson, Michael T. Nettles, and Laura W. Perna.

See also Affirmative action; Afrocentrism; Ashmun Institute; Atlanta Compromise; *Bakke* case; Black colleges and universities; *Brown v. Board of Education*; Economic trends; Employment; Freedmen's Bureau; National Association for the Advancement of Colored People; Niagara Movement; School desegregation; Talented Tenth; United Negro College Fund

Edwards v. South Carolina

The Case: U.S. Supreme Court ruling on freedom of assembly
Date: February 5, 1963

In this incorporation case, the Supreme Court held that local officials could not block an otherwise lawful demonstration because they disliked the demonstrators' political views.

About two hundred African American students marched peacefully in small groups from a church to the South Carolina state capitol, an obviously public forum, to protest the state's racially discriminatory laws. A few dozen police officers initially told them they could march peacefully but about an hour later ordered them to disperse under threat of arrest. A crowd had gathered to watch the demonstrators but did not seem threatening, and the police presence was ample. The demonstrators responded by singing patriotic and religious songs until some two hundred demonstrators were arrested and convicted of breach of the peace. Their conviction was upheld by the South Carolina supreme court.

The Supreme Court, by an 8-1 vote, reversed the convictions of the civil rights demonstrators. Justice Potter Stewart, in the majority opinion, applied the First Amendment right to freedom of assembly to the states, refusing to let the states bar demonstrations of unpopular views in traditional forums. In line with other time, place, and manner decisions, the Court used the Fourteenth Amendment's due process clause to incorporate the peaceable assembly portion of the First Amendment and to apply it to the states. Justice Tom C. Clark dissented, defending the state's action.

Richard L. Wilson

See also Civil Rights movement; *Griffin v. Breckenridge; National Association for the Advancement of Colored People v. Alabama; Wisconsin v. Mitchell*

Emancipation Proclamation

The Event: President Abraham Lincoln's Civil War declaration that slaves in areas in rebellion against the Union states were free
Date: January 1, 1863
Place: Washington, D.C.

The Emancipation Proclamation freed few slaves at the time Abraham Lincoln issued it, but its symbolic force helped transform the Civil War into a crusade against slavery.

Although the American Civil War (1861-1865) was the result of sectional conflict regarding the issue of slavery, both the Union and the Confederate governments initially denied that slavery was a war issue. The Confederate government claimed that it was fighting only to defend the principle of states' rights. The Union government claimed that it was fighting to preserve the Union of states against Confederate efforts to destroy it.

Lincoln's Cautious Approach to Emancipation

From the beginning of the war, abolitionists, Radical Republicans, and black activists urged President Abraham Lincoln to use the war as an opportunity to strike down slavery. Lincoln, though, acted in a cautious manner in the early months of the war. Until September, 1862, Lincoln refused to include the abolition of slavery as one of the Union's war aims. Furthermore, when radical commanders in the Union army ordered the emancipation of slaves in parts of the occupied South in 1861-1862, Lincoln countermanded the orders.

These actions caused reformers to question the depth of Lincoln's own commitment to antislavery. In Lincoln's defense, it must be noted that Lincoln both publicly and privately often expressed a heartfelt abhorrence of slavery. Yet Lincoln knew that a premature effort to turn the war into a crusade for emancipation would be counterproductive to the cause of freedom. An early act of emancipation would prompt loyal slave states such as Kentucky, Maryland, and Missouri to join the Confederacy and probably cause the defeat of the Union. From a practical point of view, the Union government could not abolish slavery in the South if it lost the war.

Decorated text of the Emancipation Proclamation. (Library of Congress)

Origins of Lincoln's Emancipation Policy

Lincoln was finally encouraged to seek emancipation because of the actions of the slaves themselves. During the war, some 600,000 slaves—about 15 percent of the total—escaped from their masters. Slaves understood that the advance of the Union army through the South presented them with an unprecedented opportunity for escape. Most escaped slaves sought shelter with the Union army.

The presence of large numbers of slaves within Union army lines presented Union commanders with the question of whether the slaves should be returned to their rebellious masters or allowed to stay with the army and use up its scarce resources. Most Union commanders allowed the slaves to remain with the army, justifying this decision out of military necessity. Pointing to the right of armies under international law to seize or destroy enemy property being used to sustain the war effort, Union commanders claimed the right to seize the Confederacy's slave laborers as contraband of war.

The actions of Union commanders shifted the focus of emancipation from human rights to military necessity, thereby encouraging Lincoln to adopt a general policy of emancipation and giving Lincoln an argument with which to win public support for this policy.

The Proclamation and Its Limits

Lincoln's Emancipation Proclamation, which was issued January 1, 1863, declared that slaves in areas in rebellion against the United States were free. Slaves in the loyal slave states and slaves in areas of the Confederacy already under Union control were not freed by the proclamation. Because of this fact, some commentators have criticized the proclamation, claiming that the proclamation had little impact because it sought to free the Confederate slaves who were beyond Lincoln's control and neglected to free the slaves within his control. This criticism ignores several facts regarding Lincoln's action. The Emancipation Proclamation amounted to an announcement that henceforward, the Union army would become an army of liberation. Whenever the Union army captured an area of the Confederacy, it would automatically free the slaves in that region.

Additionally, the limited scope of Lincoln's proclamation was prompted by the limited powers of the president under the Constitution. Lincoln pointed out that, as president, his only constitutional power to emancipate slaves was derived from his power as commander in chief to order the military destruction of property that supported the enemy's war effort. Slaves belonging to masters in states loyal to the Union and slaves belonging to masters in areas of the Confederacy previously captured were not currently being used to support the enemy's war effort. In making this argument, Lincoln was not being evasive or cautious in seeking the emancipation of all American slaves. One month before he issued the Emancipation Proclamation, Lincoln proposed to Congress the passage of a constitutional amendment that would have freed all slaves living in the loyal border states and in currently occupied portions of the Confederacy.

Effects of the Proclamation

In the end, perhaps two-thirds of American slaves were freed by the Emancipation Proclamation. The remainder of American slaves were freed by the laws of state governments in loyal slave states and by the Thirteenth Amendment (1865), which abolished slavery in the United States.

Harold D. Tallant

Further Reading

Lincoln's Emancipation Proclamation: The End of Slavery in America (New York: Simon & Schuster, 2004) by Allen C. Guelzo, *Slaves No More: Three Essays on Emancipation and the Civil War* (Cambridge, England: Cambridge University Press, 1992), by Ira Berlin et al., LaWanda Cox's *Lincoln and Black Freedom: A Study in Presidential Leadership* (Columbia: University of South Carolina Press, 1981), Eric Foner's *Nothing But Freedom: Emancipation and Its Legacy* (Baton Rouge: Louisiana State University Press, 1983), John Hope Franklin's *The Emancipation Proclamation* (Garden City, N.Y.: Doubleday, 1963), and James M. McPherson's *Ordeal by Fire: The Civil War and Reconstruction* (2d ed., New York: McGraw-Hill, 1992) discuss the proclamation and its effects from a variety of viewpoints.

See also Abolition; Civil Rights Act of 1866; Civil War; Confiscation Acts of 1861 and 1862; Draft riots; Fourteenth Amendment; *North Star, The*; Race riots of 1866; Reconstruction; Slavery; Slavery and the justice system; Thirteenth Amendment

Employment

African Americans have historically been discriminated against in both hiring and promotion. Race relations will improve as African Americans become more prominent in positions of high responsibility.

African Americans continue to be confronted with the historical factors that produce racial discrimination in employment. Three salient factors contributing to racial discrimination in employment are trends in historical antecedents, educational level attainment, and employment and unemployment rates. Much excellent scholarly research provides data on these factors. In James Blackwell's *The Black Community: Diversity and Unity* (1975) and Talmadge Anderson's *Introduction to African American Studies* (1994), the authors provide historical and empirical data that more fully explain these areas.

Historical Antecedents

The first African American laborers were indentured servants who were brought to Jamestown, Virginia, in 1619. From the beginning, African Americans were not afforded a level playing field in employment. The seminal work by John Blassingame, *The Slave Community* (1972), offers a very good account of this period. Because the contemporary notion of rates of employment and unemployment is not relevant for slave labor, it is not possible to compare the work of African Americans and that of whites during the period of institutional slavery in America, which lasted from the mid-seventeenth century through 1865, more than two centuries.

Following slavery, most African Americans were involved in farm labor at very low wages. The majority lived in the South and often worked as sharecroppers or day laborers. In the first quarter of the twentieth century, in an effort to escape the rigid de jure (legal) segregation that restricted their opportunities for employment in the South, African Americans began moving to the North in search of better jobs in record numbers. Finding themselves in the midst of the rapidly growing Industrial Revolution, African Americans began to acquire jobs that paid wages that far exceeded those they could receive as farmhands in the South.

After World War II, more African Americans acquired skilled and professional jobs. Although in the 1990's, the wages earned by African Americans were still below those of white workers, they had slowly but steadily increased relative to those of whites. According to the U.S. census, the African American median family income was 58 percent of that of whites in 1972. By 2001, that percentage had only increased to 66 percent. It is this trend that best reflects an important relationship between the races in the area of employment.

Educational Attainment Levels

The most pervasive trend in African American and white employment is that the former has always lagged behind the latter. In both percentage of employed and earnings, African Americans compare poorly with whites. Analysis of employment data from the 1960's into the 1990's shows that African American unemployment rates were double those of whites. As reported by Claudette E. Bennett in *The Black Population in the United States*, the unemployment rate for African American men in 1994 was 14 percent; the rate for white men was 6.7 percent. In that same year, African American women were unemployed at 12.1 percent while white women had an unemployment rate of 5.5 percent. Two factors substantially contribute to this disparity: educational differences and discrimination in hiring and promotions.

Educational attainment is perhaps the highest social goal among Americans. It is generally believed that success in life, especially employment, is directly correlated to the level of education a person obtains. Since 1940, the disparity between African Americans and whites in educational attainment for grades K-12 has narrowed greatly. By 1998, the median years of education among the two groups was about equal. By that year, the percentages of whites and African Americans having completed high school was 88 percent.

However, the percentage of whites with advanced degrees remained nearly three times that of African Americans. The educational inequality at the post-high-school level places African Americans at a disadvantage when attempting to qualify for professional jobs. Some of the proposed remedies include improving physical facilities in urban and rural schools, providing equivalent educational resources for all students, improving teacher quality and teacher training, enhancing school-community relations, and hiring and promoting substantially more African American faculty and administrators.

Unemployment Rates

Two factors stand out in any description of the African American experience in hiring and promotion in the United States. The unusually high rates of unemployment (official and hidden) and a modest presence in senior management positions point to major disparities between black and white people. Hidden unemployment refers to those persons discouraged in seeking employment and those who are involuntary part-time workers. The National Urban League estimates that the hidden unemployment

Racial prejudice and discrimination have historically consigned the most poorly paying menial jobs to members of racial minorities, particularly African Americans.
(Library of Congress)

rate for African Americans may be nearly double that of the official reported rate.

Independent of gender, the unemployment rate for African Americans has continued to be more than double that of whites. This reality has held despite affirmative action, set-asides, and minority hiring policy programs. Similarly, the median per capita income for African American households and families has remained greatly below that of whites. Wealth owned by African Americans is less than 1 percent of that owned by whites. In the area of median worth of household, the U.S. Bureau of the Census reported in 1988 that African American worth was only 23 percent that of whites for families consisting of married couples. For female-headed families, African American families' worth was only 3 percent that of whites. Three times as many African American female-headed households live in poverty as those headed by white women.

Even within the corporate structure, African Americans have faired poorly. The federal Glass Ceiling Commission reported in 1995 that African Americans experienced disproportionately high resistance to advancement to high-level decision-making positions when compared with whites with similar education and training. Many of the experiences faced by African Americans in the corporate business environment are presented by George Davis and Glegg Watson in Black Life in Corporate America: Swimming in the Mainstream (1985). In a capitalist system in which employment and maximum fulfillment of human potential are vital to the accumulation of wealth, unfair employment practices have denied African Americans full opportunity to develop and maintain favorable conditions of wealth when compared with whites. With increasing national public policy that severely dampens affirmative efforts to level the playing field in hiring and promotion, the need for better education and employment seems less likely to be met.

Joe R. Feagin and Melvin P. Sikes argue in their book Living with Racism: The Black Middle-Class Experience (1994) that African Americans have been adversely affected by the racist hiring and promotion practices in the area of employment. However, most critical has been a failure of the nation to capitalize on an opportunity for a productive investment in African American human capital.

William M. Harris, Sr.

Further Reading

James Blackwell's *The Black Community: Diversity and Unity* (New York: Harper & Row, 1975), Talmadge Anderson's *Introduction to African American Studies* (Dubuque, Iowa: Kendall/Hunt, 1994), and John Blassingame's *The Slave Community* (New York: Oxford University Press, 1972) examine slavery and various historical factors that contribute to workplace discrimination against African Americans. Statistics on African Americans and employment are found in Claudette Bennett's *The Black Population in the United States* (Upland, Pa.: Diane Publishing, 1995). Two books dealing with African Americans in the workplace are George Davis and Glegg Watson's *Black Life in Corporate America: Swimming in the Mainstream* (New York: Doubleday, 1985) and Joe R. Feagin and Melvin P. Sikes's *Living with Racism: The Black Middle-Class Experience* (Boston: Beacon Press, 1994). *Social Goals and Educational Reform* (Westport, Conn.: Greenwood Press, 1988), edited by Charles V. Willie and Inabeth Miller, and *A Common Destiny: Blacks and American Society* (Washington, D.C.: National Academy Press, 1989), edited by Gerald David Jaynes and Robin M. Williams, Jr., suggest education reforms.

See also Affirmative action; Agriculture; Economic trends; Education; Equal Employment Opportunity Act of 1972; Equal Employment Opportunity Commission; Fair Employment Practices Committee; Great Migration; Sharecropping

Equal Employment Opportunity Act of 1972

The Law: Federal legislation that prohibited government agencies and educational institutions from discriminating in hiring, firing, promotion, compensation, and admission to training programs

Date: March 13, 1972

Landmark legislation helps redress historic discrimination against women and members of minorities in hiring and promotion.

The Equal Employment Opportunity (EEO) Act of 1972 was an omnibus bill appended to Title VII of the Civil Rights Act, which had been enacted on July 2, 1964, to meet a need for federal legislation dealing with job discrimination on the basis of "race, color, religion, sex or national origin." The 1964 act was charged to enforce the constitutional right to vote, to protect constitutional rights in public facilities and public education, to prevent discrimination in federally assisted programs, and to establish an Equal Employment Opportunity Commission (EEOC). Title VII did not, however, give comprehensive jurisdiction to the EEOC.

A series of laws and executive orders has built up over the years to add to the momentum against discrimination in all areas of American life. With enactment of the Fourteenth and Fifteenth Amendments, the Civil Rights Acts of 1866 and 1875, and a series of laws passed in the mid- and late 1880's, the government and the president, in theory at least, gained sufficient authority to eradicate racial discrimination, including employment bias. No president, however, used his constitutional power in this regard. With the peaking of the Civil Rights movement in the early 1960's, the pace of progress toward equal opportunity accelerated. President John F. Kennedy's Executive Order 10925 established the Committee on Equal Employment Opportunity, the predecessor of the EEOC. Numerous other executive orders by succeeding presidents followed, each chipping away at discrimination in employment.

Antidiscrimination Legislation

The first modern federal legislation to deal specifically with employment discrimination, however, was the Equal Pay Act of 1963. As a result of this act, more than $37.5 million was subsequently found to be due to 91,661 employees, almost all of them women, for the years between 1963 and 1972. Then followed the momentous Civil Rights Act of 1964, which contained the provision for equal employment opportunity that would be expanded with the 1972 law.

The push for the Equal Employment Opportunity Act was a natural result of many forces in the early 1970's: The economic disparity between white men, on one hand, and members of minorities and women, on the other, had become more apparent and disturbing. Women and members of minorities were generally last hired and first fired, with little chance for promotion. Yet, one-third of the U.S. workforce were women. Although most women worked in order to support themselves and their families, many people still considered their employment to be expendable and marginal. This was especially true for poor women, minority women, and female heads of household. Female college graduates earned only slightly more per year than the average white man with an eighth-grade education. In the 1960's, female-headed households were largely black women with one thousand dollars less than their white counterparts in annual median income. The median annual income for white women in 1971 was slightly more than five thousand dollars, and for non-white women, four thousand dollars. African Americans in general suffered more from lower salary and lower job security and benefits because, in part, they either were discouraged or, in many cases, were not permitted to join labor or professional unions. In 1972, some 88 percent of unionists—about 15 million—were white, while only 2.1 million were from minority groups.

Combatting Unemployment

Another motivation to push for the EEO Act was unemployment. In 1971, the general unemployment rate was close to 6 percent as compared to 3.4 percent as recently as 1969. Rates of joblessness were highest among the veterans returning from Vietnam (12.4 percent), and in cities with high minority populations such as Jersey City (9 to 11.9 percent) and Detroit (6 to 8.9 percent). The U.S. Department of Labor reported in 1972 that one-fifth of all wage and salary earners were unionized and males outnumbered females four to one.

The unemployment issue had plagued government and business ever since Congress passed the Employment Act of 1946, which declared, among other things, that it was federal policy to promote "maximum employment."

On March 13, 1972, the EEO Act was passed by Congress, and on March 24, it was signed into law by President Richard M. Nixon. Primary responsibility for eliminating employment discrimination was entrusted to the Equal Employment Opportunity Commission. Congress increased EEOC's authority dramatically by giving it power to issue cease-and-desist orders, to receive and investigate charges, and to engage in mediation and conciliation regarding discriminatory practices. Jurisdiction of the EEOC was extended to cover all companies and unions of fifteen or more employees, private educational institutions, and state and local governments. The EEOC found broad patterns of discrimination. It resolved most of them and referred unresolved cases to the attorney general, who had authority to file federal lawsuits.

Affirmative Action

Affirmative action became one means to promote equal employment opportunity. It was a controversial measure from the start. Opponents of affirmative action viewed it as preferential treatment or "reverse discrimination," often invoking the decision in *Griggs v. Duke Power Company* (1971), in which the Supreme Court noted that Congress did not intend to prefer the less qualified over the better qualified simply because of minority origin. Proponents of affirmative action believed that when properly implemented, the policy did not do away with competition but, rather, leveled the playing field to create equal *opportunity* for jobs in hiring, on-the-job treatment, and firing policies. Affirmative action, according to proponents, meant a conscious effort to root out all types of inequality of employment opportunity, such as unrealistic job requirements, non-job-related selection instruments and procedures, insufficient opportunity for upward mobility, and inadequate publicity about job openings.

The U.S. Civil Service Commission provided technical assistance to state and local governments in developing affirmative action plans and provided training manuals for the purpose. The thrust of EEO guidelines, however, was that gender, racial, ethnic, national origin, or religious status alone should be avoided as an employment consideration. Women and members of minorities had taken the lead in getting the EEO proposal through Congress, thus making EEO a women's and minority issue.

The EEO Act dealt with areas where discrimination had been blatant, such as hiring and promotion by small businesses and by police and fire departments, as well as admission to local unions such as branches of the longshoremen in the Northeast and Southeast. Discrimination in some areas was so blatant that the federal appeals courts actually had to order hiring of members of minorities to rectify the situation. For example, after the passage of the EEO, Minneapolis hired its first minority-group fireman in twenty-five years.

The EEO Act also dealt with various forms of discrimination against women, such as denying employment because there were no toilet facilities for women. The act required that women receive equal opportunities for sick leave, vacation, insurance, and pensions. It also became illegal to refuse to hire or to dismiss an unmarried mother as long as unwed fathers were holding jobs. Newspaper classified sections were no longer permitted to segregate help-wanted listings under male and female headings. Only a few jobs, such as that of actor, could be proved to have a bona fide occupational qualification on the basis of sex.

Opposition

Opposition forces focused on the confusion created by the passage of the EEO Act. Many of the existing labor laws protecting women and members of minorities seemed to become invalid in the context of the act. For example, the classic prohibition on work that would require a woman to lift more than a specified maximum weight could not stand. Qualification for employment would have to be based on ability to meet physical demands, regardless of gender. Banning women from certain jobs because of the possibility of pregnancy appeared to be impermissible. Leaves or special arrangements for the rearing of children would have to be available to the father, if the couple decided he was to take over domestic duties. In fact, "Men's Lib" became a new trend in the 1970's. Women's campaigns for full equality prompted men to reassess their own situation. The result was that "liberation" was becoming an issue for both men and women.

Men began moving into jobs once reserved for women, seeking alimony from wives, and demanding paternity leaves. The Supreme Court ruled that airlines could not limit flight attendant jobs to women, and most airlines began hiring some male stewards. AT&T had filled 25 percent of its clerical positions and 10 percent of its telephone operator positions with men by 1974. More men enrolled in nursing schools.

On the other hand, by the time the EEO was enacted in 1972, 31 percent of black families were headed by women. One decade later, in 1982, this figure had grown to 45 percent as compared to 14 percent of families headed by white women in the same year.

The EEO Act worked in tandem with or initiated investigations into other areas of discrimination, such as education. For example, by the late 1960's, more than a decade after the Court struck down "separate but equal" laws, more than 75 percent of the school districts in the South remained segregated. This meant markedly disproportionate employment opportunities for African Americans.

Impact

Armed with its new authority, field investigators, and two hundred newly hired lawyers, the EEOC was able to respond effectively to complaints of discrimination. Within a few weeks of assuming its new, authoritative position, the EEOC had filed suits against many big companies. The actionable charges of sex discrimination surged from 2,003 cases in 1967 to 10,436 by June of 1972. Sex discrimination cases, in only three years from 1970 through 1972, increased by nearly 300 percent. By June 30, 1972, however, only 22 percent of cases involved sex discrimination and 58 percent racial and ethnic discrimination, with 11 percent involving national origin and 2.5 percent religious discrimination. In 1972, the EEOC forced employers to give raises to some twenty-nine thousand workers, mainly women, after finding violations of the law. The total underpayment of wages amounted to about fourteen million dollars.

Much of the business sector objected to the EEOC's efforts, contending that the new law would permit employees to file class-action suits without the employer's being given fair notice of the identity of its accusers. Such criticism protested that as many as eight different laws gave employees an unfair advantage in pressing charges. Nevertheless, companies—including many large corporations that did work for the government—were forced to change their employment policies to comply, and the composition of the workforce began to change. The Equal Employment Opportunity Act, along with subsequent follow-on legislation, opened the door for many women, African Americans, and members of ethnic minorities to rise out of poverty and begin a movement toward middle- and upper-middle-class status that later would begin to change the power structure in the United States.

Chogollah Maroufi

Further Reading

Blumrosen, Alfred. *Modern Law: The Law Transmission System and Equal Employment Opportunity*. Madison: University of Wisconsin Press, 1993. Statistical and historical account of discrimination in employment; considerable discussion of the Equal Employment Opportunity Act of 1972 and its aftermath.

Equal Employment Opportunity Act of 1972. Washington, D.C.: Government Printing Office, 1972. The actual text of the Equal Employment Opportunity Act, which became law on March 13, 1972.

Libeau, Vera A. *Minority and Female Membership in Referral Unions, 1974*. Washington, D.C.: Equal Employment Opportunity Commission, 1977. Considers the special problems of women in trade unions and how they deal with job discrimination.

National Committee on Pay Equity. *Recommendation to EEOC*. Washington, D.C.: Government Printing Office, 1983. Specific proposals made to the EEOC regarding the question of equal pay for equal work.

Sedmak, Nancy J. *Primer on Equal Employment Opportunity*. 6th ed. Washington, D.C.: Bureau of National Affairs, 1994. Basic information regarding the identification of discrimination in employment and related legal remedies, explained in under-standable language.

Twomey, David. *Equal Employment Opportunity Law.* 2d ed. Cincinnati: South-Western Publishing Co., 1990. An illuminating discussion of legislation concerning discrimination in employment, with considerable attention to the Equal Employment Opportunity Act of 1972.

See also Affirmative action; Civil Rights Act of 1964; Economic trends; Employment; Equal Employment Opportunity Commission; Fair Employment Practices Committee

Equal Employment Opportunity Commission

Identification: Created by the Civil Rights Act of 1964, the EEOC monitors workplace compliance with civil rights legislation
Date: Established 1964
This commission investigates complaints of discrimination based on race, ethnicity, sex, age, religion, national origin, or disability.

Increasing numbers of cases being brought under the Civil Rights Acts of 1866 and 1871 and the Fourteenth Amendment in the 1950's and 1960's encouraged passage of the Civil Rights Act of 1964 to provide protection for workers against discrimination in the workplace. The Equal Employment Opportunity Commission (EEOC) was created to investigate complaints and to provide legal remedy to those victimized.

Initially, the EEOC focused on cases of racial discrimination in the private sector. The landmark Supreme Court decision in *Griggs v. Duke Power Company* (1971) forced employers to show the job-relatedness of employment requirements. In 1972, the Civil Rights Act of 1964 was amended to include the public sector as well as the private. Affirmative action programs were created during the 1960's and 1970's, and the EEOC monitored their implementation and operation. EEOC regulatory efforts were very broadly focused and, through consolidation of complaints into class actions, the agency was able to address broad categories of discrimination.

Judicial interpretation of the Civil Rights Act of 1964 expanded the focus of the commission to include sex discrimination and sexual harassment cases. EEOC guidelines addressed issues such as sex-based job classifications ("pink collar" occupations) that limited employment opportunities for women. The concept of comparable worth was addressed by the EEOC in the 1970's. A lack of presidential support for equal employment opportunity during the 1980's, however, slowed the process of reducing sex discrimination and addressing issues of sexual harassment. In 1979, the *Regents of the University of California v. Bakke* case challenged the validity of affirmative action programs, and the status of such programs was being hotly debated as the decade ended.

Under Presidents Ronald Reagan and George Bush, the EEOC was much less active than it had been during the 1960's and 1970's. Under the direction of Clarence Thomas, who was appointed chairman by President Reagan, the commission was much less aggressive in investigating complaints and declined to pursue sex discrimination complaints based on the concept of comparable worth. The imposition of quotas to rectify cases of long-term discrimination and the consolidation of broad classes of discrimination were effectively ended. The handling of cases one by one severely limited the effectiveness of the EEOC. The Civil Rights Act of 1991 reaffirmed the principles of equal employment opportunity and affirmative action, although the use of quotas was discontinued.

William L. Waugh, Jr.

See also Affirmative action; *Bakke* case; Civil Rights Act of 1964; Civil Rights Act of 1991; Economic trends; Employment; Equal Employment Opportunity Act of 1972; Fair Employment Practices Committee; *Griggs v. Duke Power Company*

Evans v. Abney

The Case: U.S. Supreme Court ruling on restrictive covenants
Date: January 29, 1970
The Supreme Court imposed a racially neutral principle to decide a question of the legitimacy of race-based restrictions on parkland donated to a municipality.

Justice Hugo L. Black wrote the 6-2 majority opinion upholding a decision of a Georgia court that a park built on land donated to the city of Macon explicitly for use as a whites-only park had to be closed and the property returned to the heirs of the person donating the land. Previous decisions made it clear that Macon was barred on equal protection grounds from operating the park on a racially restrictive basis. Because the benefactor had been explicit in his instructions, the Court decided the only proper course of action was to return the land to the heirs.

Although African Americans were still denied access to the park, so were whites, thus preserving racial neutrality. Justices William O. Douglas and William J. Brennan, Jr., dissented, and Thurgood Marshall did not participate.

Richard L. Wilson

See also Segregation

Fair Employment Practices Committee

Identification: Committee formed to investigate complaints of discrimination that arose from Executive Order 8802
Date: Spring, 1941
Although the committee was somewhat successful in its endeavors it was disbanded by 1946. The federal government did not establish another organization devoted to eliminating racial discrimination in employment practices until the Civil Rights Act of 1964.

In the spring of 1941, as the United States prepared to enter World War II, African American leaders pressured the administration of Franklin D. Roosevelt to eliminate segregation in the armed forces and discriminatory hiring practices in the booming war industries. A. Philip Randolph, president of the Brotherhood of Sleeping Car Porters, the largest black labor union, threatened a massive march on Washington, D.C., by a hundred thousand demonstrators under the banner Democracy Not Hypocrisy—Jobs Not Alms. Roosevelt, hoping to avoid an embarrassing racial protest that might divide the Democratic Party and his administration at a time when he needed unity for his war-preparedness program, moved to head off the March on Washington movement by meeting with Randolph and Walter White, president of the National Association for the Advancement of Colored People (NAACP).

On June 25, 1941, a week before the planned march, Roosevelt issued Executive Order 8802. It prohibited discrimination by employers, unions, and government agencies involved in defense work on the basis of race, creed, color, or national origin but made no mention of desegregating the armed forces. Roosevelt established the Fair Employment Practices Committee (FEPC) to investigate complaints and redress grievances stemming from the order. Randolph and White accepted the compromise arrangement and called off the march.

Although African Americans hailed the FEPC as the greatest step forward in race relations since the Civil War, Roosevelt initially gave the agency little authority. Underfunded and understaffed, the FEPC at first could do little more than conduct investigations into complaints received and make recommendations, relying on the powers of publicity and persuasion to achieve change. In mid-1943, however, amid mounting concern that manpower shortages were hurting the war effort, Roosevelt beefed up the agency by giving it the authority to conduct hearings, make findings, issue directives to war industries, and make recommendations to the War Manpower Commission to curb discrimination.

Impact

The FEPC had a mixed record of accomplishment in eliminating racial discrimination in the war industries and government agencies. It resolved less than half of the eight thousand complaints received, and employers and unions often ignored its compliance orders with impunity. Although African American employment in the war industries increased from 3 percent in 1942 to 8 percent in 1945 and the federal government more than tripled its number of black employees, such changes had more to do with wartime labor shortages than FEPC actions. Nevertheless, the FEPC scored some significant successes. In 1944, federal troops broke up a strike by white Philadelphia transit workers and enforced an FEPC directive that African Americans be upgraded to positions as streetcar operators. At war's end, despite the FEPC's shortcomings, African American leaders and white liberals hoped to transform the committee into a permanent agency. In 1946, however, southern Democrats in the Senate filibustered a bill to extend the FEPC and killed the agency. Although several northern states passed their own Fair Employment Practices acts, the Senate again blocked bills to create a permanent FEPC in 1950 and 1952. Not until the Civil Rights Act of 1964 did the federal government establish another agency devoted to eliminating racial discrimination in employment practices.

Richard V. Damms

See also Brotherhood of Sleeping Car Porters; Civil Rights Act of 1964; Defense industry desegregation; Economic trends; Employment; Equal Employment Opportunity Act of 1972; Equal Employment Opportunity Commission; Military desegregation; National Association for the Advancement of Colored People

Fair Housing Act

The Law: Federal legislation that prohibited discrimination in housing

Date: April 11, 1968

This law helped to break racial enclaves in residential neighborhoods and promoted upward mobility for members of minorities.

The Civil Rights Act of 1866 provided that all citizens should have the same rights "to inherit, purchase, lease, sell, hold, and convey real and personal property," but the law was never enforced. Instead, such federal agencies as the Farmers Home Administration, the Federal Housing Administration, and the Veterans Administration financially supported segregated housing until 1962, when President John F. Kennedy issued Executive Order 11063 to stop the practice.

California passed a general nondiscrimination law in 1959 and an explicit fair housing law in 1963. In 1964, voters enacted Proposition 14, an initiative to repeal the 1963 statute and the applicability of the 1959 law to housing. When a landlord in Santa Ana refused to rent to an African American in 1963, the latter sued, thus challenging Proposition 14. The California Supreme Court, which heard the case in 1966, ruled that Proposition 14 was contrary to the Fourteenth Amendment to the U.S. Constitution, because it was not neutral on the matter of housing discrimination; instead, based on the context in which it was adopted, Proposition 14 served to legitimate and promote discrimination. On appeal, the U.S. Supreme Court let the California Supreme Court decision stand in *Reitman v. Mulkey* (1967).

Johnson's Efforts

President Lyndon B. Johnson had hoped to include housing discrimination as a provision in the comprehensive Civil Rights Act of 1964, but he demurred when southern senators threatened to block the nomination of Robert Weaver as the first African American cabinet appointee. After 1964, southern members of Congress were adamantly opposed to any expansion of civil rights. Although Johnson urged passage of a federal law against housing discrimination in requests to Congress in 1966 and 1967, there was no mention of the idea during his state of the union address in 1968. Liberal members of Congress pressed the issue regardless, and southern senators responded by threatening a filibuster. This threat emboldened Senators Edward W. Brooke and Walter F. Mondale, a moderate Republican and a liberal Democrat, respectively, to cosponsor fair housing legislation, but they needed the support of conservative midwestern Republicans to break a filibuster. Illinois Republican senator Everett Dirksen arranged a compromise whereby housing discrimination would be declared illegal, but federal enforcement power would be minimal.

In the wake of *Reitman v. Mulkey*, the assassination of Martin Luther King, Jr., on April 4, 1968, and subsequent urban riots, Congress established fair housing as a national priority on April 10 by adopting Titles VIII and IX of the Civil Rights Act of 1968, also known as the Fair Housing Act or Open Housing Act. Signed by Johnson on the following day, the law originally prohibited discrimination in housing on the basis of race, color, religion, or national origin. In 1974, an amendment expanded the coverage to include sex (gender) discrimination; in 1988, the law was extended to protect persons with disabilities and families with children younger than eighteen years of age.

Title VIII prohibits discrimination in the sale or rental of dwellings, in the financing of housing, in advertising, in the use of a multiple listing service, and in practices that "otherwise make unavailable or deny" housing, a phrase that some courts have interpreted to outlaw exclusionary zoning, mortgage redlining, and racial steering. Blockbusting, the practice of inducing a white homeowner to sell to a minority buyer in order to frighten others on the block to sell their houses at a loss, is also prohibited. It is not necessary to show intent in order to prove discrimination; policies, practices, and procedures that have the effect of excluding members of minorities, women, persons with disabilities, and children are illegal, unless otherwise deemed reasonable. Title VIII, as amended in 1988, covers persons who believe that they are adversely affected by a discriminatory policy, practice, or procedure, even before they incur damages.

The law applies to about 80 percent of all housing in the United States. One exception to the statute is a single-family house sold or rented without the use of a broker and without discriminatory advertising, when the owner owns no more than three such houses and sells only one house in a two-year period. Neither does the statute apply to a four-unit dwelling if the owner lives in one of the units, the so-called Mrs.-Murphy's-rooming-house exception. Dwellings owned by private clubs or religious organizations that rent to their own members on a non-commercial basis are also exempt.

Enforcement

Enforcement of the statute was left to the secretary of the Department of Housing and Urban Development (HUD). Complaints originally had to be filed within 180 days of the offending act, but in 1988, this period was amended to one year. HUD has estimated that there are about two million instances of housing discrimination each year, although formal complaints have averaged only forty thousand per year. The U.S. attorney general can bring a civil suit against a flagrant violator of the law.

According to the law, HUD automatically refers complaints to local agencies that administer "substantially equivalent" fair housing laws. HUD can act if the local agencies fail to do so, but initially was expected only to use conference, conciliation, and persuasion to bring about voluntary compliance. The Fair Housing Amendments Act of 1988 authorized an administrative law tribunal to hear cases that cannot be settled by persuasion. The administrative law judges have the power to issue cease and desist orders to offending parties.

HUD has used "testers" to show discrimination. For example, a team of black and white people might arrange to have an African American apply for a rental; if turned down, the black tester would contact a white tester to ascertain whether the landlord were willing to rent to a white instead. That testers have standing to sue was established by the U.S. Supreme Court in *Havens v. Coleman* (1982).

Under the administrative law procedure, penalties are up to $10,000 for the first offense, $25,000 for the second offense, and $50,000 for each offense thereafter. Attorney fees and court costs can be recovered by the prevailing party. In 1988, civil penalties in a suit filed by the U.S. attorney general were established as up to $50,000 for the first offense and $100,000 for each offense thereafter.

Title IX of the law prohibits intimidation or attempted injury of anyone filing a housing discrimination complaint. A violator can be assessed a criminal penalty of $1,000 and/or sentenced to one year in jail. If a complainant is actually injured, the penalty can increase to $10,000 and/or ten years of imprisonment. If a complainant is killed, the penalty is life imprisonment.

Impact

The effect of the 1968 Fair Housing Act has been minimal. Without a larger supply of affordable housing, many African Americans in particular have nowhere to move in order to enjoy integrated housing. Federal subsidies for low-cost housing, under such legislation as the Housing and Urban Development Act of 1968 and the Housing and Community Development Act of 1974, have declined significantly since the 1980's. Conscientious private developers are confronted with the text of a law that aims to provide integrated housing but proscribes achieving integration by establishing quotas to ensure a mixed racial composition among those who seek to buy or rent dwelling units.

Michael Haas

Further Reading

Ingrid Gould Ellen's *Sharing America's Neighborhoods: The Prospects for Stable Racial Integration* (Cambridge, Mass.: Harvard University Press, 2000) is an analysis of integration and housing. James A. Kushner's *Fair Housing: Discrimination in Real Estate, Community Development, and Revitalization* (Colorado Springs, Colo.: McGraw-Hill, 1983) is a compendium of legislation and litigation. George R. Metcalf's *Fair Housing Comes of Age* (New York: Greenwood Press, 1988) is a comprehensive evaluation of the precedent, purposes, and problems of enacting, implementing, and enforcing fair housing legislation. *The Fair Housing Act After Twenty Years* (New Haven, Conn.: Yale Law School, 1989), edited by Robert G. Schwemm, evaluates the political and social impediments to achieving nondiscrimination in housing.

See also Civil Rights Act of 1964; *Reitman v. Mulkey*; Restrictive covenants; Segregation; *Shelley v. Kraemer*

Fifteenth Amendment

The Law: Amendment to the U.S. Constitution forbidding discrimination in voting rights on the basis of race, color, or previous condition of servitude. Section 2 gives enforcement power to Congress

Date: 1870

The U.S. Supreme Court has used the Fifteenth Amendment to decide many cases involving discrimination in access to voting, especially after the passage of the Voting Rights Act of 1965. The law and the Court's interpretive decisions ended racially discriminatory voting restrictions in the United States.

The original U.S. Constitution tied the right of individuals to vote in federal elections to state election laws. A person who was eligible to vote in elections for the lower house of the state legislature was entitled to vote in federal elections. The result was that eligibility to vote was determined by state, not federal, law. If a national decision on voting rights was to be made, a constitutional amendment such as the Twenty-fourth, which ended poll taxes, was required.

In 1868, after the Northern victory in the Civil War, the Fourteenth Amendment established citizenship and civil rights for the newly freed slaves. On February 3, 1870, the Fifteenth Amendment was adopted to prevent state governments from denying freed slaves the right to vote. Its language however, is much broader, because it prohibits denial of the right to vote "on account of race, color, or previous condition of servitude." Section 2 of the amendment gives Congress the power to enforce its terms by remedial legislation.

Discriminatory Laws

Immediately after the ratification of the amendment, Congress passed the Enforcement Act of 1870, which made it a crime for public officers and private persons to obstruct the right to vote. Enforcement of this law was spotty and ineffective, and most of its provisions were repealed in 1894. Meanwhile, beginning in 1890, most of the states of the former Confederacy passed laws

---

The Fifteenth Amendment

SECTION 1. The right of citizens of the United States to vote shall not be denied or abridged by the United States or by any State on account of race, color, or previous condition of servitude.

SECTION 2. The Congress shall have power to enforce this article by appropriate legislation.

---

that were specifically designed to keep African Americans from voting. Literacy tests were a major disqualifier because at that time more than two-thirds of adult African Americans were illiterate. At the same time, white illiterates were allowed to vote under grandfather clauses, property qualifications, and "good character" exceptions, from which African Americans were excluded. Racially discriminatory enforcement of voting qualifications became the principal means by which African Americans were barred from the polls.

In the absence of a statute, the only remedy for these discriminatory practices was case-by-case litigation. The Supreme Court, in case after case, struck down the discriminatory state practices. Grandfather clauses were invalidated in *Guinn v. United States* (1915). The state-mandated all-white primary was outlawed in *Nixon v. Herndon* (1927); party-operated all-white primaries were forbidden by *Smith v. Allwright* (1944) and *Terry v. Adams* (1953). The Court held in *United States v. Thomas* (1959) that phony polling place challenges to African Americans seeking to vote—by the time the challenges had been resolved, the polls had closed—were improper under the Fifteenth Amendment.

Racial gerrymandering was forbidden by *Gomillion v. Lightfoot* (1960). In that case, Alabama had redefined the shape of the city of Tuskegee so as to exclude all but four or five of its four hundred African American voters, thus denying this group the opportunity to influence city government. The Court also dealt with discriminatory administration of literacy tests in several cases, most important, *Schnell v. Davis* (1949), in which Justice William O. Douglas, writing for the Court, remarked that "the legislative setting and the great discretion it vested in the registrar made it clear that . . . the literacy requirement was merely a device to make racial discrimination easy."

Voting Rights Act of 1965

The mass disfranchisement of African Americans could not be reached efficiently or fully by means of individually brought cases. Although some of the discriminatory state practices were halted, every voting registration decision could be made on the basis of race if voting registrars wished to do so. Against this background, Congress passed the Voting Rights Act of 1965. Section 2 of the Fifteenth Amendment provided constitutional authority for this law, which was aimed at "ridding the country of racial discrimination in voting," according to the statute's preamble. The law forbade a number of discriminatory practices. Literacy tests were "suspended" for five years in areas where voting discrimination had been most flagrant. To deal with voting discrimination through outright intimidation and violence, the law provided for federal voting registrars and protection by federal marshals.

African Americans marching in New York City to celebrate the ratification of the Fifteenth Amendment in April, 1870. (Library of Congress)

The first important cases arising under this law came to the Court in 1966. In *South Carolina v. Katzenbach* (1966), the Court held unanimously that the most important provisions of the Voting Rights Act were constitutional. Chief Justice Earl Warren wrote that "the record here showed that in most of the States covered, various tests and devices have been instituted with the purpose of disenfranchising Negroes, have been framed in such a way as to facilitate this aim, and have been administered in a discriminatory fashion for many years. Under these circumstances, the 15th Amendment has clearly been violated." Because Congress's power under the amendment is remedial, this finding of fact was necessary to invoke federal power. The broad construction of Congress's power to deal with discrimination in voting in *South Carolina v. Katzenbach* established an important precedent to which the Court consistently adhered.

Voting Rights Act of 1970

Congress renewed the Voting Rights Act in 1970 and extended the literacy test ban to the entire country. The extension reached New York State's English-language literacy test, which had the practical effect of disfranchising many Puerto Rican voters. The English-language literacy test had been in place long before any substantial Puerto Rican migration to New York City had taken place. The extension was upheld by the Court in *Oregon v. Mitchell* (1970). Although the justices disagreed on some aspects of the new law, they were unanimous in upholding the constitutionality of the literacy test ban, even though there was no showing that New York had attempted to discriminate against Puerto Ricans. However, in *Rome v. United States* (1980), the Court became enmeshed in the question of the extent to which Congress may control state and local government under the Fifteenth Amendment. The question arose as to whether the remedial power reached only deliberate attempts by states and municipalities to deny Fifteenth Amendment voting rights or whether it was the effect of state practices on African American—and by extension, other minority group—voting that authorized federal action. The Court has not fully settled this extraordinarily complex constitutional question. Congress renewed and further extended the requirements of the Voting Rights Act again in 1982, this time for a period of twenty-five years.

The effect of the Court's Fifteenth Amendment decisions coupled with the broader provisions of the Voting Rights Act has been immense. In 1961 only 1.2 million African Americans were registered to vote in the South—one-quarter of voting-age African Americans. By 1964 nearly 2 million were registered. In 1975 between 3.5 and 4 million African Americans were registered to vote in the South. By the end of the century, although electoral turnout among African Americans and other persons of color in the United States is still lower than that of whites, the gap has nearly been closed. Formal legal discriminatory barriers to voting no longer exist.

Robert Jacobs

Further Reading

Conscience and the Constitution: History, Theory, and Law of the Reconstruction Amendments (Princeton, N.J.: Princeton University Press, 1993) by David A. J. Richards provides an analysis of the Fifteenth Amendment. Jack Greenberg's *Race Relations and American Law* (New York: Columbia University Press, 1959) offers a good place to start for a comprehensive view of the constitutional rules before the passage of the Civil Rights Act of 1964 and the Voting Rights Act of 1965. John Braeman's *Before the Civil Rights Revolution: The Old Court and Individual Rights* (New York: Greenwood Press, 1988) discusses the developing jurisprudence of the Court in the area of civil rights. For insight into the inner workings of the Warren Court, Bernard Schwartz's *Inside the Warren Court* (Garden City, N.Y.: Doubleday, 1983), with Stephen Lesher, is based not only on the documentation but also on personal acquaintance. *Compromised Compliance: Implementation of the 1965 Voting Rights Act* (Westport, Conn.: Greenwood Press, 1982) by Howard Ball, Dale Krane, and Thomas P. Lauth contains one of the first important discussions of the remedial versus effects morass in which the Court finds itself.

Using cases, Daniel Hays Lowenstein's *Election Law* (Durham, N.C.: Carolina Academic Press, 1995) analyzes how the Supreme Court has treated questions regarding electoral structures and processes. J. Morgan Kousser's *The Shaping of Southern Politics: Suffrage Restriction and the Establishment of the One-Party South, 1880-1910* (New Haven, Conn.: Yale University Press, 1974) and *Colorblind Injustice: Minority Voting Rights and the Undoing of the Second Reconstruction* (Chapel Hill: University of North Carolina Press, 1998) analyze the right to vote in the South, covering the Reconstruction era in the first volume and the post-World War II years in the second. Michael Dawson's *Behind the Mule: Race and Class in American Politics* (Princeton, N.J.: Princeton University Press, 1994) examines voting rights in connection with race as does Abigail M. Thernstrom's *Whose Votes Count? Affirmative Action and Minority Voting Rights* (Cambridge, Mass.: Harvard University Press, 1987).

See also Civil War; Fourteenth Amendment; Gerrymandering; *Gomillion v. Lightfoot*; Grandfather clauses; *Guinn v. United States*; Ku Klux Klan Acts; *Lassiter v. Northampton County Board of Elections*; Poll taxes; Reconstruction; *Smith v. Allwright*; *Terry v. Adams*; Thirteenth Amendment; Twenty-fourth Amendment; Understanding tests; Voting Rights Act of 1965; White primaries; *Yarbrough, Ex parte*

Film history

Cinematic representations of African Americans have been the subject of debate and contest since the inception of the film industry. Struggles over stereotypes within film and over who controls the production of images of African Americans are firmly linked to broad cultural understandings and conceptions of race.

The social and political stakes of film for African Americans were dramatically expressed early on, in the reception of D. W. Griffith's 1915 film *Birth of a Nation*. As the first full-length feature film, *Birth of a Nation* helped inaugurate the studio system, and Griffith's work as director supplied some of the basic elements of cinematic grammar. The film represented African Americans in purely stereotypical roles (as happy and loyal slaves, mammies, bucks, and brutes) while glorifying the Ku Klux Klan. Because the film was released while lynching was at its peak, the material it treated raised some concern, and the National Association for the Advancement of Colored People (NAACP) protested the film. As Ed Guerrero notes in *Framing Blackness* (1993), screenings of the film were often preceded by people dressed as members of the Klan riding through towns, and there was a march of twenty-five thousand Klansmen through Atlanta, Georgia, on opening night. Although the NAACP was not able to prevent the film from being shown, it did succeed in bringing enough political and economic pressure to make Hollywood executives think twice before producing a film that celebrated organizations like the Klan.

Although *Birth of a Nation* may have presented an unusually virulent form of racism, stereotypical cinematic representations of African Americans would predominate in mainstream films for decades to come. However, these films never existed without contest or debate. Some African Americans believed that the best way to counter stereotypical representations was to protest in the courtrooms and streets; others decided to produce their own images.

In the late 1920's and 1930's, a series of "race films" that were produced, written, and directed by African Americans attempted to present more realistic images of African Americans. Oscar Micheaux was the most famous of these filmmakers, releasing thirty-four films during a thirty-year period. Micheaux and the other independent black filmmakers who were his contemporaries had very limited resources, and it was not always clear that their representations were any less stereotypical than those of their mainstream counterparts. Nevertheless, they did manage to address black themes and to provide exposure for a large number of black actors while explicitly addressing a black audience.

Civil Rights, Black Power and Blaxploitation

Although this early independent black film industry started to decline in the face of increased competition from Hollywood studios and the economic toll of the Great Depression, some of its concerns were eventually addressed by mainstream cinema.

From the end of World War II through the 1960's, the Civil Rights and Black Power movements increasingly targeted Hollywood and helped create an environment in which some of the earlier depictions of African Americans were increasingly untenable. Stereotypes such as "mammies" and "bucks" never disappeared from Hollywood films, but they were eventually supplemented with more nuanced images of African Americans. Although mainstream films in the years immediately after *Birth of a Nation* tended to support the ideals of segregation, Hollywood films in the 1950's and 1960's had an integrationist ethic, which was marked most clearly by the growing stardom of African American Sidney Poitier in such films as *Edge of the City* (1957) and *The Defiant Ones* (1958).

At the height of the Black Power movement, African American audiences expressed dissatisfaction with integrationist narratives that failed to address the contemporary realities of racism. This, coupled with black political power and the severe financial

In the film To Kill a Mockingbird *(1962), based on Harper Lee's novel, a southern lawyer (Gregory Peck, front left) defends a poor African American (Brock Peters, front right) falsely accused of rape. Its depiction of the justice system is considered so authentic that it is used in the training of lawyers.* (Museum of Modern Art, Film Stills Archive)

problems that were facing the Hollywood studios, led to a new wave of black-centered films that were released in the late 1960's and early 1970's and were labeled "blaxploitation" films because they were cheaply made and generally relied upon the same kinds of sexuality and violence that Hollywood used in its "exploitation" films.

Some of the most famous blaxploitation films, including *Sweet Sweetback's Baadasssss Song* (1971), *Shaft* (1972), and *Superfly* (1972), featured supermasculine black heroes who often had to fight against an oppressive social system. Occasionally, these heroes were women, including Tamara Dobson and Pam Grier in films such as *Cleopatra Jones* (1973) and *Coffy* (1973), who were just as macho as their male counterparts, Fred Williamson and Jim Brown. Although the depictions of strong African American heroes who were able to confront the problems surrounding them appealed to many African Americans, the films were criticized and protested for their tendency to reproduce stereotypical images of African Americans as prostitutes, pimps, and violent drug dealers. By the mid-1970's, the genre had died out, as Hollywood studios discovered that they could court African American audiences without relying on black-centered films.

Backlash and Beyond

In the late 1970's and the 1980's, a conservative backlash against African American protests and gains (in the cinema as well as in the broader society) produced a series of films that openly relied upon racial stereotypes. However, films in which African Americans are presented solely as stereotypical or peripheral figures (such as the *Rocky* series, 1976-1990, or *Caddyshack*, 1980) were eventually joined by a series of new black independent films made by people such as Robert Townsend and Spike Lee. Townsend's *Hollywood Shuffle* (1987) was an explicit critique of Hollywood's representations of African Americans. It follows the career of a young and talented black actor who finds that there is plenty of work available in Hollywood, but only in stereotypical roles, as pimps, muggers, and so on.

The most powerful African American filmmaker to emerge in the 1980's was Spike Lee. Lee's first commercial film, *She's Gotta*

Have It (1986), which was criticized for its depiction of black sexuality and its apparent acceptance of a black woman's rape, nevertheless presented African Americans as fully realized human beings in a black-centered world. However, it was Lee's 1989 film *Do the Right Thing* that established him as one of the most important and influential directors of the decade. The film, which follows events that lead to the death of a black man at the hands of white police officers, had tremendous box-office success although it was also the subject of immense controversy. It is widely credited with enabling the success of a variety of 1990's black filmmakers such as Matty Rich, the Hughes Brothers, and John Singleton.

The 1990's saw a proliferation of black-centered mainstream and independent films. Some of the most interesting of these films (such as Cheryl Dunye's *The Watermelon Woman*, 1997, and John Singleton's *Rosewood*, 1997) were intended, in part, to question or correct Hollywood's past treatment of African Americans. Others, such as Kasi Lemmon's *Eve's Bayou* (1997), depict African American social worlds without any apology for the omission of white characters. Of course, African American characters were also present in a wide variety of films in which they were not always central to the narratives, and black stereotypes resurfaced and were reconfigured in seemingly endless varieties. *Just Cause* (1995) and *A Time to Kill* (1996) in particular are remarkable for the ways in which they critique, reconfigure, and redeploy the figure of the black brute/rapist. The tension between and within films in the 1990's serves as a condensed history of the always contested cinematic representations of African Americans.

Jonathan Markovitz

Further Reading

Donald Bogle's *Bright Boulevards, Bold Dreams: The Story of Black Hollywood* (New York: One World Ballantine Books, 2005) provides a fascinating examination of African Americans in the film industry. Bogle's *Primetime Blues: African Americans on Network Television* (New York: Farrar, Straus and Giroux, 2001) is a notable analysis of the role of African Americans on television. Bogle's *Toms, Coons, Mulattoes, Mammies, and Bucks* (New York:

Continuum, 1992) provides the most thorough investigation of African American stereotypes in film. Ed Guerrero's *Framing Blackness* (Philadelphia: Temple University Press, 1993) is an excellent analysis of the ways in which blacks have been defined by film and have struggled to define themselves in that medium. Robert Lang's *The Birth of a Nation* (New Brunswick, N.J.: Rutgers University Press, 1994) and Fred Silva's edited collection *Focus on "The Birth of the Nation"* (Englewood Cliffs, N.J.: Prentice-Hall, 1971) provide extended discussions of the importance and legacy of *Birth of a Nation*. Lisa M. Anderson's *Mammies No More* examines changing cultural representations of black women.

See also Cowboys; Harlem Renaissance; Ku Klux Klan; Literature; Lynching; Music; *Roots*; Stereotypes

Fourteenth Amendment

The Law: Amendment to the U.S. Constitution that provides legal protections for individuals against state violations of civil rights
Date: Ratified in July, 1868
The Supreme Court used the due process and equal protection clauses of this amendment in order to expand both the number and breadth of rights protecting individuals. More than any other amendment, the Fourteenth provided the basis for the range of rights that Americans came to take for granted during the twentieth century.

The Fourteenth Amendment to the U.S. Constitution, ratified by Congress in 1868, was part of the plan for Reconstruction following the Civil War (1861-1865) and was formulated by the Republican majority in the Thirty-ninth Congress. Before Congress met in December, 1865, President Andrew Johnson had authorized the restoration of white self-government in the former Confederate states, and the congressmen and senators from those states waited in Washington to be seated in Congress. The abolition of slavery had destroyed the old compromise under which five slaves counted as three free persons in apportioning representation in the House and the electoral college, and the Republicans wanted to make sure that the South did not add to its numbers in the House and thus profit from rebellion.

Between December, 1865, and May, 1866, the Republicans attempted to hammer out a program that would accomplish their purposes in the South, unite members of their party in Congress, and appeal to northern voters. Given the diversity of opinion within the party, this undertaking proved to be difficult. Radical Republicans wanted African American suffrage, permanent political proscription, and confiscation of the property of ex-Confederates. Some maintained they were authorized in these actions by the Thirteenth Amendment, which, they believed, gave Congress the power to abolish the "vestiges of slavery." Moderate Republicans, on the other hand, feared political repercussions from African American suffrage, as such a requirement

The Fourteenth Amendment

SECTION 1. All persons born or naturalized in the United States and subject to the jurisdiction thereof, are citizens of the United States and of the State wherein they reside. No State shall make or enforce any law which shall abridge the privileges or immunities of citizens of the United States; nor shall any State deprive any person of life, liberty, or property, without due process of law; nor deny to any person within its jurisdiction the equal protection of the laws.

SECTION 2. Representatives shall be apportioned among the several States according to their respective numbers, counting the whole number of persons in each State, excluding Indians not taxed. But when the right to vote at any election for the choice of electors for President and Vice President of the United States, Representatives in Congress, the Executive and Judicial officers of a State, or the members of the Legislature thereof, is denied to any of the male inhabitants of such State, being twenty-one years of age, and citizens of the United States, or in any way abridged, except for participation in rebellion, or other crime, the basis of representation therein shall be reduced in the proportion which the number of such male citizens shall bear to the whole number of male citizens twenty-one years of age in such State.

would result in beginning the Reconstruction process over again. Many moderates also believed that an additional amendment to the Constitution was needed to provide precise authority for Congress to enact civil rights legislation.

From deliberations of the joint committee and debate on the floor of the House came the Fourteenth Amendment. Many Republicans believed that the proposal was in the nature of a peace treaty, although this view was not explicitly stated. If the South accepted the amendment, the southern states were to be readmitted and their senators and representatives seated in Congress; in other words, Reconstruction would end. Republicans presented a united front during the final vote as a matter of party policy. Because the amendment was an obvious compromise between radicals and moderates, it was too strong for some and too weak for others.

SECTION 3. No person shall be a Senator or Representative in Congress, or elector of President and Vice President, or hold any office, civil or military, under the United States, or under any State, who, having previously taken an oath, as a member of Congress, or as an officer of the United States, or as a member of any State legislature, or as an executive or judicial officer of any State, to support the Constitution of the United States, shall have engaged in insurrection or rebellion against the same, or given aid or comfort to the enemies thereof. But Congress may by a vote of two-thirds of each House, remove such disability.

SECTION 4. The validity of the public debt of the United States, authorized by law, including debts incurred for payment of pensions and bounties for services in suppressing insurrection or rebellion, shall not be questioned. But neither the United States nor any State shall assume or pay any debt or obligation incurred in aid of insurrection or rebellion against the United States, or any claim for the loss or emancipation of any slave; but all such debts, obligations and claims shall be held illegal and void.

SECTION 5. The Congress shall have power to enforce, by appropriate legislation, the provisions of this article.

The Amendment

The Fourteenth Amendment became the most important addition to the Constitution since the Bill of Rights had been adopted in 1791. It contains five sections.

Section 1, the first constitutional definition of citizenship, states that all persons born or naturalized in the United States are citizens of the United States and of the state in which they reside. It includes limits on the power of states, by providing that no state may abridge the privileges and immunities of citizens, deprive any person of life, liberty, or property without due process of law, or deny to any person within its jurisdiction the equal protection of law. This section was intended to guarantee African Americans the rights of citizenship, although the amendment's framers did not define exactly which rights were included. Nor did they define "state action" to specify whether the term meant only official acts of state government or the actions of individuals functioning privately with state approval.

The courts later interpreted the due process clause to extend the rights of the accused listed in the Bill of Rights, which had applied only to the federal government, to the states. They expanded the notion of equal protection to include other categories, such as sex and disability, as well as race. They also interpreted the word "person" to include corporations as legal persons; under this interpretation, corporations found protection from much state regulation.

Section 2 gives a new formula of representation in place of the old three-fifths compromise of the Constitution, under which five slaves were counted as equal to three free persons in determining a state's representation in the House of Representatives and the electoral college. All persons in a state were to be counted for representation, but if a state should disfranchise any of its adult male citizens, except for participation in rebellion or any other crime, the basis of its representation would be reduced proportionately. While not guaranteeing suffrage to African Americans, this provision threatened the South with a loss of representation should black males be denied the vote.

Section 3 declares that no person who has ever taken an oath to support the Constitution (which included all who had been in the military service or held state or national office before 1860) and has then participated in the rebellion can be a senator or representative or hold any civil or military office, national or state. This disability could be removed only by a two-thirds vote of both houses of Congress. This section took away the pardoning power of the president, which congressional Republicans believed Andrew Johnson used too generously.

Section 4 validates the debt of the United States, voids all debts incurred to support rebellion, and invalidates all claims for compensation for emancipated slaves.

Section 5 gives Congress authority to pass legislation to enforce the provisions of the Fourteenth Amendment.

The correspondence and speeches of those who framed the Fourteenth Amendment do not support any theories of economic conspiracy or ulterior motives. The framers desired to protect the former slaves and boost Republicanism in the South by barring old Confederates from returning to Congress and the electoral college with increased voting strength. They hoped to do this without threatening the federal system or unduly upsetting the relationship between the central government and the states. At the same time, Republicans wanted to unify their party and project a popular issue for the approaching electoral contest against Andrew Johnson.

William J. Cooper, Jr.
Updated by Mary Welek Atwell

Further Reading

Michael J. Perry's *We the People: The Fourteenth Amendment and the Supreme Court* (New York: Oxford University Press, 1999) is an important contribution to the literature on this subject. *Conscience and the Constitution: History, Theory, and Law of the Reconstruction Amendments* (Princeton, N.J.: Princeton University Press, 1993) by David A. J. Richards provides an analysis of the Fourteenth Amendment. Michael Les Benedict's *A Compromise of Principle: Congressional Republicans and Reconstruction, 1863-1869* (New York: W. W. Norton, 1974) emphasizes the Republicans' concern that the Fourteenth Amendment maintain the role of the states in the federal system. LaWanda Cox and John H. Cox's *Politics, Princi-*

ple, and Prejudice: Dilemma of Reconstruction America, 1865-1866 (New York: Free Press, 1963) posits that civil rights, rather than merely partisan politics, was the central issue during Reconstruction. Harold M. Hyman and William Wiecek's *Equal Justice Under Law: Constitutional Development, 1835-1875* (New York: Harper & Row, 1982) includes a thorough discussion of the Fourteenth Amendment as a logical and necessary extension of the Thirteenth Amendment. Donald E. Lively's *The Constitution and Race* (New York: Praeger, 1992) focuses on the association of attitudes toward race and constitutional interpretation.

See also Black codes; *Brown v. Board of Education*; Civil Rights Act of 1866; Civil Rights Act of 1964; Civil Rights Acts of 1866-1875; *Civil Rights Cases*; Civil War; Disfranchisement laws in Mississippi; Emancipation Proclamation; Fifteenth Amendment; Reconstruction; Thirteenth Amendment

Free African Society

Identification: Movement founded for a dual purpose—to serve the black community's religious needs as a nondenominational congregation and to function as a benevolent mutual aid organization

Date: Founded in 1787

Place: Pennsylvania

The Free African Society was the first major secular institution with a mission to aid African Americans.

Both the origins of the Free African Society and the long-term repercussions of its founding form an essential part of the religious history of African Americans. The original organization itself was of short duration: About seven years after it was organized in 1787, it disappeared as a formal body. In its immediate wake, however, closely related institutions emerged that tried to take over its proclaimed mission.

Generally speaking, prior to the 1790's people of African slave origins who managed to obtain their individual freedom had only one option if they wished to practice Christianity: association, as subordinate parishioners, in an existing white-dominated church. Several churches in the American colonies before independence, including the Quakers and Methodists, had tried to identify their religious cause with that of the black victims of slavery.

Richard Allen

Richard Allen, born in 1760 as a slave whose family belonged to Pennsylvania's then attorney general, Benjamin Chew, was destined to become one of the earliest religious leaders of the black segment of the American Methodist Church. As a youth, Allen gained extensive experience with Methodist teachings after his family was separated on the auction block in Dover, Delaware. Allen was encouraged by his second owner, Master Stokeley, to espouse the religious teachings of the itinerant American Methodist preacher Freeborn Garrettson. Allen's conversion to Methodism was rewarded when Stokeley freed him at age twenty to follow the calling of religion. His freedom came just as the Revolutionary War ended.

For six years, Allen worked under the influence of Methodist evangelist Benjamin Abbott and the Reverend (later Bishop) Richard Whatcoat, with whom he traveled on an extensive preaching circuit. Allen's writings refer to Whatcoat as his "father in Israel." With Whatcoat's encouragement, Allen accepted an invitation from the Methodist elder in Philadelphia to return to his birthplace to become a preacher. At that time, Philadelphia's religious environment seemed to be dominated by the Episcopal Church. This church had been active since 1758 in extending its ministry to African Americans. It was St. George's Methodist Episcopal Church, however, that, in the 1780's, had drawn the largest number of former slaves to its rolls. Once the circumstances of the second-class status of African Americans became clear to Allen, he decided that his leadership mission should be specifically dedicated to the needs of his people. Within a short time, he joined another African American, Absalom Jones, in founding what was originally intended to be more of a secular movement than a formal denominational movement: the Free African Society.

Absalom Jones

Absalom Jones was older than Allen and had a different set of life experiences. Born a slave in Delaware in 1746, Jones served for more than twenty years in his master's store in Philadelphia. He earned enough money to purchase his wife's freedom, to build his own home, and finally, in 1784, to purchase his own freedom. He continued to work for his former master for wages and bought and managed two houses for additional income. His success earned for him great respect among other free blacks and opened the way for him to serve as lay leader representing the African American membership of St. George's Methodist Episcopal Church.

Traditional accounts of Jones's role in the founding of the Free African Society assert that, when Jones refused to comply with the announcement of St. George's sexton that African American parishioners should give up their usual seats among the white congregation and move to the upper gallery, he was supported by Richard Allen, in particular. The two then agreed that the only way African Americans could worship in an environment that responded to their social, as well as religious, needs would be to found an all-black congregation. Some sources suggest that Jones's reaction to the reseating order was the crowning blow, and that Allen previously had tried to organize several fellow black parishioners, including Doras Giddings, William White, and Jones, to support his idea of a separate congregation, only to have the idea rejected by the church elders.

Organization Goals

Whatever the specific stimulus for Allen's and Jones's actions in 1787, they announced publicly that their newly declared movement would not only serve the black community's religious needs as a nondenominational congregation but also function as a benevolent mutual aid organization. The latter goal involved plans to collect funds (through membership fees) to assist the sick, orphans, and widows in the African American community. Other secular social assistance aims included enforcement of a code of temperance, propriety, and fidelity in marriage. It is significant that a number of the early members of the Free African Society came to it from the rolls of other Protestant churches, not only St. George's Methodist Episcopal congregation.

The dual nature of the organization's goals soon led to divisions in the politics of leadership. Apparently, it was Allen who wanted to use the breakaway from St. George's as a first step in founding a specifically black Methodist church. Others wished to emphasize the Free African Society's nondenominational character and pursue mainly social and moral aid services. Within two years, therefore, Allen resigned his membership, going on to found, in July, 1794, the Bethel African Methodist Episcopal Church. Although this move clearly marked the beginnings of a specifically African American church with a defined denominational status, Allen's efforts for many years continued to be directed at social and economic self-help projects for African Americans, irrespective of their formal religious orientation.

By 1804, Allen was involved in founding a group whose name reflected its basic social reform goals: the Society of Free People of Color for Promoting the Instruction and School Education of Children of African Descent. Another of Allen's efforts came in 1830, when Allen, then seventy years of age, involved his church in the Free Produce Society in Philadelphia. This group raised money to buy goods grown only by nonslave labor to redistribute to poor African Americans. It also tried to organize active boycotts against the marketing and purchase of goods produced by slave-owning farmers, thus providing an early model for the grassroots organizations aimed at social and political goals that would become familiar to African Americans in the mid-twentieth century.

The Free African Society passed through several short but key stages both before and after Richard Allen's decision to remove himself from active membership. One focal point was the group's early association with the prominent medical doctor and philanthropist Benjamin Rush. Rush helped the Free African Society to draft a document involving articles of faith that were meant to be general enough to include the essential religious principles of any Christian church. When the organization adopted these tenets, in 1791, its status as a religious congregation generally was recognized by members and outsiders alike. More and more, its close relationship with the Episcopal Church (first demonstrated by its "friendly adoption" by the Reverend Joseph Pilmore and the white membership of St. Paul's Church in Philadelphia) determined its future denominational status.

After 1795, the Free African Society per se had been superseded by a new church built by a committee sparked by Absalom Jones: the African Methodist Episcopal Church. This fact did not, however, prevent those who had been associated with the Free African Society's origins from integrating its strong social and moral reform program with the religious principles that marked the emergence of the first all-black Christian congregations in the United States by the end of the 1790's.

Byron D. Cannon

Further Reading

Carol V. R. George's *Segregated Sabbaths: Richard Allen and the Emergence of Independent Black Churches, 1760-1840* (New York: Oxford University Press, 1973) includes discussion of the African American churches' eventual abolitionist activities. Mwalimi I. Mwadilitu's *Richard Allen: The First Exemplar of African American Education* (New York: ECA Associates, 1985) focuses on the career of Richard Allen, including his functions after 1816 as the first bishop of the African Methodist Episcopal Church.

See also African Methodist Episcopal Church; American Anti-Slavery Society; Baptist Church; Black church; Black codes; Freemasons in Boston; *Liberator, The*; National Council of Colored People; Pennsylvania Society for the Abolition of Slavery

Free blacks

Definition: African Americans who were not slaves during the era of slavery

Free African Americans of the antebellum era wielded profound influence upon black society in the post-slavery United States.

In 1860, an estimated 500,000 free people of African ancestry resided in the United States; of these, approximately half lived in the slaveholding South. Most of these free blacks were former slaves who had purchased their freedom or were freed in their masters' wills, but a significant minority were freeborn. Their experiences varied by region; those in the northern states, although limited in economic opportunity, enjoyed greater political and social freedom than their counterparts in the South, where demand for black labor was greater but free blacks were regarded with suspicion. The majority of free blacks lived in extreme poverty; however, a small but significant number achieved modest prosperity and a few attained substantial wealth, in some instances purchasing plantations and becoming slaveholders.

Free African Americans of the antebellum period exerted profound influence upon black society in the post-slavery United States. The abolitionist rhetoric of former slaves such as Frederick Douglass and Samuel Ringgold Ward influenced later generations of black activists, and the activities of free southern blacks set precedents for race relations and relations among African Americans after emancipation. The political and legal restrictions placed on free blacks by fearful southern whites in the antebellum period provided a blueprint for racial oppression in the South during the era of segregation.

Michael H. Burchett

Further Reading
Robinson, Cedric J. *Black Movements in America*. New York: Routledge, 1997.

See also Civil War; Emancipation Proclamation; Freedmen's Bureau; Freemasons in Boston; Slavery

Freedmen's Bureau

Identification: Agency established by the federal government to assist newly freed African Americans in making the transition from slavery to freedom
Date: Established on March 3, 1865

The bureau's ability to perform its varied tasks was impeded by several factors. Consequently, African Americans developed extensive self-help networks to address their needs.

In 1865, Congress created the Freedmen's Bureau, a temporary agency within the War Department. The bureau, also known as the United States Bureau of Refugees, Freedmen, and Abandoned Lands, was administered by General Oliver Otis Howard from 1865 until it was dismantled by Congress in 1872. The primary objective of the Freedmen's Bureau was to help newly freed African Americans to function as free men, women, and children. In order to achieve this goal, the bureau was expected to assume responsibility for all matters related to the newly freed slaves in the southern states.

The bureau's mission was an enormous undertaking because of limited resources, political conflicts over Reconstruction policies, and a hostile environment. The work of the bureau was performed by General Howard and a network of assistant commissioners in various states, largely in the South. The Freedmen's Bureau attempted to address many of the needs of the newly freed African Americans, including labor relations, education, landownership, medical care, food distribution, family reunification, legal protection, and legal services within the African American community.

Labor and Education

In the area of labor relations, the Freedmen's Bureau dealt with issues such as transporting and relocating refugees and the newly freed persons for employment, contract and wage disputes, and harsh legislation enacted by some states. Concerning the last issue, many southern states had passed laws, called black codes, that required adult freed men and women to have lawful employment or a business. Otherwise, they would be fined and jailed for vagrancy, and sheriffs would hire them out to anyone who would pay their fine. Given the scarcity of jobs, this policy resulted in former slave owners maintaining rigid control over newly freed African Americans. Another discriminatory law gave the former owners of orphaned African Americans the right to

Northern antipathy toward the Freedmen's Bureau can be seen in this 1866 political advertisement that a Pennsylvania candidate for Congress published to attack his opponent's support of the bureau. (Library of Congress)

hire them as apprentices rather than placing them with their relatives. Again, this law resulted in the continuation of free labor for many southerners. The Freedmen's Bureau has been criticized for the failure of its agents to negotiate labor contracts in the interest of the newly freed. The bureau was frequently accused of protecting the rights of the southern planters instead.

Obtaining an education was extremely important to the newly freed African Americans. They knew that learning to read and write would enable them to enter into contracts and establish businesses, and would aid them in legal matters. The Freedmen's Bureau provided some support, by providing teachers, schools, and books and by coordinating volunteers. The bureau also made a contribution to the founding of African American colleges and universities. Southern opposition to educating African Americans was a result of the southerners' fear that education would make African Americans too independent and unwilling to work under the terms established by their former owners. Therefore, southerners instituted control over the educational administration and classrooms and the entire system. Southern planters used various methods to exert control: frequent changes in administrative personnel, the use of racial stereotypes regarding the intellectual inferiority of African Americans, and educational policy decision making based on paternalism and self-interest. Consequently, educational opportunities were significantly restricted for African American youth.

Property and Other Rights

The newly freed African Americans were eager to acquire property. They demonstrated their interest in owning their own land as individuals and formed associations to purchase large tracts of land. Their sense of family and community was the basis for their strong desire to own land. The Freedmen's Bureau was initially authorized to distribute land that had been confiscated from southern plantation owners during the Civil War. The Freedmen's Bureau also attempted to provide for the social welfare of the freed persons. The agency was noted for rationing food to refugees and former slaves; it assisted families in reuniting with members who had been sold or separated in other ways during slavery.

Protecting the rights of the former slaves was a major task of the Freedmen's Bureau. Republicans believed that African Americans should have the same rights as whites. However, many southern states enacted black codes that severely restricted the civil rights of the freed men, women, and children. These laws, exacting social and economic control over African Americans, represented a new form of slavery. When state legislation prohibited African Americans' equal rights, the bureau attempted to invoke the 1866 Civil Rights Act, which offered African Americans the same legal protections and rights as whites to testify in courts, to own property, to enforce legal contracts, and to sue. The bureau found it extremely difficult to enforce the Civil Rights Act and to prosecute state officials who enforced laws that were discriminatory against African Americans.

A shortage of agents and a reluctance among bureau commissioners to challenge local officials contributed to the agency's limited success in enforcing the Civil Rights Act. Finally, the Freedmen's Bureau also established tribunals to address minor legal disputes of African Americans within their own communities. In many instances, freed slaves were able to resolve their own problems. When they could not, they presented their legal concerns to bureau agents.

The task assigned to the Freedmen's Bureau was monumental. The responsibilities of the bureau significantly exceeded the resources and authority granted to it by Congress. The bureau's ability to perform its varied tasks also was impeded by personnel shortages. President Andrew Johnson's Reconstruction policies represented another major challenge to the bureau, as they were not always supportive of the bureau's mandate and objectives. Myriad problems associated with the bureau meant that the newly freed men, women, and children were not able to receive the goods and services necessary to gain economic independence. Consequently, they developed extensive self-help networks to address their needs.

K. Sue Jewell

Further Reading

The Freedmen's Bureau and Reconstruction: Reconsiderations (New York: Fordham University Press, 1999) edited by Paul A. Cimbala and Randall M. Miller is a valuable resource. Barry A. Crouch's *The Freedmen's Bureau and Black Texans* (Austin: University of Texas Press, 1982) discusses the Reconstruction era and the Freedmen's Bureau in the state of Texas. *The Freedmen's Bureau and Black Freedom* (New York: Garland, 1994), edited by Donald G. Nieman, explores the various problems that affected the bureau. Edward Magdol's *A Right to the Land: Essays on the Freedmen's Community* (Westport, Conn.: Greenwood Press, 1977) emphasizes the efforts that African Americans pursued to acquire land and their relentless quest for self-determination.

See also Black codes; Civil Rights Act of 1866; Civil Rights Acts of 1866-1875; Disfranchisement laws in Mississippi; Education; Fourteenth Amendment; Ku Klux Klan; Race riots of 1866; Reconstruction; Thirteenth Amendment

Freedom Rides

The Event: Civil Rights movement campaign against segregation in public transportation
Date: May 4-August, 1961
Place: Southern states

The Freedom Rides, which highlighted the continued segregation of interstate bus terminals throughout the South, were met with violence that caused much of the nation to support the riders' cause.

James Farmer, the national director of the Congress of Racial Equality (CORE), an interracial, northern-based civil rights group, conceived the idea for the Freedom Rides. Modeled on the Journey for Reconciliation, the 1947 project sponsored by the pacifist Fellowship of Reconciliation, Farmer's plan called for an integrated group of civil rights activists to travel by bus from Washington, D.C., to New Orleans, Louisiana, as a means of testing southern compliance with *Boynton v. Virginia* (1960), the Supreme Court's ruling prohibiting segregation in interstate transportation facilities. Farmer believed that by demonstrating that bus terminal waiting rooms, bathrooms, and restaurants remained segregated throughout the South, the rides would highlight southern defiance of federal law and prompt federal authorities to remedy the situation.

The First Bus Ride

On May 4, 1961, seven African Americans and six whites divided into two interracial groups and boarded a Greyhound and a Trailways bus in Washington to begin their southern journey. The trip through Virginia and North Carolina was uneventful, but in South Carolina, white toughs attacked the riders in Rock Hill, and police arrested two of them in Winnsboro. Though they made it safely to Atlanta, Georgia, the situation worsened dramatically when they entered Alabama. Near Anniston, angry whites firebombed the Greyhound bus and beat the riders as they escaped from the burning vehicle. In Birmingham, a mob attacked those on the Trailways bus when it arrived at the terminal. Several riders were seriously injured, so CORE called off the rest of the journey.

Other civil rights activists, however, rushed to resume the rides, lest segregationists think that violence could derail the movement. Led by the Student Nonviolent Coordinating Committee (SNCC), the leading student civil rights organization, an integrated group of student activists converged on Birmingham. From Birmingham, the new riders traveled to Montgomery, where they were brutally assaulted by a mob awaiting them at the bus station. In the ensuing melee, John Lewis of SNCC suffered a concussion, James Zwerg, a white student from the University of Wisconsin, sustained spinal cord injuries, and John Seigenthaler, the administrative assistant to Attorney General Robert Kennedy, was attacked as he tried to protect several riders.

Federal Government Response

The violence in Montgomery forced the John F. Kennedy administration to act. As the riders prepared to travel into Mississippi on May 24, the administration arranged for National Guardsmen to ensure their safe passage into the state. Determined to prevent another violent disturbance, Robert Kennedy consented to the riders' arrest for violating segregationist ordinances in Jackson in exchange for assurances that state and local authorities would stop a white mob from forming at the terminal. As a result, the only white people on hand when the bus pulled into the station were National Guardsmen, state troopers, and city police officers. Local officials promptly arrested the twenty-seven Freedom Riders as they entered the whites-only areas of the terminal. Rather than paying fines, the activists chose to stay in jail to dramatize their opposition to segregationist laws. Subsequently, Farmer called for others to travel to Jackson to be arrested for trying to exercise their constitutional rights, and by the end of the summer of 1961, more than three hundred people, most of them African American southern students, had heeded his call and had spent time in Mississippi's jails and prisons.

The threat of renewed violence and continued arrests in Jackson inspired the Kennedy administration to pressure the Interstate Commerce Commission to issue explicit rules outlawing segregation in interstate travel facilities, a step the commission took in September, 1961. For civil rights activists, the Freedom

Rides revealed that the federal government was an unreliable partner in the struggle for African American equality. Although the rides made it clear that violent confrontations and national media attention would impel the federal government to act, they also showed that in the absence of such conditions, federal authorities would permit others to trample on African American rights. The Freedom Rides helped deepen the participants' commitment to the Civil Rights movement and to each other. Beatings, arrests, and jailings strengthened the bonds between the activists and encouraged them to see themselves as the vanguard of the militant, direct-action wing of the movement.

Gregg L. Michel

Further Reading

Original CORE Freedom Rider James Peck published an account of his experience in *Freedom Ride* (1962), and Taylor Branch offered a lengthy discussion of the Freedom Rides in his magisterial *Parting the Waters: America in the King Years, 1954-1963* (1988). The Freedom Rides are addressed in *Walking with the Wind: A Memoir of the Movement* (New York: Simon & Schuster, 1998) by John Lewis, with Michael D'Orso.

See also Birmingham March; Civil Rights movement; Congress of Racial Equality; Journey of Reconciliation; Selma-Montgomery march; Sit-ins; Student Nonviolent Coordinating Committee

Freedom Summer

The Event: Summer-long voter-registration campaign in a state in which African Americans had long been excluded from voting

Date: 1964

Place: Mississippi

With the help of one thousand volunteers from all over the country, African Americans in Mississippi endured many jailings and some deaths to break barriers and alert the nation to the reality of a social system maintained by terror.

In the early 1960's, Mississippi's elected officials were determined to preserve white supremacy and segregation. Several African Americans who attempted to register to vote or to challenge the status quo were murdered. In 1961, leaders of the National Association for the Advancement of Colored People (NAACP), Student Nonviolent Coordinating Committee (SNCC), Congress of Racial Equality (CORE), and the Southern Christian Leadership Conference (SCLC) formed the Council of Federated Organizations (COFO) to further the cause of civil rights in Mississippi.

Challenges

The COFO planned to register voters; set up freedom schools to teach African Americans job skills, African American history, and the rights of citizens under the U.S. Constitution; form community centers from which to launch challenges to segregation under the Civil Rights Act of 1964, and canvass for the newly established Mississippi Freedom Democratic Party (MFDP), which had no standing under Mississippi law. Organizing began in especially difficult towns such as McComb in southwest Mississippi. Stokely Carmichael moved SNCC headquarters to Greenwood in the Delta area of the state, where local businessperson Amzie Moore and SNCC organizer Robert P. Moses began planning for a massive effort for the summer of 1964, which would follow the violent resistance to the enrollment of James H. Meredith at the University of Mississippi in 1962 and the murder of NAACP leader Medgar Evers in 1963. Recruitment of volunteers of all races took place, mostly on college campuses, and civil rights workers began arriving long before the summer began. Many underwent orientation in Oxford, Ohio.

Three COFO volunteers—James Chaney, Michael Schwerner, and Andrew Goodman—were murdered in Neshoba County by a mob led by Sheriff Lawrence Ramey and including Ku Klux Klan members on June 21, 1964. However, the violence did not stop the COFO from carrying out its plans for community centers, freedom schools, and voter registration drives. White volunteers got most of the publicity, and their presence protected local African Americans to some extent, but permanent change was achieved by local people working in their own behalf, using the volunteers as a catalyst. Volunteers averaged slightly more than one arrest each by local authorities during the summer, and many were beaten or otherwise harassed. Publicity for the project had a major national impact. A reluctant Federal Bureau of Investigation and other agencies were forced into action to protect volunteers and local people, a role that has been much exaggerated in films such as *Mississippi Burning* (1988).

The MFDP challenge to regular Mississippi Democrats at the 1964 Democratic National Convention provided a showcase for local leaders such as Fannie Lou Hamer of Ruleville. Some disputes arose between Moses, who believed that local people should lead the movement for their own freedom, and Allard Lowenstein, who believed the COFO should form a close alliance with the liberal wing of the Democratic Party; however, COFO remained united until the summer project was over. Many volunteers stayed on to work with SNCC and other organizations that flourished in the wake of the pioneering 1964 effort.

Achievements

Freedom Summer was successful in opening the eyes of the American public to the inequities suffered by black residents of Mississippi; however, the public's concern with the state of affairs in Mississippi itself did not last much longer than the summer. The white volunteers gained considerable experience during the summer, and many of them continued to be active in other organizations. Within the COFO, the divisions between black and white activists and local and outsiders grew, causing it to disband in 1965.

The MFDP gained considerable publicity when it challenged the seating of the "regular" Democratic Party delegates from Mississippi at the party's national convention in 1964. Although the MFDP was unable to replace the official delegates with any of its own, it had a lasting effect: The 1968 Democratic National Convention featured a racially integrated Mississippi delegation.

Although Freedom Summer ended without any marked improvements in the state, by the 1990's, Mississippi had more elected African American officials than any other state, social relations among the races did not differ greatly from those in other parts of the country, and educational opportunities for African Americans had greatly improved. However, tensions between whites and African Americans remained and the poverty of the majority of the African American community was largely unabated.

J. Quinn Brisben

Further Reading

Mississippi Freedom Summer (Belmont, Calif.: Thomson/Wadsworth, 2004), edited by John F. McClymer, is an insightful examination of the drive. John Dittmer's *Local People: The Struggle for Civil Rights in Mississippi* (1994) is an analytical history of Freedom Summer. Doug McAdam's *Freedom Summer* (1988) gives the background and subsequent activities of the volunteers.

See also Civil Rights Act of 1964; Civil rights worker murders; Congress of Racial Equality; Ku Klux Klan; Mississippi Freedom Democratic Party; National Association for the Advancement of Colored People; Southern Christian Leadership Conference; Student Nonviolent Coordinating Committee; University of Mississippi desegregation

Freemasons in Boston

Identification: First African American Masonic lodge
Date: Founded on September 29, 1784
Place: Boston, Massachusetts
Since its founding, Boston's Prince Hall Masonic Lodge has provided moral teachings, aid to members in need, and even business contacts for the millions of African American men who passed through the ranks of the order.

Prince Hall, a former slave living in Boston, perceived the many benefits of belonging to the fraternal group called the Freemasons. In the thirteen colonies, many of the most prominent and respected citizens were Masons, including George Washington,

Samuel Adams, and Benjamin Franklin. As in the mother country, Masonic lodges in America stressed religion, morality, and charity to members in need and to all humankind. Many members developed business ties with their Masonic associates.

Prince Hall was born a slave in 1748. When he was twenty-one years of age, he was granted his freedom by his master. Hall entered into the trade of leather work. He pursued this calling for the rest of his life, although later, his Masonic leadership and his catering business occupied increasing amounts of his time. Tradition holds that Prince Hall fought against the British in the American Revolution. This is almost certainly true, but since several Massachusetts soldiers were named Prince Hall, details of this Prince Hall's army career are not clear.

In 1775, just before the outbreak of the American Revolution, a white Mason named John Batt initiated Hall and fourteen other free black Bostonians into the Masonic order. The fifteen initiates soon organized the first black Masonic lodge in America, calling it African Lodge. They continued to meet, but under the strict hierarchy of Masonry, a local group such as the African Lodge must be subordinate to a Grand Lodge, making regular reports as well as payments into the Grand Lodge charity fund. The American Masonic hierarchy was still evolving, and Prince Hall and his associates knew that many white Masons in the new country did not approve of black lodges or even black members.

Chartering the Lodge

On March 2, 1784, and again on June 30 of that year, Prince Hall wrote to the Grand Lodge of England asking for an official charter. This charter would confer added legitimacy on African Lodge and would give it a powerful ally. Difficulties in getting letters and money between Boston and England slowed the process of obtaining the charter, but Hall's group finally got the requisite fees to the Grand Lodge of England, and in 1787 African Lodge received its charter. The document, dated September 29, 1784, gave African Lodge the right to initiate new members and the duty of reporting regularly to the English Grand Lodge.

Some of the activities of African Lodge related directly to race. In 1787, three free African Americans from Boston were kidnapped by men who took them to the Caribbean island of St. Bartholomew and prepared to sell them into bondage. One of the three was a member of African Lodge. Prince Hall and the other black Masons of Boston agitated actively for release of their brother Mason, and for law enforcement officers to protect free African Americans from kidnapping. The petition circulated by Prince Hall helped goad the Massachusetts legislature into passing a law to punish slave traders and kidnappers. The three men won their release when the one who was a member of African Lodge gave a Masonic sign that was recognized by a white Mason living on St. Bartholomew, and the white Mason had the captors arrested and the three men returned to Boston.

Activities of the Lodge

Although the records of the early meetings of African Lodge are scarce, copies of two addresses by Prince Hall and one sermon by the lodge chaplain have survived. All three documents exhibit a strong degree of racial pride and solidarity. In his first charge to the African Lodge, delivered and published in 1792, Hall chided white Masons who claimed that the existence of black Masons would somehow make the order too common. He pointed out that that had not been the feeling during the recent Revolutionary War, when white and black soldiers had fought shoulder to shoulder. Prince Hall concluded by saying that any man who rebuked an African American man because of his skin color actually was rebuking God, who had made all people in his own image.

Hall's second charge to his lodge was delivered and published in 1797. In this address, the Masonic leader painted a baleful picture of the barbaric cruelties of slavery, and used the Bible to prove that the institution was not part of God's will. On a more optimistic note, Hall lectured his brother Masons about the nation of Haiti, where six years earlier the slaves had revolted and thrown off the yoke of French government and of slavery itself. Hall saw the revolt in Haiti as a first step by African Americans in ending the hated system of slavery.

John Marrant, a free African American minister living in Boston, became the chaplain of African Lodge. One of Marrant's sermons to the lodge was delivered and printed in 1789. As was the case with Hall's addresses, Marrant's sermon stressed what later writers would call black pride. Marrant said that African Americans should not be ashamed that their race was enslaved, since nearly every great people had been enslaved at one time or another, and such enslavement had often been the prelude to a great flourishing of that people. Marrant dipped into the Bible and into ancient history to prove that Africa had produced at least as many great civilizations as had any other region on earth.

On at least one occasion, members of the African Lodge put their pride in Africa into action. In 1787, Prince Hall circulated a petition asking the Massachusetts government to aid in returning men and women of color to Africa. Seventy-three persons signed the petition, including most members of African Lodge. The petition is one of the earliest documents in American history associated with a back-to-Africa movement. On most other occasions, however, members of African Lodge preferred to work to improve their standing within the United States.

Spreading the Word

As the free black population in the northern states continued to grow, African Lodge responded to requests to bring Masonry to African Americans in other areas. A number of residents of Providence, Rhode Island, were initiated into African Lodge and later began their own lodge with the blessings of Prince Hall and his followers. African Lodge also helped found new lodges in Philadelphia and New York. Meanwhile, all the Masonic lodges in the United States that were chartered by one of the British Grand Lodges began to have less contact with the Grand Lodges across the ocean. African Lodge was no exception. In 1827, African Lodge declared its independence of the English Grand Lodge and of any other Grand Lodge. It became the Grand Lodge for all chapters of African American Masons it founded in the United States.

The so-called Prince Hall Masonry continued to flourish long after the death of Hall in 1807. In 1995, the order boasted three hundred thousand members in the United States. For more than two hundred years, Prince Hall Masonry has provided moral teachings, aid to members in need, and even business contacts for the millions of African American men who passed through the ranks of the order. For most of that time, white Masons attacked the Prince Hall Masons for claimed irregularities in the latter's organizational history, including the history of the Prince Hall Masons' charters. Yet any alleged irregularities were also part of the history of early white lodges in the United States. While attacks on Prince Hall Masonry are less common today than they were previously, Masonry remains a highly segregated area of American life.

Stephen Cresswell

Further Reading

Crawford, George W. *Prince Hall and His Followers*. 1914. Reprint. New York: AMS Press, 1971. The classic defense of Prince Hall Masons to the charges of irregularity made by white Masonic groups.

Dillard, Thomas Henry. "History of Calumet Lodge #25 Free and Accepted Masons, Prince Hall Affiliation." *Journal of the Afro-American Historical and Genealogical Society* 10, no. 1 (1989): 22-28. A rare glimpse into the history of a single lodge of Prince Hall Masons.

Grimshaw, William H. *Official History of Freemasonry Among the Colored People in North America*. 1903. Reprint. Freeport, N.Y.: Books for Libraries Press, 1971. For many years, this book was considered the basic history of Prince Hall Masonry. Readers should be aware that it contains a vast number of unsubstantiated statements and should be used with care.

Muraskin, William A. *Middle-Class Blacks in a White Society: Prince Hall Freemasonry in America*. Berkeley: University of California Press, 1975. Sociological and historical examination of Prince Hall Masonry as a foundation of the African American middle class.

Wesley, Charles H. *Prince Hall: Life and Legacy*. 2d ed. Washington, D.C.: United Supreme Council, 1983. A careful history that does a good job of separating earlier myths about the origins of Prince Hall Masonry from documented fact.

See also Abolition; Black codes; Free African Society; Free blacks; Pennsylvania Society for the Abolition of Slavery

Fugitive Slave Law of 1793

The Law: Federal law requiring the return of slaves fleeing across
state lines
Date: Signed into law on February 12, 1793
*The Fugitive Slave Law aggravated sectional conflict between free and
slave states.*

In colonial America, the return of fugitives within and between
jurisdictions was a common practice. These fugitives were usually felons escaping from jails; persons charged with crimes; apprentices and indentured servants fleeing from their employers;
or black, white, or Native American slaves running away from
their masters. Their rendition between jurisdictions depended on
comity among colonial authorities. The articles of the New England Confederation of 1643 included a provision for the return
of fugitive slaves and servants. Like all subsequent American legislation on the topic, it did not provide for a trial by jury.

Rising Sectional Conflict

In the late eighteenth century, with the growth of antislavery
sentiment in the North and the settlement of territory west of the
Appalachian Mountains, a uniform method for the return of fugitive slaves became necessary. Article VI of the Northwest Ordinance of 1787 excluding chattel slavery provided that persons escaping into the territory from whom labor or service was lawfully
claimed in any one of the original states might be returned to the
person claiming their labor or service. The provision did not dis-
tinguish between slaves and indentured servants.

The United States Constitution of the same year incorporated
the provision, without limiting the claimants to residents of the
original states of the union. One of several concessions intended
to win support from the slaveholding states, Article IV, Section 2,
states that "no person held to service or labor in one state, under
the laws thereof, escaping into another, shall, in consequence of
any law or regulation therein, be discharged from such service or
labor, but shall be delivered up on claim of the party to whom
such service or labor may be due."

Thanks to fugitive slave laws, African Americans could never feel safe, even after reaching northern states. (Library of Congress)

In 1793, Congress decided to set federal rules for the rendition of alleged fugitives. This action was prompted by Pennsylvania's attempt to recover from Virginia several men accused of having kidnapped John Davis, a free black man. Unable to receive satisfaction, the governor of Pennsylvania brought the matter to the attention of President George Washington, who referred it to the Congress.

A committee of the House of Representatives, led by Theodore Sedgwick of Massachusetts, reported a rendition bill on November 15, 1791, but no action was taken. A special Senate committee, consisting of George Cabot of Massachusetts, Samuel Johnston of North Carolina, and George Read of Delaware, submitted a bill on December 20, 1792, establishing a ministerial procedure for the extradition of judicial fugitives. It also provided a system for the recovery of fugitives from labor or service. A claimant had to present a written deposition from one or more credible persons to a local magistrate who would order officers of the court to seize the fugitive and turn him or her over to the claimant. The bill set penalties for harboring a fugitive, neglecting a duty, or obstructing an arrest. After debate, the bill was recommitted with instructions to amend, and John Taylor of Virginia and Roger Sherman of Connecticut were added to the committee.

A Revised Bill

January 3, 1793, a revised bill was reported to the Senate by Johnston, allowing the claimant or his agent to seize a fugitive and bring that person to a federal court or a local magistrate. Oral testimony or an affidavit certified by a magistrate of the master's state sufficed to establish a claim. To guard against the kidnapping of free African Americans, residents of the territory or state in which they were seized, the new bill included a proviso assuring them their rights under the laws of that territory or state. This meant they were entitled to a judicial inquiry or a jury trial to determine their status. They were also to be presumed free, until proven otherwise, and allowed to testify on their own behalf.

After two debates, during which the proviso was dropped, the bill passed the Senate on January 18. It was entitled "An act respecting fugitives from justice and persons escaping from their masters." The House passed it with little discussion, February 5, by a vote of forty-eight to seven. Seven days later, President Washington signed the bill into law.

The first two sections of the act, known popularly as the Fugitive Slave Act of 1793, dealt with the interstate rendition of fugitives from justice. The third section provided that when a person held to labor escaped into any state or territory of the United States, the master or a designated agent could seize that individual and bring him or her before a judge of the federal courts in the state or before any magistrate of a county, city, or incorporated town. Title was proven by the testimony of the master or the affidavit of a magistrate in the state from which the escapee came, certifying that the person had escaped. The judge or magistrate then had to provide a certificate entitling the petitioner to remove the fugitives.

The act applied to fugitive apprentices or indentured servants as well as to slaves, a provision important at that time to representatives of the northern states. The act did not admit a trial by jury, and it contained no provisions for the alleged fugitives to offer evidence on their own behalf, although they were not prevented from doing so if the presiding judge or magistrate agreed.

Section 4 provided criminal penalties, a fine of five hundred dollars, in addition to any civil action the owner might have under state law, for obstructing the capture and for rescuing, harboring, aiding, or hiding fugitives.

Although many attempts were made to amend the act, it remained the law of the land until the abolition of slavery, its constitutionality repeatedly upheld by the Supreme Court. It was amended and supplemented, not replaced, by the Second Fugitive Slave Law of 1850, part of the Compromise of 1850.

Impact of the Law

The statute contributed significantly to acerbating the growth of sectional conflict within the United States. Efforts to enforce its provisions encountered immediate resistance in northern states, isolated and scattered at first but increasingly well-organized and vigorous (for example, the Underground Railroad), as slavery prospered in the Old South and spread to western lands. Many northern states passed personal liberty laws (Indiana in 1824, Connecticut in 1828, New York and Vermont in 1840). Designed to prevent the kidnapping of free African Americans, these laws provided for trial by jury to determine their true status. The effectiveness of the statute was further diminished by the Supreme Court's decision in *Prigg v. Commonwealth of Pennsylvania* (1842) that state authorities could not be forced by the national government to act in fugitive slave cases.

Subsequently, Massachusetts (1843), Vermont (1843), Pennsylvania (1847), and Rhode Island (1848) forbade their officials to help enforce the law and refused the use of their jails for fugitive slaves. Because the Fugitive Slave Act of 1793 provided no federal means of apprehending fugitive slaves, owners had to rely on the often ineffectual and costly services of slave catchers. With the outbreak of the Civil War, the law ceased to apply to the Confederate States. It was considered valid in the loyal border states until it was repealed June 28, 1864.

Charles H. O'Brien

Further Reading

Campbell, Stanley. *The Slave Catchers: Enforcement of the Fugitive Slave Law, 1850-1860*. Chapel Hill: University of North Carolina Press, 1970. Chapter 1 deals with attempts to enforce the Fugitive Slave Act of 1793.

Finkelman, Paul. "The Kidnapping of John Davis and the Adoption of the Fugitive Slave Law of 1793." *The Journal of Southern History* 56, no. 3 (August, 1990): 397-422. Discusses the incident that led the Congress to take up the issue of fugitive slaves; thoroughly examines the legislative progress of the law.

_____. *Slavery in the Courtroom: An Annotated Bibliography of American Cases.* Washington, D.C.: Library of Congress, 1985. Presents a detailed description of judicial decisions, as well as other documents pertaining to the enforcement of the Fugitive Slave Act of 1793.

McDougall, Marion G. *Fugitive Slaves, 1619-1865.* 1891. Reprint. New York: Bergman, 1969. Appendix includes the text of the Fugitive Slave Act of 1793 and many other relevant legislative and judicial documents.

Morris, Thomas D. *Free Men All: The Personal Liberty Laws of the North, 1780-1861.* Baltimore: Johns Hopkins University Press, 1974. A definitive account of the efforts of Northern states to secure individual liberty against the harsh implications of the Fugitive Slave Law of 1793.

Wiecek, William M. *Liberty Under Law: The Supreme Court in American Life.* Baltimore: Johns Hopkins University Press, 1988. Discusses the Supreme Court's interpretation of the Fugitive Slave Act of 1793 in *Prigg v. Commonwealth of Pennsylvania* (1842).

_____. *The Sources of Antislavery Constitutionalism in America, 1760-1848.* Ithaca, N.Y.: Cornell University Press, 1977. Detailed exposition of the fugitive slave provisions of the Northwest Ordinance and the United States Constitution, 1787.

See also Black codes; Bleeding Kansas; Compromise of 1850; Fugitive Slave Law of 1850; Kansas-Nebraska Act; Missouri Compromise; Northwest Ordinance; Proslavery argument; Slave codes; Slavery and the justice system; Underground Railroad

.